The Intestines of the State

The Intestines of the State

Youth, Violence, and Belated Histories in the Cameroon Grassfields

NICOLAS ARGENTI

THE UNIVERSITY OF CHICAGO PRESS   CHICAGO AND LONDON

NICOLAS ARGENTI is research lecturer in anthropology at Brunel University. He is coeditor of *Young Africa: Realising the Rights of Children and Youth.*

The University of Chicago Press, Chicago 60637
The University of Chicago Press, Ltd., London
© 2007 by The University of Chicago
All rights reserved. Published 2007
Printed in the United States of America
16 15 14 13 12 11 10 09 08 07   1 2 3 4 5

ISBN-13: 978-0-226-02611-4 (cloth)
ISBN-13: 978-0-226-02612-1 (paper)
ISBN-10: 0-226-02611-6 (cloth)
ISBN-10: 0-226-02612-4 (paper)

Library of Congress Cataloging-in-Publication Data

Argenti, Nicholas.
  The intestines of the state : youth, violence, and belated histories in the Cameroon grassfields / Nicholas Argenti
     p. cm.
  Includes bibliographical references and index.
  ISBN-13: 978-0-226-02611-4 (cloth : alk. paper)
  ISBN-10: 0-226-02611-6 (cloth : alk. paper)
  ISBN-13: 978-0-226-02612-1 (pbk. : alk. paper)
  ISBN-10: 0-226-02612-4 (pbk. : alk. paper)
  1. Oku (African people)—History. 2. Oku (African people)—Politics and government. 3. Oku (African people)—Social life and customs. 4. Slavery—Cameroon—North-West Province—History. 5. Marginality, social—Cameroon—North-West Province—History. 6. Young men—Cameroon—North-West Province—Attitudes 7. Young men—Cameroon—North-West Province—Psychology. 8. North-West Province (Cameroon)—History. 9. North-West Province (Cameroon)—Social conditions. I. Title.
   DT571.058A74 2007
   305.896'36—dc22

                                                              2007011955

FOR ALEXANDRA, CHIARA, AND QUENTIN

AND

FRANCIS WANJEL (1947–2006),

ntshii nda, master carver, teacher, friend. Mort, sauf en moi.

He shouts dig this earth deeper you lot there you others sing up and play
He grabs the rod in his belt he swings it his eyes are so blue
Stick your spades deeper you lot there you others play on for the dancing

—Paul Celan, Todesfuge, 1952

Contents

Note on Orthography

E blam Ebkwo (or Əblam Əbkwo), the language of Oku, has recently been transcribed by the Oku Language Society (Kenchinten əblam əbkwo). My own usage, however, was developed before that of the OLS, according to a system I devised based on the International Phonetic Alphabet (IPA). Because it is the system most likely to give a clear impression of the pronunciation of Eblam Ebkwo to those not familiar with the language, and because it is the one I have used in previous publications, I have largely retained it for this book. I deviate from it, however, when using terms that have been written down for some time already in Oku, including, for example, place-names, personal names, the name of the language itself, and terms that have been used in the literature on the Grassfields for some time, such as the term for a local ruler, which is properly əbfɔn in Eblam Ebkwo but which I transcribe as *fon,* in keeping with the widely accepted spelling in the region as a whole. Unless otherwise stated, I produce the plurals of such terms in English, with the addition of a final *s,* rather than by applying the appropriate noun-class prefix. In the case of Eblam Ebkwo words that are not previously established in the literature on the Grassfields, I provide the term in the singular. When I provide two terms in a row in parentheses—for example, (*əbfɔn, təfɔn*)—the first term is the singular, the second term the plural.

In addition to the letters of the Roman alphabet, the IPA signs I use are the following:

Ə, ə   as in the French *peu, feu,* or *le*

Ɛ, ɛ   as in the /e/ of "let"

γ   a soft /g/, as in the Flemish pronunciation of "Ghent"

Ŋ, ŋ   as in the /ng/ of "flying"

ɔ   as in the /o/ of "hot" or "pot"

The digraph /sh/, as in "ship," is used in place of ʃ in the IPA to keep in line as much as possible with the orthography now being established in Oku. /r'/ at the end of a word marks a glottal stop that sounds somewhere between the English /r/ and /k/, or the Dutch hard /g/ as in *dag*. The Roman /u/ denotes the sound of the /oo/ in "food" or the /ou/ in the French *clou*. /r/ is not alveolar as in English but a voiceless velar fricative. The elongation of a sound is marked by doubling the relevant letter or by a /~/ above it. To my knowledge, there are three tones in Eblam Ebkwo. I do not note them except in cases where they are phonemically determining, as in *bá* (high tone, meaning "father") and *bà* (low tone, meaning "leopard"). This orthography is in accordance with the general alphabet of Cameroon languages (Sadembouo and Tadadjeu 1984), with the exception of my replacement of the recommended /z/ prepalatal voiced fricative with the Roman /j/. Accordingly, I replace the recommended prepalatal voiced affricate /j/ with the digraph /dj/.

Preface

The Grassfields area, roughly corresponding to the present North West and South West provinces of Cameroon, is made up of about fifty chiefdoms of various sizes, each with its own language.[1] Many of these chiefdoms are renowned for their masquerades as well as for their elaborate hierarchies headed by kings, who are known throughout the region by variations on the term *fon*. These hierarchies are generally centralized in the palace in the capital and divided into a tripartite system composed of the *fon*, a regulatory society of commoners including servants, advisers, and a judiciary body known as *kwifon*, and the society of royal eligibles—the *fon*'s sons and his predecessor's sons—sometimes referred to in the literature, as in local pidgin, as "princes." Both the *kwifon* regulatory society and the royal eligibles are divided into ranks according to complex title systems that confer unequal decision-making powers, as well as sartorial prerogatives, on their occupants. These palatine courtly societies are marked by a stark concentration of wealth among the *fons* and the few elites gathered around them, and this wealth is measured in the form of people, and in particular in wives, of which the *fons* of the greatest chiefdoms of the Grassfields possess hundreds.

My research was conducted primarily in the Grassfields chiefdom of Oku (known to the Oku people themselves as Əbkwo), over an initial period of two years. A two-month pilot study in 1991–92 permitted me to narrow my attention down to the chiefdom of Oku, a relatively small, remote polity of about 65,000 people, renowned for its carving and traditional medicines as well as for its relatively well-preserved primary montane forest, which until the 1970s still sustained leopards. I returned to Oku after a three-month interim period in London for a further uninterrupted twenty-two months from 1992 to 1994. Since the aged *fon*, Sentie, had died while I was in London following my pilot study, I rushed back to Oku to witness the enthronement of the new *fon,* Ngum III, at the palace: the first such ceremony to take place since 1956. On April 1, 2006, Ngum III passed away, and the ceremonies described in this book took place again. In 1992, after two months and the end of the enthronement ceremony, I moved to the smaller village of Jikijem, where I lived for the remaining twenty months of my time in Oku. Roughly speaking, the first half of this period, apart from my focus on language acquisition, was dedicated to studies of village and palace hierarchy, mostly through informal and semistructured interviews, and of the organization of death ceremonies and masked dance, mostly through participant observation. I also studied domestic rituals and healing practices throughout my stay. I conducted interviews at first in West African pidgin, which I had learned in London before my departure, and then in Eblam Ebkwo, the language of Oku, as I became more familiar with it. In the second half of this period I took on the additional task of working with carvers, to one of whom, Francis Wanjel, I was apprenticed (see Argenti 2002a). Francis, to whom I was indebted for a year of companionship as well as for so much of what I came to understand about Oku, passed away very soon after my latest visit to Oku in June 2005, and this book is dedicated to his memory.

Acknowledgments

This book has been in progress for more years than I care to admit, during which time I have become indebted to a great many people. Blithely disregarding the critique of Western models of chronological time that this book puts forth, I start with the beginning and thank first of all David Zeitlyn for piquing my interest in the Grassfields by alerting me to the wonders of the sultanate of Fumban when I was a doctoral neophyte at Oxford looking for a region on which to focus my studies. As luck would have it, Oxford has housed an extraordinary concentration of Cameroonists over the years, all nurtured by Sally Chilver—the grande dame of Grassfields studies. I cannot possibly thank her enough for all the help she has so selflessly offered to me over the years: first in convincing me to devote myself to the region, and then in supporting me ever since my return from the field with her untiringly perspicacious readings of my work, her constant advice and inspiration, and, most of all, her devoted and delightful friendship. I must also thank Shirley Ardener in the same breath, who has been a source of unstinting moral support for just as long and invited me to present seminars at which I received invaluable feedback on early versions of some of the chapters finally presented here. At University College London, where I moved from Oxford to follow my studies on Cameroon, I am indebted to my supervisors Mike Rowlands, Bruce Kapferer, and Susanne Kuechler for their time and input. I am also exceedingly grateful to Phil Burnham for instruction in language acquisition before my departure and for support and advice while I was in the field, and to Buck Schieffelin for stimulating conversations and encouragement throughout the writing. I am also very grateful to Nigel Barley and to John Mack for British Museum funding and the encouragement to extend my research outside Oku to the chiefdoms of Bamessing and Babessi.

In Cameroon, I recognize my everlasting debt to all the people of Oku. Never before, nor since, have I been received with such warmth or self-less generosity as I was in this hinterland chiefdom. My gratitude goes to His Royal Highness Fon Ngum III, sadly departed, who made my studies possible, received me most graciously even as recently as last year, and patiently taught me a great deal about Oku. I am also indebted to his wonderful family for the warm hospitality they have always accorded me. While still in Elak, the capital of Oku, I was introduced to the village of Jikijem by Philip and Nicolas, sons of Mbu's compound, who found me a place to stay in the quarter of Mbok-Jikijem. I thank them and all the other people of that remarkable compound, including its head, Fay Mbu Yang Daniel, who never fails to go out of his way for me, and the sadly departed musician of national renown Francis Dom, who was also a son of Mbu Bey and a valuable friend. I must then thank Babey Joseph Baba, in whose compound I stayed for my whole time in Oku barring the first two months, and who was always much more than a host. His whole family also know full well all that they have done for me and how much they will forever mean to me. With reference to Jikijem, I must also thank Babey Theresia Ntshi and Bah Emmanuel Tokoh, both of whom transcribed songs, prayers, interviews, and other texts for me. I am also grateful to Ndong of Yundji Bey, Tshie Kelam, for his friendship and support, and to his mother and sadly departed father.

Finally, I thank Njakoi John Bah: the standard anthropological appellations of "language informant" or "research assistant" fail to do justice to the role John played in the coproduction of works that have been signed only by me but that are in reality authored by us both (not that I blame him, of course, for my errors and oversights). John has continued to conduct research and to publish articles of his own in ethnographic journals ever since I left the field in 1994. He has published on customary marriage (1998), burial (2000), the Oku palace (2004), and Oku ritual (2005). I have not the room here to thank him adequately for all the help he offered me in the field, and since, in the writing up of this work, but only point the reader to the preface I wrote to his latest article, in which I was happily able to make the full weight of my debt to him explicit (Argenti 2005b). In addition, I thank those members of John's family who never failed to help and support me, including his wife Anna, his brothers Sam and Moses and their wives, and his late mother and father, whom I sorely miss.

Outside Jikijem, my gratitude is due to Francis Wanjel, to whom I was apprenticed as a carver and to whose memory this book is dedicated, and to his brother Peter Meyunneghe. Francis actually sought me out to make me his apprentice at the point that I had resigned myself to the idea that I would not find a master carver willing to take me on, and I am indebted to him for the hundreds of hours he spent so patiently with me in his workshop in Manchok, teaching me not only how to carve and what it means to be a carver but, at the same time, the language of Eblam Ebkwo. In Elak, I also thank for their companionship Ellen Weinreb, Toby Quantrill of the Kilum Mountain Forest Project, and Father Ozwald Holzer, all of whom never failed to raise my spirits. I am also indebted not only for logistical help and companionship, but also for his invaluable critical advice on my work, to Father Hermann Gufler, who has now lived in Oku longer than I have and begun to publish on it in his own right (see Gufler and Bah 2006). I am also grateful to Jeremy Avis for friendship in the field and afterward, and for his advice on the ethnomusicological aspects of my research since my return. In Bamessing (Nsai) I am grateful to Ueli Knecht and his family for their hospitality. In Bamenda, I acknowledge the hospitality, help, and support I received from Patrick Mbunwe Samba, tragically assassinated in April 2003, and from Lucy Davis and her family. In Yaoundé, I express my wholehearted gratitude to Rowena and Bill Quantrill. I am also deeply indebted to Margaret Niger-Thomas for inviting me to the University of Buea and for her very generous hospitality there.

Too many people have commented on drafts of this book for me to mention, but among them I especially thank Rob Aitken, Jean-François Bayart, Karin Barber, Andrew Beatty, Stephan Feuchtwang, Eric Hirsch, Thomas Fillitz, Paola Filippucci, Silvia Forni, Christraud Geary, Peter Geschiere, Anne Hugon, Miles Irving, Adam Kuper, Tanya Luhrman, Peter Pels, Barbara Plankensteiner, Ivo Quaranta, Janet Roitman, Ute Roschenthaler, Ramon Sarro, Marina Temudo, Daniel Jordan Smith, Jean-Pierre Warnier, and Helena Wulff. I am additionally indebted to John Peel for having made available to me a manuscript detailing the testimony of a recaptured slave of Grassfields origin that he recently discovered in the Church Missionary Society archives. The book has additionally benefited from members of the departments of anthropology at the University of Frankfurt am Main, the University of Kent at Canterbury, the London School of Economics, Manchester University, and Vienna University, where parts of it were presented.

Last but not least, how can I ever acknowledge my debt to Alexandra Argenti-Pillen, who more than anyone else has had to put up with the incompatibilities of writing a book and maintaining some semblance of a normal family life? I thank her not only for her support in this thankless task but for the additional burden she has shouldered of providing me ever since I first met her with inspiration and guidance, and with more than one critical revision of this work. Like me, it has been radically ameliorated by her attention.

I gratefully acknowledge research funding from the Fondation Dapper, Paris, and writing time provided by a Princess Diana/Royal Anthropological Institute fellowship at the Brunel University Centre for Child-Focused Anthropological Research from 2001 to 2002, and by an Arts and Humanities Research Council Research Leave Scheme grant in 2004–5. I am also grateful to Mission 21, Basel, for permission to reproduce photos from their archive.

Centuries of Youth: Remembering, Incorporation, and the Reclamation of History

He reproduces it not as a memory, but as an action: he repeats it, without knowing, of course, that he is repeating, and in the end, we understand that this is his way of remembering.—Sigmund Freud (1926, 150)

Every group ... will entrust to bodily automatisms the values and categories which they are most anxious to conserve. They will know how well the past can be kept in mind by a habitual memory sedimented in the body.—Paul Connerton ([1989] 1998, 102)

The object of loss is written across the bodies of the people, as it repeats in the silence that speaks the foreignness of language.—Homi Bhabha (1990, 315)

The desire to forget is strong, but ... the memory of "sixty million and more" [African-American slaves] is somehow encrypted within us, in our time and in our bodies.—Peter Nicholls (1996, 63)

There was a place in Africa that was known about by European traders and missionaries for centuries before any of them were ever able to reach it—or even to locate it with any precision. This place was famed for one commodity above all, a commodity whose quality was praised as highly as its abundance: its slaves. Although the coastal areas of the Slave Coast were on the whole only lightly populated, this mysterious hinterland region—known only to those at the end of a long chain of indigenous middlemen—supplied men, women, and children to the transatlantic trade for centuries. Ships' captains knew neither where this region might lie nor what it was called. Only in late 1889, five years after the Germans had signed an annexation treaty with a small group of coastal Duala for a protectorate they named Kamerun, did they expedite a reconnaissance force inland to try to discover the source of this prodigious supply of manpower—a supply that the German colonial forces, industrialists, and merchants would soon commandeer for their own use (Austen 1996b; Austen and Derrick 1999; Rudin 1938). When, after an arduous journey, the first German caravan finally arrived at the cool highland plateau ringed by volcanic peaks that surmounted the steamy forests of their fledgling colony, they named the place *Grassland* and drew up lucrative contracts with a local chief for the exclusive supply of manpower (see Chilver [1966] 1996). After a brief period of German rule, the region would be divided between the French and the British during the First World War, from which time the British section, bordering southeastern Nigeria, would come to be known as the Grassfields.

From a Western point of view that has received curiously little scrutiny over the decades, colonial occupation brought an end to slavery in Africa. From the point of view of the victims of slavery and the slave dealers alike in the Grassfields, however, the arrival of the Germans in the Grassfields simply cut out the need for middlemen, and the young men and women who were once supplied by local rulers through a long chain of intermediaries to the European slave traders on the coast could now be supplied in situ to the German labor recruiters and their agents, who put them to work as caravan porters or as agricultural laborers in the industrial plantations that they set up in the devastatingly malarial lowlands of the territory. Far from shrinking, the numbers of young people coerced into forced labor outside their chiefdoms—a substantial proportion of whom did not survive their ordeal—increased dramatically in the German period. Under such conditions, massive fissures would emerge in the social fabric of the Grassfields chiefdoms, pitting youth against their elders more desperately than ever before and giving rise to recurring mutinies, insurrections, and political movements that would continue to inform the politics of contemporary Cameroon, and even to threaten the national security and cohesion of the nation state, into the twenty-first century.

One of the unintended consequences of the German missionary presence was to further exacerbate the tensions between youth and elites by giving the former a voice and a political platform that they had never before enjoyed. Although the vast majority of young people were forced to serve the German military or the traders, some were educated in seminaries, made literate, and even given salaried employment in the church or the local administration. These "interpreters," or *tapenta* as they were known in pidgin, became such a force in the region that they inspired an eponymous youth movement that seriously destabilized the region and threatened chiefly hegemony. Unaware that the monster was largely one of their own making, the missionaries railed against the depredations of these unruly bands of youths. By their own accounts, the *tapenta* rampaged through the Grassfields, accumulating acolytes as they went and rejecting their exploitative association with any chiefdom in favor of a new imaginary identity of extroversion that associated them with the recent European invaders, their sartorial styles, bodily deportment, and language. All of these things the youths appropriated with an ease and exactitude that often alarmed their teachers more than it flattered them, and threatened to destabilize the hegemony of the chiefs and elites in the region.

Despite young people's ongoing history of struggles against marginalization and of resistance to oppression in the Grassfields, not a word was ever spoken to me about slavery or forced labor for the duration of my stays in the region. So complete was the silence on this issue, despite the fact that other aspects of the past are regularly recounted in myths and stories, that it was conspicuous by its obstinate discursive absence.[1] Has the past then been forgotten in Cameroon? Was the violence of the institutions that upheld the hegemony and the economic and military power of the elites of the expanding states of the Grassfields so totalizing that it effectively obliterated all trace of itself? Or might there be other, untold ways in which the past perdures and informs the present? Although the dark period of the slave trade and its colonial aftermath spawned a discursive silence on the subject of slavery, it also witnessed the birth of ritual practices that are still embodied and performed by the youth and elites of the Grassfields to this day. Among these we must count one of the richest and most complex masking traditions on the continent. These masked dances were of two main types: those belonging to the palaces, and those owned by the lineage heads of the outlying villages of the chiefdom. All were performed by young men, many with the participation of women as unmasked coperformers. The palace masks were performed by young men who had been forcibly recruited from the villages for service in the palace. These men formed the policing body known as the *kwifon* society, members of which often abducted other youths for sale into slavery. The village lineage masks, however, depended for their dancers entirely on the young men who were most likely to be abducted for sale into slavery. By its very nature then, in its very membership, and from its very inception, this performative tradition encapsulated the oppositions, struggles, and tensions of the slave trade in the Grassfields—a trade that took the form of an intestine war waged not only between the chiefdoms of the region but even between the youth and elites within each one of them. Not for nothing is the palace of the chiefdom of Oku known in all its ambivalence as "the intestines of the state" (əbtɔɔ kətum; Bah 2004, 436). Similarly, in the chiefdom of Bafut, the area surrounding the palace is called Momela's—"Center of the country" (Chilver and Kaberry 1963, 5).

However silent the people of Oku might be on the subject of slavery, centuries of trading in human beings remains palpable today in other ways: the myths and nondiscursive bodily practices of the chiefdom are impregnated with veiled references to the institutions of slavery and to their effects on the young people who were once most imperiled by them. The mythic memories and the bodily practices of the Grassfields together form a body of social memory.[2] This body of social memory is not monolithic or unidimensional, however, but undetermined, conflicted, and heteroglossic. It pits youth and elders against one another in a mutually antagonistic embrace and has done so for centuries. This conflicted body of social memory still informs contemporary discourse and embodied practice, driving the development of youth movements and political processes at the local and national levels in contemporary Cameroon, and loading the present with the weight of the past.

The history of modernity in Cameroon is in fact inseparable from the history of slavery, which marked the inception of modernity in Africa and still informs the social relations of its societies to this day. The inequities that pitted youth against predatory elites in the era of the transatlantic trade still now scar the social fabric of Grassfields communities, where indefinite bachelorhood and celibacy, unemployment, and emigration still constitute the experience of the maligned and marginalized majority. This occurs not only because the young constitute the absolute demographic majority, but because they can only age to the extent that they accumulate the wealth and power needed to be recognized as adults in these conservative palatine hierarchies. The masked performances that were once deployed to address the unspeakable violence of the slave trade as it unfolded are still relevant today because the power relations first conceived by the transatlantic slave trade still obtain in the present. The dances of the Grassfields are therefore not commemorative of a past that is dead and gone; they are not commemorative practices that explicitly evoke a past from which contemporary generations can clearly delineate themselves. The past is not "another country" in Cameroon—it is everywhere present in the relations of structural violence that continue to divide and polarize communities on the basis of social judgments of age and seniority. In the ambiguity and the polyvalence of their unspoken embodiment, the dances address the inequities that persist in the contemporary social relations between youth and elites in the Grassfields today.

Because the slavery and forced labor of the precolonial and colonial periods are not generally discussed openly, because they do not take the form of verbal testimonies, it could be said that these practices do not constitute a body of memories for contemporary generations of Cameroonians, that slavery and the past of oppression and extreme violence have been forgotten. And yet, through such practices as the masked dances that ludically pit youths against elders in the public celebrations of the Grassfields today, the silent ghosts of the past are brought back to life and remembered in the bodies of the maskers and their melancholic acolytes. The big men who once traded in slaves and the marginalized youths who once formed their capital have not gone away, and the relations between them are still characterized by iniquity, antagonism, suspicion, distrust, and periodic open conflict. The embodied practices originating in the precolonial period thus reify it in a present that still bears many structural similarities to that past, fusing the past and the present in the performance of the dance. Slavery as such might not constitute a body of verbal knowledge in the Grassfields today. As the last generation of those with firsthand experience of slavery die out, so do cognitive memories of this period. But the contemporary social relations of inequity and exploitation that still bind youths and elders to one another in the present perpetually recall the past by reinscribing its social polarization in the present, giving to long-standing embodied practices a contemporaneity that makes of them not merely a body of social memory but the site of an ongoing struggle between the generations—a struggle in which contemporary oppression is inscribed and reified in the bodies of the people by means of dances that were first inspired by the extreme violence of the eras of the slave trade and of forced labor.

Commemorative ceremonies, as quintessentially modernist practices, inscribe historical events in chronological time in order to separate their participants from the past by means of an imagined unilineal forward progression. Because the palaces and the big men of the Grassfields, now joined by the new elites of the state, are still pitted against their own youth, however, the violence of the past perdures in the present, and its silent encryption on the bodies of the people has yet definitively to be told, to be rendered monolithic, and to be settled into a distinct and delimited past into which it can be forgotten. There has been no "truth" or "reconciliation" in Cameroon, and the masked dances of the Grassfields reveal not a break with the past, nor its containment in a petrified body of "culture" or "heritage" (Argenti 2005a; Appadurai 1990). Rather, the ambiguous mythical histories and the agonistic dances of the Grassfields bear witness to the underlying social and political continuities in the relations between youth and elites that belie hegemonic modernist discourses and imaginaries of revolutionary historical transformation and progress. These practices bear witness to the lived experience of extreme violence, political and economic polarization, and the social costs of state formation and inculcation into the global economy—lived experiences that obdurately perdure across the centuries of the Grassfields, triggering what Richard Werbner (1998) has termed "postwars of the dead." Where modernist commemoration instigates closure by representing one authoritative, definitive, and final version of the past, the ambiguous and ambivalent embodiment of the dances of the Grassfields bears witness to a past that is fraught with tension, to struggles that have not yet ended, and to a story that is not yet concluded.

The last word concerning the past of the Grassfields has not yet been spoken. Because the full meaning of the violence has yet to be resolved, its full catastrophic impact accounted for, the violence of the past is still palpable—ever present in the bodies of the people. It is a story yet to be told, to be concluded. The trade in human life and the coercion of the people into forced labor, which were the cornerstones of state formation in the Grassfields, have happened, but they have not yet ended, and with every dance they happen again in their raw and irreducible immediacy and their conflictual ambivalence. Because the extreme violence of the past in the Grassfields remains irreducible and subject to conflicting interpretations, revisions, and appropriations, it is in fact part and parcel of the present. In other words, the past of the Grassfields is belated; what it will have been has yet to be told. The dance is not the commemoration of what was; it is the struggle to define what the violence of the past will have been. With every return of the dry season, when the recent dead are commemorated in the dances of the palaces and in the villages of the Grassfields, the unrestful dead of the more distant past also wake from their fitful slumbers, emerging from the forests and the waterways, where they wait disconsolately on the doorstep of the other world. Forever caught between worlds, they return to show us what we will come to know, what will be remembered—later.

The Making of Youth in Africa

In an infantilization that recurs throughout Africa, those denied a toehold on the ladder of elite hierarchies are systematically represented as children, adolescents, younger siblings, or bachelors; such depictions are rhetorical devices that make the exploitation by elites pass for strict-but-fair paternalism and that also serve to ridicule the complaints of the exploited as the tantrums of ungrateful toddlers. It is to these people—the men and women excluded from the lowest levels of the pyramidal hierarchies of the Grassfields and facing lifelong bachelorhood, penury, and servitude—and to the history of their confrontations with authority that this book is devoted.[3] But in what sense can a negatively constructed category be taken as a demographic reality? Can those defined by what they lack—power, wealth, status, and consequently the protection and basic security to which full members of society are entitled—really constitute a social group?

The means by which local elites and national governments alike portray and interact with those they term their "children" or "youths" today are strongly influenced by the social history of people classified as "young" in precolonial societies. Although differences certainly exist from one society to another, young men and women in precolonial Africa were and often remain subordinate to the overarching power of male elders, and this subordination is typically expressed and played out at the local level by treating all social subordinates as children. Bayart ([1979] 1985) has termed these classificatory children "social cadets."[4] Men were therefore classified as children not as a result of their biological age (which still today is of little significance throughout much of the continent) but rather because they had not achieved the level of economic importance that would permit them to acquire wives, to build their own compounds, and to become economically viable agents. Biological adults, and in extreme cases even old men, can thus to this day be classified as children (Bayart 1989, 149; Toulabor 1992, 134). Relative seniority is not calculated simply on the basis of age but by means of a complex, multilayered assessment of an individual's economic power, social connections, kinship and affinal ties, gender, esoteric knowledge, membership in secret societies and military organizations, position in the hierarchy, and so on. The category of "youth" was and is therefore a moveable feast, a derogatory term masquerading as flattery and used by those in positions of power to define ever-shifting groups of subordinate people. What youth have in common is not their age but their exclusion from power and their dependence on the "men," "fathers," or "elders" in their societies. Bayart's term "cadet" thus usefully distinguishes this category of people from biological children, allowing us to see through the obfuscation encouraged by the euphemistic use of infantilizing terms to refer to the poor and the powerless in an iniquitous and polarized economic and political environment.[5]

In other words, African political hierarchies are said to be gerontocratic not because men (and to some extent women) accumulate power as a function of growing old but, on the contrary, because they can only grow old to the extent that they have successfully accumulated wealth and power. Women are particularly disfavored because, whereas a minority of male cadets are destined to become elders, submission to elders is a permanent rather than a temporary aspect of women's lives (Balandier 1974; Bayart [1979] 1985, 234ff.; and 1992, 54; Marie 1976; Meillasoux 1981).[6] The advent of colonialism brought about new orders of power that encouraged young men to express their frustrations and to seek an escape from their exploitation. Although some of the changes brought about as a result of colonialism seem to have been advantageous to young men and women, others were undoubtedly deleterious. The main advantage of the onset of colonial authority for a minority of young men stemmed from the need of the new bureaucracy for skilled labor: literate clerks, secretaries, and low-ranking officials who could keep the machinery of government working at the national and local levels. A small minority of young men throughout the continent were quick to take on the opportunities presented by the new balance of power. Gaining an education in one of the mission schools suddenly came to be seen as a ticket to freedom from protracted subordination to one's elders (Jindra 2005; Rowlands 1993). Rather than wait half a lifetime for the necessary wealth to obtain a wife or to gain entry into the traditional hierarchy, the young men who were about to become the "new elites" of the continent could now seek salaried employment from a third force that was independent of local authority, indeed superior to it.

For some young men, colonial occupation thus came to represent an emancipation of sorts, and these are the men who gained the most at independence, moving overnight into the posts left empty by departing European civil servants (Bayart 1989, 151; Geschiere 1997, 36). The great majority of young people did not have such opportunities, however, and for this majority, taking a chance as a laborer in one of the colonial industries was the only way of earning an income, albeit at a shocking personal risk. As I discuss later, the mortality rates on the plantations and in the mines of Africa in the early 1900s exceeded those of a war zone and even those of the Nazi labor camps of the Second World War. Despite the risks, however, some youths survived their time as laborers and returned to their communities to found a category of "new elites." This historical juncture thus marks one of the factors contributing to the adoption of the concept of "youth" as a category of political significance in Africa: no longer children but not yet elders within the classificatory systems of their societies of origin, the new elite had to be accommodated as a major new political force.

Of course, only a minority of the emerging youth of Africa were destined to become overnight success stories of emancipation, enrichment, and political empowerment. Even at the local level, the few success stories represented a problem: young men who had gained entry to the colonial and postcolonial government were no longer clearly answerable to their elders, which led to sporadic social unrest and irreversible changes within local hierarchies struggling to incorporate the new elites (Geschiere 1997, 164; Goheen 1996, 145, 161).[7] But more serious problems have arisen from the great majority of young people who sought entry to the new order but were not granted it. Deeply frustrated by the false promise of emancipation represented by mission-school educations that led to nothing, coerced into forced labor by the colonial forces, recruitment agents, and their proxy chiefs (Bayart 1989, 99–100; Chilver and Röschenthaler 2001; Geschiere 1997, 34ff.; Kilson 1966; Mbembe 1985, 90–98; Olivier de Sardan 1984), and unable to find salaried employment in the urban centers, Africa's young people spawned a rural exodus that continues to this day (Banya and Elu 1997) and engaged in millenarian movements and revolts that occasionally took on anticolonial proportions (Kramer [1987] 1993; Ranger 1975; Rouch 1955; Stoller 1989, 1995; Seekings 1993; Toulabor 1992). More often than not, however, they vented themselves locally as perpetrators of petty crimes or attacks against elders and elites (Bayart 1992, 50–51, 87; Joset 1955; Seekings 1993; Warnier 1993, 73, 199–200, 217–18).

Indeed, apart from a few exceptions, Africa's new youth were systematically divested of the right to accede to eldership as reinvented by the state, and the state can thus be seen to have reproduced rather than re-

placed local gerontocracies. Like the colonial order, the postcolonial state
has participated in a dialectical relationship with local elites, each sym-
biotically providing legitimacy for the other, and one of the outcomes of
this partnership has been the emergence of "youth" as a salient category
(Argenti 2004, forthcoming). The term "youth" has thus gained its notorious connotations not only because it was a negatively defined category
(demarcating a group whose members are neither children nor properly
adults or elders, and who are likely not to conform to the status quo) but
because of the failure of colonial and postcolonial governments to offer
any alternative to the traditional eldership they had supplanted other
than the equally exclusivist and divisive sphere of capital accumulation.
The resilience of the problem of "youth" thus cannot be laid on the doorstep of "traditional" African societies as if they were hermetically sealed
entities. Rather it denotes a liminal category resulting from the insertion
of African societies into the global economy—a process first introduced
in the seventeenth century by means of the transatlantic slave trade, perpetuated through the colonial period by means of the institutionalization
of forced labor, and further into the postcolonial period by the forced
introduction of neoliberal economic principles. Far from being eradicated,
the old category of the child has been subjected to a cancer that has made
it grow out of all social proportion. In many contemporary African states,
the rhetoric of the "father of the nation" has the effect not of implementing a policy of concern regarding youth but rather of infantilizing and thus
of disciplining the great majority of the population (Seekings 1993; Van
Dijk 1998, 1999).[8]

Rather than resolving the problems faced by young people in African
societies, then, colonial and postcolonial forms of authority have exacerbated them. Despite the construction of a new minority of "elites" or
évolués—indeed, partly because of it—power has not devolved significantly to young people, who now represent a marginalized majority group
in Africa.[9] Authoritarian forms of leadership and nation-building coupled
to the economic crises and the World Bank- and IMF-sponsored restructuring programs of the past twenty years have served to create a climate
in which the exclusion of young people from local and state power has
become once again as brazen and acute as it was in the colonial period.
Just as the desperation of marginalized cadets led them to the plantations
and the mines in search of paid employment during the colonial era, the
chimera of economic salvation presented by emerging neoliberal free-
market economies has once again led to significant out-migration from

rural communities toward the towns and cities. As mentioned earlier, this "rural exodus" was soon identified as a major problem (Bayart 1989, 41–55; Mbembe 1985, 84; Warnier 1993, 118). Although a few of the migrants managed to find employment of one kind or another, the great majority met only the severe shock and disillusion of a life of unemployment in which petty crime, prostitution, and "management" or "*débrouillardise*" in the informal sector had by the 1980s become the only modes of survival (De Boeck 1998; Devisch 1995a; Gandoulou 1989a, 1989b; Mbembe 1985; Vigh 2006; Waage 2006). Economic marginalization and political exclusion finally resulted in the 1990s in the prodemocracy movements that swept the continent, but the search for social justice was to be a futile one.[10]

Political Economies of Performance

Despite the ontological, epistemological, cultural, and historical connections between the politics of youth and the "art" of masking, a review of the literature on African masking and performance on the one hand, and of studies of childhood and youth on the other, would reveal little overlap between these two fields of study. The subject of dance has generally been ignored by mainstream anthropologists, who are consequently dependent on the excellent research carried out in departments of art history, museum studies, ethnomusicology, folklore, sociology, or cultural studies.[11] Meanwhile, the study of youth and of youth movements in Africa has largely become the preserve of sociologists and political scientists, with anthropologists only lately beginning to express an interest in the social dimensions of such movements.[12] In fact, the political and the embodied aspects of youth, which we so often separate from one another as studies of activism, militancy, or social deviance, on the one hand, and of dance, performance, ritual, or possession, on the other, are often but two sides of the same coin, and they carry an excess or supplement that transcends the procrustean imposition of Western disciplinary parameters. The dyadic polarization between the political and the cultural (the former always hailed as causal and virile, the latter often feminized and derided as representational—with the Platonic implications of representation as imitation, illusion, and falsehood—and therefore as epiphenomenal) has been imposed by an academic territorialization that is beholden to Western concepts and categories that do more to obfuscate than they do to clarify the study of either field.

In the chapters that follow, performance is made central to the study of social reproduction and social transformation by bridging several disciplines, including those of anthropology, political science, psychology, history, philosophy, and art history. If I make use of theories and methods from all of these disciplines, it is not out of a collector's passion for accumulation. Rather, it is only by triangulating in such a manner that one is likely to be able to produce a clear map of a phenomenon that is not reducible to the delineations and boundaries of Western academic or popular categories—a case paradigmatically made by Said (1995) with respect to the Western representations of the Middle East—but instead represents an inherent aspect of being-in-the-world, a being that is necessarily *at once* social, political, psychological, historical, cosmological, and aesthetic.[13] Just as the Nigerian proverb states that one cannot see a masked dance without moving oneself (Argenti 1992), so too the history of youth that I delineate here cannot be seen in the round from a single interpretative point of view.

It is perhaps ironic that dance and performance were never more central to the ethnographic project than in the heyday of the functionalist school of anthropology, which is more often remembered today for a reductionistically mechanistic approach to social formations than for its omnivorous appetite for a wide-ranging, inclusive spirit of ethnographic enquiry. The functionalist analyses of the 1920s and 1930s, in which ritual and performance were theorized as the pillars upholding the social fabric, mark some of the most notable attempts that anthropologists made systematically to enquire into the political underbelly of dance, the power of performance, or the art of politics. Studies by Radcliffe-Brown (1922) on the role of dance among the Andaman Islanders, by Malinowski ([1925] 1948) on magical rites, by Evans-Pritchard (1928) on Azande dance, and by Margaret Mead (1928) on Samoan children's dances represented, each in their own way, an avant-garde and seminal transcendence of disciplinary boundaries that would come to influence subsequent generations of anthropologists interested in the connections among power relations, social reproduction, and performance. These analyses naturally focused on the role of dance in social reproduction, leading Mead (1928), for example, to see dance as a form of social apprenticeship or education for Samoan girls, or Radcliffe-Brown to emphasize its Durkheimian integrationist force.[14] Because functionalist analyses were concerned with the contradictions between the individual and society, however, they were also to varying degrees influenced by Freud's emerging concepts, and took from these the notion that certain desires, appetites, or passions could be displaced or sublimated to another field. Thus the notion of dance as a form of apprenticeship or of social integration was overlaid with a theory of performance as a "safety valve" allowing for the release of tensions and the negotiation of contradictions in society.[15]

The view of performance as providing a safety valve can be seen to have influenced a later generation of anthropological analyses of performance that theorized dance and other embodied phenomena as a form of catharsis. I. M. Lewis's ([1971] 1989) wide-ranging work on possession rites thus suggested a relationship between the social exclusion of women and their tendency to become possessed. Max Gluckman's theory of "rituals of rebellion" (1963, 1965), in which subjects in Swaziland invert the social hierarchy by insulting and ridiculing the king once a year at the first-fruits ceremony, similarly posits performance as a cathartic release of tensions that might otherwise have spilled over into real violence.[16] Crucial as these studies were to theorizing the links between performance and social reproduction, however, they never entirely shed the functionalist mould in which they were cast. As Todd Sanders (2001) demonstrates in a critique of Gluckman's (1963) thesis, the theory of rituals of rebellion is predicated on the functionalist principle that the elements of obscenity and role reversal they evince are strictly delimited in time (ritual versus profane time), and again, they act as mere safety valves, ultimately reinforcing the status quo rather than providing the means for the marginalized to question or to challenge it in earnest.[17] Gluckman states this most clearly himself when he says that while "rites of reversal obviously include a protest against the established order ... they are intended to preserve and strengthen the established order" (1965, 109).[18]

Turner's analyses of rites of passage departed from previous approaches by moving from a theory of instrumentalism that theorizes dance as facilitating or precipitating certain social outcomes to one that was essentially meaning based or representational. Nevertheless, his work retained the notion of social solidarity and an essentially ahistorical approach to social reproduction as central tenets. Applying Van Gennep's 1909 work *Les rites de passage* to the initiation ceremonies of the Ndembu of northwestern Zambia, Turner (1967) divided the rite into the three phases of separation, transition (or limen), and incorporation. In keeping with the liminal symbolism of the transitional phase, Turner saw the boy's circumcision ceremony as "a complete reversal of the natural order ... [in which] the status hierarchy of secular society is temporarily in abeyance"

(1967, 192–93). As in Gluckman's Swazi case study, the novices are permitted to heap insults on the circumcisers. Explicitly distinguishing his approach from Gluckman's (1963), however, Turner warned against seeing this as a "rite of rebellion." Nevertheless, in arguing as he did that rites of passage were predominantly repressive, and that they served to bring together opposing factions, play down conflicts, and restore the equilibrium that was threatened by the ambiguous status of pubescent boys in the society (1967, 265–67), Turner could be said simply to have been shifting the functionalist emphasis on social reproduction to a spiritual plane that was equally teleological.[19] Moreover, as Edward Schieffelin ([1976] 2005) and Zoila Mendoza (2000) clearly demonstrate in relation to the *gisaro* dances of the Kaluli of Papua New Guinea and the mestizo masquerades of the Peruvian Andes, respectively, dance is not epiphenomenal: it is not a narrative *about* the social world but integral to its creation and transformation in a genuinely open-ended manner.

In keeping with the focus on social solidarity and reproduction in all these works, functionalist theories, theories of rites of rebellion, and theories of rites of passage, while good at describing static situations, all ultimately fail to account for the social transformations introduced by the colonial encounter and the postcolonial condition, and for the serious and unprecedented forms of exclusion, oppression, and economic exploitation, and the resulting resentment and alienation of young people and other marginalized social groups to which these have so often led (Argenti 2002a; Comaroff and Comaroff 2005; Cruise O'Brien 1996; Herzfeld 2003; Sykes 1999). The historical transformations introduced by the insertion of Africa into the world market—first of all by means of the slave trade—followed by Africa's subjugation by military expeditions, and the restructuring of its societies under colonial regimes, followed in turn by the replacement of these regimes with equally autocratic postcolonial forms of government, all presented young people with problems (and occasional opportunities) that were unprecedented. Unlike the changes introduced by the seasons, by agricultural work, by physical maturation, or by the life cycle, the extreme violence of these revolutionary and often catastrophic changes could not be accounted for by representations understood as timeless, self-contained, and as predictably repetitive as the ritual inversions of rites of rebellion or the momentary reversals of the liminal phase of rites of passage.

Even if they operate from a position of subjection, Africa's cadets have not simply been reduced to "docile bodies" by the domination and repression to which they have been subjected by local and national elites over the centuries. Ever since the advent of colonial influence in Africa, the people confronted with these new forms of authority have abounded with grassroots methods for appropriating the forms of power with which they were confronted. Many of these social movements have been reviled by colonial authorities and postcolonial elites alike for their alleged "irrationality," for the disturbing elements of satire they seemed to evince, and for the passions that the leaders of such movements were able to arouse in their acolytes. The widespread Mammi Wata cults of coastal West Africa and the Bori cult of Niger (Drewal 1988; Masquelier 1992)—not to mention countless witchcraft associations such as the *famla'*, the *msa*, or the *djambe* of Cameroon that I discuss in subsequent chapters—are typical in their reification of the powers of seduction of the material trappings of Western wealth and modernity, seemingly making available to their Faustian devotees the fabulous riches that the majority of Africans can only dream of, and yet which are regularly paraded in front of them by the elites of their countries. Although these cults are believed to be of great social value to their adherents, they are the subject of suspicion and anxiety to outside observers, encapsulating as they do, in the seductive persona of the siren or of the witch bearing gifts, both the attractions and the dangers of the pursuit of wealth without regard for social norms. If these forms of worship have a dark side, then, it is because the history of capitalism in Africa has also evinced a dark side. Africa's insertion into the global economy is drenched in the blood of the slave trade (as are, of course, those of the nation-states of Europe and America), and such cults permit their adherents to express their misgivings about the consequences of unfettered capitalist accumulation today through the use of bodily practices first sedimented by the violence done to previous generations of enslaved cadets.

Some social movements have made their political ramifications clear for all to see. For example, from the 1950s onward in Niger and then in Accra, Ghana, the Hauka movement immortalized in Jean Rouch's film *Les maîtres fous* revolved around individuals who became "possessed" by particular representatives of the French colonial administration, mimicking their forms of dress and their strange bodily comportment in ways that the authorities found deeply disturbing (Olivier de Sardan 1982, 1984, 1993; Rouch 1955; Stoller 1984; 1989, 147ff., 195; Taussig 1993, 240).[20] Again underlining the tendency of the continent's youth for pragmatism over idealism, the young participants in the Ode-lay masquerades of Freetown, Sierra Leone, cultivate close links with the city's politicians at the same time as they implicitly satirize them by appropriating their titles and exaggerating their forms of attire and the wealth to which they have access (Nunley 1987). For example, some of the militaristic titles adopted by the young members of an Ode-lay society include the "Director for defence and communication," the "Representative to the United Nations," and the "Special envoy from the O.A.U. [Organization of African Unity]" (Nunley 1987, 64).[21] This masquerade group and others in Freetown have abandoned the use of masks altogether in favor of military dress. As Nunley makes clear, the groups' military aesthetic underscores the close contacts that politicians have with such masquerade societies and objectifies the political power that these groups and their supporters wield by way of their symbiotic relationship.

These examples suggest that African masking is not adequately accounted for by means of static and bounded theories of social reproduction. Masking in Africa bears witness to social change as much as it does to reproduction, and to contacts between peoples as much as to the identity of a single social group. As Gluckman, Turner, Ottenberg, and many others have observed, masking is often engaged in by all the social strata within a group, bringing the dominated and the dominant together in a single carnivalesque event. However, this does not necessarily mean, as has so often been assumed, that masking promotes social solidarity. Rather, it has often been appropriated by the dominated—including women, the young, or otherwise marginal members of the community—who have used it to bear witness to their oppression at the hands of colonial invaders, postcolonial oligarchs, patrons, elders, and elites. Masking does not mask social inequalities; it *un*masks them. It was not because it provided a convenient safety valve or a ritualized and predictable containment of political frustrations that the French colonial authorities in Niger banned the Hauka and imprisoned its practitioners. Nor does the irreverent mimesis of the clientelism, the crime, the violence, and the desperate survivalism of life in Africa's cities today as embodied in the Ode-lay masks support theories of emasculated, ritualized rites of rebellion or of inversions performed by a momentarily liminal group that is about to be returned to the social fold.

From Terror to Farce: The Grotesque Body and the Politics of Mimetic Appropriation

The corpus of African ethnography is particularly striking for the prevalence to be found in it of examples of ordinary peoples adopting the cultural idioms of their colonial masters. This phenomenon often appears tragic and ignominious in equal measure where those engaged in the representation of colonial power have been harshly victimized by it, and yet such situations are not unusual. In one of the classic descriptions of such an event, Terence Ranger (1975) describes the Beni *ngoma* dances of East Africa, which were clearly influenced by the brass marching bands of the British military, complete with titles, ranks, and military-style uniforms with which to compliment the brass and drum music and the marching dances. Closely inspired as they were by the British military, however, Beni dances also included something that antedated the colonial experience: the competitive call-and-response jokes and insults typical of long-standing Swahili dances. Pointing to the relationship between the experience of colonial oppression and performative enactment, Ranger (1975, 10–14) records that the first Beni dances emerged in the settlements of freed slaves, in which settlers built large and elaborate replicas of battleships that then became the centerpieces of these prototypical dances. As they marched around their ships in bits of discarded uniform, shouting orders and firing rockets from makeshift portholes, they seemed to be performatively remembering the violent process of capture, enslavement, and enshipment and the further violence of interception by the British fleet and forced resettlement in coastal missionary villages. Ranger compares this embodied remembering to the mimicry of Nazi guards by concentration camp inmates in World War II. As Bruno Bettelheim has described (1943, 448), some inmates of the work camps adopted old scraps of German uniform they happened to find or sewed replicas of them for themselves. But whereas Bettelheim concludes that these prisoners had internalized the ideology of the Gestapo, Ranger questions the notion that the Beni *ngoma* dances may be nothing more than the reenactment of the trauma of subjection to "absolute power." On the one hand (1975, 20–21), he notes that Beni dances were not static repetitions of an original traumatic event but that they regularly evolved, constantly incorporating new choreographic elements, musical forms, lyrics, and costumes. On the other hand, he points out the pleasurable, joyous ethos that these dances evinced irrespective of their symbolically violent content and the catastrophic status of their original referents (15).

Fritz Kramer provides a more explicit example of this type of appropriation, the de Gaulle dance of the Fang of Gabon, which was danced in large European-styled summerhouses by men and women dressed in European colonial costume. Just as in the Beni dances, this dance featured dignitaries, including the president, the customs officials, or the police magistrate, who took their places under a French flag. At the climax of the dance, de Gaulle himself would appear in a resplendent uniform, together with Eboué, the governor general, and General Pétain. In a mimicry of military drill and colonial bureaucracy, de Gaulle would inspect the dancers' clothes, impose fines, and watch the women's dances as if on the parade ground. Despite the potentially sinister subject matter of this dance, however, Kramer follows Ranger in stressing the sense of joy that the dance evoked: "Despite this military ambience, the dance was concerned with love and seduction; . . . the dancers sang by way of welcome: 'De Gaulle, o! come, take the village; De Gaulle, you're the man I cry for'" ([1987] 1993, 131).[22]

The Hauka movement of Niger mentioned earlier also emerged during and clearly in response to the French colonial period. Échard (1991, 1992), Fuglestad (1975), Olivier de Sardan (1982, 1984), Stoller (1989, 1995), and Taussig (1993, 240) all emphasize the subversive, political significance of this performance, during which the dancers would become possessed by the spirits of colonial administrators. The widespread Mammi Wata cults of coastal West Africa and the Bori cult of Niger (Drewal 1988; Masquelier 1992; Onwuejeogwu 1969; Smith 1954) could be cited as examples of similar movements, representing as they do for their devotees the powers of seduction of the material trappings of Western wealth and modernity, and seemingly making available to them the fabulous riches that the majority of Africans can only dream of, yet which are regularly paraded in front of them by the elites of their countries. A more recent example of a performance genre that reenacts the experience of the power of the state is provided by John Nunley's (1987, 64) work on Ode-lay masquerade societies mentioned earlier.

The equally young, marginal, and unemployed *sapeurs* of Brazzaville provide another recent case. These young *aventuriers* or *sapeurs* have developed a desperate culture of extroversion around the cult of the foreign and are regularly referred to as "delinquents" by the elites whose exorbitant European designer style of clothing and general hedonism they mimic (Gandoulou 1989a, 1989b; MacGaffey and Bazenguissa-Ganga 2000). Participation in this movement is only possible by travel to Paris, where aspirant *sapeurs* undergo extremes of penury to save the money with which to buy the requisite set of designer outfits needed to return to Brazzaville. There, they display their new *gamme,* the complete range of outfits they hope will gain them entry (however illegitimate and fleeting) into the space of the elites.[23] Gandoulou (1989a) makes the point that the *sapeurs* of Brazzaville are not involved in an act of mere parody of the Europeans or the Congolese elites they emulate but in an attempt to appropriate some of the trappings of modern power.[24]

The members of Air Youth, a youth association and dance group of the Grassfields chiefdom of Oku, wear blue track suits and red berets—the latter a reference to the national paramilitary police's uniform—and perform a dance that, once again, embodies all of the signature gestures of the national government (all of which are inherited, in turn, from the old colonial administration of Cameroon): shaking hands, saluting, and the obligatory military inspection by the sergeant carrying a decorated stick that is at times shaken like a ceremonial dance-spear or Dane gun but at other times smartly swung and pointed like a drill sergeant's swagger stick (Argenti 1998). In her description of one of the Zionist churches of the Tshidi of South Africa, Jean Comaroff (1985, 202–28) likewise notes the use by dancers and their acolytes of uniforms influenced not only by the Christian church but also by modern military attire; she also highlights the ambiguous use of brass staffs to connote, at once, the cudgels used in old initiation rituals, bishops' staffs, the Rastafarian "rod of correction," and military dress-swords (226). In all of these cases—the de Gaulle dancers, the Hauka initiates, the Ode-lay maskers, the *sapeurs,* the Mbaya dancers, and the South African Zionists—it is clear that although outright emulation or mimicry is not the object (that is, the dancers do not want to *become* the colonial officers, whom they fear as a source of violence and oppression), neither is satire: these performances do not seek to ridicule their exemplars so much as to appropriate them—a process that entails the transformation of the exemplar.

The performances and possession rites described here may be thought of as modernist in their self-conscious departures from local canons of style and tradition and in their references to exogenous sources of power and domination. But performance genres that might at first glance be thought of as long-standing and unblemished by the ravages of time and the pernicious interventions of global forces also have histories, points of origin, and connections to transregional forces that tie them too into the tentacular reach of the black Atlantic.[25] The "timeless" or "traditional" masks and rites found in the slave-hunting grounds of the Western world may not be modernist in their aesthetics, but they are certainly modern in their references to historical processes that bind Africa to Europe and the Americas across an Atlantic corridor of political, economic, and cultural relations that has for centuries exploded locality, traduced boundaries, and problematized homogeneous notions of space, place, and time. In its dialectical engagement with world histories and global processes, African masking has always been modern. Once masking is itself conceived as a response to modernity—albeit preexisting colonial domination and, in many instances, even first contact with Europeans, though not with European trade—one need no longer differentiate between specious (and ultimately romantic) divisions of masking into "traditional" and "modern" or "innovative" styles, and one is freed from searching for authentic, premodern forms of masking, from which deviations represent failed emulations and de facto corruptions.

The question remains, then, of how masking relates to memory and history. The examples I've given all have one thing in common that makes them good points of departure for examining this question: they clearly are reenactments of events that their participants (or their elders or ancestors) have lived through; at the same time, however, they all introduce *something new* to what they enact. On one level, the performances described could all be said to recall the violent events that have triggered them, and to lead to the surrender of their participants to the realities that they evoke, but—*at the same time*—they transform these realities, introducing new elements to them that dramatically change their significance while nevertheless leaving the events they refer to untouched—untouchable. Similarly, to witness or to participate in the masked dances of the Grassfields is to be thrown powerfully back into the violent events that have inspired them, to be brought face to face with the slave raiders, to be marched once again to the coast. At the same time, however, these dances *are not* the slave raids, they *are not* the forced marches—they are dances. As such, they are full of the joy, the passion, and the transcendent pleasure of dance. To the horror of its exemplar, the dance introduces—precisely by means of incorporation—what Bakhtin ([1957] 1968) terms grotesque realism.

In his paradigmatic work on the carnivalesque elements of Rabelais's writing, Bakhtin delved into the history of carnival in Europe from prehistoric times to the Renaissance.[26] Where the business of the medieval church and state were represented in spiritual, ascetic terms, carnival celebrated the corporeal, the sensual, and the humorous. Although the festive life that had once been integral to religious devotion was relegated to the people and made a part of folk culture in the medieval period, it nevertheless remained uniquely important, generative, and seminal of social reproduction despite its impure and low status. Medieval carnival was not merely a cultural festival but constituted an inherent part of social life itself. Carnival was no less real than the periods of Lent with which it contrasted; it was not a satirical representation of the serious but its other side—its festal dimension that was ever present in the social body of the people. The chaotic reversals, inversions, blasphemies, and uncrownings of carnival were not a temporary hiatus in the business of the state; they were its very engine and source of strength. Where the church and state lauded permanence, immutability, and stability, carnival invited change, renewal, and rebirth. Where the state and church were hierarchical, monolithic, and petrified, carnival was open-ended, heterogeneous, and inclusive. In Bakhtin's "grotesque realism" ([1957] 1968, 18–21), as he terms Rabelais's literary celebration of the generative degradation of carnival, the power of the state is incorporated in the body of the people—a body that is not individual but communal—and in this very incorporation, the state itself is reconstituted and transformed. This amalgamation is why in grotesque realism all that is bodily becomes grandiose. Grotesque realism celebrates degradation. In this genre, the earth and the lower regions of the human body alike are not only negative elements but regenerative ones too: impure and profane, but fertile and seminal.[27]

In a manner similar to that of the political transformations of the medieval carnival, the dance in the Grassfields—also centrally concerned with death, burial, and mourning as well as with farce, celebration, and survival—transforms the serious, oppressive aspects of the slave trade that it incorporates and plays on the ambiguity of this double inscription. Between being and not being, art and life, exemplar and reenactment, trauma and play, the dance brings the past into presence as the new and transforms the death of close kin into the celebration of long dead ancestors and the revelation of political oppression.[28] The dance thus represents a heterogeneous, living form of historical remembering that stands as the very antithesis of monolithic memorializing histories.[29] In their doubled, indeterminate relation to history, the mimetic performances of the Grassfields confound Manichean binary oppositions between authenticity and copy, truth and falsity, primary event and repetition, restituting the sensuousness of experience to that which has fallen outside discursive memory.[30]

The Ghosts of Others: Inenunciability, or the Presence of the Past

Communities ravaged by internecine violence do not tend to elaborate explicit discourses about their predicament, but they sometimes adopt indirect and ambiguous forms of speech and representation. In some communities, it is not necessarily "good to talk," and if the children of the Grassfields "talk back," they do not do so in ways that one might expect them to. Cadets do not verbally berate their elders or their chiefs, nor do they even complain about them privately to each other that often.[31] But a social sphere that has been cleansed of direct, referential forms of speech—in which allusions to violence and domination are masked in both senses of the word—raises serious questions for historians: if crimes, wars, acts of political violence, and various forms of political oppression are never spoken about, how are they remembered? To what extent is it possible to have a history of the unsaid? In a context in which events and phenomena are not spoken about, one might be tempted to ask to what extent the ineffable and the unremembered can be thought of as part of social reality in any significant way. Such doubts give rise to perhaps the most sinister question of all: if unremembered events are not part of social reality, then perhaps they never really happened? Commentators on the crimes against humanity for which the twentieth century will be remembered have noted this magical effect of totalitarian regimes, which have not only perpetrated atrocities but have also ensured that these atrocities remain in essence largely unspeakable.[32] In the aoristic words of Maurice Blanchot in *The Writing of the Disaster* (1995, 42), one of the central questions with which this book is preoccupied is therefore how one is to "keep watch over absent meaning."

Otherwise put, discursive silence cannot be assumed to point to an epistemological silence: the descendants of those who suffered through the space of death that the hunting grounds of the Grassfields were at the time of the slave trade, and of those who labored and died in the plantations and on the forced marches of the caravan porters of the colonial era are silent today about these catastrophes and their contemporary postcolonial predicament alike not because they do not *know* of them, but because they are forced to bear witness to their excessive nature in radically alternative ways. Although it may be tempting from an empirical point of view to dismiss that which is not made explicit (and thus effectively to erase it from the historical record), we are called upon to recognize that peoples find ways of bearing witness to the silences of their histories— ways that are found where language and discursive memory break down. Moreover, as anthropologists and historians, we are now called upon to develop the analytical methods to bear witness to these silent witnesses.[33] In keeping with segments of other West and central African communities ravaged by slavery and later exposed to colonial exploitation, the cadets of the Grassfields may not speak of their past, but they live with it—or, to put it more precisely, it lives with them and *in* them: ever present in their bodies, palpable and unforgotten.

Writing a political history of slavery and colonialism in the Grassfields, as has been observed with writing histories of transatlantic slavery more generally, is a process fraught with difficulty. This difficulty, however, is due not only to the practical obstacles arising from the lack of records, the illiteracy of the protagonists, or their political powerlessness and consequent inability to ensure that testimonies were heard and records were kept. More importantly, it arises from the fact that regimes of terror such as those that turned the Grassfields into human hunting grounds from the seventeenth to the early twentieth centuries, transforming the region into an anarchic and amoral zone of plunder in which social structures and ordered cosmologies were radically undermined by the effective collapse of security and the regular disappearance and death of close family members, eventually culminating in the serious depopulation of the area, are somehow beyond the scope of historical record. This point raises the fundamental question of the very possibility of constructing coherent histories of catastrophe, disaster, massacre, or genocide—whether for those involved or for professional historians. I have just stated that the silence of survivors and their descendants cannot be assumed to evince an ignorance or a failure to remember, but it is also true that the violence of history may problematize and fragment knowing, requiring us to conceive of alternative epistemologies of remembering.

The possibility that the peoples of the Grassfields may be haunted not only by their own ghosts—that is, by the memories of their immediate ancestors—but by the ghosts of others descended from a more distant past begs important questions regarding the possibility of taking account of embodied experience and remembering in standard historical discourse, with its scaffolding of linear, progressive temporality.[34] What does a fragmented temporality called forth by performative or embodied remembering imply for the possibility of historical representation? Is not historical representation predicated on leaving the past behind, when in fact the most inescapable feature of violent pasts is that they will not be left behind because they exist in the perpetual present of the struggles and cleavages they have spawned?[35] These problems lead Cathy Caruth (1991c, 182) to envisage "a history that is no longer straightforwardly referential," and Lyotard (1990) to argue that standard narrative histories do violence to histories of violence. In purporting to reinstate the positivist chronology separating the original violence from its later representation or performance—causal effect from secondary affect—such positivist history is false to subjective experience. It "instantly occults what motivates it, and . . . is made for this reason" (1990, 16). This is history as memorialization, which courts forgetting by attempting to place a too-easy closure on events that will not stay where they belong in time and refuse to be forgotten: "the present is the past, and the past is always presence" (16).

The transfer of achronological to chronological time, or from remembering to memory effected by narrative organization, can be described as a form of memorialization. Representing in words and images what has not yet attained a definitive form or meaning, but remains the site of an ongoing struggle, gives a single, inevitably essentialized meaning to what is in fact undetermined and thereby constitutes a means of forgetting. The violence characteristic of all stages of modernity—beginning with the humanitarian catastrophe perpetrated by the emergence of a global economy indissoluble from the Atlantic slave trade in the seventeenth and eighteenth centuries—calls for a means of social representation that will somehow amount to more than a paradoxical obliteration of that which it purports to disclose. I argue in the following chapters that the effects of the slave trade are still felt in Cameroon to this day not despite but *because* of the nondiscursive, sensuous, corporeal, embodied nature of practices to which they have given rise, and which together amount not to memorial ceremonies but to living practices of remembering. To depict without essentializing this silent world of the unsaid and the undetermined that stands outside of time, I delineate the foundations of a new history of violence in three closely related ways: first, by examining the ways in which victims of violence and their descendants bear witness to their past and to the presence of their past; second, by structuring this work itself as an act of bearing witness in its own right; and third, by offering it to my informants as a potential new way to bear witness through texts.

If this work is to avoid the trap of building monuments and mausoleums in which to entomb memory and to consign it to oblivion, it must do so through a history that records the implosion of time and the encryption of violent events in ourselves and in our bodies. Therefore, in the chapters that follow I delineate as nearly as possible a lived history of the Grassfields that attests to what lies beyond narrative representation in the violent past/present of the slave trade and colonial occupation and remains forever to-be-remembered, like "an interminably deferred debt" (Lyotard

1990, 28).[36] To date, histories and ethnographies of the colonial world—like the myths of origin they describe—have largely confined themselves to representing what we might call, following Homi Bhabha's "Time of the Nation" (1990), the Time of the King. Taking forward Bakhtin's model of the chronotope as the time-space of the nation, Bhabha identifies the discursive construction of the modern nation as an a priori historical presence about which the state instructs the people. This is "pedagogical" or "empty" time, which is presented as undifferentiated from the past, which in turn is unilineal, "continuist," and "progressivist" (1990, 303, 309). It is a form of time in which the past is used in an attempt to create the space of the modern nation by means of a narrative of origins, development, and progress, which again involves more forgetting than it does remembering. Within this chronotope, difference from essentialized foreign others is stressed with the same aim of emphasizing historical continuity, so that "the difference of space returns as the Sameness of time" (300). In contrast to this "pedagogical" time-space, however, another, "performative" time-space is created by the people that bears witness to their incommensurate, subjective experience of time, history, and national identity. This performative time—which we could call, in contrast to the Time of the King, the time of the people—is "non-sequential," "problematic," "ambivalent," and "chiasmatic" (299, 293), attesting to mixed origins and forgotten or suppressed episodes of state-sponsored violence, which give memory a "ghostly" or "double" aspect as they seem to recur in the present (295).[37]

Where empiricist, evidential discursive forms have largely ignored performative time, or the time of the people, fictional writing has come to the fore. An entire genre has now emerged known as testimonial writing, or *testimonio*, which attempts to address the social history and the human cost and consequence of regimes of terror on the social fabric of victimized communities. Thus Christine van Boheemen-Saaf (1999) has written a critical analysis of James Joyce's work as a means of conveying the inexpressible trauma of colonial occupation, the pathological effects of which are inscribed into Joyce's very language. The emerging Latin American genre of *testimonio* is similarly oriented toward addressing wounds that have yet to heal because they have never fully been acknowledged. Unnold's (2002) work on the *testimonio* of the Pinochet regime in Chile makes this point clearly, pointing out that although the atrocities of the Nazi regime culminated in the relative closure afforded by the Nuremberg trials, in Chile "official" versions of history still prevail despite the change in government, and the untold suffering of that era is still veiled by revisionist state-sponsored versions of the past. A dominant model of the past that publicly and explicitly confronts the abuses of the Pinochet regime has not yet been unequivocally established. As Unnold puts it, *testimonio* establishes itself as an alternative representation of history, challenging the truthfulness and completeness of official representations (2002, 41), and the genre should therefore be seen not as fiction but as nonfiction (18). What the violence of political repression achieves is not only its effects on the bodies of the tortured but on the body of society, which is torn apart by the cleavages resulting from the fracturing of families, the diasporic dispersal of refugees, and the guilty silences of unacknowledged crimes and betrayals. In such circumstances, works such as those of Isabelle Allende, including *The House of the Spirits,* serve to bridge the gulf between the past and the present and to retrieve from oblivion the unacknowledged suffering of the past that still lingers in the present.[38]

Toni Morrison's (1987) novel *Beloved,* set in the United States during the period of slavery, stands out in this genre of writing as one of the foremost illustrations of the effects of political violence on remembering. It manages where history fails by depicting its effects in the person of Beloved: an apparition that straddles time periods and haunts the house of Sethe, a character based on factual reports of a woman who killed her baby girl in a desperate attempt to save her from the slave owners who were about to apprehend them after their escape from captivity. On one level, Beloved the young woman is the ghost of the baby girl, returned in the flesh as if she had only been absent. She thus embodies in a concrete, corporeal sense the memory of her violent death at the hands of her mother. However, Beloved also suffers from intrusive memories and flashbacks that hint to other pasts: of having lived in sexual bondage to two slave owners, a father and son. These are clearly not the baby girl's memories but someone else's. Moreover, she also has recurring but vague, indeterminate memories that appear to represent an abduction in the African hinterland, and others—more horrific still, despite their poetic aestheticization—of the Middle Passage, which link her with previous generations of slaves who were taken from the ports of the African Slave Coast. Because these memories are indeterminate, they represent or refer to many historical periods simultaneously, and in this manner Toni Morrison is able to convey the lived experience of slavery more effectively than orthodox histories of Atlantic slavery have been able to. Because of the "re-memories" to which Beloved subjects her "mother" Sethe, insatiably forcing her to recount more and more of their past lives, Sethe is "wrapped in a timeless present" (Morrison 1987, 184).[39]

As a result of the bloody legacy of slavery, time can no longer constitute a full present for "freed" slaves such as Beloved. History itself is transformed by these events and countless others like them, and the ghost of Beloved thus represents a postmodern historicity in contradistinction to a now impossible metaphysical history. This postmodern historicity is invoked to address a time fragmented by the looping effects of violence and political oppression, which prevent people from living their lives in a unitary and secure metaphysical present, condemning them instead to live—over and over again—in different times with recurring but unresolved, indeterminate experiences. But embracing postmodern historicities does not imply that we need abandon all claims to the past. On the contrary, it is precisely positivist metaphysical histories that fail to account for the indeterminacy—and therefore the continuing relevance—of the past in the present. This is not only the case with reference to those who lived through the Shoah, through Hiroshima or Nagasaki, or through American slavery, but perhaps still more urgently for those in nonliterate societies presumed to be "without history." Those descended from the survivors of the slave trade in the hinterlands of the African Slave Coast would seem to be in double jeopardy: not only, given their lack of a tradition of scriptural record-keeping, are they in danger of being essentialized as a "people without writing" (Manganaro 1990), but they have largely responded to the period of slavery with an unplumbed silence (Austen 2001; Baum 1999, 16; Shaw 2002, 8–9).[40]

In contrast to the majority of ordinary discursive practices, dances are polyvalent, labile, and ambiguous in their references and in the experiential and emotional effects they bring into play. Many dancers in the Grassfields may know the basic referential elements of the dances in which they participate, such as what animals or types of person the masks they wear represent, but the magical or supernatural effects associated with the dance and the elements of danger in the performance highlight a realm of experience that participants are unable to bring to full consciousness or to express verbally. Likewise, the elements of dance that come close to the experience of possession blur the boundary between the voluntary and the involuntary aspects of bodily remembering and liken dance to witchcraft affliction or possession. And the passionate, transcendent sensations of pleasure, pain, fear, and sorrow that are achieved by the dancers and their acolytes cannot be visited again in language afterward. (People seldom speak about a dance, and when they do, it is only in the most mundane and practical fashion.) Rather, it is *the dance itself* that they repeat over and over again.

I have suggested that the practice of dancing brings to life and transforms memories of extreme violence by introducing a third term or a
supplement to the binary oppositions of verbal discourse. In his reading
of Plato's *Phaedrus,* Derrida ([1972] 1997) elaborates the functions of
this third term in ancient Greek thought. The word *pharmakon* as used in
the work of Plato has been translated in Western texts by the single term
"drug," but Derrida shows that its meaning was originally much richer and
more ambiguous than this reductive translation suggests. The *pharmakon*
referred not only to drug or cure but to their opposites: poison, infection,
and illness. Derrida goes on to show that writing itself was thought of
as a type of *pharmakon,* "a 'recipe' (*pharmakon*) for both memory and
wisdom" ([1972] 1997, 71). But the *pharmakon* of writing is critiqued by
Plato as representing a remedy that is also a poison, introducing as it does
a mimicry of speech (*logos*) and a pretence of memory. In Plato's critique,
writing is "the miserable son" (145) of speech, evincing "the distress of the
orphan" (77). It is good only for re-memoration, recollection, or commemoration (*hypomnēsis*), not for living, knowing memory (*mnēmē*). Writing
is "not a remedy for memory, but for reminding" (102). Plato thus presents
writing as a suspect, magical form of mimesis, with the consequence that
in Western culture, mimesis has ever since been denigrated as a problem
or a failure. But Derrida critiques Plato's supposition that memory could
exist in a pure form, without any sign or supplement: a *mnēmē* with no
hypomnēsis. Writing, like painting (another of the meanings of *pharmakon* is "paint" or "dye")—or, in our case, dance—introduces the play of
difference; it is "parricidal," but not without connection to its "father"
(164). Derrida thus concludes that there cannot be any representation
without transformation.[41] The mimetic—what imitates—is not imitative:
it is new. As such, it can paradoxically be mimetic of what remains in the
future, to come. The double can precede the simple, and representations
can be indeterminate before they are presented again as reductions (190).
In this manner, the supplementarity of dance makes it forward looking
and anticipatory, imitative of a future to come.

The people of the Grassfields exist today—and have done so since
the advent of the colonial era—in a political system whose local policing
institutions are all doubled by those of the state, and in which the state
has appropriated *fons* as local government and ruling-party representatives. The cadets of the Grassfields are now answerable not only to the
palace authorities but also to the national government and the security
forces that represent it at the local level. Because the state has failed in

the past decades to live up to young people's hopes for education and employment, and because the Anglophone Cameroonians of the Grassfields find it particularly difficult to gain entry into a Francophone-dominated government, the cadets of the Grassfields are now doubly marginalized: first by the "traditional" authorities of the chiefdom, and second by the national authorities. Young people's response to their marginalization at both levels has been to seek alternative avenues to political influence in opposition political struggle, but these attempts have been so brutally suppressed by the state that the contemporary predicament of youth has come to stand more in continuity than in contrast with the violence of the precolonial and the colonial eras. Although the government legalized opposition parties in 1990, the basic tenets of multiparty politics are ignored with impunity by the ruling elite.[42]

The reproduction of the authoritarian condition of postcolonialism—itself a reproduction of colonial violence, which was in turn seen as a continuation of slavery—has arguably been most strongly marked in the North West Province, where, following both the 1992 election and the subsequent banning of foreign observers from the 1997 election, the Anglophone region of Cameroon was subjected to a wave of repression. No sooner was the 1992 election result announced than John Fru Ndi, the SDF presidential candidate widely believed to have won the election, was placed under house arrest and the entire North West Province was placed under a state of emergency. These maneuvers allowed the armed

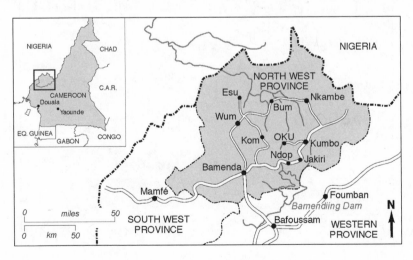

FIGURE 1. North West Province.

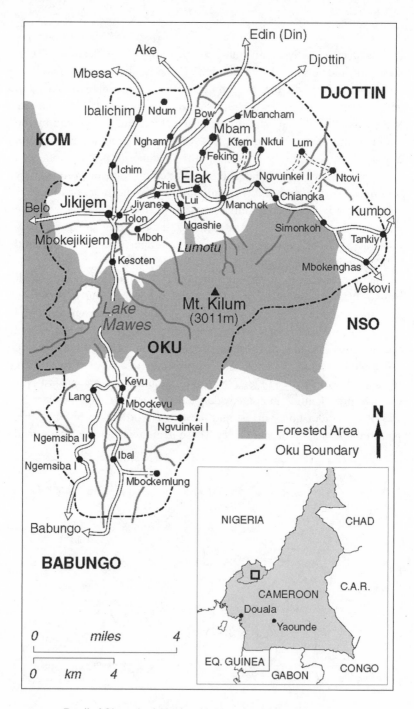

FIGURE 2. Detail of Oku and neighboring chiefdoms, North West Province.

forces a free hand in establishing a regime of repression against all SDF officeholders, party members, and suspected supporters, and mass arrests of suspected SDF sympathizers at all levels of the organization took place (Amnesty International 1992; *Africa Confidential* 1997; Takougang and Krieger 1998). Even the official launch of the SDF in 1990 was marred by serious state-sponsored violence as 2,000 troops fired tear gas and live bullets at the marching supporters, killing six young adults. Indeed, it is primarily the young and the cadets alienated by the ruling party who have flocked to the opposition SDF, making of this political party another youth movement in the mould of preceding youth insurrections that have punctuated the history of the Grassfields at regular intervals.

Again, during the 1992 occupation, gendarmes opened fire indiscriminately in a crowded marketplace in the chiefdom of Kom, sending people fleeing over the border into Oku. Cases of beating and rape were commonplace throughout the North West Province during the 1992 occupation, and they were repeated during a second incursion in 1996–97. The violence of the paramilitary forces was so acute on this occasion that the population of Oku was forced to flee into the surrounding forest, retracing the steps of their ancestors, who had escaped into the mountains to seek refuge from raiding Chamba slave catchers, or later, as members of the floating population, to evade the impositions of oppressive chiefs and colonial labor recruiters. During pro-SDF party rallies and peaceful demonstrations, party members are often assaulted by the gendarmerie, whose tactics range from the use of water canon and tear gas to beatings with truncheons and even the indiscriminate use of firearms against unarmed demonstrators (cf. United Kingdom Home Office 2001, 6, 26; U.S. Department of State 2001, sec. 1.c; 2003). On October 1, 2001, in the town of Nso', paramilitary police opened fire on a crowd of demonstrators marching in support of the Southern Cameroons National Council;[43] the police indiscriminately killed three people and seriously injured several others. Rank-and-file members of opposition parties are also regularly arrested during such events and then held in detention for extended periods without charge or trial.[44]

In such a political context, embodied practices that evoke the struggles and confrontations between cadets and elites remain emotively charged as commentaries on the present, revealing more continuities than they do breaks with the past and traducing discourses of progress and development as they bear witness to a political landscape that is still now the site of an ongoing struggle between youths and elders, marginalized cadets

and political elites. The dances performed by the cadets of the Grassfields
bear witness to the fractured temporality that they embody, enabling them
to keep watch over the silent, unspoken violence of their predicament.
At the same time, however, their experience does not go unchallenged,
and the performative embodiments of the palace masks forever threaten
to introduce a modernist, linear temporality—the Time of the King—according to which, practices of memorialization would consign the past to
a monolithic set of memorial practices, forgetting the violence of the past
in order to dissimulate the violence of the present.

Kings, Slaves, and Floating Populations: Discourses of Centrality and Marginality in the Precolonial Era

The transformation of the real into the unreal is part of the process by which man conceals from himself the human origin of his own violence, by attributing it to the gods. — René Girard ([1972] 1977, 161)

Vitality is regained ... a conquered vitality obtained from outside beings. ... It is through this substitution that an image is created in which humans can leave this life and join the transcendental. ... They become part of permanent institutions, and as superior beings they can reincorporate the present life through the idiom of conquest or consumption. — Maurice Bloch (1992, 5)

No greater power can be claimed by a political or military leader than that he can conquer a territory and then himself become the source of the fertility on which that territory depends. — David Lan (1985, 102)

"Nowhere do the multiple possibilities for constructing any history come into such obvious confrontation as in accounts of beginnings." So warn Ralph Austen and Jonathan Derrick (1999, 5) at the outset of their monograph on the Duala of coastal Cameroon in a remark that could equally have been made with reference to the hinterland Grassfields. In looking back at the body of foundation myths that serve as the oral history of the polities of the Grassfields and the source of legitimacy of the ruling elite, what strikes one foremost is the lack of credibility for many of the assertions they contain, with the ubiquitous claims to origins in the Tikar plateau to the east of the Grassfields first among these.[1] Clearly then, the myths of the Grassfields cannot be seen as constituting an oral history or an oral tradition in any straightforward sense (cf. Vansina 1985). Nevertheless, they can be seen to encapsulate a body of subjective experience relating to the past, and in this sense to constitute a body of social memory.

In this chapter and the next, I place these myths in relation to what we might call the "objective evidence" (sparse as it is) covering the political developments of the eighteenth and nineteenth centuries, and suggest possible interpretations for the iconic events to which the myths refer, such as the genesis of states in the massacre of endogenous populations and the inevitably foreign origins (or claims thereto) of the ruling elite. In chapter 3, I analyze the witchcraft discourses of the Grassfields in a manner similar to my analysis of the myths of origin, placing them in the context of the slave trade that clearly contributed to their genesis and their present structure. From chapter 4 onward, I turn to my observations of contemporary masked performance to support my interpretations with a body of cultural practices that seems to embody all of the conflicts and contradictions that reside at the heart of state formation in the region. Although I delve into the past, my aim is not to produce a history of the Grassfields but to analyze from an anthropological standpoint the ways in which the past continues to inform social relations between youth and elites in the present.[2]

My focus on two bodies of conservative ritual practice—myths and masking—sheds light on the role these practices played in the past during the eras of slavery and colonial occupation. These ritual practices are still very much alive today, however, and this study ultimately highlights the social effects that the bodies of memory that these practices nurture and maintain continue to have in the present. Looking at foundation myths, witchcraft discourses, and palace masking as so many strands of the same discourse, I explore the legitimating effects that these practices had for the elites who deployed them. I also highlight the appropriations these practices have undergone at the hands of the marginalized youth, who had little to gain from exclusive hierarchies and the increasingly onerous demands the members of those hierarchies made upon their peoples. Such marginalized youth have for centuries aggressively and creatively reinterpreted the canon of Grassfields discourses, subjecting social memory to revisions, doublings, and veiled critiques that make of these ritual discourses and embodiments today the rich, disjunctive, labile, and irreducibly polyvocal genre that they are.

Things Hidden since the Foundation of the World

The same discourse that places Grassfields chiefs, known as *fons*, centrally within their polities paradoxically represents them as outsiders, strangers, or liminal characters of one sort or another. Origin myths of the royal lineages of the Grassfields inevitably describe wandering hunters lost in the forest and moving restlessly from place to place for a protracted period before settling in what would become the kingdom of their children.[3] Chichi, one of the first leaders to be remembered in the Oku origin myth, is memorialized as a wanderer who uprooted his people from their homeland and led them on a peripatetic journey through the forest. According to some versions of the myth, Wu Chichi and Chie, his two successors, continued this wandering exile for a further two generations, fleeing from slave raiders as they went. Chie is the first hero of the myth to reach present-day Oku. His son Ngang is remembered as a savior of his people, protecting them against invading "strangers of the bow-and-arrow"—mounted slave raiders coming from the north. Two of his descendants, Nyaya (Ever-away-from-home) and Nei, are both spoken of in many versions of the origin myth as returning to the itinerant ways of their predecessors: hunting in the forest for extended periods of time before settling down to rule the kingdom. Nei is said to have died in the forest by falling from a cliff during one of his hunting forays. When myths of origin do not associate early fons with the forest per se, they often ascribe to them magical powers to inhabit bodies of water or caves located within forests. Such is the case of the legendary Mkong Mote of Oku, reputed to have saved the polity from the claims of the fon of the neighboring Kom people by entering into the sacred lake Mawɛs and being chosen by its eponymous resident goddess.[4] In Oku the crater lake Mawɛs is said to be the dwelling place of the ancestors, who come out in their "day" at night, at which point the lake drains away to reveal their village. Otters are endemic in the crater lake, where their amphibious and nocturnal existence leads them to be associated with the other world of ghosts, spirits, and ancestors. In accordance with their presumed closeness to the gods and the ancestors reputed to reside in the bottom of the lake and in the wild untenanted areas of the polity, otters, whenever they are accidentally trapped by hunters, are given a burial ceremony as a human being would be.[5]

   In Oku, all new fons enact their close relationship to this sacred crater lake through the circumambulation of the lake they undertake after their enthronement, a walk that reenacts the mythical descent of the legendary

Mkong Mote into the lake (Bah 2000, 2005). In keeping with the exogenous origin of the king's lineage and his close association with the forest surrounding the polity, the palace itself is mirrored in another, secret palace hidden inside a part of the forest known as Lumotu—a thin corridor of primary forest extending down from the main body of the Kilum forest toward the palace in Elak (Argenti 2002a). The palace of Lumotu is essentially a scaled-down version of the palace in the capital, Elak, in which the fon normally resides. It is said that this second palace was built in the forest after Mkong Mote—echoing his emergence from the sacred lake Mawes in the founding myth of Oku—emerged from his grave in the palace at Elak shortly after his burial, and, having assumed the form of a snake, traveled to the forest site, where he preferred to be interred. The fon and his entourage make an annual pilgrimage from the palace in Elak to the one in Lumotu to this day. Through the use of myths of foreign or sylvan origin, feral forms of address, retreats to the forest, and the propagation of the belief that they are *finte*—capable of transformation into dangerous animals—the kings of Oku and their entourages are constructed as liminal figures, with one foot in this world and another in the chthonian world of the forest and its sacred lake. Nor are these myths considered mere constructs by those who keep them alive today. Fay Keming of Eghok Ntul, one of the highest-ranking members of the palace hierarchy, told me he had once seen snake tracks in the dust of the palace *kwifon* compound.[6] He was adamant that they had been left by the recent passage of Mkong Mote from the site of his original grave.

Not only are the mythical leaders of the Grassfields said to have traversed or dwelled in the region's forests, but contemporary leaders are credited with keeping close ties to this realm. In addition to the sylvan origin myths, the small patches of primary forest that are still today sedulously preserved near many of the region's palaces ensure that contemporary fons literally live in the forest.[7] The ties that bind fons to the world of the forest are most strongly evinced, however, in the animality that distinguishes them quite radically from the rest of the population. Fons of the Grassfields proper as well as of the forest belt to its south are renowned for possessing doubles in the form of large forest mammals, and they are accordingly addressed by their retainers and pages as Leopard (*bà*) or Bush Cow (*nial*). When the fon addresses the public, attendees punctuate his speech with regular praise names derived from the bellowing of wild animals, such as the sound "*mbee*," the call of the bush cow. Others blow into elephant tusks when the fon is about to appear in public, thus announcing his imminent arrival with a call uncannily reminiscent of the elephant's bellow. When the fon does appear, he is literally covered in the exuviae of his forest transforms: elephant-tail hair or porcupine quills protrude from his crown, leopard teeth and claws adorn his neck, otter and leopard furs are bound around his waist, bangles of ivory hang from him, and when seated on his throne, he holds a cup carved from a bush-cow horn and rests his feet on elephant tusks.

In accordance with the primary representation of fons as leopards, the royal eligibles—the princes from among whom fons must be chosen—are known as "children of the leopard's bed" in many of the regional languages. Until the extinction of the last remaining large forest mammals in the 1970s, any royal game killed in the forest was brought to the palace so that the fon could participate in its mock funeral and then in its cleaning, butchering, and distribution among the palace elite and the lineage heads. A fon's demand for ivory from a chief constituted a demand for the political submission of his people, and its refusal an act of rebellion (Chilver 1961, 253). Fons kept the leopard teeth and claws, the bush-cow horns, and the elephant-tail hair as articles of personal adornment that constituted a royal prerogative. Many of the trade goods that the palaces of the Grassfields monopolized were also forest products or products of the forest edge: camwood, palm oil, and a certain wood and seed pod of which small quantities are scraped into ablutions essential to all the major rituals of the Grassfields (known as *ǝm-kan* in Oku). In addition, the long-standing predilection of fons for carving and smithing associates them with two forest resources—iron ore and wood (Argenti 2002a). Fons dressed in their full ceremonial costume of animal and forest by-products intended to look otherworldly to their subjects. Just as the origin myths situated the origins of their ancestors in distant foreign lands, so too the ceremonial dress of the fons was composed of products of the forests and borderlands on the margins of the Grassfields.[8] So strong and consistent is the association of the ruling dynasties of the Grassfields with the forest that—whether they belong to the forest belt as do the southern chiefdoms or to the deforested savannah plateaus of the northern highlands—we can appropriately refer to the states of the Grassfields as forest cultures.

Why this association of fons with forests? Despite the paternalistic and peaceful image that fons are at pains to cultivate, forests have been inscribed on the social imaginary over the centuries as a space of violence. The wild animals that the forest nurtures and that still roamed part of the Grassfields until the 1960s reify other, greater dangers that have emerged from there over the centuries in the form of marauding armies and slave-raiding parties. And although the wild alters of the fons (the leopards, bush cows, and elephants) are meant to underline the legitimacy of the fons in the social imaginary, it seems that it was their military might and their legacy of violence that was the main source of concern to the majority who were excluded from the palace hierarchies. The careful distinction made between the fon and the *kwifon* regulatory society in the palaces of the Grassfields serves to elide and to disremember the coercive aspects of leadership and its history of violence. Careful as living fons are not to be personally polluted with contemporary acts of violence, their hegemony has historically been based on a discourse of violence and practices of coercion that must be deniable but nevertheless communicated, and that are all the more potent for being unremembered in the myths. Only by this means have fons been able at once to project an image as protectors of their people while enforcing their coercive powers over them. The schizoid image of fons as both hunters and wild animals serves to embody this paradox, while their representation as green men or forest dwellers obfuscates the contradiction and naturalizes the violent aspects of fonship.

Raiders or Refugees? The "Work of Kings" in the Grassfields

Although the origin myths credit the originary traveling leaders with populating their newfound territories with members of their own, exogenous lineages, the proto-fons of the Grassfields are acknowledged to have settled not in untenanted places but among autochthonous peoples. Often known in the origin myths as in contemporary kinship and rituals of state as the "people of the earth" or the "fathers of the land" (*ghel ntie*), the descendants of these autochthonous peoples still preserve distinct identities and separate lineages, and are considered essential to the performance of rites organized by the palaces. Nevertheless, these peoples are often considered inferior and are demeaned in cultural memory by those who identify with the lineages of the newcomers.[9] In contradistinction to the transcendent identity of rulers as those who have the capacity to bridge existential and economic spheres, claims to primary residence are not a source of political legitimacy in the Grassfields but rather a justification for the subjugation (and perhaps once the ritual scapegoating) of certain lineages within centralized hierarchies. As the Oku origin myth makes clear, the foundational rulers of Grassfields polities were credited with saving their peoples from the attacks of slave raiders in their places of origin. The same myths that present these leaders as saviors, however, also depict them as foreign aggressors, overpowering by ruse or by force the autochthonous populations of the lands they eventually settled in.

Historical sources record that in the course of the eighteenth and nineteenth centuries, heterogeneous groups generically known as Ba'ni (Mudi, Peli, Bali, Bali-Chamba), and later BaNten, BaTi, and Fulani, who were mounted slave raiders in the service of vassals of the emirates of Adamawa, Muri, and Bauchi to the north of the Grassfields, attacked many of the Grassfields polities. These attacks radically destabilized local populations, sparking an "unprecedented stampede" (Warnier 1975, 384) of whole groups in the search for safer territory and permanently altering settlement patterns in the area (Awasom 1984; Chilver 1961; Chilver and Kaberry 1963, 1968; Fardon 1988, 86–89; Kaberry and Chilver 1961; Mbembe 1996, 44–46; Van Slageren 1972, 74ff.; Warnier 1975, chap. 3 and 384–85). The chiefly states of the Grassfields seem not to have developed in response to the attacks of these mounted slave raiders, however, but to have predated them. If anything, the military campaigns of the invading raiders had the effect of destabilizing the region and triggering the movement of vulnerable people between states rather than of consolidating settlements or facilitating the emergence of more elaborate, centralized hierarchies. The origin myths that record the presence of autochthonous people therefore in all likelihood refer to migrations that took place before the slave raids of the eighteenth century, but the indeterminacy of the oral narrative enables it to encompass the events of the slave trade that were to come after its inception.

Although origin myths such as that of Oku suggest that the ruling dynasties that came from the east were themselves fleeing early, pre-transatlantic forms of slave raiding and helping to protect their people against further raids, the later Chamba raids seem rather to have had the effect of transforming elements of these diasporic populations into raiders themselves. As raiding parties progressed over a period of decades through the savannah of the present border area between Nigeria and Cameroon and southeastward into the Grassfields, their membership revolved as leaders of the original parties died, quarrelling factions set off in different directions, and elements of subjugated peoples were included in the raiding party. If Tikari groups ever did set off from the Tikar plateau in the direction of the Grassfields, as the origin myths allege, it seems likely that they came not simply as refugees but as raiders accompanying the Chamba bands that had sacked their own settlements (Chilver 1964; Fardon 1988, 88; Nkwi and Warnier 1982, 85; see Bopda 2003, 44, for the same phenomenon among the proto-Pahouin).[10] By the nineteenth century, this process was so entrenched in Grassfields political culture that the largest chiefdoms staged full-scale annual military campaigns for the recruitment of slaves from neighboring peoples (Warnier 1995b, 257–58). In at least one chiefdom, Bamum, these annual wars of capture were so much an institution as to be considered the "work of kings" (Tardits 1980, 800–817).

Whatever their exact composition, the population movements of the eighteenth and nineteenth centuries significantly destabilized the region. In the first place, it seems that the lineages present in the Grassfields before the arrival of exogenous groups suffered massacres, enslavement, and political oppression at the hands of the newcomers. Furthermore, as just mentioned, peoples who had become mobile as a result of Chamba and Fulani mounted slave raids became slave raiders themselves, either on their own behalf or as mercenaries in the pay of the more powerful Chamba and Fulani bands. And although the myths represent exogenous fons in paternalistic terms as benevolent protectors of the people over whom they came to rule, the true picture is one in which disenfranchised factions seem to have moved—as often as not among gangs of armed slave raiders—away from polities in which they had been bypassed for succession or had suffered at the hands of violent slave raiders, and settled into neighboring or more distant polities. Because the encounters between exogenous bands and locals introduced new struggles for land and control over people, the migrating bands often reproduced in the ensuing violent upheaval the same destabilization of local communities that had caused their own flight.[11] Once this vicious circle had been set in motion, it became difficult to distinguish between the victims of slave raiding seeking protection in the rugged landscape of the Bamenda highlands, on the one hand, and its perpetrators on the other.

The origin myth of Oku, for instance, records the demise of the autochthonous Ntul people of Kidjem, who were present when the first exogenous leaders arrived. According to the myth, the Ntul were dispatched en masse by the goddess Mawɛs, who turned herself into a lake and drowned them in revenge for their refusal to house her. The myth closely associates the goddess Mawɛs with the fon Mkong Mote, who had pointedly offered her a place to live in his kingdom that she had declined. In some versions of the myth, the massacre is completed when the Oku fon Mkong Mote enters the lake along with the leader of the Ntul, and Mkong Mote kills the Ntul leader with Mawɛs's connivance (cf. Davis 1991). Other versions of the myth blame the death of the Ntul less cryptically on the Oku people themselves. In these versions, the fon of Oku burns the Ntul to death in a fire, either by coaxing them into a house which he then locks and sets fire to, or by surrounding them with a magical fire when they are harvesting grass in a field (Argenti 1996, 16n8). The survivors of this massacre are reported to have scattered across the region, founding the villages of Njinikijem, Kijem Keko (Babanki), and Kijem Kitingo.[12] The neighboring polity of Kom shares a similar origin myth in which its ancestors are burned to death in a house by their neighbors from the chiefdom of Babessi (Shanklin 1985, 147). The Bangoua (Bangwa) origin myth replaces fire as the weapon of choice with a pit trap. Pradelles de Latour (1985, 33) relates the myth as follows: one of the successors of a foundational Bangwa hunter-king invites all the neighboring leaders to a feast, at which he places those he considers his enemies in a house laden with dishes arranged over a pit trap concealed under the floor. As the floor gives way and swallows up the enemies, the Bangwa king has them interred and has himself proclaimed king of the land by the other leaders present.[13] Whatever the variations among these myths, they all render ambiguous the moral status of the victims of slave raids by implicating them in their turn as the perpetrators of further atrocities.

The origin myths do not emphasize the generosity of the founding ancestors so much as their cunning and violence against the autochthons they conspire to decimate and to rob of their land. Accounts of the genesis of Grassfields polities thus seldom fail to record the grim massacres that enshrine the power of the sylvan intruder over the original settlers[14]—and the euphemistic style of the accounts, which suggests that the victims were killed by magical means or by proxy in the person of a deity, lends an air of legitimacy to the violence of the conquering hero. Although these autochthonous people (perhaps themselves the subjects of recent migrations or small-scale population movements) are often derided in the social imaginary as uncivilized "wanderers" (ironically, since the early Grassfields fons are themselves memorialized as wanderers), they seem to have been the victims of attack by a population that would usurp their territory and found the ruling lineage. The violence of the encounter seems to have become lodged in the social imaginary not as a massacre but as the very genesis of a people whose legitimacy is based on their exogenous origins, their cunning, and their unremembered violence as much as on their status as victims and refugees.

It is curious that, despite ample evidence, scholars of the Grassfields have not to date remarked on the sacrificial aspect of the origin myths, nor linked this discourse of genesis by genocide to the human sacrifices of foreign captives and slaves that took place during the annual dance in all the major states of the Grassfields until the eve of the twentieth century. We know that in the expanding conquest-states in particular, human sacrifice was practiced until colonial intervention in the late 1890s. Chem-Langhëë and Fomin (1995, 198, 199) state that the Banyang killed slaves to accompany their masters when they died and that a slave was killed to mark the climax of the war dance (*etogobi beti*). Esser (1898, as cited in Chilver and Röschenthaler 2001, 74, 78) states that thirty slaves had just been killed to honor the Banyang chief of Miyimbi, who had died six weeks before his arrival. Chilver (pers. com., Sept. 12, 2002) remembers that Bafut informants spoke openly to her about the sacrifice of slaves in 1959–60, with one of them concluding that "it all seems like a dream now." The Bafut sacrificed slaves on the occasion of the annual Ebin or Lela dance (Chilver and Kaberry 1963, 29); they also sacrificed royal wives on the occasion of the death of the fon (Chilver and Kaberry 1963, 29). The hostile encounter between Bafut and the neighboring chiefdom of Bali and its German allies in the late nineteenth century seems to have led to an increase in the ritual sacrifice of slaves in Bafut (Ritzenthaler 1966, 38, 42). Chilver (1963, 102–3; pers. com., Sept. 12, 2002) further mentions a report of 1917 in the Buea archives by a Leftenant Melcomb reporting the sacrifice of slaves among the Bagham. Njoya (1995, 232) mentions the live burial of slaves and royal wives with the deceased fon among the Bamum. The coastal Bakweri sacrificed slaves in a ceremony known as *eyu,* which was intended to dispose of a man's wealth at his death (Ardener [1970] 1996, 247). In the vast majority of cases, the slave to be sacrificed was obtained from a distant polity, often by capture.

In the powerful expansionist chiefdom of Mankon, dozens of people accused of witchcraft were sacrificed through an ordeal during the period leading up to the annual "dance of the king." The last sacrifice of this kind is remembered to have taken place in 1919. Those who were accused of witchcraft and submitted to the ordeal were predominantly foreign women married to Mankon men, and cadets.[15] The accused were fetched in their houses on the morning of the ordeal by the mask known as Mabu and his *kwifon* society acolytes, stripped of their clothes, and brought to the palace. There they were made to drink a decoction of palm wine mixed with the powdered bark of a tree known as *ngu* (*Erythrophlaeum guineense*), which contains a substance related to prussic acid and is likely to trigger cardiac arrest. Once they had drunk the decoction, the accused were made to run out of the town, beyond the trench that marked its boundary, to a promontory known as the "hill of *ngu*." There they were made to run around the hill until they either threw up the poison or succumbed to it and dropped to the ground (Warnier 2007, chap. 8).

Given this context of slave raiding and human sacrifice, the emphasis of the myths on the foreign origins and the itinerant past of the early fons can be seen to associate them in veiled terms not only with slaves but with the exogenous slave raiders that many of them in fact served as mercenaries, and their foundational journeys were marked by massacres that were regularly commemorated thereafter. Like the violence of nation building and the elaboration of predatory hierarchies, however, the odium of the sacrifice did not reflect on the fons and the palatine elites but rather on their victims, who were vilified as outsiders, criminals, and witches. As Warnier puts it, they were the excrement of the fon (2007, chap. 8)—an expression that further enriches our understanding of the appellation of the palace as the intestines of the state. Despite the hegemonic discourse that divorced the fons and their entourage from their own acts of violence, however, the authority of the leaders of the emerging states of the Grassfields always retained traces of their association with foreign invaders—if not of the fact that they had themselves been foreign invaders or were descended from them. As Homi Bhabha notes of the modern state, the violence involved in establishing the polity was subsequently forgotten, but it was never altogether eradicated: "It is this forgetting—a minus in the origin—that constitutes the *beginning* of the nation's narrative" (1990, 310).[16]

Deleterious to human security as the raiding of the eighteenth century was, its effects were overshadowed by a still more insidious process of depopulation: the local abduction of cadets for sale by their own elders. While the former process had resulted in armed conflict and the overt capture of vanquished peoples, the latter saw local leaders feeding on their own people, selling them into slavery by stealth on a piecemeal basis. It was thus the proliferation of the long-distance slave trade and not the Fulani slave raiding of the early eighteenth century that opened the way for increased political centralization and the development of quasi city-states in the region. It has been noted that the villages of the Grassfields were heavily fortified, but this defensive machinery was aimed inward rather than outward: it was designed to keep people in rather than to avert external attacks. Moreover, the defensive earthworks were only constructed in the mid-nineteenth century, thirty years after the last large-scale Fulani raids had taken place (Warnier 1985, 138, 271; 1995b, 263–64; pers. com., October 2003; cf. Chilver 1961, 1964; Masquelier 1978, 62). By this time, the risk that one would be kidnapped and spirited away in the dead of night was greater than that of falling victim to a full-scale raid. Moreover, the fons' habit of preying on their own people increased the risk of their subjects' voluntary flight, so the fortifications also served as reassurance to the fons that their subjects would not leave of their own volition.[17]

In a further example of the predatory practices of elders upon their own people, middle-aged Oku people are aware of grandmothers of theirs having been bought as slaves for a sum of cowries from the neighboring chiefdom of Kom and married—probably in the late nineteenth or early twentieth century.[18] As a result, Oku people who know they came from another chiefdom, but not from which compound or lineage there, are presumed to be the descendants of slaves since these were denied links with their compounds of origin after they were bought.[19] In this sense, Kopytoff and Miers's (1977) argument that the freedom that leaders took from their subjects was of little value in comparison with the protection from abduction and enslavement that they offered in return needs to be nuanced with respect to the Grassfields case. In the context of organized external raids typical of the eighteenth century, it is certainly the case that belonging to a strongly centralized polity became ever more important and that the lack of strong lineage ties of the disenfranchised cadets would not have been a source of independence to be valued but of insecurity to be feared. By the nineteenth century, however, raids decreased in frequency, and illicit internecine abduction became ever more common. This transformation then triggered an ever-increasing displacement of populations of disenfranchised people seeking security in escape and independent resettlement rather than in the dubious protection offered by predatory elders.

Once in place, exogenous lineages had to compete for territory, entering into alliances with neighboring groups and waging war on others in a pattern of temporary and unstable alliances that perpetuated a circuitous or Brownian movement of peoples within the region not unlike that ascribed to the mythical hunter kings and their bands of followers. The origin myths are clearly of great antiquity, predating the slave trade of the eighteenth and nineteenth centuries. Nevertheless their indeterminacy allowed them to anticipate future events and, in retrospect, to account for events that they predated. Conversely, however, in discussing human sacrifices in archaic terms in the form of foundational acts of violence, they project back in distant "empty" time what is in fact (also) a recent past. The emergence of the state in the Grassfields is also more recent than the myths suggest. The vertical elaboration of settlements into proto-city-states with power centralized around palace hierarchies resulted not from the external attacks of the Fulani raids of the eighteenth century but rather from the insertion of Cameroon into the global economy. As we have seen, this began with the transatlantic slave trade in the sixteenth century, but it really took hold on local economy and demography in the nineteenth century as the industrial plantations created an insatiable need for labor on the coast. Despite this defensive centralization, however, the widespread political instability and the condition of cultural plurality created by migrating groups led to the formation of increasingly mixed and plural populations that often included lineages from many different origins. The contradictions inherent in the interdependence of processes of centralization with increased population movement seem paradoxically to have encouraged the formation of strong, exclusivist cultural identities (including the greatest language density in Africa, serving to differentiate minute groups of people from one another). Given the available evidence, it seems likely that these identities only began to emerge in the course of the eighteenth century and that their value was twofold: at the internal level, they afforded a means for validating recent and fragile alliances in archaic mythical terms that appeared self-evident (as the expression widespread in the Grassfields puts it, "we speak with one mouth"), while at the level of external relations they served to distinguish neighboring groups of lineages one from another and to justify their territorial claims.

State Formation and the Floating Population

The political and demographic instability engendered by Ba'ni and Fulani raids thus perpetuated rather than attenuated the pattern of population movements first initiated by fleeing refugees and refugees turned raiders. As the nascent centralized hierarchies excluded more than they included in their parsimonious dispensation of titles and the redistribution of wealth that went with them, centralization was weak, and it was limited by processes of fission engendered as disenfranchised men and women exercised Hirshman's "exit option" and sought better patrons (Hirschman 1970, as cited in Warnier 1993, 118; 1996). Warnier (1975, 385) thus aptly terms the roaming bands that resulted first from raiding and later from internal predation and exploitation the "floating population" of the Grassfields.[20]

Warnier (1975, 375) illustrates the turbulent liquidity of the demographic situation with one simple set of statistics: in the nineteenth century, between 20 percent and 55 percent of married women in any one polity had come from another one. Furthermore, because each wife took a young male agnate with her to her new home, each external marriage entailed the movement of two people (378). Moreover, the population movements of young men may have exceeded those of women. In a situation in which fons could routinely mobilize 5–10 percent of the women under their suzerainty as wives, and lineage elders all had more than ten wives each, the majority of young men were doomed to a life of bachelorhood and the resulting liminality of childlessness (Warnier 1995b, 261). So strongly is childlessness stigmatized to this day in Oku that death ceremonies are not performed for men who die before having married and fathered children, and their houses and goods are burnt rather than passed on to anyone else. Until recently, their corpses were thrown into the bush rather than buried. Asked why bachelors were not buried or mourned, I was told it was "because they had never become people"—a slogan otherwise used with reference to slaves.[21] The options open to this marginalized group were to remain working for their lineage elders in the hopes of receiving their first wife as recompense, in their thirties or forties[22]—an obligation that many lineage elders failed to live up to anyway—or to leave their compounds and polities in search of work and patronage in another part of the Grassfields. The fission sparked by the genesis of centralized identities was, however, moderated by the negotiation of strong diplomatic and economic ties linking emerging states to one another. Alliances forged by the ruling lineages of neighboring polities were reclassified as blood bonds in origin myths that defined allies as sibling lineages descended of one mother (or of one father, in the case of weaker diplomatic ties).[23]

The two distinct spheres of trade that obtain in the Grassfields to this day probably emerged at this stage: a sphere of exchange in which household goods and foodstuffs were exchanged within the Grassfields was supplemented by a long-distance sphere of exchange in prestige goods reserved to members of the elite palace hierarchies (Dillon 1990; Rowlands 1979; Warnier 1985). The trade in prestige goods was engaged in by the elites of the Grassfields on behalf of the fons, who gave some of the elites permission to trade on their behalf. Not only did this closed sphere of exchange supply the fons, the palace treasuries, and the elites themselves with the goods that marked their power to rule their polities and lineages, but it formed the very basis for the emergence of centralized elite hierarchies in the region (Rowlands 1979). Probably from the very start of their availability in the Grassfields, Dane guns and other items of European manufacture originating from the coastal trading centers of Douala, Limbe, and Old Calabar were reserved for the prestige sphere of exchange. These guns cannot have been coveted for strategic purposes alone. They were so time-consuming to load, so dangerous to use, and so completely undependable for the eight months of the rainy season as to be almost useless as weapons, and they therefore did not afford their owners a simple military superiority over their enemies (Rudin 1938, 311–12; Warnier 1980). Rather, the guns represented the links that the fons who were able to procure them entertained with their allies in the Grassfields and—more importantly still—with the trading networks that connected their remote hinterland chiefdoms to the Europeans and their suppliers on the coast (Warnier 1980, 1985).

In contrast to the local foodstuffs of the subsistence sphere of exchange (thought of by their cultivators as local even when they were of foreign introduction, such as maize, manioc, bananas, plantains, potatoes, sweet potatoes, tobacco, groundnuts, avocadoes, mangoes, chili peppers, and so forth), the prestige goods obtained in the long-distance trade were all exogenous, with the great majority of them European. Moreover, the elites who hoarded them did not attempt to elide but rather stressed the foreign origin of these goods. Just as fons were strongly identified with the forests of the borderlands of the Grassfields and the wild animals and foreign peoples that lay beyond them, so too the items that marked their links with exogenous hierarchies and long-distance trade networks were represented as goods of exotic origin. One of the local terms used to refer to prestige goods was the adjective *mǝkale, makala,* or *makara,* a term commonly used by scores of language groups from the Cameroon coast right through to the hinterland Grassfields and whose central meaning was "European" or "white man" (Ardener 2002; Argenti 1998, 2001, 2004, 2005a). The coastal Duala middlemen who represented the source of the European goods similarly represented themselves as Europeanized, with European prestige goods—and European culture—among the imports that they amassed and redistributed to the hinterland during the period of German colonialism if not before (Austen and Derrick 1999, 121, 133–34; Wirz 1973a, 192). Prestige goods were thus to all intents and purposes "white man goods," and—as discussed in the next chapter—palace treasuries became repositories of items understood to be of European origin: beads, ceramic toby jugs, vases, Dane guns, and cloth were supplemented after colonial contact, from the late nineteenth century into the early twentieth, with objects of German military and ceremonial attire, including swords, spiked helmets, body armor, uniforms, and boots (Argenti 1998; Geary 1983, 1996b).

Because word had got back to the hinterland polities that *məkale* goods originated from the hulls of European trading ships, the goods came to be thought of in the Grassfields as having emerged from the sea, and the Europeans who brought them were thought to have their homes in that watery realm.[24] This emic representation of the trade in prestige items was sanctioned in the origin myths, which also connected fons to sacred bodies of water, themselves representations of the realm of the ancestors. In this manner, the trade in European prestige goods evinced the connection of the fons and their elite traders with the world of the ancestors, and origin myths that had predated first contact were brought in ex post facto to refer to a later historical era. Because Grassfielders themselves obtained prestige goods through trade with the middlemen of the forest zone to the south of the Grassfields, *məkale* goods were also thought of as forest goods, with a double origin in the ships that were seldom if ever seen by Grassfields elites themselves and in the forests of the Bamileke polities of the southern Grassfields. These forests, already supplying the Grassfields with the forest products essential to palatine rites and the legitimation of the fons, now also came to be seen as the origin of another range of prestige goods essential to the promulgation of centralized hierarchies, and another layer of signification accrued to the image of the forest-dwelling hunter-king. Just as the early leaders of the emerging states of the Grassfields were legitimized through their association with exogenous warlords, so too in the late nineteenth and early twentieth centuries, the fon of Bamum and his palace elite, who had recently converted to Islam and adopted the gowns and turbans of the northern emirates, now took to dressing in German military uniforms to mark the arrival of the Germans with whom they rapidly forged a strong alliance (Geary 1988a, 1996a, 1996b). Throughout the centuries, the power that Grassfields rulers wielded always depended on their external alliances—so much so that it was not unusual for the fons and their courtiers to dress in the clothes of foreign invaders.

Just how did fons and their chosen acolytes in the palace hierarchies accumulate the wealth needed for exchange in the prestige sphere? The title system of the emerging states of the Grassfields depended on the harnessing of women's and young men's labor by the elites, a system that ensured the marginalization of the majority of the population and the condemnation of the cadets to a lifelong "childhood" bereft of wives and children (Argenti 2002b; Bayart [1979] 1985, 1989; Warnier 1993). As mentioned earlier, one of the principle means by which young men's labor was successfully extracted from them without remuneration was through a promise of deferred payment in the form of a wife. If a lineage head had ten wives and fifty children (the average), however, the likelihood that he would indeed be able to provide all of his twenty or twenty-five sons with a wife was slim. In practice, the elder sons would be provided with wives, but the large-scale polygamy central to the title system doomed a high proportion of young men to lifelong bachelorhood. Similarly, because customary law forbade the division of property upon a lineage elder's death, his landholdings were often passed on to a single son, forcing the remaining siblings to disperse in search of other opportunities. This practice remained in effect during the colonial era (Le Vine 1964, 63; Tardits 1960, 123).

The heads of extended lineages depended on the accumulation of goods from the local sphere of exchange in order to accumulate the wealth needed for investment in the long-distance trade.[25] The dividends of profit in the regional sphere could thus be transformed into accumulation in the prestige sphere, which would in turn be invested in the accretion of titles in the palace hierarchy, finally contributing to increased centralization and more complex social stratification. Over time, however, increasing centralization led to inflation in the cost of accession to higher positions within the palace hierarchies, leading in turn to ever-greater exploitation of the subordinates in the lineage. Those with nothing to loose who chose to opt out of such lineages fed the ranks of the floating population. Disgruntled wives who felt they were excessively exploited by their husbands might also decide to leave them, and they might join the floating population in an attempt to begin a new life in a neighboring polity. Members of this itinerant demographic group were often suspected of having been banished from their places of origin as a result of criminal activity, and they were viewed with some apprehension. Members of the floating population were also presumed to harbor subversive feelings of jealousy regarding their original lineage elders—the "fathers" they had opted to abandon—and this filial treachery was seen to go hand in hand with witchcraft. Those who roamed from place to place were therefore attributed supernatural abilities that made the members of settled populations ambivalent about them.[26] From a sociological perspective, however,

the floating population was nothing more nor less than a structural out-
come of the process of increasing centralization and the hypertrophy of
the elite palace hierarchies to which it led, with the available women and
capital flowing into fewer and fewer hands.

In a sense, the floating population represented not only a symptom of
this problem but also a palliative for it—a system of labor redistribution
that could be domesticated by elites according to a patronage system expressed in terms of classificatory kin. Disgruntled bachelors left their compounds and lineages of birth to seek out elite patrons in neighboring polities who had something to offer in return for labor. As bachelors settled
and married in their new patron's compound, they became "sons" of their
adopted lineage. This uxorilocal form of marriage was disadvantageous
to men in comparison with the virilocal norm, but at least it represented
a way out of bachelorhood and a foot up onto the lowest rung of the
hierarchical ladder. It was not without reason, however, that the floating
population was an object of fear throughout the region. As the elite system became increasingly top-heavy, and wealth and women accumulated
in the hands of ever-smaller groups, titled elders had little to offer to the
workforce they referred to as their "children." Although these outsiders
might be accommodated to great profit by expanding lineages and polities
hungry for manpower, they could as easily destabilize local relations, and
represent a source of insecurity and even of insurrection. In a pattern that
repeats itself all over Africa today, the exploited young men who represented the victims of the elite title system were pressured to reproduce the
conditions of their own marginalization. As the only way out of lifelong
"childhood," they set off in the footsteps of the ancient fons of the origin
myths to claim land of their own and to set up independent lineages. As a
result of this struggle for power, the vast majority of cadets were placed in
a position of dire insecurity, while a minority of cadets regularly swelled
the ranks of the elites, exacerbating the appetite for labor of the elite hierarchies while depleting the capacity of the cadets to satisfy it.

Fons, Strangers, Slaves

The resistance of cadets to the appropriation of their labor by the elites
thus revealed contradictions in the process of hierarchization in the Grassfields—contradictions that could only be resolved by the introduction of
a panoply of more coercive measures than classificatory kinship and the

putative obligations of "children" to their "fathers." For lack of a more precise term, this host of institutions has come to be known in English as slavery. The slave trade—in both its internal and long-distance forms—introduced to the classificatory kinship system the element of coercion needed to tame the tendency of the floating population toward insurrection and flight. At one end of the scale, some domestic slaves were traded only once as a debt payment within a lineage or between two allied lineages in a system that was not unlike today's indentured labor agreements that are euphemized as fosterage. These domestic slaves were kept not by dint of force but remained where they were because there was nothing exceedingly wrenching or onerous about being transferred as part of a debt settlement within one's lineage or affinal network. Such domestic slaves seldom had anything to gain from attempting to return to their compound of birth, and they served much the same function in their new compound as they had in their natal compound before their transfer.

As Warnier (1995b) graphically illustrates in his semifictional case, however, adolescents and young men with weakened links to their local communities, who were perhaps already mobile or residing with affinal kin outside their natal villages and language areas as foster children or baby-sitters, presented easy prey for dealers or opportunists, who sold them to traders who would in turn resell them in polities in need of labor.[27] These slaves often remained where they were sold despite harsh conditions because they feared recapture by neighboring peoples, or because—having been taken as children—they simply did not know the way back to their home communities.[28] In a foreign-language area where they had no kin, those sold into slavery could not protest or arrange for their return, and they remained with their new "fathers" and often learned their captor's language. As time passed, these slaves were absorbed into their communities as classificatory kin and sometimes allowed to marry "free" women from the lineage. Their children, in turn, were born with all the rights of other members of the lineage. The distinction between members of the floating population and slaves was thus moot—a matter of a continuum rather than an antithesis, with the former the most likely people in the Grassfields to be turned into the latter.

If the domestic slave trade represented a short-term solution to the labor shortage that limited the accumulation of prestige goods and titles for the elites of the Grassfields, the long-distance slave trade represented a more radical solution. When the elites traded slaves to dealers and middlemen, it was not on a slave's labor that they intended to capitalize but on the sale of the slave's person; slaves traded in the long-distance networks can thus be described as chattels. Their owners' sole intent in selling them was the accumulation of the prestige goods offered in exchange (Rowlands 1979). In some cases, local currency, such as cowries or brass rods, was used that could be converted into prestige goods at a later stage. In other cases, the prestige goods themselves, such as Dane guns, European cloth, or Venetian beads, were given as payment for the slave. The nineteenth-century missionary and linguist S.W. Koelle, who interviewed hundreds of slaves in Sierra Leone to produce an early classification of African languages ([1854] 1963), has recorded a myriad of ruses through which generations of young Grassfields men and women, then referred to collectively as Bayon, from a region variously known as Mbirikum, Mburikum, or Mbudikum, were captured. As we saw at the outset, where these young people came from was a complete mystery to the coastal slave traders, European merchants, and missionaries (and a secret closely guarded by the middlemen who passed the slaves through the hinterland trade routes) until the late nineteenth century, when the first German expedition finally reached the famed highland plateau renowned as an inexhaustible source of manpower. In the Atlantic trading ports of the Gold Coast, Bayon slaves were especially valued for their obedience, honesty, and hard work, and evidence suggests that they were traded in large numbers over centuries (Chilver 1961; Hutchinson [1861] 1967, 322; Hutter 1902, 260; Koelle [1854] 1963; Van Slageren 1972, 74; Warnier 1995b, 253; Wirz 1973a).

In 1848, the missionary John Clarke, in his *Specimens of Dialects,* mentioned a place he named

Balap ... in the Bayung country, near to Bafimbo, Ba'njiang, Bafot, Bamangku, Basangang, Baku and Ba'njo; these are all inland countries, in the unexplored interior of Africa. They are said to be, from a two months' journey, to a six months' inland, eastward from the sea. An armed people called *Bali,* mounted on horses, wearing clothes, and with spears and guns, overrun these lands, and destroy, or enslave the inhabitants.... When they reach a Town, they surround it, and set some of the huts on fire; the fire spreads, and the terrified inhabitants fly—some fight and are slain—many are taken prisoners—and the aged and sick are speared, or left to perish for want!—the young children are torn from the arms of the mother, and thrown into the burning huts: the prisoners taken by them are sold as slaves, and sent towards the north, and the land is laid desolate for years. The *Bali* move with their tents and camels [*sic*] towards another Town, when that which they have previously taken supplies them no longer with food; and in this manner up to 1846, the following Towns had been destroyed—Balitshet, Bafot, Ba'ntshop, Batshebilung, Balabalung, Ba'nya, Balunti, Ba'ngo, Ba'mboba, Basung, Babaset, Bazit, Ba'mbavi, Batshwilun, Ba'nbavi, Bazirinkong, Baiyaque, Barante, Bangia, Bafimbo, Basanga, Baku, Bamugku, Bambu, Ba'nzhiang, Balap. (1848, 74–75)

A few years later, T.J. Hutchinson quoted from a letter received from Reverend Anderson, a missionary in Duketown, Old Calabar, dated July 22, 1856:

There is a people, or country, or both, far on the other side of Qua, called Mbafum. Some of them are sometimes brought as slaves to Old Kalabar. I have long wished to ascertain the position and distance from Old Kalabar of a country called here Mbrikum, Mburikum, or Mbudikum. Many of them are brought here as slaves. They are more liked in Old Kalabar than many brought from other countries. They are peaceable, honest, energetic; they represent their country as being three months' journey from Old Kalabar—as being destitute of large trees, and as being not far from some "big watery," on which ships are visible. Their country is much infested by men who "wear trousers and ride on horseback,"—I suppose some Moorish tribe—and who are called Tibare [Tikar, here used to refer to the mixed Bali groups?]. (Hutchinson [1861] 1967, 322)

By all accounts, the precolonial process of state formation in the Grass-fields, such as we can reconstruct it, led to a situation in which travel out of one's own polity, whether over the longer term as a member of the floating population or even for short journeys as a farmer, trader, or traveler, was fraught with the danger of capture and enslavement.[29] To say that early slave raiding destabilized the Grassfields region is an understatement. Warnier (1985, 127) describes the slave raids of the eighteenth and nineteenth centuries organized by the Chamba and Fulani as nothing short of terrorist campaigns designed to weaken and demoralize local communities in order to render them more susceptible to further raiding. Because the polities of the Grassfields had not developed into full-fledged states and were not organized into any sort of confederacy, several groups of palace elites took to raiding during the eighteenth and nineteenth centuries on behalf of the external aggressors. These local raiders reproduced the methods of their long-distance patrons, multiplying the terrorist campaigns and exacerbating the insecurity of the region. They even went so far as to sell their own subjects into slavery, despite laws prohibiting such acts. Warnier (1975, 381–82) reports that the fear of being sold into slavery by one's chief was one of the key factors that drove young men from their chiefdoms. Despite the pollution incurred by killing a king, two of the chiefs of Bambili were put to death by their subjects for selling their own people. And those spared by their own fons still could be captured by a neighboring one. The fact that Hutchinson ([1861] 1967, 327–28) refers to reports of the Mbudikum people as "living in the tops of trees"—probably because they posted constant lookouts for slave raiders—gives some idea of the extremities to which Grassfields peoples had to go to protect themselves from recurrent raiding.

In their works on slavery in the Grassfields polities of Nso', Bamum, and Kom, respectively, Chem-Langhëë (1995), Njoya (1995), and Nkwi (1995) either elide or deny the existence of nineteenth-century wars whose primary purpose was the capture of slaves. However, Jeffreys (1963, 81), Van Slageren (1972, 77), and Warnier (1975) reveal not only that external forces such as the Fulani and Chamba raided in the region for slaves but that local polities rapidly joined forces with these raiders or made pacts with them in the early nineteenth century, raiding their own neighbors on behalf of the Fulani and Chamba to supply them with slaves. Clarke provides evidence of this from the testimony he collected from Grassfields slaves:

> A powerful Native Chief had united with the *Bali,* and was assisting them in the destruction of the tribes around. Those who fly before the enemy hide themselves in the forests and in the wilderness by day, and go to the provision grounds of the countrymen by night, to obtain food. This is soon perceived, and their unfeeling neighbours shew no pity—the slave-hunt commences, and all who were taken are secured by their cruel countrymen. There is no mercy to succour; no wisdom to unite for mutual defence against the common foe: the poor starving and forlorn creatures are captured, and sent to the nearest slave market;—they are sold and driven in the frightful slave "coffle" to the next, and so onward from one market to another, and from one land to another, until they are sold to the sea side Trader, and by him to the slave-buyer, to enter the Baracoon of the European! . . . Some survive and are sold to the Cubian, or Brazilian Planter; and such drag out their remaining days in a state of slavery. (1848, 74–75)[30]

By the end of the eighteenth century, some 7,000 slaves a year were being exported from Old Calabar for the Atlantic trade. From the names in the registers, it seems that a high proportion of these came from the Grassfields. Additionally, a slightly smaller number per annum of Grassfields captives were sold into the transatlantic trade from what is now the port of Douala (Austen 1983, 1995; Austen and Derrick 1999), and 5,000 slaves a year were being sent as tribute to Yola by the Fulani of Adamawa to the north of the Grassfields, many of these the result of slaving expeditions into the Grassfields, an area treated by the lamibe as a "pagan slave-march" (Chilver 1961, 237, 239). These figures give us, for the eighteenth century, approximately 16,000 to 18,000 slaves exported per annum. Armed slave raiding in the eighteenth and early nineteenth centuries, followed by the regular sale of slaves to the long-distance slave trade by local elite slave traders, transformed the Grassfields from a largely peaceable region in the early eighteenth century into a chaotic, unstable, violent, and dangerous place of terror from the second half of the eighteenth century well into the twentieth.

Let us return now to the forest, and in particular to the political construction of the forest in the chiefdoms of the Grassfields. Forests were not only a conduit for inanimate prestige goods but also for slaves: the forest gave slaves to the polity, but it also took free men, women, and children from the polity, swallowing them into the murky realm of the long-distance slave trade. Widespread witchcraft beliefs in the "secret of the shadows" (*minang bachye* in Mankon, *famla'* among the Bamileke) to this day associate death with slavery, conceived of as a passage into a forest witch market, a secret plantation, or an underground realm of darkness (cf. chap. 4). The generalized association of the ambiguous, marginal status of the slave with a symbolic form of death (Kopytoff and Miers 1977, 15) is especially poignant in Cameroon, where the fate of those caught up in the long-distance slave trade was known to involve deportation by Atlantic slave traders to an unknown world beyond (or beneath) the sea. The belief that these traders intended to eat the slaves in cannibal feasts held deep under water, or to sell them to their compatriots abroad as food, was widespread among Grassfields slaves and freemen alike.

For members of the floating population, forests therefore remained more than ever a realm of death, a borderland into which one's people were swallowed up on their way to the other world of slavery.[31] Because, for criminals, being sold into slavery was a punishment imposed interchangeably with the death penalty, and because such a punishment could only legitimately be imposed on convicted criminals as a result of the derogation of their social status as citizens and lineage members, slavery was to all intents and purposes a surrogate form of death. So strong was the association of enslavement with death in the chiefdom of Nso' that mock burials were performed for those sold into slavery (Chem-Langhëë 1995, 180n9), whereas Bamileke slave traders commonly checked under the armpits of slaves before buying them for the traces of earth that would reveal that the slave had been acquired by a sorcerer from the realm of the dead and recently unearthed from his grave (Sanduo [1955], as cited in Van Slageren 1972, 78).

The forests of the Grassfields, as they were imagined, represented in stark terms that which the palace never revealed in the light of day. This imagined forest represented the watery realm of the night, which served as a bleak reification of the coercive powers of the fons as its most feared inhabitants. It projected the control of fons over slaves and commoners in the prestige economy onto a naturalized, sylvan backdrop. Because slavery was represented in the social imaginary of its potential victims as a form of cannibalism, the fon-as-leopard was the forest's dominant predator, with slaves as his prey.[32] Indeterminate as it was, the image of slavery as a form of cannibalism came to be used in a plural, disjunctive, or doubled way, at once as a hegemonic discourse by slave-trading elites and as a counterhegemonic critique by slaves, all of whom reproduced images of slavery in terms of the ingestion of human beings.[33] Forests were not only the true home of fons but also the natural dwelling place of slaves, where each group occupied its preordained niche. Like fons, slaves were considered to be sorcerers capable of transformation into wild animals (Njoya 1995, 231); like fons, slaves were "foreigners."[34] Both extremities of the social hierarchy were thus encapsulated in this metaphorical realm. Although the special relationship of fons with the forest legitimized their hegemony by evincing their connection to the ancestors, it also served to underline the affinity of slaves with the wild and the dead—thereby underlining their liminality. Economic relations that pitted elites against commoners and slave dealers against slaves thus came to be reified in terms of the forest surrounding the polity, and nature was made to stand for the violence of a culture in which the base unit of currency was the human being.

CHAPTER THREE

Masks of Terror and the Subjection of Cadets

If no one commits any misdeeds, what will the elites get to eat? — Mankon proverb (as quoted in Warnier 2007 [trans. mine])

In their elaboration of discourses of power, the palatine elite of the Grassfields had more than myths in their armory. All of the major rituals that took place at the palaces—whether the enthronement of new fons or queen mothers, or the rites of commemoration for members of the royal family or of the *kwifon* society—were punctuated with the sudden appearances of the many palace masks, which would come bursting into the palace courtyard one by one, without warning, as the ceremonies progressed. I cannot provide here a full inventory of the innumerable palace masks of the Grassfields, so I concentrate in this chapter on four of the masks belonging to the palace *kwifon* society in the chiefdom of Oku.[1] Apart from the palace masking group Fuləŋgaŋ, and in contrast to the majority of masks belonging to the lineage groups of Oku described in later chapters, all of the palace masks emerge from the palace on their own, accompanied only by their unmasked acolytes. These masks do not dance, as do all those that perform in groups, nor are their sorties accompanied by music, bar the loud urgent calls with which the acolytes egg on their masks. These are not beautiful masks to behold but dark, fearsome creatures with a redoubtable and excessive tendency to violence. As I describe later in the chapter, the performances of these masks, far from being enjoyable in a straightforward fashion, engender a tension between attraction and repulsion, presenting themselves to the public almost as a challenge or a provocation. This chapter explores why such masks can be a source of pleasure and attraction to those who come to see them, despite their being universally acknowledged as dangerous, frightening, and repulsive.

The major palace festivals held on the occasion of the enthronement of new fons, the commemoration of lost ones, or the "crying" of "mothers" and "fathers" of past fons, attract large audiences throughout the Grass-fields. Apart from the small minority of senior members of the palace hierarchy who have a role to play on such occasions, the vast majority of the people who attend such celebrations come to see the performances of the palace masks or to take part in the dances of the lineage masking groups, which are not part of the palace but all of which are required to attend such ceremonies in a show of devotion to the palace. Despite the large size of the crowd at such events, often numbering in the thousands, those attending are not often a representative cross-section of the population but are largely cadets—"murmuring children" (*yondε war'*) or "arms/hands" (*əbkoy*), as they are known, that is, the young unmarried men who swell the ranks of the floating population. Elders, adults (married compound heads), and women are all in the minority. When I asked palace elders why cadets were so disproportionately represented among the audience members, they argued that things were different now: in the past all the adults in the polity would have performed their duty and come to the palace. At that time, "children" were not even allowed to attend such ceremonies. Things had come to such a pass, however, that tradition and ritual were no longer regarded with the respect they were due, and the palace masks had gone from being the sport of kings to the plaything of children.

The question then emerges as to why the audience of the palace masks would be composed almost exclusively of those who have profited the least from the limited dispensation of wealth and titles from the palace. As we shall see, the performances of these masks seem to consist mainly in heaping indignities on the people assembled at the palace, reifying in the most grossly concrete and physical terms possible the subjection of the majority to the might of the palace elite. As we have seen, however, the poetics of performance is indeterminate and ambiguous—open to many possible interpretations and experiences. This chapter explores how these performances, which involve the cadets integrally in the violent chases they effect through the palace courtyards, may have played into the palatine discourse of power in the period of the slave trade, and how they may conversely have been appropriated by the cadets and members of the floating population. Finally, the chapter considers how today's performances of the palace masks bring the past back into play in the contemporary political relations between members of the palace hierarchy and cadets.

Domination and Pleasure: The Ambiguous Attraction of Palace Masks

In Oku, as in many of the Grassfields polities, the palace mask Mabu has three different personas.[2] The most notorious of these was known as Mabu of Death (*Mabu eykuo*) or Mabu Kill-Person (*Mabu yui wel*). Forbidden from the colonial era onward, *Mabu eykuo* was the palace lictor mask, or executioner. When a person tried by *kwifon* was found guilty of a crime punishable by death, he or she was led by Mabu along with several *kwifon* members to a particular point where a river flows over a cliff edge. The condemned was then left, tied hand and foot, on a rock in the middle of the waterfall, where eventually he or she would lose balance and be washed over the cliff. Not only was the identity of the executioner hidden by the costume, then, but the method of execution allowed the *kwifon* society as a whole to pretend that its hands were not soiled with the blood of Oku's citizens. Today at trials the *kwifon* society still condemns people to severe beatings, although it delegates the corporal punishment to the plaintiffs and their family members attending the hearing.[3] The other two personas of Mabu are known as Mabu of Injunctions (*Mabu kəlaŋ*) and Mabu Spear-Goat (*Mabu ntəm bvəuy*). The former of these is the persona Mabu adopts when it is sent out by *kwifon* to inform someone that he or she is being summoned to a trial at the *kwifon* compound. The third persona, Mabu Goat-Killer, redresses crimes deemed to have been committed not against individuals but against *kwifon* or against the polity as a whole. In such cases the *kwifon* members on the expedition catch a goat belonging to the offender, which Mabu then symbolically touches with its spear (hence its name, *ntəm*, "to spear/shoot/kill"); the goat is then taken back to be consumed in the *kwifon* compound. Unlike the *kwifon* masks I describe later in the chapter, Mabu is also a member of the *kwifon* masking group known as Fuləŋgaŋ.

When traveling outside the palace, Mabu elicits some of the most marked avoidance behavior among passersby of any mask. Anyone walking toward Mabu along the path it is using strives not to set eyes on it,

FIGURE 3. Mabu entering the palace courtyard followed by its entourage of *kwifon* society members.

let alone come into physical contact with it. Forewarned by its unmistakable birdlike whistling, passersby run to hide in the undergrowth or take shelter in nearby houses long before it arrives. The time at which Mabu is "hottest," however, is arguably not during its punitive expeditions but when it attends the death ceremony for a member of *kwifon,* the palace regulatory society. I attended just such a ceremony in 1993 for a young member of *kwifon* who was seen to have had an inauspicious, premature death. Soon after I arrived, Mabu appeared in one of its "hot" states. Once in the courtyard, Mabu refused the rooster it is customarily offered by the compound head on such occasions and instead, in a full-blown charge, sprinted toward the crowd of mourners lurking in the coffee bushes. Given the steep gradient of the hill behind the compound, the unevenness of the rocky ground, and the obstacles presented by the tall coffee bushes and the scraggly undergrowth, everyone was taken aback by the speed with which the barefooted mask suddenly sprinted out of the courtyard in pursuit of the mourners. Like so many chickens before a diving hawk (I choose the metaphor advisedly, as the mask is dressed in a gown of stiff, brown raptor feathers), the mourners scattered before the charging mask with every symptom of blind panic. The assault, which went on for some ten minutes, resulted in cuts, bruises, and a ceremony in total disarray before Mabu was finally appeased.

FIGURE 4. Mabu at the palace turning on its acolytes, who crouch in submission.

Oku men and women alike not only fear being beaten or speared by Mabu but sincerely believe that contact with the mask would expose them to its harmful medicines. Seeing the mask sprinting toward them at full speed, cudgel and spears poised above its head, people simply flee. Despite the fact that commoners greatly appreciate Mabu's performance in the palace grounds, the mask elicits a marked repulsion when on a punitive expedition. Even inside the palace courtyard, where Mabu is understood to be at its least violent, the members of the assembled crowd keep a weary distance from it, leaping away from the mask when it lunges toward them as they might from a dangerous animal. This behavior clearly raises the question of why many people go out of their way to see the mask perform despite its repellent and fearsome reputation. For although Mabu is undoubtedly one of the most feared masquerades in Oku, inevitably turning its spectators into victims of its charges, it is also paradoxically one of the most appreciated of the palace's many masks.

People rationalize the ambiguity of their feelings by maintaining that the mask is dangerous in some contexts and not in others: it can be "hot" (*lumɔ*) or "cool" (*ezɔɔle*), depending on the situation. When Mabu is in a cool state, such as at the palace memorial celebrations, it is said that the mask is "not angry." Nevertheless, this does not stop it from charging at the crowds assembled at the palace whenever it comes out of the *kwifon*

FIGURE 5. Mabu at the palace followed by a *kwifon* society attendant playing its clapperless double bell.

enclosure. Despite local informants' protestations that the mask is less an-gry at such times, the many personas of Mabu clearly are not considered to apply to different masks but to the same one. The delight that cadets take in participating in the performance of Mabu—running from it with the same mixture of dread and delight as Spanish youths might from the bulls at Pamplona—is very much informed by their experiences of its two current personas, Mabu Goat-Killer and Mabu of Injunctions, and by col-lective memories of the executioner, Mabu of Death. Indeed, knowledge of this particularly sinister persona of the mask is still current, kept alive by the stories about Mabu that youths recount to one another in hushed tones.

Nevertheless, the fear of Mabu that fleeing youths evince is overlaid with a sense of the outrageous hilarity of the mask's defiance of social norms, and a description of the effect of Mabu that does not recognize this ambivalently pleasurable emotion would only be telling half the story. Indeed during any of its sorties, anyone who reaches what they think is a safe distance from the mask cannot help but stifle giggles at the expense of those within the mask's reach. And those on the other side of the court-yard who have the opportunity to watch the events unfold from a comfort-able distance are not simply horrified; rather, their horror is tinged with a sense of awe, grudging admiration, and bewildered amusement. Those who have just witnessed Mabu on one of its stampedes typically tell each other stories for the rest of the day about what happened to whom: how so-and-so got his flip-flop stuck under a coffee-bush root and was unceremoniously run over by the hurtling mask, how someone else flung her basket of cornmeal high in the air with a piercing shriek as she leaped out of the mask's way with an alacrity that belied her considerable bulk, and so on. After any of Mabu's sorties out of the palace, its ravages become more pleasurable with each increasingly caricatured retelling, without, for all that, entirely dispelling the aura of danger, distress, and shock that the mask never fails to evoke by its presence.

The ambiguous representation of Mabu as both human and animal, civilized and wild, hunter and hunted, and the ambivalent emotions that the mask arouses among ordinary commoners throughout the Grassfields closely correspond to the essential elements of the elite discourse of power discussed earlier in the context of the myths of origin. Although Mabu the wild beast confronts the people of the Grassfields with the inhuman danger of the liminal stranger allegedly lurking in the bush on the periphery of the polity, Mabu the hunter reassures the citizens that the palace protects them from this exogenous threat. One single mask thus contains both opposing aspects of the discourse typical of state formation in the Grassfields, the logic of which runs something like this:

1. It is not us (the elite slave traders) who represent the source of the terror that faces you.
2. An unseen enemy (the disenfranchised cadets of the floating population) threatens us from without (and even those who might live in our compounds are symbolic strangers).
3. We will protect you against this threat to the state (by enslaving more cadets).

In the era of the slave trade, masks thus embodied the (ill)logic of a discourse by means of which palatine hierarchies elided the coercive effects of their hegemonic control, transposing the terror that they instigated themselves with their slaving activity onto their own victims. Thus, although the objects of terror in the original Chamba and Fulani raids had been the raiders themselves—still vividly remembered a century later by Jean-Pierre Warnier's and Michael Rowlands's informants—the local palatine elites who later abducted people by ruse and stealth rather than by organized raiding portrayed those they enslaved as the sources of danger and instability while presenting themselves in paternalistic terms as protectors of their people.

For this deception to work, palace elites had to foster a xenophobic discourse that literally demonized the floating population that supplied them with their victims, while simultaneously naturalizing the elites' appetite for members of this demographic group. What could the palace have wished to achieve in displaying the sinister and ambiguous figure of Mabu to the people during the period of the slave trade? Mabu the hunter was also Mabu the bird of prey, and Mabu the ape, at once human and in-human, hunter and hunted—trader and slave: while the gown of Mabu is made of raptor feathers, its mask is always said to represent an ape. Only through such an irreducible figure, capable of containing contradic-tory and irreconcilable entities in one performance, could the palace elide the contradictions of its discourse, effectively transposing the violence of the slave dealer/hunter onto the foreigner/ape. If the hunter was also, at the same time, the (hunted) ape, could we be sure which was hunting the other? Which held the spear? Rather than say that Mabu is *both* animal and human, it is more precise to say that it is *between* these categories, that it reverberates unstably between these poles of its identity. The mask does not "contain" a hunter with a spear separate from a bird of prey or an ape, nor does it conjoin them entirely. Rather, these otherwise discrete categories oscillate in the mimetic supplementarity of the mask, which is always beyond reduction.

By means of this supplementarity, the separate figures that the mask alludes to become fused (*con*fused). Is the foreigner/ape not also—at the same time and in the same mask—wielding a spear and threatening the people? And were those who saw this mask in the period of the slave trade, or who see it now, capable of differentiating between the hunter and the hunted, the attacker and the victim? As Mabu bore down on a young man in the crowd, forcing him to kneel on the ground as he raised his spears menacingly over his bowed head, who was the young man meant to fear? The palace elite? Or the apes of the forest and the foreigners they represent—members of the floating population from whom the elite were purportedly protecting him? Both of these were equally plausible read-ings of the mask,[4] ultimately transforming slaves from victims into per-petrators—the perpetual threat lurking just outside the chiefdom. Like Derrida's *pharmakon,* the opposing definitions are contained within the single indeterminate figure and are only notionally separable (Derrida 1993). This ambiguity sets up a dialectical process between the mask and its victims/spectators whereby the opposing readings of the mask serve to naturalize and to justify the schizoid representations of the status of the cadet in the palatine discourse as at once loyal subject and potential slave. Perhaps the young man kneeling before Mabu was himself the foreigner, the ape, in relation to whom Mabu became the benevolent protector of Oku, saving the people from the threat in their midst. But if the young man was seen—or saw himself—as a local person and a loyal subject, in other words as *a person,* then Mabu would reciprocally shift in this game of mirrors back into the exogenous threat, the sylvan beast that justified the territorializing violence of the palatine elite. The indeterminacy of the mask thus elicits a corresponding indeterminacy in the very identity of those it confronts. By means of the mask's fusion of opposites, the palatine elite could thus project their asocial behavior as slave hunters and slave dealers onto their victims, who were made to take on the fearsome and undomesticated attributes resulting from the elites' own predatory practices.

Despite Mabu's reputation as an executioner, another of the palace masks known as Nkɔk has a still more fearsome reputation. The startling, inscrutable appearance of the mask's amorphous and eyeless headdress projects an unmistakable sense of menace that its cudgels quite needlessly underscore. Its rustic bludgeon and the sylvan, otherworldly "basket" it carries on its back—a badly decayed, mummified otter elliptically referred to as a woman's farming basket (the eponymous *nkɔk*)— serve to associate it with the realm of the forest and the wild, while ambiguously referring to the nurturing role of women as farmers. Whenever it comes out of the *kwifon* enclosure, Nkɔk never takes long to break free of its restrainers, whose the purpose is therefore rhetorical: a means of emphasizing the belligerence of the mask as it overpowers them rather than a way of reining it in. Once these restrainers have been dispatched, Nkɔk is free to rampage at will. From the moment of its first appearance, the audience members know exactly what to expect, and with an ambivalent mixture of anxiety, dismay, and high-spirited jocularity, they prepare to dodge its assaults. Each time the mask charges at the crowd, a corridor suddenly bursts open in front of it as the body of people is rent asunder, only to be redistributed in a new form as the disfigured mask turns to make another charge. As Nkɔk runs wildly at the crowd, it is capable of sending people running pell-mell by the hundreds, at times leaving the crowded palace courtyards all but deserted in a matter of seconds. The stampede it causes in such situations can rapidly become more frightening than the mask itself. As with Mabu, the only way to appease the wrath of the mask is for the fon to offer it a live fowl.[5]

FIGURE 6. Nkɔk in the palace courtyard restrained with ropes by two attendants.

Where Mabu seems like a hunter with animal qualities, Nkɔk is first and foremost the wild beast rendered all the more sinister by the hints at its human characteristics. The rough black gown of Nkɔk conceals the masker's body right up to his wrists and ankles, like a catsuit. All that remains visible of the masker are his hands and feet. Even the outline of its body is broken up and confused by the gigantic, inanimate black head-dress from which great hanks of black webbing and ragged bedraggled cloths hang recklessly to the ground, dragging through the rainy-season mud like the decomposing flesh of the amphibious otter on its monstrous back. On the sliding scale from humanity to animality, Nkɔk stands still closer to the realm of the wild. Like Mabu, however, Nkɔk sets up a tension between irreconcilable opposites that is at the heart of the grim fascination it elicits. Its weapon, a gigantic bludgeon so roughly hewn that it seems like an objet trouvé from the most tenebrous of forests, links it at once to the realm of undomesticated animality and simultaneously—because it is a weapon—to the world of the civilized and the human.

Further blurring categories, the otter tied onto the mask's back is not only referred to as a (woman's) farming basket but also as a "child," because it is carried on the back in the way that small children usually are. Nkɔk thus conjoins elements of the male—in the form of the hunter or warrior—with the female—in the form of the mother/farmer. Because of this blurring, and also because it is masked by a male performer, it is a transvestite mask and a grotesque confusion of the domesticity and nurturance that the mother represents with the violence of the male hunter or the wild beast. Not only as an animal, but as a dead and decomposing one, the mummified otter is a preposterous travesty of the proper human mother–child relation, conjoining impossible opposites in one: the familial and the foreign, the wild and the domesticated, the animal and the human, nature and nurture, violent masculinity and caring femininity. In this sense, the references of Nkɔk parallel those evoked by Mabu, but to these Nkɔk adds another set of opposites—the living and the dead. Apart from the corpselike appearance of Nkɔk with its trailing bits of leprous flesh echoing the decomposition of its insanely ignored child, the fact that the child is an otter—let alone a decaying corpse—strongly evokes the realm of the dead.

As we have seen, otters are endemic to the sacred crater lake Mawɛs in Oku, and because this lake is associated in myth with the realm of the dead, the otter's ability to live at once above and beneath the surface of the lake affords the animal a sacred status as a being that transcends the ordinary boundaries between the realms of the living and the dead. Because otters are considered benign and sacred in Oku, their deaths must be mourned as one mourns for human beings when they are accidentally caught in a hunter's trap. The decomposing otter tied to Nkɔk is therefore shocking in the disrespect it shows for this hallowed, almost human "child," but it simultaneously underscores in blatant and concrete terms the ability of Nkɔk, and by implication the palace elite more generally, to move between the realms of the living and the dead.[6] The mask thereby serves implicitly to give the sanction of the ancestors to the actions of the palatine elite. It is notable that the rites of enthronement for fons and the investiture ceremonies for many of the elite titles in Oku involve treating the initiand like a child (that is, keeping him in seclusion, leading him by the hand, feeding, washing, and rubbing him with camwood, and so forth), and that many elites mark their status by wearing otter-skin belts.

Charge at them as Nkɔk may, however, the members of the crowd—again inevitably composed of a majority of young men—are far from incensed at their maltreatment. Although they are undeniably frightened and seriously discomfited, they nonetheless admire Nkɔk and enjoy the mask's ravages even as they become its victims, laughing nervously and shouting exclamations of almost adulatory disbelief as they run from it. Those standing at a distance let out the special ululation reserved for raising the alarm in the event of a fire by tapping the palm of the hand on their mouths as they shout a high-pitched cry. Others, pointing to this or that trampled person or fleeing group, call out exclamations of dismay, "yəvəuy! yəvəuy!" or "ɛmɛɛyɛɛ!" and laughing in horrified wonder even as they condemn the mask. These exclamations of dismay are certainly not insincere, but they nevertheless contain a rhetorical element. The young men's cries of disbelief, by emphasizing the danger that audience members face, do not evince disapproval or indignity so much as grudging praise for the mask. Likewise, when asked to describe the mask, these young men inevitably qualify Nkɔk as "bad" (bɛmə), again an ambivalent, nuanced term with mixed connotations of disapproval and praise for a source of power comparable to the contemporary African American use of the word. Although the display of the might of the mask is an experience of discomfiture and fright for those within striking range, its emotional effect on the audience of young men is ambivalent and complex, with the indeterminate references of the mask serving to elide and to project the political and economic violence of the palatine hierarchy into the realm of the wild, and then to further absolve it by association with the realm of the all-forgiving ancestors.

One of the less-often seen of the palace masks belonging to the *kwifon* society, Aga, only comes out on the occasion of the death ceremony for a fon or a queen mother (*nɔ ntɔk,* "mother of the palace"). Even in these cases, it is reputed only to appear just before sunset in perfect weather. It is preceded in its sorties by an unusual coterie of outriders made up of the *kwifon* members who have paid the heavy dues to join its society. Aga society members are easily recognized by their unique caps, embroidered bags, and curious walking sticks to which they have special rights and which are a part of their everyday dress.[7] Significantly, the bag of Aga members differs from the that carried by ordinary men in two ways: it has no shoulder strap but two small loops and, most importantly, as with the gowns of certain masks, its surface is interwoven with human hair. This second characteristic makes it a much-feared object that has special prohibitions attached to it—in particular that no one must come into contact with it apart from its owner, who cannot take it into any house but his own. Aga members come out of the kwifon compound into the palace courtyard before a sortie by the mask itself.[8] On these occasions they remain recognizable, but members of the assembled crowd to whom they speak must pretend not to know them. Just as those who recognize the identity of a masked dancer are required to uphold the suspension of disbelief ac-

FIGURE 7. An outrider of Aga.

cording to which masks are not simply costumed dancers but rather wild creatures, so too an even more radical suspension of disbelief is called for in the case of Aga members: although they are clearly recognizable, their ceremonial disguise marks them as being removed from their usual social status, a general condition known in Eblam Ebkwo as *tshiese*. In this state, the Aga members loose their quotidian social identity and cannot be referred to by name. Furthermore, they seem to loose the ability to speak, save to call out repetitively the name of the mask that their presence announces—"Aga! Aga!"—as if it were a madman's compulsive cry or the bellowing of a wild animal more than an act of human speech.

As Aga's outriders fan out, roaming around the compound courtyard and repetitively crying out their mask's name, they confront people, placing themselves squarely in front of them, planting their large ceremonial spears in the ground, and wordlessly demanding money from them with an outstretched hand. They are so insistent that it is almost impossible to get away from them without making an offering. Their mood is almost maniacally jocular, but their unblinking wide open eyes and the smiles pasted to their faces do not relate in any way to the mood of those they choose to pester, and the facial expressions that would in other circumstances connote bonhomie thus become subtly sinister and threatening, evoking the psychopathology of dissociation. Because the "patrons" they accost are not allowed to speak to them or even to make eye contact, the Aga members' merriment is entirely one-sided and quite unrelated to the objectified giver, who is not cajoled so much as intimidated. The relationship between Aga members and those from whom they beg thus inverts the normal patron–client hierarchy of the begging relationship, with the elite beggar/client coercing the commoner giver/patron, who is ritually inferior to the beggar—an armed "beggar" who belongs to one of the most feared of the palace secret societies. One cannot help but wonder how this performance would have been perceived when the palace was actively involved in the abduction of freemen for sale into slavery, and what the coins that the Aga members dropped into their dreaded bags of human hair would have been seen to stand for: the slave trader's payment? the vulnerable cadet or fearful father's protection money? Again, the imprecision of the reference is the key to its salience, and the fear and ambivalence the performance evidently evoked remain palpable to this day.

After the comic/sinister sortie of its outriders, the large ponderous mask of Aga moves slowly and with the utmost economy of gesture from the *kwifon* compound and toward the center of the palace courtyard; the crowd is suddenly still, echoing the silence of the somber procession. Although most of the palace masks are accompanied by attendants, some of them playing musical instruments and egging the masks on with calls or attempting to "cool" them with entreaties when they threaten to get out of hand, the Aga procession progresses in complete silence.[9] When it reaches the center of the deserted courtyard, one of the group of acolytes who form a human curtain around it signals to the crowd to turn away. Pressing against the walls of the buildings that line the courtyard in order to get as far as possible from the mask, the members of the crowd turn their backs to the procession, facing the courtyard walls to avert their gaze from the mask. Aga's attendants, having abruptly abandoned all pretence of good humor, are suddenly angry and watchful, ensuring that everyone has their back turned to the center of the courtyard as a goat is sacrificed at Aga's feet, the blood from its throat seeping into the ground of the courtyard.

FIGURE 8. Aga on its way from the *kwifon* compound to the palace courtyard.

As mentioned in the previous chapter, we know that in many Grassfields polities, human sacrifice was practiced up to colonial intervention in the nineteenth century. Could it be that this sacrifice of a goat has replaced such human immolations in Oku? As I describe later, a goat is also sacrificed (albeit symbolically) for a new fon in Oku by the palace elite as part of the fon's enthronement ceremonies. As the largest of the sacrificial animals, the goat would have been the natural choice to replace human beings once slaves became harder to obtain and the colonial authorities monopolized the right of execution. Röschenthaler (2006, 81, 88) notes the association of slaves with goats in Ejagham sacrifices, and Fomin and Ngoh (1998, 42–43) point out that slaves were forbidden to witness the live burial of fellow slaves alongside deceased Banyang elites. As in the sacrifice performed by the Aga initiates, those attending were made to turn their backs when the slave was beheaded. Putting paid to any doubts, Röschenthaler was explicitly told by Ejagham informants that the ritual still takes place but that since the colonial era a goat is made to stand in for a slave. As once was the case with slaves, the executioner is meant to decapitate the goat with a single blow of his cutlass. The same sort of slippage operates further down the sacrificial scale in Oku today, where one or two bags of salt are accepted as replacements for a goat in ritual use and are even referred to as a "goat" for the purpose of the offering. In the

FIGS. 9 and 10. The acolytes of Aga perform its sacrifice while the audience members are made to turn their backs.

same manner that salt equals goats in initiation ceremonies and dowry gifts, it would seem that goats equal slaves in sacrificial rites.[10]

As with Mabu and Nkɔk, this third *kwifon* mask appears to sediment unspoken memories of slavery, in this case by reenacting the buying followed by the sacrifice of slaves occasioned by royal burial and memorial ceremonies. How else can we explain why the sacrifice of the goat at the feet of Aga elicits such a pronounced sense of sinister dread that the entire population averts its gaze as the animal's throat is slit (despite the fact that goats are routinely killed in the Grassfields without their slaughter attracting any attention), if not for the fact that this immolation reenacts the human sacrifices of past enthronement ceremonies? Similarly, although the mask itself is considered fearsome and dangerous in the extreme, it is not said by the audience at the palace to be ugly. Indeed, its headdress is invisible, the mask itself masked by the vegetation surmounting it and the smoke emerging from it. If it is not what can be seen that induces dread, then it must be what is hidden: what the mask did when all were made to turn their backs, and what it does now that evokes at the same time as it veils what it did then. Conjoined with the attraction of the ambiguously jovial preliminary begging engaged in by its outriders, Aga elicits the same contradictory emotions of fear and attraction as do the other *kwifon* masks, making use of humor and revelry to draw the crowd into the reenactment of human sacrifice.

As with the Aga initiates, no one dares to address the jesters of the *kwifon* society known as *nokan,* nor does anyone let on that they know who the jesters are, despite their faces being plainly visible. Like Aga's outriders, they are removed from their usual social status (the condition referred to as *tshiese*) and accordingly thought to be highly dangerous. Although they wear no headdresses as such, the *nokan* jesters are also categorized as masks (*əmkum*) in the Grassfields, and despite their buffoonery they are thought of as among the most dangerous of masks.[11] In Oku, the special status that masks occupy is connoted by the notion that they are *tshiese*. With respect to masks, the term refers to the medicinal properties that render an object dangerous; crops or other property can thus be protected by certain medicinal objects called *tshiese*. With respect to individuals, however, being *tshiese* implies a divestment or dissociation from one's social identity. In such a state, whether one is masked or not, recognizable or not, is immaterial: in either case onlookers are required to behave as if the *tshiese* individual was simply absent and that someone or something else was standing in their place. Like slaves, then, *nokan* appear human, but they are removed from normal social relations and responsibilities and divested of their personhood—depersonalized.

As Richard Dillon (1990) points out with respect to the Grassfields chiefdom of Meta, the palace jesters' military role as spies necessitated an inversion of the normal behavior of soldiers during military campaigns. In contemporary performances too, their role inverts the ordinary behavior of the other palace masks and simultaneously parodies the behavior of the palace elite. The jesters capitalize on the ludic potential of being depersonalized, traducing status distinctions by approaching titled lineage elders (who cannot normally be looked in the eye, let alone touched) and tugging on their beards or playing with their ceremonial caps and beaded leopard-tooth necklaces. Their method of humor is invariably to stigmatize difference, whether it be a bald head, an elite's beaded necklace, or my use of a camera and notebook. Although it is a serious transgression to address a palace jester, running from one or displaying any sign of fear is considered shameful and ridiculous by members of the assembled crowd. The stricture against addressing the jesters and the concomitant stricture against evading them thus put the individual who becomes the butt of their jokes in a tense situation: unable to move away from them and simultaneously forbidden from engaging with their jokes, one is forced simply to bear their mockery as best one can. As with the Aga society members, the joking relationship is thus completely one-sided, at the expense of the disempowered victim of the joke.

Like Shakespearean fools, the *nokan* capitalize on the tension created by their intimidating humor, taking advantage of their removal from social norms by behaving in a foolish, joking manner that never truly allays the weariness to which their license gives rise.[12] A clearer reference to their antisocial ethos is evident in the behavior they exhibited in the days

when the market in Elak, the capital of Oku, was situated on the edge of
the palace grounds: at that time, they would steal from the market stalls
with impunity. In contemporary Oku, although palace jesters no longer
perform any military duty, they still appear on the occasion of the death
ceremony for any *kwifon* member or member of the royal family. Recalling the "child" of Nkɔk, the jesters often appear carrying carved figures
referred to as their "children" (*wan nokan, yon nokan*). These anthropomorphic representations are blackened but have their faces rubbed in
white kaolin, like the *nokan* themselves. In a travesty of the caring role
of the parent, the *nokan* are fond of using these figures provocatively for
making suggestive jokes, lifting their "children's" loincloths to present
their genitals in mock invitation to members of the crowd. In a form of
humor typical of the *nokan,* they also occasionally give their "children" to
young members of the crowd, who are forced to "babysit" for them until
the jester returns for it, sometimes offering the caregiver a small present
of food that they have just stolen from a market stall. I once saw a young
boy, forced into the role of "babysitter" (*eblii wan*) for a jester standing
disconsolately in the palace courtyard for over an hour in the pouring
rain, holding the jester's statue while everyone else took shelter in nearby
buildings.

FIGURE II. A *nokan* with its "child."

FIGURE 12. The procession of the *nokan*.

After milling about for some time individually, the palace jesters come together for their group procession, known as their *enar'*, around the main palace courtyard. During the procession, their leader taps a monkey's skull that he holds on a stick, letting the skull bob absurdly about as he shuffles slowly forward. Behind him come the rest of the palace jesters in a long single file. In accompaniment to their leader (*kam*), they thump their ungainly sticks together or drag them along the ground like a host of fools. As they proceed slowly around the courtyard in their pathetic and disordered shuffle, their leader calls out phrases, speaking in tongues and in foreign languages in a high-pitched voice, to which the others respond in unison with a falsetto giggle: "hi! hi! hi!, ho! ho! ho!" Once again, the crowd's response to this procession is highly ambivalent, with the audience members not sure whether to laugh or to recoil as they see the ghastly ashen creatures filing mutely past.

The high-pitched laughter that the jesters emit in answer to the indecipherable calls of their leader as they proceed around the courtyard recalls the "whinnying or high, mocking laugh" of Dogon masks, which Calame-Griaule (1986, 535) understood in terms of their knowledge of death and their supposed supernatural powers.[13] Barley (1983, 73) has pointed out that among the Dowayo just to the north of the Grassfields, clowns are thought hilarious but nevertheless liminal, and therefore dangerous. They too speak in high-pitched voices and "are mediators between the living and the dead . . . half male, half female, half Dowayo half Fulani," and therefore associated with the wild. As in the Grassfields, one is not allowed to show one's annoyance at these jesters but pretends not to notice them. Not only do the jesters of the Grassfields speak in high-pitched, otherworldly voices, but their speech is itself largely incomprehensible. The odd timbre and incomprehensibility of their speech and the inappropriateness of their laughter are associated by the commoners at the palace with the voices of the dead anomalously emerging from the forest, which is their proper place.

Many elements of the jesters' attire and performance also refer to the forest, but one of their prime connections to the forest is their apparent madness. In the Grassfields, madmen (in common with witches and those gifted with supernatural powers) are reputed to wander in the forest for extended periods of time. When they return, their hair is unkempt and knotted, their clothes are torn and disheveled, and because they are unwashed, their skin has taken on a grayish or whitish tone caused by the accretion of a layer of dead cells on its surface. Because the forest is the site to which gifted children, thought of as "single twins," go to meet with their otherworld siblings, and because the ghosts of the dead are thought to reside there among the trees, madmen (*yel ejar'en*)—although they provoke nervous laughter—are treated with the caution and respect that one reserves for those believed to possess supernatural powers. Madness, in other words, is not at all associated with idiocy in Oku; madmen are likened to healers, soothsayers, witches, and witch-children in their close connection to the Other World. Above all, however, the speechlessness and high-pitched gibberish of the jesters relate them not only to animals but to foreigners, whom they intentionally parody by speaking in tongues.

Although the palace jesters' costumes leave them recognizable to those who know them, even their closest friends shun them, and they, for their part, seem to recognize no one. Again, in the absence of any convincing disguise or any truly threatening behavior, the only explanation for the apprehension caused by these foolish masks must lie beyond their immediate appearance or behavior. One of the main reasons for the dread these figures elicit despite their harlequinesque behavior may lie in what they recall: as I discuss later in the chapter, throughout the Grassfields, jesters used to function not only as spies and scouts but also as slave catchers. Known as *gwe, bagwe, begwe,* or *bigwe* on the Bamenda plateau, *nɛkiɛ* in Bamessing, *bugwɛ* in Bafut, *megwe* in Meta, and *sam'su* in Baham, the sinister society of jesters had its analogues throughout the chiefdoms of the Grassfields. Skilled at playing the roles of madmen, fools, or drunks, these scouts were sent out by the palace authorities to gather intelligence in foreign polities of the region, where they were ignored and allowed to roam freely on the presumption that they were harmless. The German explorer Eugene Zintgraff—the first European to reach Bali in 1889— was the first to describe the *gwe* or *bagwe* scouts, with whose assistance he went into the fatal battle against the chiefdoms of Mankon and Bafut in 1891: "These scouts, about 40 in Bali, were a remarkable institution. They seemed to play the fool, and at dances sat on the ground near the Fon, pretending madness. They in fact acted as spies and were intelligent fellows" (Zintgraff 1895, as translated in Chilver [1966] 1996, 26). In 1898 the German speculator Max Esser, following in Zintgraff's footsteps, was entertained by a group of these jesters in the palace of Bali. He noted that although they were generally assumed to be fools, they were "recruited from amongst the most intelligent people of the country . . . who wander freely . . . inside the country of neighboring peoples, observing everything with a sharp eye" (Esser 1898, as translated in Chilver and Röschenthaler 2001, 91; cf. Kaberry and Chilver 1961, 361). Despite the fact that the jesters make people laugh with their antics, the dread and suspicion they simultaneously inspire inhibit people from ever offering gifts of small change to them, as they often do to dancing masks. The perception of palace jesters as an exceptionally dangerous type of mask is further illustrated by the fact that *kwifon* members consider swearing by them the most binding oath of all, the breaking of which is believed to result in death.

Seduction and Violence in Masking and Slavery

Whether with respect to the palace or the jesters (all considered "masks"— *əmkum*—in the Grassfields), the onlookers (typically the cadets excluded from the palace hierarchy) try by all means to get as much distance as possible between themselves and the mask, all the while ensuring that they get to see events unfold. They are torn, in other words, between the desire to witness events and the concern to avoid becoming targets of the masks. These masks consistently break free of their restrainers and charge the crowd, causing people to flee in all directions. Because each of the two public courtyards is enclosed on three sides by buildings, the crowd soon comes up against the palace buildings in its attempt to flee from a charging mask, resulting in scrambled heaps of people amassing against the periphery of the courtyard. It is hard to exaggerate the panic struck by a mask charging the crowd in such a confined space. Because those closest to the mask are the most frightened, they run the fastest and often end up running over the slower members of the crowd farther back from the mask. The movement of the frightened members of the crowd outward from the periphery of the palace masks and their uncomfortable containment within the palace walls effectively denude the participants of any control over the masks. If the appearance of palace masks recalls that of undomesticated beasts, their movements suggest the strength, bulk, weight, belligerence, and unpredictability of animality rather than its beauty, its agility, or its grace. And although the palace masks engage the members of the crowd in a dialectical relationship that makes them something more than passive members of an audience, the masks also deny the crowd members the opportunity to participate on equal terms, implementing a totalizing subjection that makes them something less than subjects.

Once a mask has stormed the crowd and sent its members stampeding toward the perimeter of the courtyard, scores of people are left sprawled on the ground, others crouched in submission at the feet of the looming mask, while others still are pressed so hard against the courtyard walls that they are nearly buried in the mass of bodies. It would clearly be inappropriate to describe such a performance as a dance, which begs the question how we are to understand it. Clearly, on one level, the palace masks can be seen as ends in themselves, as confrontations staged (or rather not staged, and therein lies their ambiguity) between the palace elite and the young commoners in the audience. But the fact that these events constitute not only a straightforward confrontation but also, at the same time, a performance begs the question of *what* is being performed, *what* is being enacted or *re*enacted—what is being remembered? There cannot be a performance of nothing, a reenactment of nothing, a memory of nothing. As we have seen, there was a time in the past of the Grassfields, not so long ago, when exogenous warriors—not "people" (*yel*) but monstrous "strangers of the bow-and-arrow" (*balak enuin*) as they are remembered in Oku—burst into the polity from the surrounding bush, sacking the villages, terrorizing the population, and making away with long lines of prisoners. Then came the time when the fons of the smaller chiefdoms of the northern Grassfields entered into pacts with the raiders, undertaking to supply them annually with some of their own subjects in return for peace. The palace elite thus took over the coercive role of exogenous enemies and began to prey on their own people.

The performances remember what language does not, and where language is specific, concrete, and referential, these reenactments return the past to the present in an ambiguous, open-ended, and indeterminate form that allows the palatine elite and the cadets each to engage with it on their own terms. In their ambiguous indeterminacy between humor and terror, pleasure and violence, and their mimetic reenactment of the unspeakable horrors of the slave trade, these performances place themselves between the event and the dance, allowing the palace authorities to harness the between-character of mimesis to appropriate the unforgotten events of the past and to redeploy them in defense of the palatine discourse of state formation. In this light, the performances of the palace masks can be seen as an erasure as much as a memory of the past—transforming what they embody in the act of doing so. A catastrophic failure of the fons to protect their subjects, culminating in the tragic transformation of fons from protectors of their "children" into slave traders, is thus re-presented only as an intrusion into the community by sylvan beasts, or alternatively as the identification and expulsion of inhuman "witches" and floating outsiders from within the social body.

When Mabu comes into a compound to mourn the loss of a deceased member of the *kwifon* society, it often strikes or knocks over one of the veranda posts supporting the roof of the house of the deceased. This practice is widespread in the Grassfields. Malcolm Ruel (1969, 214) reports on his Banyang informants' memories of an earlier time, when Tui, the executioner mask, would inflict serious physical damage to the compound when it came to mourn a member of its society. All of this suggests that the Oku mask's relatively contained act symbolizes an earlier period when the performance was still more chaotic than it is today, resulting in the literal rather than the symbolic destruction of the compound. Ruel describes how

Tui … makes its appearance by entering the community or settlement from outside, as though having come from a journey. When it enters a settlement all the inhabitants are expected to flee, shutting themselves indoors. The gowned figure and its attendants then make a show of destructive power. Nowadays it is restricted to rampaging through the deserted settlement ... but in the past it is said that more material damage was done, to houses or to their thatched roofs. (214)

By means of the same slippage, this less contained, more chaotic appearance of the mask in the early colonial period may recall an earlier, still more anarchic event—the slave raid of the precolonial period. Then too the Banyang raiders entered the community from outside, with everyone fleeing before them or shutting themselves indoors. The houses were then destroyed or set alight and the prisoners taken away.

In the light of the earlier analysis of the role of the goat sacrifice made by the Aga maskers, Mabu Goat-Killer's taking of a goat from those who have been fined by the palace *kwifon* society can also be seen to recall its erstwhile role as an executioner. In the same process whereby the goat killed by Aga can represent a slave, so too Mabu's appetite for goats recalls his role as an executioner. Moreover, when "killing" a goat, Mabu only touches it with its spear rather than killing it, and this symbolic death marks the appropriation of the goat (which is bound and led away alive) by the *kwifon* society. Likewise, alleged witches and criminals were not always killed once they had been condemned to death. Rather, they or other members of their compounds could be abducted by Mabu and his henchmen and sold into slavery as a form of execution by other means. It is to this practice that the Mankon proverb quoted in the epigram to this chapter alludes; what the elites got to "eat" as a result of the misdeeds of the cadets were the cadets themselves.[14]

Dispatching those who had been condemned to death into an exile of slavery reveals that slavery was equated with death, that it effectuated a social death. And because exile involved first of all disappearance into the forest surrounding the polity, the forested borderlands of the Grassfields came to be associated with the realm of death, insatiably swallowing up members of the community who were never to be seen again. Once again, the palatine discourse operated a displacement by means of which its own internecine consumption—a *guerre intestine* if ever there was one—was projected onto the forest. In another hint of the symbolic value of the goat, one of the rites performed at the enthronement of the new fon of Oku in 1992 was known as "hitting the goat" (*tɛl bvəuy;* cf. Argenti 1999a). Soon after the new fon had first been presented to the people, he was made to stand in a clearing with all the palace elite lined up on his left. A goat

FIGURE 13. The ceremonial striking of the goat during the installation of Fon Ngum III of Oku in 1992.

was brought out and, as it was led past them, was ceremonially struck by each as it passed. Even though the slaps dealt to the goat were harmless, those involved in the ceremony interpreted their actions as an execution and spoke gleefully of "killing the goat."[15] Just as a harmless tap can stand for a deadly blow, so too a goat can stand for a human being, recalling the time when slaves were killed to mark the death of a chief.[16]

As we have seen, Mabu is explicitly referred to as an ape in several polities, and its mask clearly resembles a stylized ape's head. Oku informants invariably told me that the mask of Mabu was that of a *fəbuk,* a forest-dwelling primate that they pointedly stressed was strong enough to overpower a man with ease.[17] That one aspect of Mabu should represent an animal stands to reason in that its animality could serve as a projection of the violence of the palace, but why an ape? Perhaps because an ape was a particularly apt trope for a slave. Taken as a complex whole, the languages of the Grassfields operated a slippage between the terms for "ape" and "slave," with the referent of each term shifting from chiefdom to chiefdom so as to blur the boundaries between them. The root of the word for "slaves" throughout the conglomerate of Grassfields polities that spoke Ring languages was *-buk* or *-bu',* with the prefixes changing according to the different noun-class systems of each language (Warnier

1985, 127). The term is likely to be etymologically related to the name by which slave traders on the coast referred to the region: Mburikum—the land of slaves. In a subgroup of Ring languages including Oku, Nso, and Kom, however, the primary meaning of the root *-buk/-bu'* does not refer to slaves but to apes. This subgroup uses words with the root *-kɔt* or *-kɔs* for "slaves." The term for "slave" in Oku is thus *kəkɔ́s*, perhaps related to the verb *kɔ́ɔ́*, "to catch," and to *kəkɔ́ɔ́*, the "forest"—literally the "place of catching," that is, the hunting ground. Again, the Eblam Ebkwo root *-buk* refers to apes: *fəbuk* (sing.), *əmbuk* (pl.). In the neighboring polity of Kom, also in the Ring-language subgroup, the term for "slave" is *akɔs*. In Nso', the term for "slaves" is *kwàn*, perhaps (as in Oku) related to the Nso' terms *kô*, "to catch," and *kóóri*, "to catch a group of people" (Chilver, pers. com.). The term *kwan* was perhaps also related to the term for "monkey": *kán*. Apes, meanwhile, are referred to in Lam Nso' as *kibu'* (with the glottal stop replacing the final *k*), again using the *-bu'* or *-buk* root that refers to slaves in other Ring languages.

	Ring languages	"ape"	"slave"
Group 1	Oku (Eblam Ebkwo)	*fəbuk*	*kəkɔ́s*
	Kom (Itang Ikom)	*achum*	*akɔs*
	Nso' (Lam Nso')	*kibu'/kan*	*kwàn*
Group 2	Bambui (Aghombə)[18]	*nkɔ*	*abu'u*
	Babungo[19]	*fəbú'*	*bu'*
	Bamessing/Nsei (Kenswei Nsei)	*bachoŋ*	*bɔ'*
	Other Ring languages		*-buk/bu'*

Thus, one subgroup of Ring languages (group 1 in the table) would appear to differentiate between "ape" and "slave" with the use of the root *-kɔs* to refer to slaves and *-buk* or *-bu'* to apes. In light of the neighboring Ring languages of the Grassfields, however (group 2 in the table), the roots *-bu'* and *-buk* (and therefore the Oku name for the mask Mabu) become more ambiguous, referring to slaves as well as to apes. The prefix *ma-* refers to greatness or might in some Grassfields languages. If one takes into account the tendency of secret societies in the Grassfields to conceal meanings by using the terms of neighboring chiefdoms, the name Mabu can be seen to refer not only to a "great ape" but also—through the mechanism of reference to other languages, which serves as the coding for secret societies—to a "mighty slave." In other words, it is only if one adopts a monolingual perspective that one can assume that the terms for "ape" and "slave" were clearly discrete in the Grassfields. If, however, one takes into consideration the multilingual perspective of Grassfields people themselves, on the one hand, and the practice common to secret society members of introducing privileged spheres of communication by veiling their speech in the languages of other chiefdoms, on the other, it becomes clear that the terms "slave" and "ape" were used ambiguously as plays on one another and did not in fact refer to discreet spheres of meaning.[20] The Rosetta stone in this multilingual system is provided by Babungo (see group 2 in the table), in which language the root for both "slave" *and* "ape" is *-bu'*.

Before their extinction through hunting and deforestation, apes were of course forest-dwelling creatures in the Grassfields, and one of the only animals likely to pose a threat to hunters, trappers, or others who went to the forest. Because they were placed in the same category as apes, palace masks and slaves were equally represented as forest-dwelling, nonhuman, wild creatures that, in both cases—despite their disturbingly human form—posed a threat to the polity, and in particular to those who inhabited its borderlands. But Mabu is an ape with human characteristics. In addition to the unmentionable but universally known fact that the mask is performed by a human being, it carries spears and cudgels, like hunters or warriors. While its most obvious characteristics would have related it to animals, then, it was also in a sense a human being—that is, a citizen.[21] Inimical to any totalizing identification, Mabu dances between species, between humanity and animality, between offensive and defensive violence, between freedom and capture, trader and slave. Because Mabu is indeterminate, it becomes overdetermined.

In the southern chiefdoms of the Grassfields, those to whom fons gave permission to trade in slaves on their behalf were given an object known as a slave rope with which to symbolize their prerogative (Dillon 1990, 34; Warnier 1975, 163; 1985, 134–35, 189–90, 245; 1995b, 259). Taking slightly different forms in different polities, this object was woven of raffia fibers interspersed—as with the bags of Aga members—with human hair. These ropes were thought to give the palace slave dealers the power to overcome slaves, instantaneously draining them of their strength, and it was understood that dealers enslaved people simply by touching them with the rope (Rowlands, pers. com.). The possession of other people's hair is still associated with witchcraft in the Grassfields today and presumed to afford the witch power over its original owner. (For this reason, the bags that are used to contain nefarious medicinal substances are often woven of human hair, and people are careful to collect their hair when it has been cut, so that it should not fall into the wrong hands and be used against its original owner). Short in length, slave ropes were not whips or functional weapons, nor could they be used to bind people in literal terms. Rather, they marked their owners as those possessed of the power to bind people by magical means. In the same manner, many of the palace masks still possess short cudgels or longer bludgeons that they swing menacingly at the other masks and spectators, thus reifying the supernatural dangers of contact with them. In one contemporary Oku masquerade, the symbolic potential of these weapons is rendered more explicit still by the use of a short baton that not only references the cudgels wielded by masks (and thus the slave rope from which they are in part descended) but also the modern military officer's swagger stick (Argenti 1998).[22]

More commonly, certain masks in each of the lineage masquerade groups dance with whisks fashioned from horsetails. In the case of masks belonging to the royal Mbele lineage, these whisks are gifts from the fon to the masking group and are said to originate from the tails of the horses of Fulani slave raiders killed in battle in the nineteenth century. The whisks thus celebrate the protection from slavery afforded by the palace in the past, but at the same time they retrace the erstwhile provision by some fons to their elites of slave ropes and other forms of rights to trade in slaves.[23] The hair of the slave ropes is likewise echoed in the human hair woven into the gowns of the lead dancers of lineage masking groups (although not, interestingly, in those of the palace masks, which are predominantly feathered) and in the plat of human hair—said to be medicated—that often hangs from the back of the lead dancer's headdress. In the northern Grassfields polities beyond the Ndop plain, including Kom, Nso', Bafut, and probably Oku, the right to trade in slaves was conferred by the fon not by means of a slave rope but by the gift of a royal market bag (*kibam ke way ke fon;* cf. Chem-Langhëë 1995, 185; Chilver 1961, 242; Chilver and Kaberry 1963, 11; Nkwi 1995, 245).[24] The bags of the wealthiest elite within *kwifon* who belong to the Aga society—again woven with human hair in the manner of the slave rope—may have been that chiefdom's version of the royal market bag.

In a more literal connection between masks and slaves, the *nokan* described earlier are known to have engaged in snatching women, children, and adolescents to sell into slavery on behalf of their fons. Nor were these abductions always marked by physical violence—as with the palace masks and the performances of the jesters in the palace today, the skill of the *bigwe* really depended on their ability to attract and seduce their prey into following them of their own volition. Through the use of flattery, feigned amiability, and small gifts of food, the jesters sought to lead their victims farther and farther from their native villages, until they eventually reached a place distant enough for their victims to be bereft of protection. Without kin, in a place whose language they did not understand, and so far from home that they could not find their way back, they would be discreetly sold by the *bigwe* to a slave trader before they realized what had taken place.[25] The palace jesters' skill at speaking in tongues and speaking foreign languages no doubt gave them a practical advantage abroad, but it was their embodiment of exogenous personas that—as with the palace mask Mabu—paradoxically associated them with the slaves they hunted.

Slave capture and the performances of palace masks thus had this in common: they both depended for their success on luring people by seduction, despite the dangers they personified. In this light, the "children" that the jesters carry about with them take on a sinister significance, evincing for all to see the travesty of the caring role that the jesters so suavely affected when seducing children away from the safety of their compounds to sell them into slavery—a form of seduction that is now sexualized in the suggestive jokes that the jesters play with their "children." In this vein, it is interesting that slave dealers, always keen to euphemize their activities, often referred to slaves as their "children," and even told them soon after buying them that they intended to treat them as they would their own children, signifying that they would be given a place in their new master's compound rather than being sold on to the coastal Atlantic slave traders.

The testimony of Josiah Yamsey (Nyamsi), a recaptured slave of Grassfields origin, as recorded by the Rev. Johnson in Sierra Leone in 1820, eloquently attests to this practice and deserves lengthy quotation as it has not previously been published:

> My Master did not pretend to sell me but kept me & pretended to be fond of me, did use me better than others had done, gave me plenty to eat. One day he ... took me to a very bad place where the people eat slaves & there he sold me for what I cannot tell.... I stayed at that place a few days then the man carried me away again to another place, and there sold me for a piece of Cloth and a little salt to a Trader.... He was very kind, carried me to his farm a long way & made me understand that he would not sell me again. I was glad of this & worked very hard in my master's farm. But one day he take me again & carried

me to another Town & sold me for Gunpowder. ... The man who bought me
made me a fool again, he made me understand that I should be like one of his
children to which he pointed. I thought I was at length come to rest. ... I came
home one day from the farm having worked very hard all day & I thought
my Master was well pleased with me, but when I came into the home I saw a
stranger sitting & my Master was preparing something to eat for that man; &
I saw that that man gave my Master a piece of blue Cloth. ... The next morning he sent for me & I was carried away to his place. (J. Yamsey, as quoted in
Johnson 1820)[26]

Feigned affection for one's slaves, a ploy used time and time again in
the course of a slave's life as he or she was traded from market to market,
ensured that slaves remained docile and hardworking. In another parallel
with the installation of new fons, such periods of good treatment facilitated the recuperation of sickly slaves exhausted from their travels and
thus resembled the fattening period of the fon's internment inside the palace before his first public display—always rubbed in camwood, as slaves
also were at the time of their sale.

The similarities between slaves and palace masks discussed so far are
summarized in the following table:

Slaves	Palace masks
dehumanized	dehumanized
forest dwelling	forest dwelling
"floating": of indeterminate allegiance	uncontained/unrestrained
"apes"	Mabu the ape
"dead"	the white/dead jesters
"fools," "children"	palace jesters: "fools," "child-minders"
slave ropes, hair bags	cudgels, whisks, hair gowns

The similarities between slaves and fons can be summarized as follows:

Slaves	Fons
dehumanized	dehumanized
forest dwelling	hunters/wild animals
"floating"/foreign	wandering/foreign
double (witches)	double (transforms, finte)
apes (homicides)	leopards/elephants/bush cows (homicides)
otherworldly, "dead"	reborn, sempiternal
victims of the slave rope/bag	owners of the slave rope/bag
refugees	refugees turned raiders

The Hunger of the Palace

One of the political advantages of slavery to centralized hierarchies in the Grassfields was that it could be used to elaborate a discourse of difference in which members of the floating population could be circumscribed and contained by expansionist states while simultaneously remaining liminal, and therefore tradable.[27] Cadets, those banished from their homes, and other members of the floating population lived under the constant threat of enslavement by the various palace elites, but they in turn represented a threat to the elites: roaming unpredictably and lacking any definite allegiance to a single lineage or palace hierarchy, they called into question the centralizing practices of the emerging states of the Grassfields. By enslaving cadets and other outsiders, expansionist states managed at once to contain the flow of this disenfranchised population while nevertheless demonizing it by institutionalizing its alterity as evidence of the ineradicable difference and fearfulness of neighboring peoples, all the while eliding the fact that their own histories and peoples were irreducibly hybrid and composite.[28] In this manner, they managed to impose closure and a sense of boundedness in the Grassfields despite, and even by means of, the flow of dissenting cadets exercising the "exit option" (Warnier 1993, 118)—a flow to which they had themselves given rise by alienating their youth and scouring the region for slaves. In a word, it was by spreading instability in the region and nurturing fear and alienation among their people that the elites of the emerging states of the Grassfields managed to territorialize a region that was characterized above all by the flow of populations in a political landscape of overlapping borderlands and weak allegiances. Slaving begat insecurity, insecurity begat terror, and terror was harnessed by the palace elites to bolster monolithic discourses of bounded identity.

The liminality of the fons served to reify and to naturalize the predatory aspects of their relationship to their people. In an economic context predicated on the ability to straddle economic spheres and to transform wealth into prestige goods, prestige goods into human capital, and human capital into political power, the power of the fon to transform himself and to move between human and animal worlds at will embodied his status as the legitimate ruler, despite his predation upon his people. The transitions between economic spheres that the fon and his acolytes monopolized and the coercion they implied were naturalized in terms of his transformations into forest animals and the domesticating powers that this transformational capacity signaled. By emphasizing their transcendence of local boundaries,

Grassfields rulers and palace elites propagated allegories that naturalized their monopoly over access to the prestige economic sphere, which in turn reinforced their hegemony and promoted further centralization, the further elaboration of the palatine hierarchy, and the development of ever-stronger local identities.

Because the prestige sphere of exchange was based on the long-distance trade in which slaves traveled outward in exchange for goods of exogenous origin, the putative forest origins of the fons naturalized their affinity with the exotic prestige items they hoarded.[29] As mentioned earlier, the power of the fons was mythologized in terms of a historiography of exogenous aggression upon those who would become their subjects, but their continuing hegemony depended on the conversion of the external alliances and sources of wealth to which they claimed exclusive access into the fabric of an identity bounded in culture and territory. Fons could not nurture legitimacy on the basis of their liminal status and their acquisition of exogenous sources of wealth alone, still less on the predation of their own people; rather, their hegemony depended on a discourse of domestication and transformation of exogenous trade goods and people for local redistribution as the bounty of the palace.[30] The association of fons with forests attested not only to their liminality, then, but also to their unique powers of domestication—powers that they wielded by dint of a liminality that bound them to those at the opposite end of the hierarchy: slaves, cadets, and other members of the floating population.

The commoners, women, and cadets of the Grassfields, for their part, fitted into the palatine economy not only as sources of labor but potentially as prestige items of exchange. Although they represented a source of wealth to the fons and titled lineage heads who could attract, capture, or buy them, they were also a potential source of instability in that they introduced to the polity a floating population that might never be successfully domesticated and that might ultimately destabilize the elite hierarchy rather than strengthen it. Like the animals of the forest brought home by the hunter or the enemy heads brought home by warriors, slaves were said to be "eaten" by elite traders who nurtured the body politic by domesticating the foreign. The intense colonial and scholarly speculation regarding the practice of cannibalism in the Grassfields (e.g., Esser 1898, as quoted in Chilver and Röschenthaler 2001, 73; K. Knutson ca. 1912, as quoted in Ardener 2002, 119)—as well as local slaves' own beliefs in the practice (cf. J. Yamsey, as quoted in Johnson 1820)—should be seen in light of the wider discourse of eating as a form of subjection rather than a literal practice. Likewise, the significance of the reported practice of ingestion of small pieces of flesh from vanquished enemy combatants represents an example of this wider discourse of subjugation rather than an end in itself: in nineteenth-century warfare as in sports today in the Grassfields, the victors were said to have "eaten" their opponents. The use of cannibalism as a metaphor for witchcraft activity in contemporary Cameroon similarly builds on the wider discourse regarding eating as a form of political domination (Bayart [1979] 1985; Geschiere 1997; Rowlands and Warnier 1988; Warnier 1995a, 1995b).

The trope of ingestion thus served to mark the preeminence of the palatine hierarchies—the intestines of the state—in a context characterized by population movement, high linguistic density, and an intense cultural pluralism that belied the homogeneity of the myths of origin. And if the incoming slave population had to be domesticated, dissenters within the polity could conversely be expelled from the body politic: banished to the forest as the proper realm of those who failed to integrate into the palace hierarchy. By absorbing foreign captives into the polity and integrating them to some degree while expelling the "excrements of the fon" (Warnier 2007)—the "strong-heads" (Goheen 1996, 56; Van Slageren 1972, 105) and "recalcitrant wives" (Njoya 1995) who questioned the political order—the fons could appear to play a nurturing, pastoral, and eminently social role as the political fathers of the polity, while guaranteeing the expansion of the palatine hierarchy by means of the coercive extraction of labor from one's own cadets and subjugated neighbors alike. The palatine control over the slave trade recast as the shadow play of culture over nature thus allowed the fons to appear to be resolving a threat that they had in fact created. Those watching the shadow play were shown only fearful wild animals from a realm of encroaching darkness overcome by the heroic hunter-kings. But as the lynchpins of elite hierarchies that spread insecurity throughout the region by preying on their populations and giving rise to successive waves of emigration and demographic instability, the hunter-warriors—like their ambiguous palace masks—were themselves creatures of the forest.

Despite the close connection of many current fons with the national government, the new elite, world religions, and Western forms of education, the esoteric association of fons with wild animals shows no signs of abating in the popular imagination today. One of the most striking means by which these rulers still underline their connection to the realm of the wild is through the use of the palace's masks. Although they may have lost their primary forests, their leopards and elephants, and their control over the slave trade and the death penalty, none of the leaders of the Grassfields has relinquished these ambiguous objects of fascination and terror. These masks not only stand as the clearest connection among fons, palace regulatory societies, and the cultural construct of the forest, but they effectively bring the wild realm of the forest into the kingdom itself. As wild creatures of sylvan origin, the masks of the palaces of the Grassfields stand as living testimony to the fons' power to entrap the forces of the borderlands surrounding the polity within the confines of the palace. Palace masks thus address the paradox of the stranger-king: successfully contained within the palace walls but periodically breaking out to brutalize the people, the masks simultaneously enact the domestication and the redeployment of exogenous sources of terror, reminding people of the political forms of coercion that their fear of nature reifies.

As the palace masks run randomly through the crowd without constraint, they momentarily impose the topography of the forest directly onto the palace. Like the elephants and bush cows that once trampled people's farms with impunity, and occasionally rampaged through their compounds, the palace masks move unhindered by any human intervention and perpetually threaten uncontained outbursts of violence. Those who step into the palace precinct enter the very core of the body politic, but at the same time they enter a world periodically and paradoxically exempt from social norms and outside the domestic order. In a political situation of flux, uncertainty, and fuzzy allegiances, palaces present themselves as centers of power in an inevitably disputed landscape.[31] The better to do this, however, enthronement ceremonies and royal memorials become shadow plays of anarchy, nurturing millenarian spectacles of chaos in which the very core of the state is swallowed up by the encroaching wastes around it. The rampages of the palace masks can thus be seen as a form of propaganda before the name: a revelation of the full horror of the forces supposedly encroaching upon the chiefdom, and a justification for the political coercion and violence necessary to keep these forces at bay. Using the logic of the hair of the dog, the palace masks are more chaotic and wild than the inhuman forces that threaten the polity from without, and the *fon* himself is a transform of a predatory beast.

Because the dances of the palace masks are indeterminate, their violence can be made to encapsulate this fusion of oppositional categories at the center of the polity: they can refer at once to the threat from without and to the response from within—foreign attack and local defense, insurgency and counterinsurgency in one self-justifying spectacle of power.

The masks evince the status of the palace as at once the residence of the urbane, statesmanlike fon, on the one hand, and of his animal transform, which cohabits with his sylvan masks on the other. The palace is at once a domesticated "home" and a wild space in which the relations of power dividing the elites from the cadets are naturalized, in both senses of the word, by means of an idiom of power that represents the subjection of cadets and the enslavement of the marginal in terms of the domestication of the wild, the expansion (*kǝkwuiye*) of the lineage, and the reterritorialization of the borderlands of the polity. As the core of the polity, the palaces of the Grassfields have always been at once places of safety and of danger, of domesticity and the wild, of nurture and predation, of fecundity and insatiable hunger.

Discourses of nature or of the wild clearly played key roles at the heart of the forest cultures of the Grassfields, then, but these discourses were not for all that monolithic. The indeterminacy at the heart of the spectacle of state as embodied in the palace masks helped to construct a discourse with which to legitimate state violence, but this very indeterminacy also left the door open for alternative readings. In other words, the mimetic representation of the violence of the palace put into play a set of images that could be appropriated by the victims of palatine domination to forge oppositional identities and to lend coherence to the histories of dispersal, fragmentation, and oppression of diasporic peoples. To the marginalized cadets who gleefully came to confront the masks at the palace, the indignities heaped on the people by the stampeding masks reflected on the palace authorities more than they did on the threat supposedly posed by the cadets themselves. In its indeterminacy, the violence of the masks could thus be appropriated and overdetermined by the victimized cadets and read as a graphic demonstration of the unprovoked belligerence of the palatine elite.

Although I have thus far discussed the palace masks predominantly in terms of the totalizing subjection of the cadets that they facilitated, it is also clear that the pleasure that cadets experience in the course of these performances was more than a mere trap set by the mask to attract its victim—a form of false consciousness promulgated by an all-powerful state. Goading the masks as they did into revealing their true nature, and forcing the palace authorities to reenact their exploitation of their youth for all to see, the cadets were not only seduced but also seducing. Pointed in the wrong direction, the magician's mirrors could reveal what they were designed to hide. If the elites of the expanding states of the Grassfields deployed the myths of origin and the terror masks of *kwifon* as a centrifugal force binding exogenous forces to the polity, cadets saw them as a vindication of their centripetal tendencies. Today, the masks of *kwifon* no longer execute people or sacrifice slaves, but they are still the object of a visceral fear that cannot be explained by the actual dangers they pose. Despite their threatening and belligerent demeanor, palace masks seldom hurt audience members in earnest. If the masks remain truly fearsome today, then, it is because they remain overdetermined, impregnated with resurgent traces of their past—reenacting (re-presenting) as dance what was first presented as violence.

CHAPTER FOUR

Aurora colonialis: German Imperialism and the Modernity of Slavery

Very early the Germans realized that the best asset they had for the exploitation of the resources of the Cameroons was the native, for without his labour nothing could be done. — Harry Rudin (1938, 316)

The penetration of the Whites by and large intensified the trade in human lives. — Jaap Van Slageren (1972, 78 [trans. mine])

They say I'm buying people. — Eric de Rosny (1981, 110 [trans. mine])

Labor Recruitment in the Grassfields

Not only was the abolition of the internal trade in slaves put forward as one of the conditions of British trade with the kings of the Cameroon River in 1843 (Rudin 1938, 17), but antislavery rhetoric later featured strongly as a justification for Germany's annexation of the territory in 1884 (Eckert 1999, 133; Rudin 1938, 395–96). One might therefore have expected slavery to come to a definitive halt soon after the arrival of the first German governor, von Soden, in 1885. One might likewise have expected slavery to come to an end in the Grassfields with the extension of German suzerainty into the hinterland under the subsequent governors Zimmerer (1891–95) and Puttkamer (1895–1907). In fact, as Lovejoy and Hogendorn (1993) have made clear for northern Cameroon and Nigeria, slavery suffered a "slow death" in Cameroon, continuing well into the mid-twentieth century. Rudin (1938, 389) makes it clear that the German

colonial administration under successive governors right up to the First
World War held the view that internal or domestic slavery was "no great
evil in the Cameroons, and would solve itself in time."[1] Even as Rudin
was writing these words, however, the use of domestic slaves of Grassfields origin was still a feature of Duala society.[2] As late as the 1940s and
1950s, accusations of slave origin could still be used as legal justification
for preventing persons from owning land in Douala. Indeed, the stigma of
slave origin is a factor in Duala society to this day (Eckert 1999, 140). The
Banyang of the Cross River, likewise, continued to smuggle slaves during
the colonial era by disguising them as carriers in trade caravans (Chem-
Langhëë and Fomin 1995, 194–95).[3] In the Grassfields itself, lineage and
compound heads were still engaged in the trade in slaves as late as the
1930s.[4]

Nor was the perpetuation of slavery in Cameroon throughout the colonial period simply a factor of administrative apathy. In fact, slavery in
German Kamerun was a matter of debate in the Reichstag from 1891 to
1902, in which year the sale and exchange of slaves within the Kamerun
protectorate was finally forbidden, although the status of existing slaves
was not altered (Austen [1977] 1995; Austen and Derrick 1999, 118; Rudin
1938, 392–93). In practice, however, the colonial administration had little
power to enforce even this limited decree. In the north of the territory
especially, its influence over the Hausa was tenuous and its military power
insufficient. In the Grassfields and throughout the hinterland, troops
were made available for the suppression of the trade in slaves, but it was
deemed wiser by the colonial administration—which feared that freeing
slaves on a large scale would cause social upheaval—to use them instead
to protect the interests of German traders (Rudin 1938, 396). Moreover,
it is clear that a fundamental contradiction existed between the stated
humanitarian aims of colonial annexation of the Kamerun territory and
the social effects of the economic and political transformations wrought
by colonial contact. In other words, colonial contact not only failed to
stem the trade in slaves; it actually exacerbated it in several ways.

Elizabeth Chilver (1961, 238) notes a statement to the Parliamentary
Committee in 1847 that "the palm oil trade in the Cameroons rivers had
practically ousted the Atlantic slave trade, though it continued on a small
scale at Bimbia." The effect of replacing the European demand for slaves
with a new demand for palm oil, however, did not put an end to slavery
but rather internalized it as demand grew for the services of oil collectors,
processors, and carriers (Chilver 1961, 237; Austen and Derrick 1999, 118,

120; Wirz 1973a).[5] In addition to the plantations set up and managed by the Duala themselves, German traders set up their own large-scale commercial plantations for which they also needed labor. Labor was so scarce along the coast that it was seen by prospective investors as the key issue determining the viability of investment in agricultural enterprises in the territory (Chilver 1967, 491; Chilver and Röschenthaler 2001). The arrival in 1889 of Eugene Zintgraff's first government-sponsored expedition to the *Grasland* region (until then known only vaguely as Mbrikum, or Bayong country) was mainly due to the determination of the German colonial administration and the planters to find the source of the Duala's slaves and ivory and to bypass their role as middlemen and their monopoly on labor (Austen and Derrick 1999, 93–137; Chilver [1966] 1996; Zintgraff 1895). The chiefdom of Bali-Nyonga, which marked the terminus of Zintgraff's expedition, was just about the only chiefdom on the entire journey in which Zintgraff received a warm welcome. It was a noted slave-dealing state founded by a roaming band of Chamba slave raiders who had lost their horses and had only settled in the area in that generation.

Together with the German speculator Max Esser, Zintgraff returned to Bali leading a second expedition in 1896. The express purpose of this expedition was to negotiate a contract with the fon of Bali for the supply of labor to the plantations on the coast (Chilver and Röschenthaler 2001; Esser 1898).[6] The movement of such large expeditions in the interior, so threatening in appearance and placing as it did such a large demand on local supplies of food, was greatly feared and hotly opposed by inhabitants who found themselves on the new German supply route. In the course of Zintgraff's 1888–89 expedition in particular, he had had to fight his way through the Banyang chiefdoms opposed to his passage. He did so using his heavily armed Liberian Vai mercenaries and took women, children, and slaves as hostages as he went (Ruel 1969, 13). When he arrived in Bali trailing his hostages behind him, the fon Galega took him to be a slave dealer like himself and offered to facilitate his negotiations for additional local purchases (Chilver 1967, 483).[7] For the Banyang, Meta, and other chiefdoms from which he took hostages, Zintgraff's expedition represented a continuation of the slave raiding of the past, not a break.[8] The major difference for the Banyang was that until then, they, much like the Duala, had been secure in the position of middlemen in the slave trade. Now they were themselves subject to raiding by a more powerful external force.

The German presence in the Grassfields not only increased the taking of slaves under the guise of labor recruitment and for the independent Duala plantations, but it also seriously destabilized the region. The Germans engaged in a protracted series of battles and "punitive expeditions" that not only recalled the raids of the mounted Chamba earlier in the century but were widely perceived to be fought on their behalf, in the name of the Bali-Chamba. Gaining allies on the ground was one way for the Germans to overcome the intrinsic weakness of their military position in the Grassfields, but again, arming these allies and sending them out to find labor for the German plantations were in complete contradiction with their putative aim of ending slave raiding in the region. In January 1891, two Vai envoys from the German trading firm Jantzen and Thormählen who had been sent to the chiefdoms of Bafut and Mankon were murdered, and Zintgraff decided to mount a punitive expedition against the two chiefdoms—both of which were on hostile terms with neighboring Bali. Four of the five Germans taking part in the disastrous raid were killed in a counterattack, along with 170 of their carriers and hundreds of the Vai mercenaries and Bali-Nyonga irregulars (Chilver [1966] 1996, 29–31; O'Neil 1996, 88; Sharwood-Smith 1925, 62). Mankon also lost many people in the attack. Later that year, some of Zintgraff's carriers mutinied—with their Mauser rifles—from a camp in Banyang country, plundering villages on their way to the coast. At this point, the Germans signed a treaty with Fon Galega of Bali, recognizing him as the "paramount chief of the surrounding tribes of the northern Cameroons hinterland." Unbeknown to the Germans involved, their policy of dealing only with those chiefdoms they perceived as the most powerful had the effect of exacerbating the hypertrophy of the centralized military states of the region, creating military superpowers in a region in which no single chiefdom had heretofore enjoyed undisputed supremacy.

Over one hundred breach-loading rifles (an enormous tactical advantage in a region that had until then only been supplied with muzzle-loading Dane guns) were distributed by the Germans to the Bali, and the artillery officer Franz Hutter set about training an irregular corps of fifty local men that came to be known as the *Balitruppe*. Within a few months of its inception, this force was used to attack three Mankon villages, which were raised to the ground in a bloody battle that was not publicly reported by the colonial administration. The funds needed for the rifles and ammunition had been made available by the Reichstag following the 1891 Brussels Antislavery Conference. They had been intended for use in the setting up of caravan routes and stations with which to support an antislavery campaign in the interior of the protectorate (Chilver 1967, 486–87; Rudin 1938, 395–96).[9] Later that year, "battle-happy Hutter" used his force—by now 150 strong—to attack the Pinyin (also enemies of the Bali), and in June and July he used it against the Banyang. On Hutter's orders, "killers were rewarded with a fathom of cloth for each head taken" (Chilver 1967, 488). Two hundred of his soldiers claimed their fathom of cloth (Van Slageren 1972, 82).[10]

In 1912, a major operation was mounted against the Ngi, resulting in several hundred casualties (Van Slageren 1972, 508–9). The region was further destabilized by large-scale mutinies and desertions of armed Vai carriers, who roamed the region raiding villages, and by the carriers' sale of some hundreds of the expedition's Mausers in exchange for women along their route (Chilver 1967, 487; Hutter 1902, 19; Van Slageren 1972, 84). When the Germans attempted to recover the arms by force, villages that had once supplied them with food could no longer be counted on. In a vicious circle of increasing insecurity, hungry deserters from the German caravans and Bali messengers took to looting instead of trade, and labor recruitment turned to raiding as the Grassfields was plunged into a new period of instability. Between 1899 and 1910, the southern Grassfields was closed to civilian traffic because of ongoing uprisings against the Germans and the Bali, which provoked a further protracted series of retaliatory attacks by the Germans (Chilver 1967, 494; Van Slageren 1972, 86).[11] The insecurity of the region went from bad to worse in this period, due in large part to the unquestioning support of the Germans for the Bali and of their hasty recourse to military solutions to disputes between the expansionist Bali and their subjugated neighbors.

When in 1897 Zintgraff and Esser struck a deal with the fon Galega for the supply of labor to the coastal plantations, it was agreed that a proportion of five to one of the laborers would be sourced from chiefdoms recently subjected to Bali overrule (Chilver and Röschenthaler 2001, 94; Chilver 1967, 487; O'Neil 1996, 89). Subject chiefdoms that had supplied slaves in precolonial times now became the source of forced labor with the backing of the Germans (Dillon 1990, 14, 270; O'Neil 1996, 89; Russell 1980, 82). When word of the extent of the mortality of the labor recruits reached Bali, resistance rapidly grew, and Bali recruitment operations more and more took on the appearance of the manhunts of the slave raiders of the precolonial era.[12] In 1899, the German plantation recruiter Conreau was killed by the Bangwa when he returned to recruit among them after a deadly epidemic on the plantations that had killed many of their laborers (Chilver 1967, 494). In the same year, an expedition headed by the *Schutztruppe* commander Pavel attacked Bafut with Maxim guns and mortars. Over one thousand Bafut and many Mankon people were killed, hundreds were taken prisoner, and hundreds more were levied as forced laborers. As had been the practice in the precolonial wars of conquest, the Germans recompensed the aid given to them in the attack by the *Balitruppe* with the gift to the Bali officers of captured women and children. Chilver (1967, 496n43) notes that the British administration was still dealing with the civil litigation arising from this practice as late as 1936. It was also in 1899 that Governor Puttkamer sent a letter to Dominik, a military officer who was then engaged in a war of pacification in the interior, instructing him not to free the slaves of those he conquered but rather to send them and their families to the coast to work as "free" laborers (Puttkamer to Dominik, 1899, as quoted in Rudin 1938, 394n1).

How such diplomacy differed from the slave raiding that had preceded the arrival of the Germans must have been a mystery to its victims. If anything, the power of the most notorious slave raiders in the Grassfields had been consolidated, and their raiding parties—now clothed in the fig leaves of labor recruiters—were better armed than ever.[13] Only the middlemen had changed. The "labor question" and the problem of resistance to forced labor recruitment had been put to the *Schutztruppe* command by the imperial administration, and it can be seen to have been guiding their decision making at the end of the nineteenth century and into the twentieth (Chilver 1967, 495–96; Rudin 1938, 321). In addition to the recruitment of forced labor, the trade in slaves proper continued with the tacit support of the German administration.[14] During the British mandate period after 1915, the British administration had no control over Bamenda division until 1924 due to lack of manpower. In 1926, the administration was forced to send police to the border of the division to intercept slave traders on their way south into Mamfe division with their slaves, whom they were disguising as carriers (Chem-Langhëë and Fomin 1995). In this manner, the provision of forced labor for the plantations and the establishment of a cash economy in Kamerun—the very conditions that the German administration argued would lead to the end of slavery—were inseparably conjoined with the perpetuation of slave trading proper.[15]

Moreover, as the Germans rewarded the Bali for their military support by placing smaller chiefdoms under their suzerainty, the period from the turn of the century to 1907 was characterized by regular revolts against German and Bali overrule, followed by German punitive expeditions and the extraction of forced labor from the pacified chiefdoms—in many respects a perpetuation of the precolonial political order, in which subjugated chiefdoms were forced either to supply slaves to dominant states or to face further raiding.[16] Not only was the colonial means of acquiring labor perceived by both local recruiters and recruits as a continuation of the slave trade, but the form of work itself became infamous as stories of the massive death toll of plantation laborers on the coast filtered back to the Grassfields and were related in the same genre as accounts of the transatlantic slave trade had been: as a mythical form of European cannibalism. Just as they had during the days of the slave trade, Grassfields chiefs expressed anxiety about the disappearance of their youth—and low-level administrators concurred, one of them anxiously decrying the disappearance of the "flower of the population" to the coast.[17] Even the pro-German fon of Bali found it necessary to express his concern to the colonial authorities in Buea (Chilver 1967, 505–6).

The enormity of the death toll in the eyes of the people of the Grassfields in this period would be hard to exaggerate. It was well known throughout the region that laborers put to work on the large-scale cocoa plantations run by Germans were dying "like flies" and that such labor—gathered as it was through operations that Mbembe (1996, 167) has termed "anarchic"—came to be regarded as a new form of slavery (Austen 1983; Eckert 1999, 139). During 1907–8, 108 of 125 laborers of Grassfields origin died on the German plantations in a typhoid epidemic (Van Slageren 1972, 85). In 1913–14 nearly 11,000 men were recruited, of whom 2,000 were destined for the plantations and railway. Elizabeth Chilver writes that "more could not be recruited without grave economic and social damage" to the Grassfields (1963, 97). In the same year about 80,000 carriers—men, women, and children—were engaged in transporting goods for the German administration and traders on the Kribi–Yaoundé road alone, while the plantations employed nearly 18,000 "natives" (Rudin 1938, 316–17). Kuczynski (1939, 57–58) records annual death rates on the plantations during the first decade of the twentieth century from a minimum of just less than 8 percent to a maximum of 75 percent. To try to imagine the significance of such abstract figures in concrete terms, we need only recall that the annual death toll in the concentration camps of Dachau and Buchenwald during the Second World War was approximately 20 percent (Bettelheim 1943, 438) and that the death toll among soldiers at the front in the First World War—the war that gave birth to the expression "the lost generation"—was 11.8 percent to 16 percent (Becker [1983] 1985, 331;

Ferro [1969] 1973, 251).[18] The death toll in the labor camps in Kamerun gave rise to heated debates in the German government of the day. Rudin (1938, 328) notes a decree of 1900, apparently intended to mollify the reformists, ordering every plantation to have its own cemetery. As survivors of the camps returned home and word spread to the hinterland of the "appalling death rate" on the plantations, recruiters such as the ill-starred Conreau came to be seen as "agents of death" whom one should kill (Rudin 1938, 325–27).

By my rough calculation, between one in five and one in six men were working on the plantations at any one time during 1926–35.[19] In the German period, a much higher proportion than this—a ratio of eight or ten to one—would simultaneously have been involved in portage for German imperial and trader caravans (Rudin 1938, 324). By the time the British took over, the depopulation of the Grassfields was such a serious administrative concern that the German system of forced labor was gradually replaced with voluntary labor (Buell [1928] 1965, 1:685), and censuses recording births and deaths were taken from 1925. Nevertheless, these censuses showed a higher death than birth rate for Bali, Buea, and Victoria (Kuczynski 1939, 271). Warnier (1995b, 255) has estimated that some 0.5 percent of the population left the Grassfields annually in slave caravans from the seventeenth to the early nineteenth centuries. In a population he estimates at roughly 300,000, this figure implies an annual loss of 15,000 people.[20] Although serious, this figure did not lead to outright depopulation of the Grassfields, which is why the region was able to supply slaves to the coast over so many centuries. In contrast, the plantation economy of the colonial era, which engaged 10 percent of the entire male population, and forced labor, which appropriated about 80 percent of the male population on a rotating basis, including the sick and the aged, dramatically aggravated the seepage of people from the Grassfields. Its excesses have left an indelible mark in the popular imaginary of the region to this day.

The March of Death: Hunger, Disease, and Disappearance on the Caravan Routes

Austen notes that those who endorse what he terms the "myth of extreme oppression" of the German colonial era often overlook traders in favor of planters (Austen 1996b, 63; Austen and Derrick 1999, 93). Indeed, traders often complained bitterly both to the German government and to the colonial administration in Cameroon about the abuses of the plantation companies and their labor recruitment—exposing the planters to official censure and exonerating themselves from closer scrutiny in one fell swoop. Although the traders' complaints were couched in the language of enlightened humanitarianism, however, the traders themselves were in competition with the plantation companies when it came to recruiting labor (Rudin 1938, 234–37, 316, 323). As mentioned earlier, the carriers—largely employed by the traders—outnumbered plantation laborers by eight or ten to one in the colony, and the complaints of the traders are likely to have been motivated at least as much by concern for scarce labor supplies as by compassion for the laborers. One thing is certain: traders did not treat their workforce with more compassion than did planters, and the system of recruitment, care, and remuneration for carriers was just as open to abuses as was the system of plantation labor.

In the Grassfields, the difficulty of the exposed high-altitude terrain often conspired with the cruelty of insensitive drivers and their masters to achieve tragic outcomes for the porters. Indeed, the experience of hunger seems to have been one of the endemic characteristics of portage even before colonial contact. During his first expedition to the Grassfields, Zintgraff was shaken by the sight of slaves who had been captured in raids by subchiefs of the emir of Yola and who were being driven in long caravans to Banyo, to the north of the Grassfields. These were kept hungry on purpose by their drivers so that they would be too weak to escape (Zintgraff 1895, as cited in Chilver [1966] 1996, 17). His concern for the slaves of others notwithstanding, Zintgraff's own carriers were also dangerously malnourished throughout their march, depending as they did on the goodwill of often suspicious if not antagonistic chiefs and on uncertain crop yields for their food. In Bafum, two of Zintgraff's carriers died of exhaustion, and several more—in addition to some of his Banyang hostages—perished on the way from Babungo to Bambui (Zintgraff 1895, as cited in Chilver [1966] 1996, 19, 21). Esser, who accompanied Zintgraff to Bali on a second expedition in 1896, notes the difficulties that the lack of food imposed on their porters and records, not without sorrow, the death of one of the porters "from indigestion" (Esser 1898, as quoted in Chilver and Röschenthaler 2001, 76).

Although Zintgraff and Esser seem to have had some compassion for the extremities to which they put their drivers, regularly expressing concern over the difficulty in feeding their men adequately, disdain and disinterest for one's porters seem to have typified later colonial attitudes.

This stance was exemplified most clearly in the curious blindness of colonial officers and traders to the malnourishment of their porters, and the ubiquitous belief that exhaustion was malingering and that beatings were more effective than food in driving porters on. Marie Pauline Thorbecke, who accompanied her husband Franz Thorbecke on his ethnological research trips in German Kamerun,[21] offers one of the few eyewitness descriptions of caravans in this period. She states her opinion so frankly that it clearly did not seem controversial to her, suggesting that her attitude was the norm of the day:

> In Nkongsamba, the porters naturally spent the night in the open, around a fire. The weight of one porter's load is of 25 to 30 kg.[22] The start of the day always gives rise to mayhem. They fight to get hold of the lightest loads. During the whole length of the portage, certain elements try to drop behind, or to escape into the bush. Thanks to treating them regularly to the "twenty-five" [the maximum number of strokes of the whip allowed by government decree], the majority of them nevertheless manage to remain in line. At the next halt, the "chop palaver" takes place. The feed is distributed on the ground. It is only thanks to the whip that we manage to keep these people from throwing themselves on the food like animals. On the order "cargo for up" the march continues. The caravan is placed under the command of an indigenous superintendent. One wishes that control could be exclusively assumed by military officers. (Thorbecke 1914, 9–15, as quoted in Van Slageren 1972, 88–89 [trans. mine])

Rudin (1938, 235) notes that "even when the Government required that natives be whipped less frequently, there were those [traders] who said that the ultimate effect of such a policy would be a relaxation of discipline and serious harm to investments in the colony." Caravans were often too big for the villages they passed through to be able to feed the carriers. As a result, the carriers (some of whom were armed) were often so starved that they would plunder villages for food without paying for it (Rudin 1938, 333).[23]

The experience of plantation labor and of portage came together at the stage of recruitment, when the new recruits for plantation labor were herded down to the coast. At that stage, the recruits were bound to each other, just as earlier generations of slaves had been (Rudin 1938, 323, 326). As Thorbecke notes, every caravan had an indigenous leader who was responsible for keeping the caravan members together, bringing up the rear, ensuring stragglers did not melt away into the bush, guaranteeing that villagers along the route were protected from the potentially violent

FIGURE 14. "Cameroon: Caravan transporting ivory and rubber" (caption from the Basel Mission archive). Note the armed guards at the front and rear of the caravan, and the two alongside it. (Basel Mission image QU-30-0020182)

FIGURE 15. "En route from Bali to Nyasoso. The missionaries Stahl, Gutekunst and Spellenberg" (caption from the Basel Mission archive). The photograph was taken in 1907 by Gottlieb Friedrich Spellenberg (*standing in the foreground*). He is quoted later in chapter 6. Because this was a missionary rather than a traders' caravan, or a group of forced laborers, it is devoid of armed guards. (Basel Mission image E-30.25.012)

porters, and meting out beatings to offenders.[24] In principle, these leaders were to be awarded government certificates establishing their aptitude and higher pay in accordance with their responsibilities (Rudin 1938, 332). In practice, traders found it preferable to bypass these regulations. Rather than report the infractions of caravan leaders who were known for their violence and risk having their certificates revoked by the government, traders kept them on and concealed their convenient brutality. Traders also evaded the obligation to pay their porters in cash, preferring to hand out the cheap European goods they peddled instead. In addition to the effects of malnutrition, exposure, and exhaustion, the lives of carriers were curtailed by the fact that cheap rum was one of the preferred methods of payment used by white employers. Furthermore, because traders were always on the lookout for a way to outmaneuver their competitors, they systematically entered areas the government had quarantined on account of outbreaks of epidemics, sending their caravans through the region regardless. The result was that disease took a serious toll on carriers, who often spread epidemics along their routes. The life expectancy of caravan porters was said by observers on the ground to be even lower than that of plantation laborers (Rudin 1938, 324, 350–51).

For the peoples of the Grassfields, as opposed to those of the coast, the primary confrontation with Europeans was thus played out in the macabre experience of the caravan first and foremost, and of the plantation second. Not only did many more Grassfielders work and die as porters than as plantation laborers, but even those who went to the plantations necessarily did so *in* caravans; some of them were even forced by the recruiters to head-load goods to the coast on their way to the plantations (Rudin 1938, 326). Porters and plantation laborers alike were recruited by force in their villages, sometimes by plantation recruiters and sometimes by native policemen, who bound them one to another before marching them to the coast.[25] Colonial recruitment thus took the form of the *razzia,* the manhunt of the slave raiders, and the way the recruits were bound and led off by force also recalled these methods. In the memories of contemporary informants, no distinction is made between enslavement and forced labor.[26] Once entrapped in a caravan on a fixed contract of six to eighteen months, the porter found that the overriding experience was one of hunger, and the only means of survival was often looting and plunder that occasioned violent reprisals by the ever-present caravan leader and his trusty whip or cudgel. According to Knutson's memoir (as cited in Ardener 2002), many German officers took on this task themselves rather than leave it to their drivers, and to this day, the exclamation *Jaman!* (German!) connotes horror and wonder in equal measure in the pidgin of the Grassfields.

The Meat You've Eaten: Cannibal and Zombie Forms of Witchcraft

The German plantations had such a grip on the social imaginary of the Bakweri who lived in their vicinity that around the time of the First World War the Bakweri elaborated a new form of witchcraft belief to accommodate their changing economic environment. Referred to as *nyongo,* the new witchcraft involved a supernatural form of plantation slavery, with the bewitched—previously said to be devoured in cannibal feasts—now turned into slaves who were doomed to toil on a secret plantation on the nearby Mount Kupe on behalf of their industrial witch-owners. It was said that many Bakweri who appeared to die—especially children—were in fact being pledged to the witches by close relatives who sought to enrich themselves illicitly (Ardener [1970] 1996, 248ff.; Geschiere 1997, 146–51). Children obtained in this way were sent off to labor for the witches on the forested slopes of the distant mountain. Only the initiated, it was said, could see the plantations hidden by the forests and mists of the mountain. The Duala *kong* or *ekong* and the Bamileke *famla'* occult systems operate today on similar principles. According to these beliefs, witches group together in associations that replicate the form of the ordinary savings association common throughout the littoral and the hinterland, known as *njangi* in pidgin. The difference between an ordinary *njangi* and these associations is that one contributes money or gifts in kind to the former but one's kin to the latter. As with the Bakweri *nyongo* of the past, contemporary *kong* and *famla'* adepts are believed to sell their close kin to these associations in exchange for great wealth. As with *nyongo,* those sold appear to die but in fact have been spirited away by the other members of the association to work on an invisible plantation in the Manenguba mountains (de Rosny 1981, 97–111; Warnier 1995b, 269).[27] In a final but no less significant parallel, *ekong* beliefs in an economic form of witchcraft involving enslavement or forced labor have also replaced a preexisting Duala belief in cannibal witchcraft, whose victims were not put to work but rather gradually eaten alive (de Rosny 1981, 99–100). It is not hard to see how this image of pure greed—"one meat eating another" (99 [trans. mine])—provided the model for the exactions of forced labor.

As Geschiere (1997) highlights in his aptly titled work *The Modernity of Witchcraft,* the principles of these new beliefs are cast in terms of the contemporary experience of their adherents: the *kong* and *famla'* associations are said to possess otherworld bank accounts into which their members deposit the embezzled salaries of their victims, as the latter toil for them on the otherworld plantations. Ardener's Bakweri informants likewise associated the origin of *nyongo* with the arrival of the Europeans and imagined that the *vekongi*—or zombies—were taken away by the *nyongo* adepts to their secret plantation in a witch lorry. The witches themselves were easily recognizable by the modern European houses they built in the village with their ill-gotten wealth. De Rosny (1981, 101–4) informs us that the greatest of all the *éconeurs* (as those who use *ekong* to bewitch people are known) in Duala in the 1970s was said to be a highly successful Greek cloth merchant with a (visible) staff of seventy and an otherworld army of zombie slaves. On his travels to the villages around the port city of Douala, where he sought out healers and elders to inform him about traditional healing in the region, de Rosny (a French Catholic priest) became aware of a disturbing rumor that was being spread about him: "they say I'm buying people," he told his friends in bewilderment. The reply was always the same: "It's called *ekong*" (de Rosny 1981, 97).[28]

De Rosny was quick to make the connection between Europeans being cast as buyers of people and the history of the slave trade. "What has been the impact of the formidable occurrence of the slave trade, during the last century, on beliefs?" he asks, and he replies with a telling ethnographic detail: 140 years after the effective abolition of the transatlantic slave trade on this coast, many of his informants still dream at night of being led off by strangers, their hands tied, to the sea.[29] No informant tells de Rosny that these dreams are motivated by memories of the slave trade, but in the face of such nightmares, can one really hold to the belief that what is no longer discussed explicitly is necessarily forgotten? When the dead of the past resurface in the sleep of the living, threatening to drag them back down to the sea, the accursed seek help from a healer (*nganga*) to free them from the *éconeur* to whom they have been sold. The work that the slave trader once carried out is thus sustained today in the popular imaginary of the coast through the form of the nightmare about the *éconeur:* the one who steals people by stealth rather than violence and puts them to work in a second world, much as they were once put to work in the New World or, later, on the mysterious and sinister colonial plantations.[30] The space of the accursed in Cameroon is no longer lived as a simple present but rather doubled by the time of slavery, which in turn is not contained in a simple past as it resurfaces involuntarily into the chronotope of the bewitched. So pervasive is the experience of *dédoublement* in postcolonial Cameroon, of the resurgence of past violence in contemporary suffering, that it has been enshrined as a ubiquitous if invisible aspect of the natural world—for the other world of spirits and witches is not supernatural, but nearby, familiar and palpable.

In the Grassfields too, the appropriation of the fathomless wealth and power of other worlds has spawned a host of secret societies. Generally known as *msa,* these societies replicate myths from the area that tell of another world hidden beneath the surface of a lake or in an inaccessible mountain stream—local bodies of water here evidently standing in for the sea and the navigable rivers that led to the slave ports. Contemporary accounts of *msa* collected in the kingdom of Bum in the western Grassfields suggest that ordinary (nontitled) villagers are able to gain access to a world of Western modernity (known as *kwang* in Bum and *balak* in Oku) during nocturnal journeys that offer the chance to gain immense wealth (Fisiy and Geschiere 1993; Geschiere 1997, 158–64; Mbunwe-Samba 1996; Nyamnjoh 1985; Warnier 1993, 157–62). As one initiate of the sibling *famla'* society put it in the mid-1950s: "After independence we shall have our own place to go to at night where all the houses are joined up in streets."[31] Another informant excused himself to his interviewer for being tired: he had, he explained, been up all night making airplanes (Mbuy 1989).[32] As with coastal forms of witchcraft, things obtained in the watery realm of *kwang* often must be paid for with human beings from the everyday world whom the initiate bewitches. Importantly, the victims must be members of the witch's kin group—often his or her children—and they are traded for the goods imported by Europeans. Unlike victims of the later coastal forms of witchcraft, however, these Grassfields victims are not put to work but simply eaten by the other members of the coven.

Robert Pool's (1994, 150–67) detailed account of *tvu'* witchcraft in the Grassfields Wimbum village of Tabenken makes this distinction clear. Here witches are explicitly said to band together into *njangi* associations. Rather than trading money, however, they trade in human flesh—"the sweetest flesh," as one informant put it. Although some of Pool's informants refer to this trading as taking place in a *njangi* association, others suggest it occurs in a "witch market" (*nta tvu'*), once again said to be on a nearby, forested mountain (17, 159, 164). Although the market is just a stone's throw away from the village, it is visible only to initiates. Quoting

Mburu (1979, 6–7), Pool (1994, 151) states that when it is a member's turn to provide his share for the feast, he must offer one of his own close kin.[33] In a conversation with Tangwa, one of his informants, Pool playfully suggests that he himself might offer all of his Wimbum acquaintances to a *tvu' njangi* and revel in unlimited supplies of the "sweetest flesh" forever after, but Tangwa informs him that he cannot do so. How could Pool offer people who did not belong to him? Tangwa asks rhetorically. "After all," Pool concludes, "I could not just take a fowl or a goat from another person's compound in order to repay an ordinary debt, so it was only logical that I could only repay a witchcraft debt with someone who was 'mine'" (156).

Although Pool describes a situation, in Wimbum, in which the witch market and the *njaŋgi* trading fraternity that exchanges human beings seem to be different aspects of one system of cannibal witchcraft, in Oku the form of witchcraft in which one goes to a market to pick up bundles that contain one's fate is distinct from the form in which a sorcerer eats another person. In the former Oku case, the witch is known as a *wel efim* (*efim* person) and said to practice witchcraft by means of *shik efim*. The verb *shik* means "to set out" and is used most commonly to describe setting out for the farm (*shik elem*) or for the bush (*shik əbkwak*). Those who *shik efim* are also said to go to the *əbkwak efim* or "bush of witches." In this place—often said to be located in a deserted area of secondary forest or fallow farmland, or on an uncultivated mountainside—they are given mysterious bundles by witches (*ghel efim* or *efim* people). These bundles contain different fates, some good, such as wealth, and some bad, such as diseases. Once they choose a parcel from the witch market, they must run all the way home with it without looking back, and the witches in charge of the market are said to hurl projectiles at them as they run. As soon as they get home, they open their parcels and discover whether they are to be showered with fortune or misfortune. A group of young men were recently accused of *shik efim* in Oku when they suddenly took to wearing fashionable clothes. It was said that they had obtained the clothes in a bundle taken from the "bush of witches" (*əbkwak efim*). Others who have started large families or had inexplicable success with their farms have also been accused of being *ghel efim* (known in pidgin by the literal translation "witch-people-dem").

Such people are viewed with ambivalence—as daring and powerful yet mischievous, irresponsible, and antisocial. They are often the object of suspicion and gossip, but they are not loathed and excoriated in the way that cannibal witches are. Cannibals are distinct from *ghel efim* in Oku and known as kəvuŋ (sing.) or əbvuŋ (pl.). A kəvuŋ is a cannibal witch who eats other people by supernatural means. As in Pool's example from Tabenken, the only people such a witch may eat are its own family members.[34] Again, as in the Tabenken case, cannibal witches in Oku are said to be organized into njaŋgi groups, and they provide their family members to the group to eat. The person eaten does not die outright but rather weakens gradually, becoming frail, confused, and sickly. In the presence of such symptoms, diviners often diagnose attack by a kəvung. In a case that was recently heard at the palace by the kwifon regulatory society, children who had taken to playing in a stream in the village of Jikijem were accused of being əbvuŋ. It was said that they had organized a njaŋgi group of cannibal witches. One day, a teacher at a school in the village suddenly fell unconscious, and the children were accused of having eaten him in their njaŋgi group. As often happens in such cases, one of the accused boys confessed to the crime.[35] In the kwifon hearing, he explained that his partners had been fighting over the body during their illicit feast, each one entirely carried away by his gluttony. Despite his best efforts, the boy said, he had been unable to restrain them. In their frenzy, they had started a tug-of-war over who would get the teacher's head, with each trying desperately to grab it from the other to devour (kvəl) it, and this was the point at which the teacher had fallen to the ground unconscious.

The ubiquitous emphasis in Grassfields witchcraft discourses not only on cannibalism—the consumption of human beings—but on the offering of only close kin in such njangi associations or witch markets brings us back once again to the question of the slave trade. As mentioned in chapter 2, the majority of the slaves sold out of the Grassfields in the precolonial era were not captured in wars. (Although wars were common, the resulting captives tended to be kept within the Grassfields to perform a number of labor and military tasks for their new masters.) Rather, slaves destined for the long-distance trade were bought and sold by ruse on a small-scale basis. For this fraudulent but well-entrenched trade to thrive, a complicity had to exist between an outside buyer and a relative of the person to be sold. This relative, agnatic or affinal, Warnier aptly baptizes "the Judas" (1995b, 259–60).

It was precisely the close relationship between the seller and the sold that made the operation feasible. Wealth in the Grassfields was based on an economy of wealth in people, which predicated a kinship system of rights over people.[36] Those sold could not be chosen randomly by the Judas; they had to be persons over whom he had rights. This explains Nwokeji and Eltis's (2002) recent finding that it was overwhelmingly children who were sold as slaves from the Grassfields area. Most often, not only could the Judas claim them as "his," but they were also likely to be the subject of conflicting claims by another kin member. As a claim over a person came to a head, selling the person was one way of establishing one's rights and of capitalizing on the person at the same time. Like de Rosny and Geschiere, Warnier (1995b, 269) concludes that it is not hard to connect the abuses to which the political economy of Grassfields kinship systems was open with the beliefs in witch markets and cannibal *njangis* that persist today. Not only did *tvu'* and *kəvuŋ* witchcraft effectively encapsulate the fears generated by the system of rights-over-people in the era of the slave trade, but it would have gained a new salience in the colonial era in relation to new concerns about forced labor.[37]

Fear of hunger and fear of the insatiable appetites of the political and business elites are the twin demons that have haunted ordinary Cameroonians ever since the colonial period (Argenti 2002b; Mbembe 1985; Mbembe and Roitman 1995).[38] Following Achille Mbembe (1985), Jean-François Bayart (1989) has elaborated the myriad subtleties of the trope of eating in ordinary people's discourse of the dominant elite of contemporary Cameroon. As he points out, hunger not only refers to a physiological state in contemporary Cameroon but is also a total social phenomenon informing every field of political life. In Cameroon today, the accumulation of wealth or of political power—especially in its most nefarious guises as a result of crime, graft, and corruption—is routinely referred to as a form of eating. The state has thus become "a vast space where one lives and expresses a gastronomy of poverty" (Mbembe 1985, 125 [trans. mine]), and eating has become a fixation that takes on political dimensions, reifying in inescapably palpable, concrete terms the political reality of African modernity.

The discourse of hunger did not emerge ex nihilo in the postcolonial era, however, and it is possible to trace its etymological history. Not only in French but also in the autochthonous languages of Cameroon, eating and the belly connote power and its abuses.[39] In Eblam Ebkwo, the language of Oku, as in many of the languages of the Grassfields, being installed as a fon is referred to as "eating" the throne (*sə jie kətie*), and inheriting or consuming wealth is known as "eating" it. In this political cosmology, the belly is therefore the locus of power, and witches are often said to contain their power as an animal or substance residing in their belly or bowels. It is this set of tropes of eating as an economy of power, desire, and venality that lends the palaces of the Grassfields their key metaphor as the intestines or bowels of the state. The winner of a game or one who earns a diploma is likewise said to have "eaten" it. Another term specifically referring to the chewing of meat, *kvɘl* (high tone)—as opposed to *jie* of soft foods—is used with reference to the way in which witches are said to consume their victims. This form of consumption is not thought of as the total and instantaneous annihilation of the individual but rather as a gradual process akin to the actions of parasites, leaving the victim alive in appearance but a mere shell, hollowed out from the inside—like a grain of rice by a weevil, a corpse by worms, or a living person by a wasting disease.[40]

The term for eating that is specific to eating meat, which is a term used to refer to the consumption of human beings by witches, is *kvɘl wel* (eat person) in Oku and *kfër wir* in Nso'. The sinister aspects of this surreptitious and gradual form of ingestion fit nicely with the negotiations of the Judas and his associates. Not only in the present postcolonial period but equally in the precolonial and the colonial periods, ever since the era of the slave trade, "eating" has served as a trope for the predatory consumption of people or of their labor, and the consequent erosion of the social fabric of their communities. Long before victims are actually abducted, they are already doomed, walking corpses, having been pledged by the Judas without their knowledge. As mentioned earlier, the notion that middlemen of the slave trade bought their victims to sate the appetites of their European clients was widespread in the Grassfields. It was also common on the coast, not only in Douala but along the entire Slave Coast. In contrast to this cannibal model of witchcraft, the new *ekong*-type zombie discourses seem to have first emerged in the colonial era to address the new phenomenon of plantation labor. When looking at the witchcraft of the coast and of the Grassfields from the colonial era onward then, we seem to have two closely related but distinct sets of beliefs: the notion, still dominant in the Grassfields, that witches capture and trade their victims for the culinary pleasure of eating them; and the belief, most strongly entrenched in the littoral, that powerful sorcerous entrepreneurs buy victims in order to enrich themselves by putting their new acquisitions to work on invisible plantations.[41]

Noting the overriding similarities between the witchcraft beliefs found among the inhabitants of the coast and those of the hinterland of Cameroon, Geschiere (1997, 151) makes the case for a "broad regional configuration" of witchcraft beliefs in this part of Africa, perhaps as far west as the Bight of Biafra.[42] Geschiere (1997, 153) and de Rosny (1981, 100–102) make the case that the cannibal versions of witchcraft predate notions of zombie workforces in Cameroon. The belief in cannibal associations would form the basis upon which zombie notions were later elaborated as a result of the inhabitants' more intensive involvement with Europeans, who introduced trade in a cash economy and large-scale plantations. In the broad configuration that Geschiere identifies, however, one might further delineate a historical differentiation of witchcraft beliefs at a subregional level, with an emphasis on zombie forms among coastal peoples (who interacted intensively with Europeans for centuries and who witnessed the establishment of plantations on their lands) and an enduring emphasis on cannibalism among hinterland peoples. The only time Pool was told about zombie witchcraft in the Grassfields was, significantly, by a young man who had worked on the coastal plantations.

In the two years I spent in Oku, never once did I hear stories of zombie witchcraft, although cannibal forms were fairly regularly described to me in veiled terms.[43] In other words, within the broad regional configuration of witchcraft beliefs across Cameroon, the cannibal discourse seems to have undergone a transformation on the coast in the colonial period to encompass modern trading relations, but not in the Grassfields, where it still refers to cannibalism as its key metaphor. From the point of view of the people of the Grassfields—who, in contrast to the coastal dwellers, were living in the old slave dealers' hunting ground—the cannibal discourse had always been particularly well suited to addressing the transatlantic trade for the simple reason that slaves sold in the long-distance trade never returned to their birthplace: cannibalism describes disappearance better than zombification does. Transshipment was every bit as terminal as death, and the belief in cannibal slave buyers reified the annihilation of transshipment in indisputably concrete terms.

Again in the Grassfields, the period of forced recruitment for the plantations of the colonial era differed from the transatlantic slave trade perhaps most saliently in that some laborers survived the experience and returned home again.[44] Although their homecoming proved that they had not been eaten, these laborers brought back "ugly rumours" about the conditions they had survived as well as accounts of the death rates among their coworkers (Rudin 1938, 325). Furthermore, because anyone who fell ill was sent home in the hope that disease would not spread to the rest of the plantation laborers (despite government directives prohibiting this practice), people often returned to their villages in poor health, only to die soon afterward. With forced plantation labor replacing slavery proper

from the late nineteenth century, coastal populations elaborated new discourses accounting for the ambiguous position of the forced laborer. Unlike slaves, forced laborers could not be thought of as simply dead. Some
of them reappeared—literally becoming *revenants,* or ghosts. Even in their
absence, it was clear that they were not gone into the watery realm of
the European (*mukala*) but put to work on the coast instead. Although
these recruits were not straightforwardly "disappeared" into the holds of
ships in the way that their unhappy predecessors had been, they must have
seemed only slightly better off. Put to work as they were ten hours a day,
six days a week, and flogged mercilessly by their masters, only to have their
contracts fraudulently renewed when they came to an end and their salaries absorbed by extortionate company stores, they must have thought of
themselves as stranded in a liminal no-man's-land between death and their
original lives—a purgatory in which many of them were, in fact, no better
off than walking dead men waiting for malnutrition, disease, and the inevi-
table floggings to take their toll.[45] Within the terms of the coastal witchcraft discourse, the *mukala* or Europeans were seen to have found a new
use for their captives. No longer simply a culinary delicacy, they were now
a source of labor. In the period of slavery, the popular imaginary of cannibal witchcraft had represented them in terms of the gross consumption of
the whole person by cannibalism. In the period of the colonial plantations,
the insatiable and excessive consumption of human labor and the resulting
alienation of the forced laborer came to be represented by the peoples of
the coast in terms of zombification and concealment on secret plantations,
while in the hinterland, where recruiting laborers differed little in its methods from catching slaves, the trope of cannibalism perdured.

The zombie witchcraft discourses most prevalent in the littoral thus
updated extant cannibal discourses (which had stretched from the coast
to the hinterland Grassfields in the period of the slave trade) to keep
pace with economic and political transformations on the coast. The question arises, then, why the *ekong* zombie discourses of the coast and the
Bamileke *famla'* never took hold as strongly in the Grassfields as they did
farther south, and why cannibal witchcraft discourses were not replaced
with a new discourse accounting for plantation labor and caravan portage
in the Grassfields. One might hypothesize that the distance of the plantations from the Grassfields kept them a total mystery to Grassfields people,
but the stories told by returning laborers make this explanation unlikely.[46]
Furthermore, caravans –crisscrossed the Grassfields routinely and would
thus have been a familiar sight even to those who were not recruited to

serve in them. Another possibility would be that the limited intercourse of Grassfielders with the German colonial administration, planters, and traders, and the political and economic isolation that typifies the North West Province to this day make this a region with a distinct political and cultural history that is less the result of intensive intercourse with Europeans than is the history of the coast. But this supposition also fails to hold up to scrutiny: although Grassfielders were not directly acquainted with Europeans until the end of the nineteenth century, the Grassfields has nonetheless been part of global modernity for four hundred years, mainly through its violent insertion into the transatlantic slave trade, and then as a source of plantation and portage labor.

Of course one of the main distinctions between the zombie, *kong, kupe,* and *famla'* discourses, on the one hand, and the cannibal discourses on the other is that the former all explicitly account for the monetization of the exchange in people, for the alienation of their labor, and for the imbrication of slavery and forced labor in market capitalism. From the point of view of the people of the coast, captured laborers were no longer disappearing across the sea but remaining nearby. The new zombie discourse therefore had to account not only for their alienation but also for their continued, albeit liminal, presence. The cannibal discourse, however, is comparatively silent on the issue of market capitalism and alienation, and elusive in its reference to the political and economic realities it speaks to, evoking an affective, visceral response regarding people's physical disappearance first and foremost. Also, the former set of discourses was predominant among the peoples to the south of the Grassfields and along the coast—middleman societies that bought and sold slaves in the past rather than "producing" them. In the Grassfields, meanwhile, where freemen were first turned into slaves and sold outside the area as a local commodity, these discourses were much less widespread. Could it be that the zombie and cognate discourses were a middleman's discourse first and foremost? As middlemen, these societies had for centuries been cognizant with complex and sophisticated systems of trade, and the explicitly mercantile references in zombie and cognate witchcraft discourses would have appealed strongly to their colonial experience, which combined the mystery of massive enrichment by the few elite plantation owners with the liminal presence of the exploited captive laborers.

In the Grassfields, the cannibal witchcraft discourse was used by the slave providers and their victims alike. It seems to have been a discourse that spoke to the experience of fear and victimization of the commoners, young people, and children. Yet in a manner analogous to the origin myths discussed earlier, the palatine elite appropriated the discourse to justify abductions and later recruitment for forced labor: the ingrates sold out of the chiefdom were not deserving of the protection of the fon; they were antisocial witches who threatened the community with their nefarious activities. To these victims and potential victims of disappearance, the economic transformations of the trade in people in the colonial period were not its key defining feature. The zombie discourse would not have occurred to the cadets who were the targets of exploitation by the elders: what mattered were not primarily the iniquitous relations of labor into which they were being sold—as Warnier (2006) demonstrates, their lives in their natal compounds in the Grassfields were already characterized by unremunerated and exploitative labor—but the threat of disappearance, oblivion, and annihilation best expressed in the trope of illicit and gluttonous ingestion by sorcerous elites. Furthermore, the trope of cannibalism speaks to the extreme violence of slavery in the Grassfields more effectively than does the notion of the zombie. As a provider of slaves, the Grassfields region witnessed a great deal more violence than the port of Douala did. By the time slaves were in the hands of the Duala middlemen, they had already been apprehended and effectively subordinated. Moreover, the Duala were selling slaves from elsewhere and were thus impervious to the human and social cost to the captives and their communities. In the hunting grounds of the Grassfields, however, the dark work of turning freemen into slaves had to be accomplished. The requisite processes of massive and near-anarchic coercion fostered the emergence of what today would be referred to as "strong states" on the one hand and violent brigand-entrepreneurs on the other, with the two groups covertly operating as partners.

The trade in slaves therefore fostered a political climate of polarization, stratification, domination, and terror.[47] In an autocratic context in which dissenters, marginalized people, the young, women, and strangers were all regularly scapegoated as "strong heads," "recalcitrant wives," "restless children," and witches and sold as slaves or chosen as forced labor, new discourses of power and its abuse, such as those explicitly elaborated in the zombie discourses of the coast, would have been too dangerous to address openly—even in symbolic terms. If the zombie witchcraft discourses of the coast, or local variants of them, were only seldom adopted in the Grassfields, it was partly because speaking out is not an option in situations of political oppression, and the cannibal discourse is conveniently euphemistic and ambiguous.[48] The ambiguity and euphemism that cadets took advantage of in the cannibal discourse came at a cost, however. Such indetermination also enabled the palatine elite and their slave catchers and labor recruiters to apply it to their own ends.

In general, normative terms, the discourse on cannibalism identified that there was such a thing as the Judas, the lineage head who profited from selling his own biological or classificatory offspring into slavery. But who was accused of cannibal witchcraft in practice, in specific instances? As Isaak Niehaus (2005) has recently illustrated with respect to zombie beliefs in the South African lowveld and Filip De Boeck (2005) with respect to the witch children of Kinshasa, it seems that despite the normative view that elites and elders are the Judases, it is predominantly cadets and children who are accused of witchcraft in the Grassfields (Kaberry 1969, 179). Indeed, the case of the witch children of Jikijem in Oku mentioned earlier provides a recent example of this pattern. The elders' practice of accusing children and youth helps to explain the pattern of sale of youth by their elders in the past, as it would have given the elder in the family an excuse for ridding himself of his own offspring. Because the discourse on cannibalism is undetermined, multivalent, and ambiguous, it has become the site of a struggle for appropriation by both opposing factions, and the elites, as in the past when they demonized slaves and cadets as potential witches, now portray them as the Judases or cannibal witches that they themselves often were. The discourse in the Grassfields is not a leveling one, as it is on the coast, where it is elite traders and entrepreneurs (and probably, in the past, also colonial officials and plantation managers) who are stigmatized. Nor is the discourse one that is purely dominating or hegemonic, a blanket justification for the exploitation of cadets. Rather, it marks the site of an ongoing struggle.

Because the discourse of cannibalism does not relate explicitly to labor and alienation as the zombie discourse does, but to eating as a trope for antisocial greed in a zero-sum universe, it can be appropriated and deployed either by the dominant or the dominated. In practice, the poor, the destitute, the childless, and slaves are often suspected by elites of being envious of their wealth and power, and they are therefore the ones to be accused (Kaberry 1969, 179; Röschenthaler 2006). Thus in Oku the kəvung cannibal witch is typically poor and powerless. He is the person who has failed to found a large family and who may be needy. Although in practice the elite cannot be subject to witchcraft accusations, the discourse that they deployed could nevertheless also be deployed to identify them—the whole social stratum of slave traders and labor recruiters—as the true source of cannibalism in the polity. Cannibal witchcraft therefore operates disjunctively in the Grassfields, not only as a weapon of the weak but also as a weapon of the powerful; it is an opportunity for domination as much as one for resistance.[49]

Cannibalism and Remembering

The descriptions of caravans of porters in the colonial, missionary, and ethnographic literature, parsimonious though they are, indicate a substantial continuity of subjective experience between the precolonial period of the transatlantic and internal slave trades, on the one hand, and the later experience of the colonial caravan on the other. Because the forms of subjectivation involved in both eras were so similar in terms of the coercive displacement they fomented and the continual violence and excessive death toll they led to, a transformation in the witchcraft discourse that had previously accounted for the slave trade was not necessary in the colonial period. The transition from the outright sale and deportation of people to their internment in local plantations on the coast was an abstract distinction in the Grassfields, where to all intents and purposes the precolonial rounds of the slave raiders sent by dominant chiefdoms continued much as they had in the past—as did the disappearance of one's kin. In such conditions of unremitting insecurity and violence, cannibalism remained the most apt discourse by which to objectify the dominant experience of predation in the region, and this discourse would have been made all the more salient by the focus on the belly elicited by the carriers' omnipresent experience of hunger.

If the cannibal had been the perfect encapsulation of the excessive appetite of the slave trader in the precolonial era, the pervasive malnourishment of carriers would have made the position of the cannibal Judas all the more trenchant and apposite in the colonial era. In conditions of pervasive malnourishment and the dominant experience of hunger, could one's father, uncle, or fon realistically be expected to refrain from eating "the meat of others"?[50] The protracted death of forced laborers who were sent back from the plantations to their villages to die compared with the sudden disappearance of transatlantic slaves only added more salience to the cannibal discourse, according to which victims were not devoured outright but slowly gnawed at from within by the insidious and insatiable witches. On the coast, however, it is clear that the transition from slavery to a plantation economy brought about marked and concrete transformations in the daily experience of slave traders, local plantation managers, and ordinary people alike, replacing as it did the transshipment of people overseas with their incarceration in plantations near to the coastal populations' own settlements—indeed, in some cases local people were driven from their land in order to make way for plantations.

Yet one may still wonder why new discourses did not become more strongly established in the Grassfields: despite the continuity of experience with slavery, some elements of forced labor were new. After the initial *razzias* of the Fulani and Chamba in the eighteenth and early nineteenth centuries, it was not common for captives to be led off by the hundreds to the slave trade. Rather, before and during the colonial period, they were increasingly obtained and sold by stealth, one by one, to slave traders, who passed them on by the dozen. The "open season" and the violent manhunts of the colonial recruiters would not have been directly consonant with the individual nocturnal abductions that the later form of enslavement by stealth depended on. Colonial recruitment was much more intensive than slave recruitment by abduction had been, and more comparable in its overt violence to earlier forms of outright slave raiding. Furthermore, it should not be forgotten that people disappeared from the Grassfields as forced laborers in the colonial period at a much faster rate than they ever had as slaves for the long-distance trade in the precolonial period.

A full answer to the question of why a new discourse did not become dominant in the Grassfields despite the advent of forms of abduction and coercion that were particular to the colonial era cannot ignore the strong centralization and the increasingly autocratic nature of the hierarchies of the Grassfields. As mentioned earlier, in the situation of covert slave recruitment facilitated by the presence of the Judas that obtained in the Grassfields just before and during the colonial era, vulnerable individuals had been able to address their anxieties and resentment covertly in the somatized form of cannibal witchcraft discourses. In the colonial era, however, not only did the colonial authorities greatly enhance the coercive powers of certain fons and groups of elites, but the need of colonial officers, planters, and traders for forced labor simultaneously presented the elite with a new, officially sanctioned means of ridding themselves of dissenters. In other words, the centralization of the expanding Grassfields states, which effectively guaranteed optimal conditions for further slave recruitment, was intensified in the colonial era, at which point it was converted into an engine for the recruitment of forced labor.

In the precolonial era, fons and lineage heads had been responsible—at least ideally—for protecting their people from abduction and sale into slavery, and the figure of the Judas could be unambiguously excoriated as an abomination. In the colonial era, however, not only was forced labor made available to fons as a profitable alternative to slavery, but it was officially sanctioned by the nascent colonial authorities and the palatine hierarchies in a way that made it all but hegemonic and its legitimacy harder for its victims to question. Such legitimation and intensification of the coercive power of the palatine elite of the Grassfields could not be questioned in the way that the relatively small-scale, illegitimate slave abductions of the past had been. In giving fons not only the right but the obligation to recruit, the colonial authorities effectively dissociated the palaces from the checks on their powers that had hitherto been available to their coteries and subjects, and made it pointless and foolhardy to voice dissent. This is still the case today in the region: in two years of fieldwork in Oku, I never once heard anyone explicitly criticize the fon, a member of the palace hierarchy, or any of the palace guards. This is not to say that no one had any grievances against the palace. On the contrary, today resentment of and dissent directed toward the traditional rulers of the Grassfields are so widespread as to be the rule rather than the exception. Grievances, however, are only expressed in the privacy of one's immediate family or shared between close friends in hushed tones. Those who dare to speak out too freely are now accused of witchcraft and banished from the chiefdom.[51] In the colonial era, they were silenced by the palace's labor recruiters.

Thus although the zombie discourses of the coast could (and can) point transparently to the identity of the witches as planters and the new rich, regularly identifying individual elites as witches, the cannibal discourses of the hinterland have remained hazy and ambiguous with respect to the political reality of the fears they address. As Peter Geschiere points out (1997, 159–60), there is a marked political distinction between the egalitarianism of the coastal societies and the polarization and strong vertical hierarchization of the Grassfields chiefdoms. Although Geschiere emphasizes that this hierarchy placed the fon above suspicion in such a way that he could intervene in witchcraft accusations, it is clearly the case that fons were and are widely suspected of nefarious nocturnal activities against their own people but that they simply cannot be accused in explicit terms. The lability and indetermination of the cannibal discourse in the Grassfields should not simply be seen in instrumental terms as a ploy by cadets to avoid detection of their political commentary on their oppression. Nor should it be seen as a cynical trick played by the elite in order to elide their predatory practices. One notion suggests a level of self-consciousness and analytical objectification that the cadets did not possess, and the other a Machiavellian calculation by the elites that imputes to their actions an unduly reified intentionality. There are no groups of elites in the palaces of the Grassfields busily confabulating on how best to mystify the political relations of domination in the chiefdom.

In fact, one of the problems with this kind of analysis stems from its synchronic point of view, taking as it does a historical position from which to interpret what the cannibal witchcraft discourse meant to those who deployed it at the time of the slave trade. If instead we set the aporia and indetermination of the cannibal discourse in its diachronic context, we can begin to see it not only as a commentary on a whole series of decontextualized times present but, first and foremost, as a mode of remembering that reveals the true tenor of any given lived moment through references to the pasts that give it its true salience. Slavery and forced labor are not only distant events sealed off from the present in their respective discrete historical periods but also resurgent memories that continually intrude into and inform the present. Because they represent memories of extreme internecine violence and intestine struggles within the polity that have yet fully to be acknowledged and resolved, what it is that they remember is yet to be determined. The silences and aporia of the cannibal discourse therefore remember that *something* happened but not *what* happened. The cannibal witchcraft discourse doubles the violence and uncertainty of life in postcolonial Cameroon with a resurgent past that is equally violent and undetermined, irreducible and ever present in its psychic and political sequelae. In this manner, the resurgence of the past in contemporary veiled discourses of political violence is not only a symptom of the violence but, by the same token, the site of the ongoing struggle over what the violence will have been.

Moreover, the silences imposed by the extreme violence and political polarization of the Grassfields have given rise not only to veiled discourses and oral practices of remembering that link the past to a doubled and fractured present, but also to a nondiscursive phenomenon that equally addresses the experiences of both the slave trade and forced labor—an embodied set of practices that avoids the need for verbalization altogether—which brings us back to the role of masking.

CHAPTER FIVE

Embodied Histories: Royal Investiture, Masking, and Remembering

FLUMO: There are some people learn how to dance in the devil; that is the dancing devil that comes out.

[BELLMAN]: So there is no sp . . . there are several different people that can wear the devil's costume?

FLUMO: There are some people—yeah—there are some people who learn how to do the same thing, the devil to eat, how the devil eat person, and like that.

[BELLMAN]: What are they called?

FLUMO: The people who do that? Oh, they are the devil.

— B. Bellman (1984, 93)

The terms *kəkúm* (sing.) and *əmkúm* (pl.) in Oku are polysemic and cover a much wider range of referents and connotations than does the Western category of masks. Certain performers who do not wear head-dresses, such as the *nokan* of the palace *kwifon* society, are nonetheless thought of as *əmkúm*. *Əmkúm* are first and foremost persons or beings in a state of transformation.[1] Protocol requires that whether confronted by an unmasked palace jester or a masked dancer in full costume, one must pretend that one does not recognize the performer. The ordinary identity of the performer is effectively eliminated for the duration of the masked performance, and headdresses and costumes are only two among several means of achieving this end.[2] The term *kəkúm* primarily refers to any person or being thought to possess the power of metamorphosis and the ability to undergo transformations. The emphasis of the term is thus not laid on masks as objects, as it is in the West (Kasfir 1988a; Zeitlyn

1990, 57), but rather on the power of transformation and access to another world of ancestors and deities. As such, masking is a source of power and of danger that the palaces of the Grassfields do their utmost to control and monopolize.

The fact that the masks of the Grassfields have access to another world raises questions about what that world might consist of and what realm of experience it might provide access to. The etymology of the word *kəkúm* is a starting point from which to address this question: the Eblam Ebkwo verb *kùm* means "to lock," "to touch," or to be adjacent to. *Kənkùm* is a lock of any sort, whether a door lock or a padlock. *εykùm* refers to locking, touching, being adjacent to or being next in line. *Kεnkùmten* accordingly refers to a follower: the *kεnkùmten* refers to the adjacent one or to the next person in a queue or line of people (cf. Blood and Davis 1999). These words, all sharing the root *kùm*, show a close family of meanings centered around the notion of locking and of standing in line: actions reminiscent of the way that slaves and later forced laborers were taken from the Grassfields bound to each other in single file and marched down to the coast by guards. It must be noted that the root of the term for "mask," *kəkúm*, has a high tone, whereas the term for "lock," *kənkùm*, and its derivatives have a low tone. In Grassfields languages as in much of Africa, tones are phonemically determining. *Kúm* and *kùm* therefore cannot be said to represent a single root in the strict sense. Nevertheless, Eblam Ebkwo and other Grassfields languages are notable for the word play, punning, and veiled speech in which their speakers engage, suggesting that the fearsome connotations of masks—some of which are used to capture alleged witches—color the field of meanings of the terms associated with locking and vice versa. Just as the bewitched on the coast still dream of being bound and gagged and led off by guards, so too it seems that the etymology of masking in Oku recalls the slave trade of the past.

The startling equation between performers and "devils" that Bellman's informant makes in his discussion of Poro society masks, as quoted in the epigraph to this chapter, would not be lost on Grassfields people, nor would his identification of maskers as cannibals—"how the devil eat person." In Oku I have seen a masked dancer wearing the mask of a lineage elder feign to devour young members of the audience that he had got hold of. The identification between masks and cannibal witches, or "devils," common to both the Poro initiates of Sierra Leone and the maskers of the Grassfields, again points to the close connection between masking and the slave trade: where discursive references to the slave trade tend to refer elliptically to the practice of cannibalism, the nondiscursive practice of masking—the term for which is itself etymologically related to the language of enslavement—again evokes the cannibal appetite of the mask in an embodied form.

Indeed, the performances of masked dance groups (kəkúm kənɔn, əmkúm əmnɔn) bring out the association of masks with slaves (kəkɔs, əmkɔs) and caravan porters in an embodied form. In this chapter, I examine three performances closely associated with some of the major ceremonies of the palace of Oku, focusing on the significance of their present form in light of what we know of the practices that gave the slave trade its particular experiential or lived reality in the Grassfields and beyond. If one speaks of the choreography of a performance, then one also must take account of the choreographies of terror of the slave trade. Otherwise put, the work of dance is very much a physical labor, bringing to mind the suffering of extreme exertion more than the beauty one might expect of performance. This suffering is to some extent a universal aspect of dance: a single performance is painful and exhausting, even when its aesthetic seeks to hide the fact,[3] but the apprenticeship that the single performance recapitulates itself entails years of exertion and discipline. Although Western aesthetics often seek to dissimulate the laborious effort and pain of artistry, in the Grassfields the work of dance is not elided but highlighted in the performance as an integral part of its aesthetic. Not only do the performers perspire, but the masks are themselves sprayed with ablutions that are referred to as the sweat of the mask and are considered beautiful. The dance steps and movements, far from alluding to weightlessness, grace, and flight, emphasize the groundedness, weight, bulk, power, and hence the physical exertion of the dancer. The greatest compliment that one can pay a mask is that "it smashes the stones under its feet" (tshar' eti).

The "death dances" (εykwo εybinene) of Oku thus put the body to work commemorating those who died in the recent past—for these dances are performed at memorial ceremonies to commemorate the dead—in part by use of the sedimentation of long past experiences of disappearance, translocation, and transformation embodied in masked performance and ceremonial processions. In focusing at this stage on the ceremonial of the palace occasioned by a royal installation ceremony, I pay special heed once again to the use that the fon and the secret societies of the palace make of dance and processions as a hegemonic practice that serves to justify or to naturalize the subjugation of commoners, young people, and other marginal groups and to validate the autocratic power of the palace as a necessary evil at the heart of the polity.

Fuləŋgaŋ, the most prominent and prestigious of all the masking groups in Oku, belongs to the palace *kwifon* regulatory society and includes Mabu, whose solo performance I described in chapter 3.[4] The Fuləŋgaŋ group performs on the occasion of the major palace ceremonies held to commemorate the death of high-ranking royal figures, notably the death of the fon himself, the queen mother (*nɔɔ ntɔk*, "mother of the palace"), and the palace guards or retainers (*ntshii ndaa, ntshiisə ndaa*).[5] Such commemorative ceremonies are not usually held on the occasion of a death— an occasion for mourning rather than celebration—but often a year or so later. The emotive distinction between a burial and a memorial celebration is evident in the names applied to each: although both are known by the single term *cry die* in pidgin, in Eblam Ebkwo a burial is known as the "die of tears" or "tearful death" (*ɛykwo əmnshie*) and a memorial as the "die of dancing" or "dancing death" (*ɛykwo ɛybinenene*). This distinction applies not only to palace ritual but to the ceremonies performed for the majority of married men in Oku.[6]

In this respect, the ceremonies occasioned by the death of the fon are exceptional. Although no dancing takes place for an ordinary burial or "die of tears," the ceremony marking the fon's burial is closely followed by the events surrounding the installation of his successor, and this installation does involve the performance of masks. The successor is chosen in secret before the death of the fon—referred to elliptically as his "loss"—is made public. During this interim period, the incumbent fon is kept inside the palace and only emerges at the climax of the installation ceremony. The late fon Sentie, who had been installed in 1956, was "lost" on April 26, 1992, soon after my first visit to Oku in 1991–92, and I was able to witness the installation of his successor, Fon Ngum III, soon after my return to Oku in 1992. My descriptions of Fuləŋgaŋ, of the new fon's first exit from the palace, and of the twin figures are taken from that occasion as well as from the memorial celebration that was held a year later, which I also attended.[7]

The Dance of Fuləŋgaŋ

It is 5:30 in the morning on June 20, 1992. As dawn breaks, the long-expected announcement of the loss of the fon is suddenly shouted out from the palace *kwifon* compound, rending the silent mist of a cold rainy-season morning: "The sun has set! The sun has set! The sun has set!" The proclamation is immediately followed by Dane gun volleys. At first

a dense fusillade, they gradually thin, sporadically peppering the soundscape throughout the day as people make their way to the palace to join
in the events. The ceremonies that would culminate a few days later in
the appearance of the new fon from the palace are under way. As part of
these celebrations, all of the masked dance groups of the chiefdom are
called on to perform at the palace. Before the masking groups come out
to celebrate the enthronement of the new fon, however, the day is devoted
to the performances that mark the mourning of the deceased fon. Known
as *shiɛŋɔ* or "displays" in pidgin rather than "dances" (*ebin*), these involve
the sorties of single masks for solo performances such as those described
in chapter 3. Shigara, a mask from the royal Ngele society, Nkii, a royal
mask (*kɔkúm mɔ ntɔk,* "mask of the palace") belonging to the fon,[8] and
Mabu of *kwifon* each come out in turn during the day to *shiɛŋɔ,* their acolytes following closely behind them.

  The dances performed by the group mask societies began on the following day, June 21. Before any of these societies were permitted to perform, however, Fulɔŋgaŋ—the only group masquerade belonging to the
palace *kwifon* society—first had to appear. Fulɔŋgaŋ is spoken of in Oku
as the archetypal group of the chiefdom. Many say it is the oldest—a metaphor of rank in a gerontocratic society—and the most "bad" (*bɛmɔ*), an

FIGURE 16. The procession of the Fulɔŋgaŋ masks heading from the *kwifon* compound to the
palace courtyard.

ambivalent means of praising the group's medicinal powers and its awe-inspiring appearance while denoting its fearful dimension. Some attribute their fear of the mask group to the medicines that it allegedly possesses, either worn in the dried lianas hung around the necks of the lead mask and final mask or said to be contained inside the masks or rubbed onto them.[9] The most visible sign of the medicines carried by the masks are the green shoots they carry in both hands as they dance and which the musicians keep clenched between their teeth as they play the xylophone and other instruments.

Unlike the musicians of other groups, those of Fuləŋgaŋ must remain speechless throughout their performance, and the plants in their mouths ensure that they respect this rule. The plant is a species of *Dracaena* (*nkɛŋ*), known as "large *ŋkɛŋ*" (*ŋkɛŋ əbwar'en*) in normal circumstances. The name highlights the fact that this variegated species of *Dracaena* is larger than the more commonly found dark green one.[10] The long, pointed leaves of the plant are called "sword of Fuləŋgaŋ" (*fiar' Fuləŋgaŋ*) when used in this performance, and the two leaders (*kam*) of the mask group in fact dance with real swords or cutlasses.[11] Cutlasses and knives are often used in medicine in Oku, where they are considered an essential means of warding off the spells of evil wishers. As we have seen, witchcraft attacks refer back to the raids and abductions of slave dealers. The swords

FIGURE 17. Fuləŋgaŋ masks dancing around the xylophone with Mabu (*second from left*).

FIGURE 18. A Fuləŋgaŋ mask brandishing its "sword."

of Fuləŋgaŋ thus exist in the space between abduction by slave raiders
and protection from abduction, reifying both opposing memories at once.
By referring to the protection offered by the apotropaic use of local cutlasses, these symbolic weapons reify memories of the *razzias* perpetrated
by external raiders and the heroic fights against them, but at the same time
they embody memories of the illicit internal trade in slaves that Grassfields elites sometimes engaged in, engendering a tension between opposing values of the sort evoked by Mabu's indeterminacy as human/animal,
hunter, and slave.

   In spite of the general view among Oku people that a mask represents
a single, identifiable animal, many of those in Fuləŋgaŋ are polymorphic
figures made up of disparate elements from several different (identifiable
and unidentifiable) animals. This is true not only for the appearance of the

FIGURE 19. Mbi, the final mask in the Fuləŋgaŋ dancing line.
Note the cutlass in its right hand and the sword of Fuləŋgaŋ
in its left.

heads themselves, but also for the combination of certain animal heads
with feather bodies, such as the "monkey" (*kətshum*), which has a monkey's head but a body of feathers. In my position as his apprentice, I used
to spend many of my days with the master carver Francis Wanjel, to whose
memory this book is dedicated.[12] As a member of *kwifon,* he would often
play the xylophone when the group appeared. I therefore took the opportunity one day to investigate the polymorphism of *kwifon* masks and,
in particular, of Mbi—the mask occupying the last position and arguably
the most difficult one in the group to identify. To my question about why
it combined elements from different animals, Wanjel replied simply, "Because it's a strong mask, and it has things that are really bad."[13] The poly-

morphism of many of the Fuləŋgaŋ masks was so unsettling to Wanjel—his membership in *kwifon* notwithstanding—that it had become a significant aspect of the aesthetic of the performance for him. Wanjel emphasized to me that the polymorphism of Mbi was a source of preoccupation to him. "It makes me suffer!"[14] he exclaimed of the fact that certain *kwifon* masks were unidentifiable even to him.

Taking the aesthetic of Fuləŋgaŋ as a whole, the features that are exceptional to the group all share one quality—they denote exogenous origins and the mystery of foreign lands and distant worlds. To an extent, every mask group in Oku strives for this quality of transcendence, but Fuləŋgaŋ takes this aesthetic to new heights by confounding the very principles that all other groups use to achieve it. In this way, the sensation of being in the presence of the unknown and the mysterious is clearly cultivated by the polymorphism of the masks of Fuləŋgaŋ and brought out still more strongly by the highly abstract, geometric masks such as that of Mbi, the "leader of the back."[15] The name of this mask, which means "the universe," further connotes the enormity of the mystery that surrounds it, as do the two chameleons mounted on the back of its headdress. Chameleons have strong connotations of witchcraft in the Grassfields; their ability to change color and to blend into the background are seen as akin to the capacity of

FIGURE 20. Mbi (*in the background*) chasing up the penultimate mask in the line.

witches to transform themselves into animals at night. This power, known as *finte,* is shared by the fon, who is said to transform into a leopard or a snake and to roam throughout his realm at night. The transformations of the fon and of the palace masks are thus metonymic of one another, each serving to emphasize the powers of the other to negotiate other worlds.

The gowns of Fuləŋgaŋ—referred to only euphemistically as the "bags" of the masks—also stand out from the Oku canon. In the first place, many of them, including that of Mabu, are made of raptor feathers. Fuləŋgaŋ is unique in combining wooden headdresses with feather gowns and in achieving the resulting polymorphism of bird and beast.[16] The headdresses of Fuləŋgaŋ follow the group's aesthetic of exception by breaking the Oku canon yet again. Wooden headdresses generally conform to a strict aesthetic throughout the Grassfields, which includes being blackened with hot irons to give them a uniformly black glossy finish (known as their "skin") before they are used. Many of those of Fuləŋgaŋ, however, are covered with pelts of the red duiker, or *frutambo* in pidgin. The use of pelts on masks is unusual in the Grassfields, and in Oku it is restricted to those of Fuləŋgaŋ.[17] Furthermore, although the wooden headdresses of Grassfields lineage masking groups tend to be restricted to one set of about twelve different well-known types, each of them easily recognizable as an idealized type such as the young woman, the lineage elder, the bush cow, the elephant, and so forth, the wooden headdresses of Fuləŋgaŋ include many unique forms. Apart from the ambiguous Mbi—a highly stylized representation of an ape, these include a Banerman's Touraco,[18] a cricket, a dog, various monkeys, and several zoomorphic animals, including juxtaposed elements of bush cows, dogs, wild hare, chameleons, raptors, and the like.

Headdresses and feather gowns aside, the textile "bags" of the other masks of Fuləŋgaŋ are also exceptional. In the first place, many of them are red—a color that no other mask is permitted to wear. Red cloth was originally rare and valuable in Oku; it was produced by dyeing white cloth with camwood, an expensive item reserved for the prestige economy and imported from the forest zone to the south for ritual use. Camwood is used to rub the bodies of those undergoing certain rites of passage. Those who are being made into lineage heads (*nkvum*), for example, are rubbed from head to toe in camwood, as are the young virgins who attend them. In the past, these lineage heads were rubbed in camwood again for the subsequent rite of passage attending their death. When they died, the corpses of compound or lineage heads were again rubbed in camwood before burial. Today, the corpses of elites and commoners alike are wrapped

FIGURE 21. A Fuləŋgaŋ mask of an ape surmounted by chameleons and exhibiting the stooped posture typical of the
group.

in a white cloth that is gradually turned red by those paying their last respects, who rub camwood on it as they pass by the bier. The red gowns of
the Fuləŋgaŋ dancers at a palace memorial celebration thus recall sacred,
liminal states, including the liminal states of morbidity, catabolism, and
death, and would have recalled these sacred states more vividly still in the
days when red cloth was produced locally by dyeing white cloth with camwood. Second, the gowns are fringed with cowry shells along the bottom
edge—a prerogative of the fon that was once used as a form of currency
in the prestige economy. In line with the general aesthetic of the Fuləŋgaŋ
masks, the red cloth and the cowry shells worn by some of the masks also
connote connections to the world beyond the confines of the Grassfields.

Like camwood, imported red cloth was scarce and highly prized in the Grassfields in the nineteenth century and constituted a prestige item of exchange, small patches of which were woven into the gowns of the elite to mark their status.[19] Cowry shells likewise were a product of the long-distance trade. They were part of the prestige economy of the northeastern Grassfields in the nineteenth century.[20]

Heads, Bags, and Slaves

The sphere of exchange negotiated on the basis of the cowry as a measure of value included the Grassfields at its southern extremity and reached northward to the Adamawa region, in the economic zone controlled by the Hausa and Fulani emirates. Cowries—all of which were obtained from the Indian Ocean to which they are endemic and brought to West Africa by traders or on board European ships—entered this sphere of exchange in Kano in barter for prestige goods, including, significantly, slaves. From Kano, traders passing through Kontcha, Banyo, Bauchi, and Yola transported the cowries back to the south. The cowries were then brought into the Grassfields through the expanding states of Nso' and Fumban, where they were once again used to buy slaves for the northern trade route (Warnier 1985, 87–90, 143–44; Jeffreys 1955).[21] Not only in the twentieth century but also in the nineteenth, when they were still being used as currency, cowries were also used for display as part of the palace treasury. The fringe of cowry shells that decorates the hem of Fuləŋgaŋ gowns is thus directly connected to the erstwhile role of the palace in the slave trade: these are the very cowries for which "strong-heads," alleged witches, criminals, and "recalcitrant wives" were once sold to the long-distance trade. Now they are displayed on the ghostly red bodies of "mourners" or "corpses" by the palace *kwifon* society for all to see, recalling that enslavement was once conceived of as death and that slaves too were symbolically "mourned" at their sale by being rubbed in camwood.

Uncovering the myth that cowries were obtained not from the Indian Ocean but directly off the shores of the West African Slave Coast, Abiola Félix Iroko (as quoted in Hogendorn and Johnson 1986, 156, 200n33) has shown how graphically cowries can be linked to mythical reconstructions of the slave trade as a form of human consumption: in the version he collected, a human corpse was said to be dropped out at sea as bait. Over time, the cowries would attach themselves to the body in order to feed on it. The body was then pulled back out of the water so that the precious

shells could be collected from it.[22] Inaccurate though such an explanation might be from a positivistic point of view, it encapsulates in salient,
concrete, and appropriately gruesome terms the literal bloodiness of the
trade in slaves and the parasitic vampirism involved in the extractive commodification of human beings. Like myth, embodied practices can also
express the ineffable but nonetheless unforgotten elements of the past. In
his history of the Atlantic slave trade, Herbert Klein (1999, 113) explains
the way that cowries were measured in the region of the African Slave
Coast, pointing out that by the eighteenth century, "ten 'heads' made up
one 'bag' of 20,000 shells (weighing around fifty pounds) which is what
one man could carry on his head. The prime means of moving cowries in
Africa was by 'headloading'—meaning on the heads of human porters."

"Heads" and "bags" were thus measures of cowries used by slave dealers, and the terms used for the costumes of masks in the Grassfields—the
origin of many of the slaves. In Portuguese, one speaks of "heads of cattle" (*cabeças de gado*), as one does in English, and just as cattle could be
counted in heads, so too Portuguese slave traders spoke of "heads of people" (*cabeças de pessoa*) (Marina Temudo, pers. com., Apr. 19, 2006). The
price of a slave in the Grassfields in the mid-nineteenth century is hard to
estimate today but is likely to have been somewhere between 20,000 and
40,000 cowries, roughly equivalent to one or two of the bags mentioned
by Klein. In the early period of the transatlantic slave trade, however, the
value of a slave in cowries was significantly lower, probably around the
value of one head of cowries.[23] One head of cowries would therefore have
been worth one slave, and it seems likely that it would have got its name in
this way. The reference to the mask's headdress as a "head" would therefore have brought to mind the eponymous euphemism for a slave in the
period of the early transatlantic slave trade.

Cowries, furthermore, did in fact circulate in bags in the Grassfields,
with each bag containing an undisclosed number of strings of cowries
(Warnier 1985, 90). Sally Chilver (1961, 251) records that in the royal trade
of the chiefdom of Nso', cowries were issued in bags of approximately
10,000 shells. Moreover, one of the many meanings associated with the
term "bag" (*kəbam*) in Oku today is still a monetary value: FCFA 100,000
is referred to as a "bag of money" (*kəbam əbkaa*). It stands to reason that
this term is a transposition of a measure that was used for cowries before their replacement by the German mark, as Klein (1999) shows it was
throughout the coastal region. The fact that a slave's worth was equivalent
to one bag of cowries in the Grassfields thus makes it likely, in a secretive

business couched in obscurantism and negotiated in terms of euphemisms, that a "bag"—the monetary value of a slave—became yet another euphemism for a slave, just as a "head" had been in previous centuries.

In yet another association between slaves and bags, some of the Grassfields palaces—including that of Oku—symbolized permission to trade in slaves by possession not of a slave rope but of a "palace bag" (Chilver 1961, 242). In Oku, where it was known as the *kɔbam ntok* or "bag of the palace," the sight of palace bags still today elicits a sense of dread, in the same way the "bags" of masks are said to make the uninitiated barren or mad if seen when not being worn by the mask. In addition to the bags of Aga secret society members described in chapter 3 are those carried by palace servants, during royal death celebrations: the servants come out of the *kwifon* compound carrying large raffia bags on their backs in which they collect the food being prepared by the fon's wives. Those who carry the bags, known as the *kɛnsoy ɛykwo* or "basket of death," always proceed in total silence, nor can they be addressed, and the entire courtyard falls silent as they arrive to make their claim.

Like their "heads," the "bags" worn by the Fuləŋgaŋ masks thus bear an etymological as well as a metaphorical or metonymic relationship to the slaves whom they evoke. Like the mythical corpse used as bait to fish live cowries out of the sea, these masks can be seen to represent—among

FIGURE 22. The *kɛnsoy ɛykwo* taking food from the house of one of the fon's wives.

other things—the transformation of the "bag of cowries" into the slave, or rather to signify an indeterminate representation of both bag and slave at once, displayed at the palace for all to see. Encrusted with a fringe of shells along their lower edge as some of them are, the dancers' gowns might even be compared to an inverted bag of shells, full to the brim with its nefarious wealth. At the same time, the unspeakable truth that each bag (or mask) contains a human being—an abominable admission for which one can still be fined today in the Grassfields, just as one could be fined in the past for calling a slave a slave—is sinisterly clear for all to see from the arms and legs protruding from the bag. Who were these palace masks mourning in their dance if not the slaves whose cash value they wore on their gowns and seemed to contain inside their bellies? Who were these anonymous walking cadavers if not the slaves themselves—symbolically dead from the moment they left Oku territory never to be seen again?[24]

Just as the cowry shells bespeak the trade in slaves in which the palace once took part, so too the swords of the masks recall the period of the *razzias*—the Fulani and Chamba incursions. As mentioned earlier, the leaders dance with real cutlasses—one of the defining weapons of the Grassfields warrior. The masks would then embody memories of the heroic fights of the founding fons and their allies against the incursions of enemy slave raiders. The sylvan versions of these swords, held by the other dancers, then serve to propel the symbol of the warrior into the realm of the forest. The reference to the forest as the origin of the witch and the foreign invader alike once again draws a relationship between slavery and witchcraft, and connects the past of the slaves and forest-dwelling spirits and ancestors to the present of the performance. The discourse of protection and of elite heroism is not unambiguously transmitted to the members of the crowd who come to watch them dance in the palace courtyard, however. Rather, members of the audience typically fear physical contact with Fuləŋgaŋ masks, which is said to cause illness, and audience members may not dance in their presence as they do for the masked dances of lineage groups.

In the ambiguous way in which they appear to threaten rather than to protect the crowd with their cutlasses and their occult powers, the Fuləŋgaŋ masks seem to evoke not only the heroic fighters who repelled the Fulani and the Chamba but, at the same time, the invading marauders themselves.[25] Just as the transhuman Fulani of today are said to go "round and round" (*kaalə kaalə*), so too the Fuləŋgaŋ masks circumambulate the courtyard, menacingly flailing their cutlasses. The dance therefore ambivalently encapsulates both aggressors and victims in the slave trade, raiders and refugees, foreign invaders and autochthons, catchers and caught, buyers and bought. Nor should such juxtapositions be thought of as mere obscurantism or mystification; rather, they accurately bear witness to the historical fact that exogenous raiders settled and even intermarried over time with the autochthonous populations of the Grassfields that they had previously harried and terrorized. The same juxtapositions are true for the untold story of the Judas, preserving in acts of remembering the fact that slave dealers could not be castigated as evil invaders and set in Manichean opposition to heroic local elites when the latter worked hand in glove with the former—and often had to do so for the survival of the chiefdom as a whole.[26] The ambivalent Fuləŋgaŋ performance thus recalls at once both moral vectors of the slave trade in the Grassfields, and in doing so it reveals their mutual entanglement in the palatine elite.

In addition to the cowries, bags, and the swords of Fuləŋgaŋ, a further connection to slavery as embodied in the dance is attested to in the parallel loss of the social identity of the masked dancer and of the slave at the point of sale. Just as masks are explicitly viewed as nonhuman creatures that belong to another world and are only trespassing in the visible world of the living temporarily, so too a slave is "structurally speaking, simply not a person" (Kopytoff and Miers 1977, 15). Rather, he or she is a "captive outsider" (15)—precisely the way that masks are said to be in the Grassfields—and, as with masks, "the relation to him is a non-relation" (Simmel [1923] 1950, 407, as quoted in Kopytoff and Miers 1977, 15). Indeed, anonymity is so obvious a feature of masking that it either is treated in functionalist terms or is ignored altogether in the literature on masking. When the loss of identity conferred by the mask is addressed, the literature tends to focus on the advantages it offers in carrying out unsavory police activities on behalf of the palace without implicating individuals in such acts of violence. In the eyes of ordinary Grassfields people, however, masking may not only be a means of highlighting the impersonal nature of the power of the palace but, at the same time, a reminder of the desocialized and alienated position of the slave—"disappeared" and forced to leave the community forever, becoming a nonperson or a ghost (ŋkvosay) within his or her lineage. The palpable sense of dread or eeriness so effectively cultivated by palace masks thus indexes at once the coercive power of the palace and the guilty secret of the source of its wealth.

Within the terms of the discourse of the palace, this secret is effectively whitewashed by the reversal of logic referred to earlier, whereby the internal violence of the palace is projected outward, making the rest of the world appear to be the source of all difference and danger. Just as the palace discourse portraying slaves and members of the floating population as dangerous outsiders reversed the real direction of coercion, so too in this instance the *kwifon* masks and musicians allegedly need the "swords" they carry for self-protection: witches are everywhere, forever trying to ruin their performance and to harm the people of Oku. Not only does the Fuləŋgaŋ performance appropriate the alleged threat posed by a foreign invader to justify the powers of *kwifon,* but it also transforms memories of its predatory past into a necessary evil at the heart of the community: the *pharmakon*—poison and remedy in one—needed to keep invisible enemies at bay. To this end, before the dance begins, as the xylophone is being set on the fresh banana tree stems, Ngu, the lead mask of the group (*kam wɛ mbii*), stamps on a small green fruit (called *kəlun* in Eblam Eb-kwo, *solanum* sp.), whose fragments are then interpreted (*taŋ*) before the performance so that information may be gleaned as to whether the performance will be marred by witchcraft attacks and whether another death is imminent at the palace.

The projection of danger outward is further evinced by the frequent warnings of witchcraft attacks that the *kwifon* society makes during palace ceremonies. An announcement made by the society at midday on June 21, just before the opening performance of Fuləŋgaŋ at 1:30 in the afternoon, is a case in point. In the early afternoon, as the crowds at the palace had started to swell, some *kwifon* society members stepped from their compound into the main palace courtyard. At the members' arrival, the seething crowd, which stretched as far as the eye could see, stopped everything and fell perfectly silent. The *kwifon* members proceeded to make their formal announcement, which ran as follows:

There is someone on the other side of the lake trying to bring poisoned gun-powder to the palace to harm the people; heads of *manjɔŋ* (the military society) are to keep a close watch on the number of Dane guns in their group so that no treated gun can be fired surreptitiously.

Food from a women's group in the village of Jikijem is not to be allowed into the palace because it has been poisoned.

Dancing mask groups (*kəkúm kənɔn*) should not dance with spears, cutlasses, or guns but only plant stems because a plan is abreast to murder someone and take advantage of the tumult to make it look like an accident.

The people of Oku should be very friendly to the strangers present.

FIGURE 23. The *kwifon* announcement.

The people of Oku have never known how many friends [political allies] *kwifon* has. In the course of this celebration, they will find out [as allied chiefdoms send delegations to the palace].

The gist of such announcements is that if *kwifon* is dangerous, it is only in the way that powerful medicines are understood to be dangerous in the Grassfields. Like the ancient Greek *pharmakon,* the power of Grassfields medicines is ambivalent, at once harmful and curative. Any harm that they cause to the body, however, is seen to be necessary for defense against greater external pathogens or witchcraft attacks. What goes for the body also goes for the body politic: the *kwifon* societies of the Grassfields may occasionally have preyed on their people, but this is what it takes to build a strong state.

The Three Captains

The place of Mabu in this conception of protection, necessary evil, and the greater good of the polity now becomes clear. As described in chapter 3, Mabu is one of several masks belonging to the *kwifon* society that performs on its own, in a performance known as a *shiɛŋɔ,* or "display" in

pidgin. In the course of this *shiɛŋɔ*, Mabu appears as a wild predator and a
hunter but also, at the same time, as the hunted. Lineage masks not associated with the palace (discussed in subsequent chapters) possess a mask
known as the *kəshiɛŋɛnɛ*, whose role is largely consistent from group to
group and essentially twofold. The *kəshiɛŋɛnɛ* of ordinary lineage masking
groups is the only mask to appear on the occasion of a burial ceremony
(as opposed to the later death celebration). On the burial day of one of
the members of the mask society, the *kəshiɛŋɛnɛ* appears alone by the
graveside to mourn the loss of its member.[27] On the occasion of a memorial celebration, on the other hand, the *kəshiɛŋɛnɛ* of a lineage group is the
first of the group to appear. Again it comes out alone, but this affair is not
the subdued one of the burial. Its role on this occasion is to rally its unmasked members behind it, egging them on in a display of the might and
fearsomeness of the group. As the members all chant behind it, it surges
forth boldly into the crowd, making a show of leaping toward onlookers,
or back toward its members, who crouch down before it as they chant on
in urgent tones. This performance, which in the case of lineage masking
groups heralds the imminent arrival of the rest of the masks, is known as
the *shiɛŋɔ* and gives its name to the *kəshiɛŋɛnɛ* mask. Although the performances of Mabu in the palace courtyard take place independent of the
appearance of the Fulɔŋgaŋ group and do not herald its imminent arrival,
they are nonetheless known as its *shiɛŋɔ* and closely resemble the sorties of lineage *kəshiɛŋɛnɛ* masks. Like them, Mabu is armed with weapons,
which it brandishes at those who get too close to it. Like them, Mabu has
a coterie of acolytes (made up of *kwifon* members) who follow close behind it and egg it on with esoteric calls. Indeed, Mabu is so feared and so
exemplary in its performance of the *shiɛŋɔ*, with its bravado, its panache,
and its barely contained violence, that the performances of all the other
kəshiɛŋɛnɛ masks in the chiefdom could be said to be imitations or deriva-
tions of its archetypal performance.

When a lineage masking group follows its *kəshiɛŋɛnɛ* out of the secret
society house to dance around the xylophone and the assembled musicians, the *kəshiɛŋɛnɛ* takes on the task of keeping all the other masks in
line as they stamp rhythmically around the center of the courtyard. Lineage society masks are known to be unruly, and the *kəshiɛŋɛnɛ* stands beside the line, running up and down along the row of masks with an exag-
gerated stamp, keeping the others in step. For this reason, as I discuss in
subsequent chapters, we could call the *kəshiɛŋɛnɛ* the "driver" of the mask
group.[28] Mabu does not play this role for the Fulɔŋgaŋ group, however;

the masks of this group are said to be so well disciplined as to not need such supervision, which would be demeaning for a palace masquerade. Mabu therefore joins the dancing line like the rest of the masks during the performance of Fuləŋgaŋ. Nevertheless, Fuləŋgaŋ follows the pattern of the ordinary lineage dancing formation in that it has both a leader (*kam*) and another mask that follows up the rear ("leader of the back," *kam yɛ ebam*). As with the role played by the leaders of lineage groups, that of the Fuləŋgaŋ leaders is disciplinary in nature in that they set the pace for the other masks to follow, guide their progress around the central xylophone, keep stragglers from falling behind, sound out the rhythm with their ankle rattles, and so on. The *kam* at the front and the *kam yɛ ebam* at the back are common to all mask groups in Oku, but Fuləŋgaŋ is unique in that Mabu periodically takes on the dance steps of a *kam* despite being in the middle of the dancing line; these dance steps are known as *sar'* and are restricted to the lead masks of Fuləŋgaŋ.

Fuləŋgaŋ does not dance with the verve of ordinary mask groups in Oku but more slowly, with smaller steps, and only for a short period of time. And whereas other groups have a set of at least three steps that they perform to the changing rhythms of the drums and xylophone, Fuləŋgaŋ, apart from its *kamsə,* has only one. Onlookers admire its laborious shuffle as a sign of its relative seniority and venerable age, and excuse the brevity of its appearance on this basis also: old men tire sooner. But viewed from another perspective, and especially in comparison with the exuberant lineage masks, the masks of Fuləŋgaŋ seem meek and browbeaten. They dance with their heads bowed, standing close to one another. Their body language is restricted, as if they were moving under a great weight or had been sapped of their strength. The only ones to retain their freedom of movement and their vigor in this performance are Mabu, Ngu, and Mbi—the three *kamsə,* also known in pidgin as the "captains" of the group, and the latter two of which stand out for being armed with real cutlasses rather than symbolic blades of grass. The fundamental ambiguity of Mabu's identity as displayed in its ambiguous *shiɛŋə* solo performance, vacillating as it does between man and ape, hunter and hunted, slave catcher and slave, is once again embodied in the Fuləŋgaŋ performance. Although according to the Oku norm Mabu would take on the role of the driver, policing the other masks by marching alongside them with its weapons, it instead joins the line as a simple mask devoid of its weapons. In this performance, however, the second of its two contradictory roles is once again in evidence. While in the *shiɛŋə* Mabu's role as a hunter/slave catcher is belied by its appearance as an ape/slave, in its role as a dancer in the line of Fuləŋgaŋ its position as a slave is doubled and contradicted by its role as a third leader or captain/slave driver.

Contemporary informants in the Grassfields today no longer remember the German colonial period, let alone the precolonial period, in explicit terms. In the course of my interviews regarding masking, no one ever mentioned the historical (as opposed to the mythical) past, or connected masking with broader political phenomena. Rather, they nearly always meticulously stayed within the bounds of the discourse of masking: that masks (the term for which, kəkúm, makes no reference to the wooden headdress) are not people but forest beasts, that they are not controlled by people but come and go of their own volition, that their costumes are not man-made but are simply the skins of their very bodies, and so on. Nonetheless, one cannot help but wonder how those who saw Fuləŋgaŋ perform (or participated in it) in the nineteenth or early twentieth centuries might have reacted to it—in relation to what events it might have gained its salience and its emotive impact for them. Like words in a language or language itself in relation to the world, dances are not solipsistic, self-referential entities but forms of expression that become meaningful in relation to their wider context. Dance exists in the world, it is of the world, and the world of dance relates to and interacts with the everyday world in the way that the ritual sphere interacts with the sphere of mundane experience.

Looking at the relation of the three captains to the rest of the Fuləŋgaŋ masks, it is hard not to think back to Marie Pauline Thorbecke's description of the colonial caravan: "During the whole length of the portage, certain elements try to drop behind, or to escape into the bush. Thanks to treating them regularly to the 'twenty-five' [strokes], the majority of them nevertheless manage to remain in line" (1914, 9–15, as quoted in Van Slageren 1972, 88–89 [trans. mine]). Is it conceivable that people who had never experienced the forced marches of slave coffles, and then the forced labor and chastisement of caravan portage, could have developed the cultural tradition of the violent shiɛŋə performance or of the kam or "captain"? To put it another way, how could the nightmarish role of the masked "captains" wielding their cutlasses have become such a central feature of the performative culture of the Grassfields were it not for the experience of the slave raids, the slave marches, the recruitment of forced labor, and portage in the colonial caravan, all of which depended for their success on slave drivers, plantation overseers, caravan guards, and military officers? Once one makes the connection, everything falls into place:

- the slow shuffle of the masks and the hunger and exhaustion of captured slaves and colonial carriers;
- the stooped figure of the dancer gingerly balancing his unwieldy headdress, and the porter staggering under his headload;
- the necessity for policing figures, known by the English term "captains," in a masquerade performance and the fact that caravans all had armed drivers— many of them military officers;
- the uncomfortable closeness of the dancers one to another in their marching line and the strange restriction of their movements, in comparison with the fact that porters were often kept in wooden fetters after their recruitment and bound to one another during their portage or when being delivered by the recruiters;[29] and
- the etymology linking masks to locks and to coffles or defiles, and referring to their headdresses as "heads" and their gowns as "bags"—erstwhile units of currency for slaves.

If dance normally expresses the transcendence of one's ordinary physical limitations, the Fuləŋgaŋ performance imposes the habitus of slavery and colonial domination like a set of irons.[30] The root of the word for mask, *kúm,* recalling the word *kùm,* "to lock," here marks the double inscription of "followers," *kɛnkùmten,* as at once partners in a dance and "locked ones" in a caravan or slave coffle.[31]

Mbɔkə Nokan: The Slave Twins

The palace jesters' procession around the palace courtyard, the *enar' nokan* described in chapter 3, is the first *kwifon* procession to take place after theFuləŋgaŋ performance during a royal installation. On June 21, 1992, the Fuləŋgaŋ performance took place at 1:30 p.m., and the jesters' procession began at 4:40 p.m. the same day. Within the context of the associations evoked by the Fuləŋgaŋ performance between the *kwifon* society and the slave trade, it becomes easier to interpret the sense of inchoate fear, dread, and suppressed revulsion inspired by the procession of the jesters, despite their supposedly humorous disposition. Coming as it does immediately after the Fuləŋgaŋ performance, the jesters' procession may seem like a mimicry or a satire of the solemn Fuləŋgaŋ dance. Just as the jesters parody the masks they come across as they perambulate about the palace grounds on their own or in small groups, so too their procession can seem like a parody of group masking. But the apparent madness of the jesters and their baffling speech, while undeniably ludic, unmistakably associate them with the forest and the realm of the dead.

Ultimately, the *nokan* are not only jesters (a relatively unambiguous term for which there is no translation in the Grassfields); they are also, at the same time, the dead. Covered in the white kaolin that denotes death, the *nokan* wear costumes whose material culture is rustic and sylvan, made up for the most part of wild vegetation and only the most ragged and torn items of clothing. In Mbiame, one of the chiefdoms of the Grassfields with close ties to Oku, the palace jesters are so completely covered in creepers, leaves, and feathers that they are virtually unrecognizable and—like modern-day snipers—would effectively become invisible in a forest landscape. The staffs they carry with them—gigantic woody stems of twisted liana— further serve to link them to the forest. If those watching the jesters' procession in the palace courtyard spoke to me of feelings of dread and horror more than of humor, it was hardly surprising. During their procession, the sinister tricksters looked for all the world like a long line of corpses emerging from the forest. Chattering to each other in the language of the dead as they traipsed brazenly back from their proper realm into the very heart of the polity, they seemed to enact the march of death anomalously transposed from the traumatic space of the colonial past into the realm of the living.[32] Moreover, these are not just any dead. As noted in chapter 2, the forest in Oku is associated with a history of plunder and warfare that has made of it a place of danger, predation, and disappearance and that has marked it forever as the place into which whole slave caravans were swallowed as they set off on their journey to the coast. Symbolic funeral rites were held for these slaves when they were about to disappear into the forest. The dead of the forest are the unquiet dead (*ŋkvosay*) who inhabit the space left by the disappeared of the slave trade. When they come out of the forest, it is to haunt the offspring they have left behind, to make them ill, and to bestow misfortune upon them. The legacy of the Judas hangs heavy on the landscape: the dead of the forest were sold by the ancestors of those whom they visit today, and if they return against all odds from their exile to the homeland from which they were banished, it is not in a spirit of unalloyed bonhomie.

A few days later in the course of the celebrations at the palace, on the evening of June 24, the close connection between the jesters and resurgent memories of slavery would be demonstrated more clearly than ever. This connection was made in the form of a rite that is only performed by the jesters for a royal enthronement. It had therefore not been witnessed before by any except the oldest members of the population, during the enthronement of the last fon in 1956, in the British colonial era. A particular type of jester, known as the *mbɔkə nokan,* was to make its appearance in the palace courtyard. These exceptional jesters, or *nokan,* were eagerly anticipated by people who had little idea what to expect or exactly what would happen when they did appear. Finally, in the pouring rain, the young people crowded in the main courtyard started to shout that the *mbɔkə nokan* were approaching. Suddenly, to everyone's consternation and in the midst of cries of disbelief, two men (who, like all other jesters, were not referred to as men but as a type of "mask," *kəkúm*), rubbed from head to foot in (white) kaolin and naked but for a leaf covering their genitals, were led down to the front of the palace. Their wrists were bound with a length of vine with which one ordinary jester pulled them along. This driver made a show of pulling and prodding them by turns, down to the center of the main courtyard, where they were silently ordered to sit as hundreds of people crowded around them despite the driving rain and the interdiction on using umbrellas in the palace grounds. The guardian jester kept the curious from getting too close by waving his long, ungainly stick about, and he elicited gales of laughter by using it to beat down all the umbrellas in the crowd that he could get at. The two *mbɔkə nokan,* meanwhile, sat in silence, their heads down, looking frightened, vanquished, and dejected. After some time, all of the jesters came down in single file to perform their group procession again. At this point the two *mbɔkə nokan* were set free by their tormentor, and they set off running back into the *kwifon* compound.

Those chosen to be the *mbɔkə nokan* in 1992 were new members of the *kwifon* society, recruited—literally "taken," *liɛ*—soon after the new fon was appointed, although the great bulk of the new recruits would not be recruited until over a year later in a ceremony known as "the abundance of the fon" (*əblom əbfɔn*). One of the new recruits who had been appointed as a *mbɔkə nokan* told me that he had been given no choice. His colleague and he were put in a room alone with one *kwifon* member (or *ntshii ndaa*), who undressed them and rubbed their whole bodies with the kaolin (just as the fon is infantilized during his seclusion in the palace, so too these new recruits were treated like children). The color white in Oku is associated with sickness and disease, dying and death, and hence with the spirit world. Those who are unwashed and covered in dust (such as children, who play in the dust, or the insane, who seldom wash) and those

FIGURE 24. The *mbɔkɔ nokan* seated in the palace courtyard, with their guardian *nokan* (standing with stick) teasing them.

who are ill or dying are referred to as "white" or "whiting": *ɛb fəfə-fəfə*.[33] Once they have been rubbed with kaolin, the two *mbɔkɔ nokan* therefore evoke images of children, epileptics or madmen, or walking corpses. After being rubbed, the left hand of each *mbɔkɔ nokan* was tied with a creeper picked inside the traditional forest of the *kwifon* compound. These creepers were later used as the leads with which they were dragged into the center of the compound.

After returning to the *kwifon* compound once they had been "freed," the two *mbɔkɔ nokan* were made to wash and put their clothes on before being offered a luxurious meal. The food they were offered was not prepared in the *kwifon* compound, however, but in the fon's side of the palace, and the person who prepared it for them was the fon's private cook. The complexity of the symbolism associated with the *mbɔkɔ nokan* rite precludes the assertion of any one interpretation. On the one hand, the two *mbɔkɔ nokan* can be seen as embodiments of the recently "lost" fon. Fay Ndintonen, an elder based in a compound near the palace, has seen the *mbɔkɔ nokan* appear three times. Not only, he asserted, do the *mbɔkɔ nokan* stand for the lost fon, but the new fon is *himself* transformed into the lost one when he first enters the palace. At that time, he stays for two days without being washed or rubbed with oil or camwood. This results, the *fay* explained, in his skin going "white" just like that of the lost fon, and just like that of the *mbɔkə nokan*. "*Mbɔkə nokan* is for the old one," he stated, referring to the lost fon. "They are made to show that he has been sitting just like that, and he has died." Not only the *mbɔkə nokan*, then, but the new fon too are all in a sense reincarnations of the deceased fon. The close association of the *mbɔkə nokan* with the fon is also alluded to by the cords bound to their wrists. Chem-Langhëë, Fanso, and Chilver (1985, 175), who describe the burial of the fon of Nso', which neighbors Oku, specify that when the corpse of the fon is seated inside the burial pit, held in place by camwood posts and hide thongs, a creeper is attached to the wrist of the deceased fon and brought to the surface as the grave is about to be filled. For those who know of this ritual detail, the ashen twin figures look all the more like dead fons escaping the grave.

If the *mbɔkə nokan* stand for the lost fon, however, they also clearly allude to twins. Indeed, twins were sometimes buried with fons, with whom they were equated, in the Grassfields.[34] The means by which twins manage to appear in two places, two bodies, when they have only one life force (*kəyui*), was put down to the fact that—like fons—they were said to be *finte*. They could transform themselves at will into a variety of animals and had the power to be in two places at once. The fact that the *mbɔkə nokan* are twin figures therefore suggests that it was the power of twins to bridge worlds that was being tapped by their sacrifice. In the chaotic upheaval caused by the slave trade in the Grassfields, twinship would have provided a powerful representation of *dédoublement;* the division of the world into two distinct spheres and the creation of a second reality occasioned by extreme violence.[35] Moreover, their use in ritual would have provided the means to overcome the splitting effects of the slave trade, rendering the world whole again by providing a bridge between incommensurate social realities.

The close ritual connection between twins and slaves is revealed by the use of slaves, instead of twins, as sacrifices in some chiefdoms. In Bafut, for example, not only several of the fon's wives, but also some of his slaves, were buried together with the dead monarch (Ritzenthaler 1966, 164). Like twins, slaves occupied a liminal position between societies and between worlds. The fact that the *mbɔkə nokan* are fed by the fon's personal cook ironically underlines their slave status, and with it the status of the fon as the archetypal slave owner and slave trader in the Grassfields. As the nineteenth-century testament of the freed slave Josiah Yamsey (quoted in chap. 3) makes clear, slave traders customarily offered the slaves they had just bought a luxurious meal in order to win their confidence: "My Master did not pretend to sell me but kept me & pretended to be fond of me, did use me better than others had done, gave me plenty to eat." These traders were fond of reassuring their new slaves that they had no intention of reselling them but that they intended that the slaves "should be like one of [their] children."[36]

During the period of the slave trade and into the colonial period, with which it overlapped, twins were often killed in the Grassfields because they were thought to be witches, just as slaves were also feared for their powers of witchcraft.[37] The white body paint covering the *nokan,* like the binding of their hands and their subjection by a driver or guard, recalls the liminal status of slaves as quasi-dead beings. The symbolism of the *mbɔkə nokan* as at once slaves and twins is not therefore contradictory but consistent: slaves and twins alike were all part of a wider Grassfields composite category of liminal beings with access to the worlds of the living and the dead alike. It is for this access to the other world—beyond the forest and the sea, or alternatively within the forest and beneath the sea—and their ultimate unification of a universe split by the violence of slavery and colonial oppression—that slaves and twins were equally highly prized in the major rites of the Grassfields chiefdoms.

The *Kəkumndjaŋ* Procession: Caravans, Cargo, and the Wives of the Palace

On June 26, 1992, two days after the *mbɔkə nokan* were paraded in the palace courtyard, the new fon of Oku first emerged from the palace in the climactic event of the protracted ceremonies. Again, the audience at the palace speculated for days about when the procession might take place, with rumors and counter-rumors running wild as to the appointed day. That morning, however, the *kəkumndjaŋ* xylophone of *ngwiko*—a mask society from the village of Ichim that plays outside its own village only for royal death celebrations at the palace—was being played in the palace courtyard. From that moment it was certain that, barring rain, the ceremony would occur that day. After the xylophone had been played for hours, during a brief lull in the rain, the procession suddenly burst forth from the main door of the palace. At the head of the procession came the fon of Sawe, a chiefdom to the north of Oku. The fon of Sawe had been sitting in public on the throne in the palace at Elak for days and is the fon ex officio during the interregnum in Oku, the period during which the fon is "lost."

Sawe has historically been the place to which those exiled from the kingdom of Oku have fled, and even Sawe's original king is said to have arrived as the result of a miraculous accident. He had been sentenced to death in his native Oku and was being executed in the customary way: he was carried by *kwifon* (no doubt with Mabu in the lead) to the middle of a rushing torrent, where he was left, hands and legs bound, to stand precariously balanced on a stone just inches from where the torrent dives over a high cliff. Once he fell, however, he inexplicably escaped death and founded his own chiefdom on the spot where the river deposited him. This myth fits with another one that equates Sawe with the land of the dead, for surely the fon did die, and it is his spirit (*keyus*) or his ghost (*ŋkvosay*) that went on to found the kingdom. In any case, many people in Oku today still refer to Sawe as the place to which they will go once they are dead. Speaking of Sawe has thus become a euphemism for speaking of death, and those now living in Sawe are seen as the souls or spirits of those who once lived in Oku. Because Sawe can be seen as an otherworld inversion of Oku, its fon is the fon of Oku when the latter is "lost." He is the soul of the "lost" fon, for it follows from the logic of the myth that the fon, once lost, should find himself reborn as the fon of Sawe.

In the procession, directly behind the fon of Sawe came Fay Nsaanen, the second in command in the palace, and directly behind him came the new fon of Oku, followed by a long line of masks. In principle this procession was to include all the masks of the chiefdom, but in practice it represented only a fraction of them. Finally, behind the long line of masks came the fon's wives.[38] On his head, the new fon wore an arresting cap of flowing white feathers known as the *fənən mbɔŋ*. This crown is associated with the second fon of Oku, Mkong Mote, who is reputed to have obtained it at the bottom of the sacred lake Mawɛs; it is only worn by fons on the occasion of their enthronement and for the ceremonial circumambulation of the sacred lake that they perform a year afterward (cf. Bah 2005). As mentioned in chapter 2, Mkong Mote is said to have entered the sacred lake along with the fon of Kijem (in some versions the fon of the neighboring Kom or Babungo people) to have the god Mawɛs decide who the rightful ruler of the lake and the lands around it should be. In the end, the goddess kills the rival chief, or in other versions of the myth the chief is condemned to roam indefinitely at the bottom of the lake, and Mkong Mote arises from the lake triumphantly wearing the *fənən mbɔŋ* cap on his head as a sign of his blessing by the goddess. In another myth about the lake, a whole town is said to exist at the bottom of Mawɛs, with its people— the ancestors of the living people of Oku—coming to life in the night, at which point the water drains away and the town is revealed. The lake thus plays a mythic role as a parallel world of the dead, similar to that played by the kingdom of Sawe. The difference between this world and that of Sawe is that Mawɛs is an aquatic realm: the white headdress thus marks the new fon's arrival into the chiefdom from the realm with which white people are themselves associated in the Grassfields. As mentioned earlier, the sea and the navigable rivers of Cameroon (along with lakes all equally known as "big water" in pidgin, a direct translation of local terms such as *djuo eyar'en* in Eblam Ebkwo or *mámùu* in Babungo) are categorized as the dwelling place of European mermen and mermaids—their pink flesh associated with that of fish, and their hunger for men with the lack of red meat to be found in the sea. The white headdress thus marks the fon as an outsider to Oku, a changeling gifted with metamorphic powers (*finte*) as much at home in the world of the "pink/red man" (*kəmbaŋ*) or the European as in the chiefdom itself.

FIGURE 25. The new fon of Oku, Fon Ngum III, emerging from the palace in the *kəkumndjaŋ* procession (*third in line,* in the white feather headdress), preceded by the fon of Sawe (*first from left*) and Fay Nsaanen (*center*).

FIGURES 26–28. The fon's wives carrying the "things of the palace" in the procession around the courtyard.

Coming behind the masks and as it were extending their line, the wives of the palace had a special role to play in this procession. Not only did they represent the wealth of the palace in their persons, but they were the bearers of the "things of the palace" (*əbfwa ntɔk*)—the objects of the palace treasury. Grassfields palaces all possess a collection of objects known in the language of each chiefdom simply as the "things of the palace" (cf. Geary 1983). In most of the palaces, these objects are normally hidden from view—like the palace masks—and only displayed on rare occasions. In some chiefdoms, these occasions include the annual dance. In Oku, which no longer has an annual dance, they are only ever displayed for the installation of a new fon. The objects in these secret palace treasuries are notable in that they are overwhelmingly of exogenous origin or are locally manufactured with precious goods obtained through trade outside the chiefdom. The items memorialize a precolonial period in which diplomatic relations between chiefdoms were wordlessly negotiated between fons by means of gift exchanges (Rowlands 1987, 60–61; Warnier 1985, 70). Typically, subjugated chiefs were obliged to make annual gifts to those claiming supremacy over them. In other circumstances, powerful chiefs might invite a rival chief to become a subject by the giving of a very large gift meant to display his power and his mercantile connections. In wars, the palace treasury was often plundered and subsumed within the treasury of the victorious chiefdom. These treasuries were thus not simply deposits of wealth but also indices of the diplomatic and trading ties that a fon and his elites enjoyed.

The objects carried in the Oku *kəkumndjaŋ* procession were almost exclusively of foreign origin. Many of them were from the chiefdoms of the Bamileke area of the southern Grassfields, others from the powerful sultanate of Fumban—the chiefdom that held the secret of wax brass casting and served as a regional center of production for prestige items. Many other objects, however, were of European origin, gifts from German colonial officers that had been subsumed within the existing system of gift exchange and diplomatic relations. The objects from the Grassfields consisted of exotic variations on locally produced prestige goods. Objects such as elaborately carved stools, drinking cups, and house or veranda posts depicting the motif of the earth spider (*ŋgam*)—the symbol of the royal Mbele lineage—were all carved locally in Oku and are renowned throughout the Grassfields for their quality (Argenti 2002a). Several of the objects in the palace collection were carved stools, but these bore exotic motifs not usually seen in Oku, such as bats' heads, and they were studded with brass nails—an article of trade of European origin often used as decoration for gun stocks and other objects in the nineteenth century—and heavily rubbed with camwood. A series of beaded calabashes and horse-tail whisks were also revealed, attesting to contact with the Bamileke and Banyang chiefdoms to the south. While the cowries obtained from the trade in slaves and kola with the north were once the most common currency in Oku, beads were the preferred currency in the southern chiefdoms of the Grassfields. Once exported out of their economic zone, they were appropriated by the palaces and used to cover objects in the treasuries such as calabashes, statues, stools, thrones, and flywhisk handles; by being decommodified and put on display, they reified the links of the western Grassfields palaces with the southern chiefdoms. But just as the cowry shells on the gowns of the *kwifon* masks recall the slave trade with the north, so these beads attest to the trade in slaves with the southern port of Douala in that slaves passed through the Bamileke and Banyang chiefdoms and represented the main commodity exchanged for the beads. In this light, the horsetail whisks are highly ambiguous: they connote the protection from slavery evinced by the fact that such whisks are said to have first been obtained from the horses of slain Fulani slave raiders, but their bead-encrusted handles attest to trade with the Bamileke chiefdoms, with slaves the main medium of exchange.

Many of the other objects in the collection portrayed human faces: for example, the Bamoum brass drinking horns from Fumban and the European ceramic toby jugs of German or possibly English provenance. Representations of the human face are the preserve of the palaces in the Grassfields. Only the palaces or the *manjɔŋ* and *mfu'* military society meetinghouses are permitted to have representations of human beings on their lintels and posts. Only the fon can sit on a stool with human caryatids or use bowls of wood or clay with human faces incised on them. This prerogative has been transposed to the European artifacts in the Oku treasury, as it has in many of the treasuries of the Grassfields. Objects of European (or perceived European) provenance have been included in palace collections in the Grassfields at least since first contact with Europeans and very probably before. Bernhard Ankermann (1959, 297–98) described Fon Tam of Bum's mausoleum thus in the early 1900s: "On the grave, a large porcelain vase, a pith helmet, a tea pot, and a broken earthenware dish. At the head of the grave . . . was a bench, and on and below it were a carved wooden bowl, a carved wooden stool of spider design, and an old phonograph." Chilver (pers. com., 1995) writes likewise of the Bali and Big Babanki palaces: "I examined some of the Bali treasure and found Toby jugs (English, Staffordshire), red Bohemian glass carafes with

gilt stoppers, and some perfectly awful German (allegedly) Art Deco jar-
dinières. The fon of Big Babanki (Kedjom Kegu) showed me some very
pretty blue-banded lusterware (English?) jugs 'worth plenty slave.' At Bamali palm wine was being poured out of a very large brown-glazed teapot,
lid missing."[39]

Any items of European manufacture were thus reserved for the prestige economy dominated by the palaces of the Grassfields and in which
slaves were of course the main currency. It is perhaps not surprising, in
this vein, that representations of human beings were—and remain to this
day—the preserve of the fon, the palatine elite, and the military. The Germans, who entered the kingdom of Nso' in 1902, were taken aback to see
the military society houses decorated with the skulls of enemy soldiers
killed in battle (Fanso and Chilver 1996). The carvings of heads that now
adorn military society lodges were placed there when the Germans "pacified" the region, monopolizing warfare and headhunting as their private
preserve. Even though German officers such as Hutter rewarded their
own men for taking heads in battle, they forbade the taking and display
of heads by any soldiers but their own. In other words, the Germans did
nothing to diminish the emblematic value of heads as representations of
military power in the Grassfields, ensuring that they continued to be depicted not only on the architecture of palaces and military society lodges
but also on the drinking cups of kings. It is notable that they are not referred to as faces or portraits in Eblam Ebkwo but—like slaves had once
been throughout the slave coast—as "heads" (kǝtu, ǝbtu).

Drinking horns mark linage leadership in the Grassfields and are passed
from one lineage elder to the next upon the death of each one (Dillon
1990). These cups were made of the horns of the bush cow—one of the
animals into which fons are said to transform at night and whose bellow (mbɛɛ) the fon's kwifon bodyguard uses to address him. The brass
drinking horns of the Oku palace collection were precious items at the
time that the sultanate of Fumban was the only center for the lost art
of wax brass casting in the region (Geary 1983; Gebauer 1979). In this
sense, these cups would have stood out in Oku as much more rare and
prestigious even than the bush cow horns of which they are a copy. As in
the more explicit representations of slaves being physically clasped by the
king in the royal Benin brasses of the seventeenth and eighteenth centuries, the human faces depicted on the brass horns are restricted to use
by the fon and objectify his power over people—not only the power to
kill people, which he possessed in his position as a member of the kwifon
regulatory society, but the more mundane rights over people as wealth,

which Grassfields fons wielded as slave traders and later as providers of forced labor in the colonial era. All of these roles played by the fon were controversial; indeed for a fon to sell any of his own subjects into slavery was banned and seen to be a polluting "thing of the earth" (*kɔnɔɔ ntie*). Such practices were therefore seldom mentioned explicitly—they were considered outside the acceptable boundaries of the palace discourse of power. Nevertheless, they had to be communicated, so oblique representations such as those periodically revealed in the *kɔkumndjaŋ* procession made the case nonverbally.[40] In keeping with this aesthetic of coercion and terror, representations of German and later French soldiers were eagerly incorporated into the architecture of Grassfields palaces, the regalia of which had always been martial. One of the veranda posts of the palace in Oku—now lost but still in place in 1996—depicted a figure with a pink face and a blue tunic overlaid by a white cartridge belt. This enigmatic sculpture was sometimes said to represent a European soldier and sometimes the fon, in which case the cartridge belts were reinterpreted as the medicinal sashes that the fon wears across his torso (cf. Argenti 1998).[41] Just as fons had been ambiguously associated with foreign aggressors in myths of origin and masquerades, so too in the architecture of the palace they were later associated with the colonial forces to which they supplied their cadets as labor.

Just as the cowry shells that fringe the gowns of the palace masks recall the "bags" of cowries that were used to buy them, so too the bead decorations tightly woven around the palace treasures make them appear to be made of money—an aesthetic that is all the more arresting when the object is a human figure. Indeed, many of the objects in palace treasuries were human figurines covered in tight skins of beading. Many of these were said to represent fons and their wives, but by means of the aporia and ambiguity characteristic of the aesthetic of the Grassfields, they simultaneously could not have failed to recall the slaves whose bodies were themselves representations of the bead-wealth for which they were traded. Fon and slave thus came together again in the "things of the palace." The statement of the fon of Big Babanki, quoted earlier, is startling because it voices discursively what is usually a form of practical knowledge excluded from open discussion: that objects of European provenance became decommodified and reserved for the prestige economy because they were "worth plenty slave." If the objects themselves are not eloquent enough testimony to the slave trade, the method of their display during the procession round the Oku palace courtyard is similarly evocative: the "women of the palace" (*ɔbkii ntɔk*), as the fon's wives are known, followed their new husband silently, performing the role of caravan porters in this somber single-file procession, trudging laboriously under the weight of their "cargo" with expressions of dejection. Tellingly, the connotations of the term "cargo," the pidgin term for imported prestige goods, were not maritime for the hinterland peoples of the Grassfields but referred to the headloads carried from the coast by porters—"Cargo fo' up!" being the order for the caravan to march. In the procession then, not only the objects they carry but the palace wives themselves seem to be reenacting the slave caravan, and at the same time to be reenacting the caravans of colonial porters who later followed in their footsteps.

If the effect of these objects on the women of the palace—whose cheerless, resigned expressions and compliant postures recalled those of the *mb ɔke nokan* twin figures—was something short of celebratory, the objects also elicited ambivalent reactions from the crowd of onlookers. Many of the ordinary villagers who came to the palace to witness the events associated with the enthronement attested to a feeling of "dry mouth" (*əbtshuo əbyumɘne*) when they saw the "things of the palace," the twin figures, and the Fulɘŋgaŋ procession. The Eblam Ebkwo expression "dry mouth" highlights the loss for words that results from amazement or wonder.[42] The term "dry" (*yumɘ*) in the expression "dry mouth" alludes not only to lack of moisture but to absence in a more general sense and connotes emptiness, lack, or disappearance. Just as one's pockets or a bag are said to be "dry" when empty, one's mouth is "dry" when bereft of words. The expression not only indicates a loss for words, however, but refers to the lack of saliva that accompanies the experience of fear. The expression therefore does not connote mere surprise so much as a sense of dread or panic and the physical effects caused by sudden fear and anxiety. It has become customary for palace elites of the Grassfields to speak in English of the "palace museum" when discussing the "things of the palace." One must bear in mind, however, that these "museums," only revealed to the public momentarily on ceremonial occasions, are not beheld by their audiences with detached aesthetic contemplation, but with awe. In many respects, therefore, these museums may be museums of fear that return to the present belated memories of past violence and concretize contemporary experiences of social and economic disparity and political polarization.

Choreographies of Captivity

From a standard historical perspective, the possibility that the events at the palace refer to more than one period at once poses questions about when these performances were developed, when they were fixed in their present form, and whether the "evidence" they provide can be trusted as accurate representations of any one chronological time period. It may seem inconsistent from such a perspective that some of the elements of the enthronement ceremony seem to refer to the chaotic precolonial period of slave raids and abductions, whereas others seem to address the colonial period of the caravans and forced labor, and it may seem still more improbable that certain specific elements of the rites refer to both at once.[43] The awkward single-file shuffle and the references to the realm of the dead common to the Fulɔŋgaŋ masks, the procession of the palace jesters, and that of the fon's wives recall the precolonial practice of locking slaves in wooden fetters after capture and while awaiting a long-distance trader, and the fact that slaves were chained to one another on their long march to the coast (Van Slageren 1972, 78). The same choreographies of captivity can, however, equally be interpreted as an embodied remembering of the colonial era of the caravans of porters and of forced laborers on their way to the coast: they too were bound to one another (although with ropes rather than chains), forced to walk in single file, and guarded by armed men who brought up the rear and beat stragglers, just as the "captains" of Fulɔŋgaŋ threaten to do today.

The "captains" at each end of the procession are doubled by the German headhunter Captain Glauning and the other colonial officers who followed him at the head of caravans of forced laborers. But these military officers were not the first to impress themselves on the consciousness of the Grassfields. Before them, there had been other captains: the captains of the slave ships who bought the cadets exported from the Grassfields to be sold to the transatlantic trade. Far from marking a failure of historical accuracy, then, the ambiguous, indeterminate title of the captain is inscribed with a plurality of meanings—it is overdetermined: by means of a single title of European origin that embodies all the unspoken memories of the past at once, it simultaneously retraces not one but two traumatic pasts upon the present. Why at once? Because the subjective experience of histories of violence in the Grassfields is itself complex, fragmentary, fractured, and only open to knowledge through its contemporary reenactments. What good would it do to introduce a notional chronology to historical events in the Grassfields when, in fact, history only happens belatedly, all at once—*in eins*—in an anterior future? The performances attendant upon royal investiture are thus shibboleths in all of the senses that Derrida (1986), following Celan, gives to the term. The value of the shibboleth lies precisely in its lack of determination and its consequent ability to refer to many events at once; in avoiding direct reference, the shibboleth highlights the connections between separate instances of political domination, remaining open even to those that have yet to happen.

Yet the value of the shibboleth to the victim of political violence can easily be inverted by the perpetrator. In the case of the investiture of Oku fons, the palace elite make use of the indetermination of the performances to promulgate a revisionist discourse that presents slaves as exogenous aggressors when they were often local victims, and local elites as heroes where they were often slave traders. Mabu, the "great slave" and the unofficial third captain of Fuləŋgaŋ, at once represents a hunter and an ape—in other words, a slave driver and caravan leader, but also at once a slave or a porter of the colonial era. By means of this indetermination, the palace *kwifon* society shifts the fear inspired by the slave driver onto the slave, making of the slave a victim twice over: first in his or her enslavement, and again in his or her scapegoating. All of the other performances discussed here operate the same discursive slippage: the *kwifon* society jesters masquerade as slaves when in fact they operated first as slave-catchers and later as labor recruiters. By collapsing the distinctions between slave raiders and their victims, they effectively project the horror of their remembering onto their victims. The ominous *kwifon* announcements likewise project the danger of attack outward from the palace (where it often originated historically in the Grassfields) to the forests—the putative home of slaves and exogenous assailants as well as of the dead.

And what, finally, of the fon himself in the Grassfields? As the head of state and mythical founder of the polity who is often said originally to have been a foreign raider and, in later incarnations, coerced into being a secret ally of Fulani and Chamba slave raiders, he represents the ultimate figure of indetermination, the *pharmakon* of state formation in the Grassfields. In Oku, he is the white-capped figure who has emerged from the lake—the realm that symbolizes at once the heart of the polity and its constitutive nocturnal other: the watery home of both Europeans and departed slaves. This other therefore contains an incommensurable duality, slave trader and slave, as does the fon himself, on whose palace veranda stood the caryatid figure that represented at once a lineage elder and a German colonial officer—the aggressor from whom, like the raiding Fulani, not all Grassfields fons managed to protect their people.

In yet another telling example of the impenetrable ambiguity of the fon, he is remembered both in local myth and in the German colonial archives as having set out to greet the first column of German officers who reached Oku—headed by Captain Glauning on his fateful 1906 expedition to Nso'—dressed as a woman on her way to the farm. The Oku people now tell this story in the genre of a trickster tale, presenting the fon as having heroically outwitted the Germans.[44] As far as the Germans were concerned, however, there was no doubt as to who this transvestite figure really was: they interpreted the fon's curious gesture as an act of subjection and passed through Oku without trouble (Chilver [1966] 1996; Fanso and Chilver 1996). The symbolism of royalty thus simultaneously represents the fon as a nurturing and protective figure and as a trickster protecting his people, while conflating him with the threats from which he is meant to protect the chiefdom, revealing the royal compromise that forms the basis of the political structure and the birth of the polity, the delineation of the boundary and its breach in one, the necessary evil lurking in the intestines of the state. Like the masks of Fuləŋgaŋ, the fon's wives bear loads for him as they follow him in single file, just as the slaves and then the forced laborers of the colonial era followed their captains.[45] Here too the shibboleth all too easily inverts its effect though, for what do these women carry in their hands if not the prestige items of wealth procured by the palace in exchange for slaves—in other words, metonyms of slaves? From this perspective, they seem to embody not only slaves but also slave traders. Revelation and occlusion, inscription and reinscription, enactment and reenactment, the irreducible pairs of the anterior future—*what will have been*—return once again with each successive royal installation, each successive remembering, to haunt the present.

From Slaves to Free Boys: Cadets' Resistance to Gerontocratic, Colonial, and Postcolonial Authority

The mass of young bachelors have never ... been the subject of special studies, despite the crucial role they played in underpinning the former hierarchies, as labour during the colonial period, as recruits to the Christian missions and, from the inception of the colonial period onwards, as rebels. — Jean-Pierre Warnier (1996, 116)

Indirect Rule and the Mimesis of Power

At the end of the nineteenth century, Bamum, one of the greatest expansionist chiefdoms of the Grassfields, descended into civil war. Finding himself in a precarious situation, the young fon Njoya decided to call on the Fulbe Ardo Umaro of Banyo for help against his enemies. The Fulbe had then only recently arrived from what is now Nigeria and were occupying the Adamawa plateau to the north of Fumban. They acceded to Njoya's request and intervened in the war some time between 1895 and 1897, putting down the rebellion and ensuring the continuity of Njoya's rule in a single decisive battle. The survivors among the insurrectionists were given to the Fulbe as booty to be sold as slaves to the north (Tardits 1980, 206–9; 1996; Geary 1996b). As a result of the spectacularly effective intervention of the Fulbe, Njoya decided to convert to Islam. This decision seems to have resulted mainly from his wish to acquire the military power of his new allies, which he deemed to be linked to their ritual practices (he had watched them praying before the battle). Among his first acts of piety were his replacement of the gown and cap typical of Grassfields fons with Muslim dress and the establishment of an armed cavalry (Njiasse-Njoya 1981, 49ff., as quoted in Geary 1988b, 22–23). By 1902, however, the Germans had arrived in Fumban, and Njoya, after a brief debate with his people, who wanted to resist their entry to the palace, formed an alliance with the nascent power.

Christraud Geary (1996b) has recorded how, from 1906 onward, Njoya forsook Muslim robes and turbans, gradually replacing them with hybrid garments that he had made by tailors attached to the palace. Within a decade, he had gone from being a Grassfields fon, to a Muslim sultan, to a Prussian *König*. In each instance, he convinced his new allies of the sincerity of his conversion, while nevertheless maintaining his hegemony as a fon vis-à-vis his subjects. In the early days of his alliance with the Germans, the new outfits he created combined elements of Muslim and German attire with traditional Grassfields royal regalia in an eclectic manner. As Njoya built up stronger ties with the German administration, however, and received more and more gifts of military regalia from them, his outfits became increasingly accurate representations of contemporary German uniforms. Between 1906 and 1908 he was photographed with his palace retainers wearing breastplates and helmets supplied by the Germans, as well as near-perfect replicas of hussar-style uniforms produced by the palace tailors (Geary 1983, illustration nos. 145–47; 1988b, 57–60; 1996b). Nor did his palace guard simply look the part for a still photograph: they also perfected military drills, which they probably learned from returning Bamum soldiers who had served in the German colonial force, the *Schutztruppe*.

At first the Germans were either delighted or condescendingly amused with this apparent show of loyalty, but by 1908 they began to be uneasy about the increasingly militarized and proficient appearance of Njoya and his soldiers.[1] The modern, breech-loading rifles that had passed into the hands of Njoya's bodyguards were often cited as a cause for concern, but just as often it was Njoya's uniforms that were cited by the Germans as an outrage. In the same period, seeing that the Germans and the Fulbe each had a religion and a script with which to promulgate it, Njoya nearly single-handedly invented a working script and established a new religion (Tardits 1996).[2] In this light, uniforms were but one part of an embodiment of the entire German ethos, and what the German administration had at first taken as a sign of adulation on the part of the *König* of the Grassfields began increasingly to look to them like an insubordinate appropriation of power. As German anxieties mounted and opinion turned against him, Njoya and his troops were ordered to stop "playing at soldiers" (Geary

1988b, 55; 1996b, 187).[3] In the same year, the Germans began to express similar worries about their other staunch allies in the region: Bali-Nyonga and the *Balitruppe* armed force under the command of their fon, Fonyonga II. The soldiers of the *Balitruppe* had also adopted local versions of German uniforms and embodied German military deportment with a precision that was nothing short of breathtaking to German observers.

One could argue that the fears of the Germans with respect to their allies in Bamum and Bali-Nyonga were unfounded. The adoption of the regalia of foreign allies has for centuries played an integral role in the diplomacy of alliance among the polities of the Grassfields and beyond.[4] Displaying the finery of foreign allies in the palace collection or on the person of the fon was a sign not of insubordination but of allegiance and friendship. Thus when the fon of Bali included items of German origin in the palace collection or when the fon of Bamum adopted German military attire, they were obeying an aesthetic of diplomacy that allied them with the new colonial power and demonstrated their respect for the Germans—a respect they believed was fully reciprocated. From the sources available to us, however, it seems that this aspect of Grassfields political relations was lost on the majority of the German administration at the time. In contrast to Njoya's view of diplomacy, the Germans interpreted the gifts they received from Njoya—including his father's throne or a copy of it (Geary 1994, 1996a)—as tribute from a pacified native ruler. Njoya, on the other hand, fully expected the German Kaiser to make use of the throne, elephant tusks, and other regalia that Njoya sent to him to transform his own appearance and thereby to display his alliance with his new partner in Africa. Nevertheless, from the point of view of western European imperialism and the stress it placed on domination over partnership, the Germans may not have been entirely wrong to express their concern: what the Bamum fon intended to negotiate was not his pacification and subjection to German suzerainty but rather an egalitarian form of cultural, political, and economic partnership.

Nor was the Bamum kingdom the only Pandora's box that the Germans unwittingly opened in their fledgling colony. As mentioned earlier, Zintgraff's arrival in Bali had resulted in the emergence of the *Balitruppe,* made up of recruits from the Grassfields kingdom of Bali who were known locally as the *basoge.*[5] These young recruits considered Zintgraff to have magical powers and were so captivated with military discipline and performance that they continued their drills throughout the rainy season (Chilver [1966] 1996, 29, 31–32). Not only was the craze for drilling rampant among the bodyguard of the fons, but it rapidly became a more wide-spread phenomenon. In November 1907 the German cartographer Moisel observed that the *Balitruppe* or *basoge* craze for drilling, which had not in any way abated, had spread to the Basel Mission school pupils:

> On the order *Stillstand* 200 or so heels clicked together and all hands were placed along where, in a German boy, his trouser seam would have been. Like-wise with other commands—*Linksum!* Battalion, march! To the right, march! Battalion halt! Eyes front! This drill made an odd impression since, apart from these words of command, the Bali lads did not understand a word of Ger-man. . . . Whenever the strong, well-uniformed and musket-armed bodyguard of the chief is drilled by a former *schutztruppe* soldier the Bali boys crowd round the spot and follow the military exercises with the greatest interest. (Moisel 1908, 267–71 [trans. E. M. Chilver])[6]

In addition to the trained palace corps of bodyguards kept by those Grassfields fons who were allied with the Germans—a corps that num-bered in the hundreds if not the thousands—schoolboys taught by the missionaries were also encouraged to adopt the bodily postures and prac-tice of the German military, and they proved to be exceptionally eager and adept pupils. This is not surprising when the demographic profile of the students is taken into account. Unlike the *Balitruppe,* whose members belonged to the palace *kwifon* society, many of the mission school pupils were commoners and slaves. The fon of Bali, who saw schooling as an-other form of forced labor, had been sending not only princes, as required by the missionaries, but also slaves and foreign children from subjugated chiefdoms to his school in order to meet the demands of the missionaries for pupils. The opportunity for such marginalized young boys to acquire a military training would have been unheard of before the arrival of the Germans, and the missionaries thus unwittingly opened the doors of the palatine hierarchies of the Grassfields to those who would in the past have been excluded from them. In addition to the school in Bali, at least two other schools in the area, those of Banyangam and Banjun, had their pu-pils dress in a uniform of khakis and red berets—essentially the same uniform as that of the German station messengers and to this day the uni-form of the national gendarmerie. According to Van Slageren (1972, 122), these pupils were seen to be "under the white man's protection," and local schoolteachers took over important positions in the *kwifon* societies.

It was perhaps the success of the militarization of the Grassfields that caused such foreboding among members of the German administration. After the first Bali irregulars, or *basoge,* had been trained, military training was no longer under the Germans' control, and the *basoge* and members of the *Schutztruppe* returning home were training their own recruits without recourse to German authority.[7] Moreover, many of the *basoge* took to using the authority they wielded for their own private ends, engaging in extortion and even the abduction of persons from subjugated chiefdoms for sale into slavery under the guise of "tax gathering" or "labor recruitment." Many members of the *Balitruppe* were in fact none other than the *bigwe* palace jesters who had been at the forefront of slave abductions in the precolonial era (Warnier 1996, 117–18). They had now fortified their symbolic arsenal of the wild with the paraphernalia and habitus of German colonial power, but they had lost none of their skills in subterfuge and deception.

The Century of Youth, 1892–1992

The Tapenta

By 1891, in an increasingly uncontrolled irradiation of devolving power, the *basoge* had given birth to the so-called *tapenta* (from the English "interpreter") or *kamenda* (from the German *Kommandant*[8]) (Rowlands 1995, 25–27; Van Slageren 1972, 84; Warnier 1993, 205; 1996). Although nominally attached to the palace of Bali-Nyonga and to the German administration, the young *tapenta* became mercenaries—armed irregulars fighting for neighboring chiefdoms and thereby severing their kinship and hierarchical ties to their kingdom of origin. The chiefs' control over young bachelors had been seriously disrupted by Zintgraff's entry into the Grassfields. As mentioned, one of the most dramatic—if unintended—consequences of his arrival in the area was the uncontrolled spread of sophisticated breech-loading rifles.[9] Not only had hundreds of these been handed out to the *Balitruppe,* but thousands more had been lost. Deserters among Zintgraff's Liberian Vai carriers had sold their weapons to villagers as they took flight. In addition, the ill-fated attack that Zintgraff had led against Bafut and Mankon with the help of Bali, which ended in the routing of the German-Bali force, provided the enemy Bafut and Mankon palaces with many rifles dropped by the German forces in their desperate retreat (Chilver 1967; Warnier 1996, 117). Although the *basoge* or the *Balitruppe* had been at least nominally under the command of the fon and allied with the Germans, the young men from other chiefdoms who acquired weapons by theft or won them in battle were far less beholden to the traditional authority structures. The *kamenda* irregulars thus marked the threshold of a downward spiral of unaccountability that threatened to destabilize the entire region and the hegemony of elders and colonial authorities alike.

Similarly, the Bamileke chiefdoms of the southern Grassfields saw the rise of the so-called free boys from the early 1900s. This youth movement resulted not from the influence of the colonial authorities, but of the missions, which educated young men and taught them trades. With these qualifications, young men soon began traveling to the coast, where they took on paid work, earning salaries that for the first time rendered them independent of their chiefs. The latter were so alarmed by the free-boy movement that they complained bitterly about the missions' activities to the colonial authorities. They pointed out that in the past youths would humbly come to lay any money they had earned at their feet, but that now, calling themselves free boys, they thought of themselves as being beyond the reach of traditional authority. In order to reinstate their authority, the chiefs beseeched the colonial authorities to send all these renegade subjects to the railway construction project near Yaoundé as forced laborers (Christol 1922; Debarge 1934, 39; Van Slageren 1972, 171–72).

Like the soldiers attached to Grassfields palaces allied with the Germans, the *tapenta* adopted variations of German colonial attire to match the militaristic titles they took on. Like the school pupils, however, their background was not an elite but a marginal one, and their unprecedented lack of accountability to hierarchical structures of authority rapidly earned them a reputation as armed brigands. Jean-Pierre Warnier writes that, although nominally attached to the palace of Bali-Nyonga, the *tapenta* "began to hold the region to ransom on their own account" (1996, 117) , and further that "neither the local Fons nor the Germans were able to block their dissemination throughout the Bamileke territory or to stop their depredations. They were recognisable by their red berets and by the multitude of young people who accompanied them" (1993, 205 [trans. mine]). Father Spellenberg, a local missionary, wrote of their activities until as late as 1914: "The appearance of the [*tapenta*] augurs nothing good. Especially the young, forming the tail of the troupe, represent a scourge for the country. Corrupted by the magic of the Whites, they attack men, women and children like wild animals. They steal anything not riveted to the ground, chickens, goats and food. Their organisation has ramifications everywhere.

When arrested, they cry out: *lef me, mi be big boy, mi be Tapenta-boy!"* (Spellenberg, as quoted in Van Slageren 1972, 84 [trans. mine]).

The *tapenta* rapidly transcended their status as youths of low social rank and confounded regional hierarchies. By donning the clothes of the Germans—including red berets, as did school pupils and the *basoge*—and wielding German guns, they evaded their servile status and set out on peripatetic journeys like the members of the floating population had before them, pledging allegiance to no chiefdom and threatening structures of authority wherever they went by attracting large bands of young malcontents. The first Basel missionaries to arrive in Bali complained bitterly of the anarchic conditions in which they had to work, speaking apocalyptically of a society turned on its head in which the elders no longer held power and "savage" youths had lost all respect for traditional systems of authority (Spellenberg 1914, as quoted in Van Slageren 1972, 84). The name *tapenta*, initially used to refer to those who were actually acting as interpreters for colonial administrators, quickly spread to describe those who could understand European languages, and finally, to describe anyone who had managed to gain the knowledge and power of the white man in any form. The term was still prevalent in this latter sense in 1958, along with the more recent appellation "America," both of which were adopted as age-grade names in the chiefdom of Bamali (Chilver, pers. com.).[10]

Just as the elite of the Grassfields were busy appropriating the infrastructure of the colonists—their churches, schools, and troops—and tailoring them to their own agendas, so too the *tapenta* and free boys eagerly took on the trappings of colonial and missionary authority in a bid to escape their position of subjugation in the gerontocratic hierarchy that had until then both depended on their labor and excluded them from influence. The missionary and colonial administrators of the time adopted the point of view of the elites on whom they depended, and it is the brigandage and the anarchic violence of the free boys that their reports stress above all. With hindsight, however, it is clear that this pan-Grassfields movement represented a key historical moment in the region—a point at which the precolonial monopoly on power previously enjoyed by the palace hierarchies was breached by the people that it was designed to dominate. Those cadets or young bachelors who in the precolonial era had had to provide labor for their lineage heads as the only way to avoid the threat of lifelong "youth," bachelorhood, and enslavement could now do better than simply seeking to minimize their exploitation by becoming members of the floating population; they could now acquire the means to incorporate and to wield new, exogenous models of military power and even seek independent livelihoods in the burgeoning colonial economy.

One of the many ironies of this confused period of political flux is that the missionaries were largely responsible for creating the social conditions about which they complained so vociferously, in which the youth could openly express dissent and seek new forms of emancipation. Cadets thus first found their voice not only because, as Father Spellenberg stresses, weapons and military discipline were made widely available to them by the colonial authorities, but because missionaries themselves handed out other forms of power without any respect for the palatine hierarchical order: they offered to young slaves and commoners symbolic capital and economic power in the form of an education that their pupils could use to become government interpreters (*tapenta*) or other functionaries and thus gain a salary independent of the elders, and they provided occult power in the form of a religious education and a secret, esoteric language (German), which their pupils rapidly mastered. All this was buttressed by baptism—an initiation ceremony demonstrating inclusion in the secret society of European colonial authority (Warnier 1996). Inspired by the nonaligned movement of freed slaves, mission school pupils soon took to calling themselves "free boys," and Warnier argues that the churches, having originally been virtual annexes of the palaces soon set themselves up (whether knowingly or not) as a countersociety, opening "a space of liberty into which the cadets precipitated themselves" (Warnier 1993, 209–10 [trans. mine]).

From around 1916 onward, the elders and the cadets, according to Warnier (1993, 211), competed in a race to appropriate the resources of the colonial presence and to exclude their competitors from them. It was becoming clear to Grassfields chiefs that they were not going to be able to hold onto power if their occult powers (including their access to the colonial authorities) were to be shared with cadets. Therefore, one of the first acts of the elders, in the vacuum left by the arrest and deportation of the German missionaries by the invading Allied Forces in the First World War, was to persecute young Christians—whom they identified with the *tapenta*—and to burn down their churches (Warnier 1996, 119). The *tapenta* and free-boy movements, Christian education, and work in the new monetary economy thus all had clear political dimensions. Far from being a mere security problem or a criminal issue, the *tapenta* represented a broad-based regional movement of protest and of rebellion by the cadets of the Grassfields. Their interventions—cultural, political, criminal—were carried out simultaneously on many fronts from the arrival of the colonial authorities onward, and their social movement was to be the first of many such youth uprisings.

The Union des Populations du Cameroun

The German occupation came to an end in 1915, when the French and the English jointly moved in to Cameroon from the south and west, respectively. With the defeat of the Germans, the temporary exclusion of the missionaries, and the consolidation of power by the new colonial authorities, the *basoge* and *tapenta* movements and the depredations of the free boys effectively came to an end. If the interwar years were calm, however, the post–World War II situation would see a recrudescence of the youth revolt. In 1955 came the maquisards, the guerrilla fighters of the insurgent Union des Populations du Cameroun (UPC). The UPC rebellion marks the first instance of a violent insurrection leading to protracted large-scale violence in Cameroon, and the movement has accordingly been identified as a modern nationalist insurrection, often vilified by the authorities of the day as stemming from cold-war communist agitation. There are, however, a number of parallels between the UPC rebellion and the youth movements that preceded it in the Grassfields. As Warnier points out (1993, 215), the "banditry" for which the maquisards of the southern part of the Grassfields (the Bamileke region) became known recalls the activities of the free boys at the end of the nineteenth century. And apart from similarities in the pattern of criminal activity engaged in by the UPC and its precursors, the UPC also appropriated exogenous forms of colonial power for which young men had become infamous during the German era. If the *tapenta* had embodied the barbarity of the Germans, they also appropriated the Germans' language. So too the maquisards appropriated the knowledge as well as the destructive power of the French, who replaced them in the Bamileke area after the First World War. Under the French, the maquisards appropriated the literacy of the colonial administration.

As latter-day hunters, the maquisards set out on a "path to the forest" (Mbembe 1996, 348 [trans. mine]), not only for tactical purposes but also in an attempt to establish a nationalist identity in opposition to the French urban administration. Just as Njoya had always introduced transformations into his mimetic appropriations of Western dress, religion, and literacy, so too the Bassa leaders of the maquisards transformed the literacy of the French, producing texts, not in French but in Bassa, that expounded their philosophy.[11] But the young UPC cadres fought not only against the French but also against the Bamileke chiefs of the southern (now French-controlled) Grassfields. Belying the doxa that this was nothing but an anticolonial, Soviet-inspired insurgency, the UPC cadres of the southern Grassfields devoted a great deal of their energy to destabilizing the Bamileke chiefs, sacking their palaces, and assassinating them or sending them into exile. Although these actions have often been interpreted as a means to an end in the fight against the French, when placed in the historical context of the free boy and the *tapenta* revolts of the previous generation they ought rightly to be seen as an end in themselves.[12] It was not the French but the Bamileke chiefs who had excluded their youth from influence, inheritance, and marriage. From this perspective, the return to the forest of the maquisards clearly recalls the deterritorialized roaming of the free boys in the early 1900s, and just as the free boys had challenged the association of the chiefs and elites to the nascent colonial authorities, so too the maquisards and their followers in the 1960s postindependence period questioned the support that the chiefs sought from the new postcolonial state, continuing their fight despite the fact that Cameroon had gained independence and thus casting doubt on the reduction of the UPC movement to an anticolonial struggle.[13]

The few works that have been devoted to the UPC have focused on the formal political aspects of the movement. Le Vine's (1964, 1971) and Gaillard's (1989) thorough political histories of Cameroon thus provide detailed and meticulous accounts of the decision making among the leaders of the party and its adversaries in the colonial administration, but little information on the grassroots social movement that propelled local youths to become members of the Armée de Libération Nationale du Kamerun (ALNK)—the fighting wing of the UPC. Richard Joseph, one of the chroniclers of the UPC, likewise admits that his 1977 analysis of the movement is a strictly political rather than a cultural or social one. Nevertheless, he concedes that "anyone who has lived through or closely studied a nationalist movement is immediately aware of the important part often played by the more popular aspects of cultural revival in such movements. The songs, the rhymes, the chants, the parodies are usually important elements in such *levées en masse*. In the case of Cameroun, however, such material is not readily available" (Joseph 1977, 202).[14] Yet it is precisely this material that provides the key to a refutation of shallow condemnations of the UPC as a mere cover for banditry or a Marxist insurrectionist movement.[15] No less importantly, it is only a focus on the cultural aspects of the UPC uprising that can highlight the continuities between this movement as it played itself out in Bamileke territory on the one hand, and the youth uprisings that had preceded it—and would follow it—in the region on the other. Not surprisingly, when Gaillard faces the task of explaining the Bamileke uprising in terms of the governing ideology of the UPC leaders, he sees only chaotic dissonance and incoherence (1989, 1:231). Willard Johnson (1970, 685), likewise noting the dissociation of the Bamileke wing of the UPC insurrection from the political ideology and leadership of the party, characterizes the violence of the cadres as "anomic." Rather than informing us about the political shortcomings of the Bamileke insurgents, however, the inscrutability of the Bamileke uprising suggests that it is not to be understood in terms of the tenets promulgated by the higher echelons of the UPC. The UPC movement had started not in Bamileke territory but among the Bassa of the forest zone to the south, and it was their leaders who had promulgated the UPC's political aims and objectives in explicit terms. The dissonance noted by Gaillard and others therefore marks not the incoherence of the Bamileke project but rather its difference from the precursors, social context, and political aims of the original Bassa insurrection of southern Cameroon.

One of the challenges involved in placing the Bamileke uprising in the broader context of the nineteenth-century youth movements that preceded it in the Grassfields is providing evidence that these distinct movements were indeed related across time through their causes, their aims, or the social profile or modus operandi of their members. Indeed, because much of the analysis (by the contemporary press as well as by historians) of the Bamileke uprising has been written in terms of the feats of destruction and violence perpetrated by hard core UPC/ALNK cadres, and their supposed Marxist foundations, one might get the impression that this political phenomenon was distinct from anything that had preceded it in the region—more beholden to international politics and to modern geopolitical struggles than to regional social processes. One need look no further, however, than eyewitness descriptions of the UPC cadres to find direct cultural parallels with the free boys and the *tapenta* of the previous generation.

René Mauries, a journalist writing in the *Dépêche du Midi* of December 15, 1956, states that the Bamileke wing of the UPC was at that time expanding from its original constituency into what he tellingly terms "the floating population" and the unemployed, to include "civil servants, plant-

ers and traditional chiefs" (as quoted in Joseph 1977, 241). Claude Tardits
(1960, 123), who conducted research in Bamileke territory during the uprising, identifies in his monograph on the Bamileke a stratum of disinher-
ited and landless "cadets" forced to emigrate in search of work or of land.[16]
The social scientist Françoise Pain similarly observed that by 1954, with
the simultaneous winding down of several major engineering projects in
Cameroon, there had emerged "a floating group of manual workers who
go from building-site to building-site and appear in any town as soon as
there is talk of work" (Pain 1959, 145, as quoted in Joseph 1977, 254). The
ethnographer Hurault, who also carried out his investigations in the midst
of the uprising, similarly refers to "frustrated and jealous non-inheritors"
(1962, 127 [trans. mine]), again evoking the landless unmarried cadets of
previous generations. And while Hurault speaks of his certainty that it
was "with horror and consternation that the great majority of Bamileke
villagers saw an armed minority come from the towns to upset their institutions by force" (1962, 132 [trans. mine]), Dominique Malaquais evokes
a massive, albeit largely nonviolent, movement of civil disobedience by
the marginalized, landless rural Bamileke cadets. This civil disobedience
included the passive protest of nonpayment of taxes and the closure of
shops and marketplace stalls (Gaillard 1989, 2:233), a form of resistance
that would be adopted by the next generation during the 1990s. The
wholesale sabotage that was inflicted on the roads can also be seen as a
form of economic protest—starving the administrative centers of the food
they normally extracted from the region—but the practical aspects of this
intervention made it both something more than an attack against the colonial administration and something less than an anticolonial struggle in
the strict sense.

Malaquais (2002, 326–33) describes newspapers of the day reporting
both men and women, by the tens of thousands, silently digging up kilometer upon kilometer of the few tarmac roads at night with their farming
implements and planting them with crops, thus transforming the infrastructure of colonial authority into the agrarian land of which they felt
they had been deprived by the state and local chiefs alike.[17] In some cases,
not only crops but entire houses are said to have germinated overnight
on these highways (332). Malaquais further makes the point (331) that
this agrarian protest reinvented a form of defensive warfare used by previous generations in the region: under threat of attack by slave raiders,
the people would dig in, building trenches hundreds of meters long that
are often still visible around the outskirts of villages in the Grassfields

today. Digging up the roads of course recalls another form of combat: the apotropaic medicine practiced by *ngaŋ* medicinal associations, which, in time of war or pestilence, sprinkle medicine across the entry points to the village to keep out witches and render enemies harmless. As I argue later, blocking the roads in this way would recur a generation after the UPC uprising, during the prodemocracy movement of the 1990s.

In fact, although only a minority of the unemployed youth ever joined the UPC and became armed insurrectionists, many more disillusioned and marginalized young Bamileke men and women tacitly supported them—together forming the river in which the fish of the UPC could swim. With their free-roaming movement unrestricted by ties to a *terroire* and an ethnic identity they had abjured, these disillusioned young men and women evoke the "tail of the troupe" of *tapenta* that Father Spellenberg had described in the same region forty years earlier. In both cases, the armed leaders represented only a minority of the movement, while an unarmed majority of young men and women took advantage of the militants to pursue their own objectives. In both cases, the political rationale of those spearheading the movement—in the first case, the pacification of the Grassfields for the German authorities; in the second case, immediate independence for a unified Cameroon—rapidly became little more than a catalyst for the mobilization of an entire stratum of the population. In both cases also, the underlying causes of the uprisings lay in the connivance of the colonial regime with chosen local elites for the exploitation of the disenfranchised cadets. As the cadets attempted to find an escape from lifelong servitude—whether through mass mobilization, passive protest, defaulting on debts to usurious elders, migration, consensual wage labor, petty crime, or finally organized insurgency—they often paid a heavy price.

The Bamileke UPC insurrection was met with the full force of the counterinsurgency apparatus that the French military had perfected in Indochina and Algeria. Entire households were rounded up into concentration camps or *camps de regroupement* (cf. Mbembe 1996, 350ff.; Gaillard 1989, 1:224), crops were burned, and suspected UPC sympathizers tortured to death (Gaillard 1989, 1:206; Malaquais 2003, 319n27). As certain UPC leaders became double agents, cutting deals with the French while continuing to fly the flag of the UPC, the southern Grassfields once again took on the topography of the *razzia,* with jester-type warlords hunting down men and assassinating elders (Gaillard 1989, 2:24–25). The French military, for their part, deployed their prisoners as forced labor on the

plantations of the palatine elite (Malaquais 2002, 319n27), a strategy recalling not only the earlier stages of their rule in the 1920s, when native
recruiters allied to the chiefs were allowed free reign, but the era of the
German occupation and before that of the slave trade, when young men
and women were similarly put to work by the local elite if they were not
sold or captured outright. In a word, by the mid-twentieth century the
Grassfields had once again become, for young people, a space of exploitation, terror, and death, and once again these conditions galvanized the
marginalized cadets—albeit this time under the political aegis of the UPC
and its armed wing, the ALNK.

The Gendarmerie

A description of youth groups in the postcolonial period and the forms of
power that they emulate must take the national gendarmerie into account
as one of their current exemplars. This paramilitary organization was established by the French in all of their African colonies, including Cameroon, and has been kept on in addition to the ordinary police force since independence in 1960. With the reunification of the previously French- and
British-controlled parts of the country after the plebiscite of 1960–61, the
gendarmerie has been deployed in the Anglophone Grassfields as well.
Their arbitrary violence, their total lack of accountability, and the impunity with which they evade prosecution for their crimes all ensure that
they enjoy no legitimacy as a police force in the eyes of ordinary people.[18]
Throughout Cameroon, but particularly in the Anglophone North West
Province, it is the gendarmes who have come to be associated most closely
with state repression.[19] During my stay in Oku, I repeatedly witnessed
the deployment of this paramilitary force. Arrests for no apparent reason, incarceration without charge, torture, looting, rape, and murder mark
their intervention in any part of the Grassfields (Amnesty International
1992, 1994, 1997a, 1997b, 1997c; Argenti 1998; Fisiy 1995, 55, 61; U.S. Department of State 2003). In March 1997, five hundred armed troops from
combined army and gendarmerie contingents were sent to Oku as part of
a wider occupation of the North West Province. Their repression was so
brutal on this occasion that the entire able-bodied male population was
forced to flee into the surrounding forest (Amnesty International 1997a,
1997b, 1997c; *Africa Confidential* 1997).

As fons become more closely linked to the government administration
and identified with the ruling Cameroon People's Democratic Movement

(CPDM) party, the gendarmes are increasingly seen by ordinary villagers as connected to the palace in one way or another. Just as the wild forces of the forest used to be unleashed by the policing masquerades of the palace *kwifon* society (whose members once executed criminals inside the forest), so it is that the Grassfields fons, trying to make light of their absorption by the state, have by and large attempted to annex the state apparatus as a surrogate "other," in the way that the fons of Bali and Bamum had once allied themselves with the Germans. But just as marginalized young men have always taken advantage of the introduction of new orders of power to free themselves from the constraints of local gerontocracies in the Grassfields, so the blatant corruption of the state is appropriated by the gendarmerie to their own ends, as the exemplar and the justification for using their weapons, uniforms, and positions as an opportunity to enrich themselves illicitly in emulation of the normative order of a felonious state (cf. Bayart 1999; Reno 1995, 2000; Roitman 1998, 2005, 2006). Unlike the ordinary, blue-uniformed police force, which is generally seen to be more benign, the gendarmes are widely accused not only of abusing their positions of authority while in uniform but also of engaging in criminal activities when off duty and of fueling the majority of violent crime in Cameroon today. Ill trained, ill motivated, and faced with a government weakened by an economic crisis, the 1994 devaluation of the CFA franc, endemic embezzling at all levels, and a crisis of legitimacy, the gendarmes set themselves up in private enterprise whenever they can, thus repeating the earlier transformation of the colonial *Balitruppe* into the anarchic *tapenta* movement.

Like the *basoge* of the German era, who had used their skills as palace jesters and licensed manhunters to profit from their official positions as representatives of colonial authority by abducting people for illicit sale into slavery, so too the gendarmes and the innumerable other uniformed security services maintained by the postcolonial state now see no reason why they should not follow the example of their employers and use their offices as an opportunity to "eat." The principle that the "goat eats where it is tethered" (Bayart 1989, 288) guides not only the actions of the elites in government but trickles down to the security services as well. As Janet Roitman (2005, 2006) explains in her exceptionally revealing work on crime in northern Cameroon, those involved in violent methods of extraction do not see their activities as illicit, even when they might agree that they are illegal. Indeed, as Bayart (1989, 290) points out, "corrupt" practices at this level of society rest on a keen political sense of injustice and inequality, and represent a social struggle. The criminal forms of extraction practiced by the gendarmes and the bandits with whom they appear to be closely associated should not, however, be taken as a straightforward form of resistance to the iniquities of the state. On the contrary, as Roitman (2006) points out in a critique of Hobsbawm's ([1969] 2000) work on bandits, the status of the security services in their capacity, in the popular imaginary, as thieves and brigands is "extremely ambivalent, being both revered and feared," and has been since the "straddling" of legal and illegal spheres of activity practiced by "brigand chiefs" beginning in the colonial era. Roitman therefore concludes that the blurred boundary between bandits and *coupeurs de routes,* on the one hand, and the state security services and functionaries on the other, and the inseparability of their shared moral economy of accumulation are such that "one cannot clearly delineate [the activities of the bandits] in terms of a counter-realm, or as instances of rebellion, resistance to the state, or acts of social justice" (2006, 259). The extractive practices of the bandits and of the state are not clearly separable from one another, and as in the case of the precolonial state in the Grassfields, we see that a notionally exogenous and vilified group of aggressors (which is in fact internal to the government or allied to it) can operate in the popular imaginary as a legitimation of the autocratic state as much as a critique of it.

As I discuss in the next section, however, when criminal gangs emerged in the Bamenda area, they were countered by oppositional forces that self-consciously sought to justify their activities in terms of a grassroots legitimacy that was opposed to the rapacious parasitism of the state. In the Grassfields, the popular perception of the state as an amoral or even immoral realm of illegal accumulation includes the gendarmerie. Despite the fact that they are perceived as acting in their own interest, the gendarmes are seen to extend the logic of consumption of the state rather than to oppose or resist it, and to reify its largely invisible and ineffable practices of appropriation in the visible realm of the road (Argenti 2004, 2005a). The association that Grassfields palaces seek with the state and the association of the Oku palace with the gendarmerie therefore belie the fon's image as a figure of protection against outside aggression and the paternalistic discourse of the palatine elite. While serving to legitimize the elite to some extent, these associations simultaneously serve to tar them with the same brush as the central government and the security forces—that is, as comparable and juxtaposed vectors of amoral and sorcerous consumption.[20]

Water among the Stones: Party Politics, Gangs, and Antigangs in the 1990s

The postcolonial state that Paul Biya, still the country's leader, inherited from Ahidjo, its first president, in 1982 was a single-party state. As Joseph Takougang and Milton Krieger (1998, 103ff.) chronicle, the birth of the Social Democratic Front (SDF) opposition party in Bamenda, the capital of the Anglophone North West Province and the northern Grassfields region, in March 1990 (notwithstanding Biya's position that multiple parties represented "a distasteful passing fetish"), effectively marked the beginning of multiparty politics in Cameroon. Far from ushering in the much-hoped-for period of liberal democracy and prosperity, however, the state's resistance to the birth of opposition parties, such as the SDF, and the failure of the SDF to change people's lives for the better sent the country deeper into an economic crisis and further alienated the most marginal elements of society: the young and the unemployed. At the same time, the political instability spawned by the failed democratization movement of the 1990s and the state's obdurate resistance to it triggered a collapse of security in and around the town of Bamenda, the capital of the North West Province.

The *ville morte* or "ghost town" general strikes that started in Douala in 1990 and were championed by Bamenda during the course of my research, echoing the UPC interventions in the Bamileke region during the 1950s, drained the government of vital revenue and dramatically crippled its ability to function over the next few years.[21] The SDF and other opposition parties quickly claimed these victories, pointing to them as evidence of the strength of their popular support. Again as with the UPC in the southern Grassfields, however, the allegiance to any particular party by the young people who made up the massive show of force in the streets of Bamenda (mobilizing up to 50,000 people in a population of 150,000) should not be taken for granted. An early portrait of the demonstrators in Douala, painted by the famous political dissident Célestin Monga, speaks of "bands of urchins (*gamins*) building barricades" (Monga, 1991, as quoted in Takougang and Krieger 1998, 127 [trans. mine]), and some of the most prominent SDF supporters in the rural areas were children under the age of ten (Argenti 2001). Echoing the practice of child soldiers, youth maskers, and traders in the informal economy throughout Africa, they took on the names of action heroes such as Sylvester Stallone, Rambo, Chuck Norris, and Arnold Schwarzenegger.[22] Pointedly, they did

not adopt the names of past heroes of the struggle against colonial occupation; more starkly still than in the UPC era, this movement was not
driven by a political ideology in the strict sense but rather—once again—
by the crystallization of youth disaffection, this time riding the vehicle
of democratization movements that happened to be driving through the
continent at the time.

Thus, rather than being a movement that clearly flagged the legitimacy
of a single political party or ideology that had given birth to it by mobilizing a sector of society, such youth protests marked a grassroots political
movement that the SDF opposition and the CPDM party in power equally
struggled to contain and to appropriate to their cause. In a demographic
category that Takougang and Krieger (1998) aptly identify as "migrants
becoming vagrants," political support was not willingly given by the young
demonstrators in starry-eyed admiration of the political leaders in either
camp. What the politicians had to contend with was a popular appropriation of power by the marginalized youth of Cameroon that was not prima
facie amenable to any political-party ideology, or to current discourses of
democracy. In other words, the unrest of the 1990s is not best conceived
of as a protracted political-party rally but rather should be rethought, in
its historical context, as a pan-Grassfields movement of disenfranchised
cadets in the mould of the many revolts that had preceded it.

In the manner that the floating population had once sought, during
the precolonial and colonial eras, to evade the unlivable conditions of
exploitation and insecurity under which they labored in the Grassfields,
and in the manner that the *tapenta* and the free boys had later openly
revolted against authoritarian gerontocracies by emulating the colonial
security forces, the largely unemployed migrant youths of Bamenda took
to the streets in the 1990s. Through the use of the nascent state against
local elites once again, their political activism evinced a disillusionment
and resentment aimed not solely at the ruling CPDM party and the economic marginalization of which it was seen as the cause, but also at the
local elders and elites and the social marginalization for which they were
considered responsible. Evidence of this dissatisfaction is seen in the
emergence of armed bands of robbers, under the aegis of the demonstrations, who preyed on people regardless of the victim's political persua-
sion. Just as the *tapenta* had emulated their German exemplars as they set
about terrorizing the Grassfields, and the gendarmes now fleeced road
users in emulation of their perception of the new elites of the central
government, people took up arms in the 1990s to enrich themselves in

the manner they imagined the political and business elite were doing. In and around Bamenda, gangs operated with impunity. During this period, robberies were a regular feature of life, with rumors rife regarding the identity of the perpetrators and their possible patrons among the political elite. Aware that neither the state nor the nascent opposition had the power to guarantee their safety in a climate of increasing insecurity and political tension, young men again took the initiative that the opposition would later claim as its own, creating self-styled vigilante "antigangs" that roamed Bamenda and the Ndop plain to the north, where the gangs were operating.

Like gang membership, the antigang phenomenon (in fact a red herring since the antigangs *were* gangs) was yet another instrument adopted by disenchanted young men for organizing under the aegis of "ensuring security." At their inception, the antigangs were welcomed by the government administration and the opposition alike. The SDF saw in them a set of shock troops that they might deploy to deal with the frankly criminal gang members who were bringing the new party into disrepute, and more generally as a tactical support force to be used to organize rallies, provide bodyguards for party leaders, and the like. The government, for its part, looked to the antigangs as a force that would curtail the activities of the criminals, who it saw as essentially inseparable from the opposition party. It looked hopefully to the antigang members as young grassroots CPDM "party militants" who would oppose the SDF in its own stronghold of the North West Province and satisfy the population that the party in power was doing something about security. These gangs, however, never addressed the threat they were meant to combat. Too unskilled to confront the sophisticated, well-armed, and well-equipped gangs, they concentrated instead on singling out lone vagrants in crowded markets—defenseless individuals who could not possibly present a threat to them and whom they could easily scapegoat as "thieves."[23]

In early May 1992, following the example of the creation of antigangs in Bamenda and Ndop, the first antigang in Oku was formed on the night of May 26 by young men from Keyon, one of the quarters of the capital, Elak. By ten o'clock in the evening they were all grouped noisily in the marketplace at Elak. Soon afterward, they began fighting with people who were accusing them of being impostors, vigilantes, or SDF militants—members of "power" groups, as they were known, after the SDF slogan "Power to the People." Later that night, after the new antigang members dispersed, the local CPDM councilor came to me to denounce them as SDF militants. I was told that he would now call on the gendarmes to have them arrested. Indeed, although the antigangs in Bamenda and Ndop could cite the existence of violent criminal gangs as their raison d'être, there were no gangs to speak of in this rural part of the Grassfields for vigilantes to oppose. This clearly begs the question of why the young men who gathered that night felt there was a need for antigangs in this part of the country, but it further calls into question why antigangs existed in Bamenda and the Ndop plain, where to my knowledge they never confronted any gangs either. Clearly, the eradication of gangs was not the aim of antigangs, even if it had played a part in their inception and their rhetoric. Regardless of this conundrum, the senior district officer in Kumbo (the nearest administrative center to Oku) had been encouraging local communities in Bui Division to set up vigilante groups, and he was in complete approval of the news I gave him of the formation of an antigang in Oku when I met him two days later. Local government functionaries were thus clearly at loggerheads with one another at this early stage of the antigang phenomenon, with some identifying them as a force they could usefully harness, others as a boon to the opposition and a criminal danger.

Regardless of the absence of gangs, antigangs continued to operate in Oku and in many other parts of the Grassfields for the next two years, setting up roadblocks at night soon after the gendarmes had vacated theirs. Dragging planks studded with rusty nails across the road every few kilometers, the gendarmes would set up makeshift roadblocks by day in order to hold up traders on their way to market and other travelers. Although this routine was (and still is) carried out in the name of security, the real purpose of these road blocks was clear to all: they represented an opportunity for an irregularly paid paramilitary force to earn their salary by fleecing road users, who were systematically forced to pay bribes for the right of passage. As mentioned earlier, the gendarmes were accordingly seen as vicious parasites and accorded no legitimacy by the population. The reaction to the nocturnal version of the gendarmes—the young antigang members—was not as condemnatory as one might expect. These vigilantes were not impostors that one could clearly oppose to a legitimate security force. In fact, many suspected the gendarmes of being "sobels" ("soldiers by day, rebels by night"—a term borrowed from Sierra Leone), who waited for nightfall to turn into the much-feared gang members from whom they were supposed to be protecting people. With no legitimate security force to compare them to, most of the people I spoke with gave the vigilante youths the benefit of the doubt. These individuals guardedly looked to the youths for protection from political and economic deficits that—in the effective absence of organized crime and in their powerlessness against a felonious but largely nebulous state—they found hard to formulate explicitly.

One morning in early June 1992 the generalized sense of apprehension regarding the unstable political and economic climate was suddenly projected onto an unfortunate scapegoat. I was called from my house—at that time still in the capital, Elak—by a hubbub outside and emerged to see a crowd of perhaps fifty people cheerfully marching down the main street in a state of carnivalesque animation. Looking strangely incongruous in the general merriment, a tall, gaunt man stood in their midst, staring sullenly ahead as he walked. An alleged thief, he had supposedly been caught red-handed stealing a fowl. It was said that he came from the neighboring chiefdom of Mbesinaku (Mbese). Under intermittent downpours, he had been marched from his place of capture—one of the outlying market villages of Oku—to Elak by a large band of hectoring vigilantes. Once there, he was paraded down the main street to the palace, then back from there to the marketplace an hour or so later. Passersby gathered enthusiastically to taunt him as his captors chanted and beat a double bell of the type used by members of the *kwifon* society. He had been stripped down to a loincloth, his ears had been cut off, and he was being made to carry a large bag of stones. I was told by some of the animated onlookers that he would later be marched barefoot from Elak all the way to Kumbo, the capital of Nso' and the divisional headquarters, a good eight hours' walk down the mountain. At each village and chiefdom boundary along the way, he would be handed from one antigang vigilante group to another. It was widely assumed that he would be killed by a mob in Kumbo (a town that had been dubbed Baghdad on account of its fierce role in the political struggle) before he was ever handed over to the traditional or state authorities there.

A little less than two months after this event, on July 27, a meeting of lineage elders, village heads, and military society officers was held at the palace. The purpose of the meeting, chaired by the newly installed fon of Oku, was to facilitate the discussion of several matters of concern to him.[24] After the official items on the agenda, however, came an impromptu vote on the desirability of antigangs in Oku. First the fon himself made a speech critical of the groups; his talk was followed by the vote—conducted by a public show of hands—which was largely against. In his opening address to the meeting, the fon had emphasized the importance of an Oku identity

over a party-political one: parties must not divide the people of Oku, he
had warned, adding cryptically: "We who are seated here are stone. Let
anyone who is water beware."[25] Later in the meeting, once the fon had
made his speech about antigangs, it was hard not to interpret this opening remark as a veiled threat to anyone who might be tempted to support
the young antigang members, or indeed the SDF party, with which he saw
them as being in league.

Whether knowingly or not, the fon had chosen an apt metaphor for the
antigangs when he described his opponents as water among the stones
of his elites. For indeed, although water is at first sight insignificant in the
face of the weight, solidity, and permanence of stone, it nevertheless has
a quietly eroding effect that is as unstoppable as it is hard to detect in the
short term. Conversely, the apparent strength of stone can turn out to be
one of its weaknesses: stones are inflexible and can be crushed or cast
aside when the need arises. Brittle as they are, they shatter under pressure.
Nor can stones, in their immobility, do much to stop the rapid movement
of free-flowing water, or to arrest its ability to change the shape of stone
as it relentlessly cuts its seaward path. Youths or cadets—known in Oku
as "rattling" or "unattached" children (*yonde war*')—are indeed like water
in the Grassfields: far more numerous than the elites, they are also much
more mobile, less individualized and identifiable. Moreover, the imperma-
nent status of cadets as a category through which individuals pass rather
than one to which they permanently adhere (ideally at least) makes of it
an amorphous, movemented, "rattling" demographic category that is hard
to identify or to pin down and therefore to control. Like the water that
babbles (another meaning of *wark*') over the stones of Oku's streambeds,
young people are notoriously weak individually, but their sheer numbers
and the apparent inexhaustibility of their supply make them a powerful
force taken as a whole. Furthermore, not only are young people everywhere in the Grassfields, but they are nowhere. Just as they are themselves
constantly deracinated, flowing across the landscape of the region, and
forever outward from their chiefdoms of origin in the Grassfields toward
the sea in their exodus to the coastal plantations and the towns, their allegiance is always in doubt, shifting, and uncertain—indeed, cadets are
today, as ever, the floating population of the Grassfields, and as was said
of them in the UPC era, they provide the water in which the fish of local
insurrections can swim.

Daniel Jordan Smith (2004) notes that the vigilante groups that sprang
up in neighboring eastern Nigeria in the late 1990s meted out much more

violence on the ordinary citizenry than did the alleged criminals they were set up to deter. In the short period of their operations, from 2000 to 2002, they extrajudicially executed hundreds if not thousands of people, regularly killing dozens at a time in public places. All the while, they enjoyed unparalleled popular support. Smith identifies the original basis of support for these vigilante groups in the generalized state of insecurity associated with the 1999 inauguration of Obasanjo's civilian government and the wider "disappointments of democracy" for which it quickly became known. In a climate of economic crisis, ongoing kleptocracy, and increasingly glaring disparities in wealth, the myth spread that the children of elites were forming criminal gangs and terrorizing ordinary people. Moreover, the police were seen to be unable and unwilling to curb the excesses of these debauched elite criminals. This myth effectively reified the popular fears, anxieties, and frustrations of the masses with a state that had lost all legitimacy and was seen to exist solely for the purpose of the illicit enrichment of the few who had access to it. Moreover, Smith points out that the mundane brutality of the state—both symbolic and actual—against its citizens spread contagiously, desensitizing people to violence by failing to restrict its use to legitimate or legal ends for the security of the state. Once a group of people could be identified as the immediate source of people's insecurity and emmiseration—even if, as in Cameroon, these were scapegoats rather than the powerful political figures that the people truly reviled—the use of violence against them was a priori justified by a political climate that had long since rendered violence banal.

In Cameroon as in Nigeria, the scapegoating of alleged thieves has not brought about the social justice or the reform so eagerly desired by the people supporting the vigilantes. None of the elites profiteering from the neoliberal restructuring programs that so impoverished the great majority of ordinary West Africans was ever affected by vigilante "operations." On the contrary, many elites gained popular support by allying themselves with them. Likewise, the professional armed robbers of the Grassfields were never truly threatened by the antigangs. Ironically, like those accused of witchcraft, it was the poorest and the most marginal members of the population who were inevitably victimized by the vigilante groups. If we understand the antigangs of the 1990s not as a reformist movement against criminality but rather place it in the historical context of youth uprisings in the region, then it may no longer be judged an unmitigated failure. In contrast to their cohorts in Nigeria, the antigang members of the

Grassfields were relatively restrained. Never to my knowledge did they kill more than one alleged criminal at a time, and they did not incarcerate suspects with a view toward executing them en masse at a later date.

Much of their activity was primarily symbolic or performative: whereas the gendarmes illegitimately blocked roads to extort money from their victims, the young antigang members blocked roads with the support of the local community, who were their kin and affines. Their interventions can be seen as a communal performance in which the adults who were not antigang members played the role of audience for a masquerade or ritual performance. Indeed, blocking roads with medicinal preparations has long been a practice used to ward off witches in the Grassfields. I have in chapter 4 outlined the ways in which such beliefs reified concrete dangers in the form of slave raiders and labor recruiters such that ritual defenses against cannibal witches reified the concrete dangers posed by slave hunters. Likewise in the era of the UPC uprising, practices of blocking paths and roads once again came to the fore. The antigangs now extended this practice deeper still into the political imaginary of the postcolony using their roadblocks to ward off the new malefactors of a sorcerous state. And while the police and gendarmerie were seen to be not only exogenous but also dangerous, corrupt, and inept, the antigang members reversed the moral order of coercive power, using it, unlike the state, for morally sanctioned—if often tragic—ends. Yet the crosscutting similarities between the antigang members and the gendarmes they emulated in their quest for alterity preclude any easy Manichaeism opposing one to the other. As Janet Roitman (2005) shows, the gendarmes have their own justifications for their illicit actions, just as the antigangs were quick to exonerate the murders they performed.

In their ambivalent appropriation of the authority of a power seen to be exogenous and amoral if not hostile, the antigangs were following in the footsteps of the *basoge,* the free boys, and the maquisards. Like them, they embodied the armory of their enemies—in this case, gangs and the state security forces—and transformed an external danger into a new, alteric way of being that sanctioned youth as a political force in the Grassfields. Not only did this latest manifestation of youth uprising in the Grassfields fundamentally challenge the hegemony of the state in the 1990s, but it simultaneously questioned the supremacy of the elders and the palace elite so closely associated with it. It is therefore not surprising that fons and elite politicians alike—despite the fact that the latter had emerged from the ranks of the cadets of the late colonial period themselves—ultimately turned against the antigang phenomenon.

Discourse/Counterdiscourse, Power/Antipower:
The Counterweight of Youth in Grassfields Politics

Jean-Francois Bayart ([1979] 1985), Peter Geschiere (1997), and Michael Rowlands and Jean-Pierre Warnier (1988) have all shown that one cannot usefully distinguish between the political and the cosmological spheres in Cameroon. The political fortunes of the elite are inseparably intertwined with their clients in their natal villages, and "local" witchcraft beliefs and value systems are used as gauges of the ethics, power, and legitimacy of national politicians and bureaucrats, and as explanations for their seemingly insatiable appetites. The political context in Cameroon is characterized by the haziness of the boundary dividing political practice at the national and the local levels, or state bureaucracy from kinship networks. It should therefore not be surprising to find that the antigangs' appropriation of power was ultimately more compatible with a long-standing pattern of youth resistance in the Grassfields than with the modernist political ideal of combating crime: the *basoge,* the *tapenta,* and the free boys had all to some extent presented themselves as new "third forces" in the mould of the colonial state—embodying its forms of discipline but deploying them to support an independent youth agenda outside both the control of the state and the legitimizing discourse of palatine authority.

This book has thus far concentrated on the hegemonic practices deployed by local elites and state bodies, and the ways in which these practices—whether masked performances and mythological discourses, or the embodiment of military discipline—were used to propagate and to support gerontocratic and colonial authority structures at the expense of the majority, whose labor these systems exploited and depended upon. But such hegemonic structures were never totalizing or unopposed by those they were intended to subdue, as the history of youth uprisings in the Grassfields demonstrates. If cadets could ever have been conceived of as "docile bodies" subjected to the totalizing hegemony of the elite, their very overt struggles against the elite in the late nineteenth and twentieth centuries call for a radical rethinking of the political significance of cadets in the eighteenth and nineteenth centuries, on the one hand, and of the ways in which memories of the violence and insecurity of this period might still inform cadets' experience of their contemporary plight on the other. Although overt forms of resistance such as popular uprisings and rebellions seem not to have been possible for cadets before the colonial period, other practices may have permitted youths to embody more subtle, covert forms of contestation and struggle from the precolonial period right up to the present. I now examine those practices, including a discussion of salaried labor as an escape from dependency for young people. I also consider the ways in which the palace masquerades I have discussed so far in terms of the discourses of power of the palatine elite may have been appropriated by the disenfranchised cadets and submitted to a counterhegemonic reading.

Although forced labor came to represent "conditions analogous to slavery" not only in the rhetoric of European reformists but also in the popular imaginary of Grassfields youth, some young men decided of their own accord to seek work on the coastal plantations early on in the colonial period. Despite the shockingly low expectations of survival for these laborers, the chance to earn a salary independent of the local elite and to escape the lifelong bachelorhood to which cadets were otherwise condemned made the journey to the coast a chance worth taking for many—and so the rivers of the Grassfields kept flowing to the sea. Thus although the German colonial authorities undoubtedly colluded with local elites and exacerbated the problem of slavery in Cameroon, the plantations they set up not only perpetuated slavery under another name but also created a new labor force, a fraction of which was even constituted by voluntary labor.[26] The essential difference between systems of slavery that had preceded colonization and the forced labor on the plantations and roads was the monetization of the labor system and the payment of salaries in a new currency that was no longer circumscribed within a restricted sphere of exchange goods: if the plantation laborers survived to the end of their contracts, and if they had not spent all of their money on food, lodging, and other extortionately priced subsistence goods on the plantation, they were left with a sum of money that they could transform into prestige goods to take back to their chiefdoms.

The prospect of so many young men managing to ennoble themselves without recourse to the palace authorities must have been a truly worrying prospect for some fons and was clearly a motivating factor in the complaints that some of them made to the German authorities to the effect that young men were being allowed to keep or spend the money they had made on the plantations rather than presenting it to their elders upon their return. As Frederick Cooper points out (2000, 119), the colonial system put an end to the transatlantic trade in slaves and gave local slaves the opportunity to flee harsh masters, to transfer their dependence to other groups, to redefine relations of dependence, and to seek salaried employment. However analogous forced labor was to slavery, forced labor was taken advantage of by those of whom it took advantage: just as Grassfields slaves who were settled in Cameroon had often managed to do well with their masters, even sometimes to thrive (Warnier 2006), so too forced and voluntary laborers managed in many instances to take advantage of the marginal opportunities presented by the "reforms" of the colonists. Even the grossest forms of colonial exploitation could be turned to youths' advantage. As Jean-François Bayart (1989, 151 [trans. mine]) puts it regarding French West Africa as a whole: "The era of the Whites became the era of insolence, when 'children,' 'their mouths on fire,' came out of their silence and, adding insult to injury, appropriated the sartorial art, the art of *'la sape'* [the practice of dressing in European designer clothing]. School, new media, and salaried employment all procured for them an empire of extroversion that each day further escaped the comprehension of the elders."

The youth revolts of the colonial era may not, however, have been entirely unprecedented. It has often been taken for granted by the colonial authorities and ethnographers alike in Cameroon that the palatine and gerontocratic systems of the Grassfields were of ponderous antiquity and stability (hence the German and later English title of king conferred on the much more ambiguous and embattled position of fonship).[27] Although the colonial era certainly provided the first opportunity for young men—and to some extent women—to bypass the elders of the Grassfields so brazenly, a closer reading of the palace performances discussed in the preceding chapters suggests that symbolic forms of domination were never unequivocal or unquestioned by the majority whose domination they naturalized.

Michel Foucault ([1975] 1977) spends the first part of his history of the French judicial system examining the performance of execution as a contested public spectacle. Although this spectacle was meant to demonstrate and to enact the ultimate power of the king over his subjects, Foucault points out the reversals and ambiguities to which such a ritual was exposed, ambiguities that would ultimately lead to its replacement with a more "humane" (and more politically effective) form of discipline.[28] In the same manner that the saturnalia of the gallows gave rise to carnivalesque outbursts of hostility to the crown that paradoxically nurtured a sense of solidarity between criminals and peasants, so too the myths of origin of the Grassfields' chiefly lines not only served the palace elite in their efforts to naturalize their domination but were also appropriated by the victims of this domination to forge oppositional identities and to lend coherence to the histories of dispersal, fragmentation, and oppression of diasporic peoples. Notably, these myths gave members of the floating population and victims of slavery the opportunity to project their marginalization in terms of the witchcraft of the forests of the spirit world. And although thus far I have discussed the palace masks predominantly in terms of the totalizing subjection of the cadets that they facilitate, it is also clear that the pleasure that cadets experience in the course of these performances is more than a mere trap set by the mask to attract its victim but rather centered on the aporetic nature of myth and performance, of whose indeterminacy cadets never failed to take advantage.

According to the doxic view of the palace authorities, the fons' embodiment of the destructive forces of the exogenous intruders afforded a means by which these forces could be transformed and redeployed to amplify the power of the state. Seen from the point of view of the palace elite, the seminal violence in which the mythical fons are alleged in the myths to have indulged and the violence of the palace terror masks exemplify the dangers that cadets and members of the floating population represent, and they consequently naturalize slavery as a positive, domesticating force. From the point of view of the cadets and slaves at the base of the pyramid of state, however, the violence of the myths and of the palace masks would have been attractive for different reasons. If the mythical fons had succeeded in founding states, it was by means of the schisms that top-heavy lineages prompted among their disaffected youth, who then set off in search of new lands to settle. What made the early fons heroes and sacred figures was not their coercive control over their people for the sake of the expansion of the elite hierarchy and the centralization of the state, but rather their status as cadets and members of the floating population set upon their peripatetic journeys by slave raids or gerontocratic domination in their homelands.

With myths as with masks, the oral canon of Oku is not only the preserve of the elite but equally of the cadets who play an active role in the propagation and the interpretation of the events that the origin myths recall. Because the telling and retelling of myths and stories are not restricted to an elite sphere of griots in the Grassfields but rather enthusiastically taken up by the cadets, the cadets are free to read into the stories of exploitation, victimization, and rootlessness of the refugees who would become fons the injustice of their own positions in the order of power. The very myths deployed as a discourse of legitimation by the elite are appropriated by the disenfranchised as a counterdiscourse. If the elite of the expanding states of the Grassfields deployed the myths of origin and the terror masks of *kwifon* as a centrifugal force binding exogenous forces to the polity, cadets could see them as a vindication of their centripetal tendencies: they too could walk in the footsteps of founding fons when they left their compounds and sought the means to found new independent lineages or nonaligned third forces.

Similarly, when cadets take pleasure in the performances of the terror masks that seem to orchestrate their own subjection—and no one has forgotten that today's masks were yesterday's executioners—they may be admiring the power of the palace elite, but they can only do so by bearing witness to its violence. Whatever the violence taking place in the palace courtyard is said by the elite to represent or memorialize, and whatever aggressor it is meant to vilify, it is perpetrated by the palace authorities, and its victims are none other than the cadets, the marginalized youth of the chiefdom itself. For them, the masks are not a *performance* of violence whose original instance occurred in another time and another place. The masquerades are not an inconsequential folkloric play depicting foreign aggressors and foreign victims. The violence is not performed—it is real; it is not a text *about* something—it simply *is*. The masquerade happens in the present, in the palace, and its violence is perpetrated by the palace *kwifon* masks on the cadets of the chiefdom. For the cadets, the masquerade is not primarily a commemorative event or a performance; it does not represent anything but rather engages the cadets in a confrontation that is itself the originary event—not the memory but the source of the memory, not the representation of the event but the event itself confusing past and present in its perpetual recurrence.

Although the palace compound is renowned for its strict codification of behavior and the humility (not to say the humiliation) it imposes on visitors, the effect on cadets of being subjected to the onslaught of the palace masks is ambiguous and indeterminate. Youths take great pleasure in succumbing to the blind panic of fleeing from the masks. Why then is this violent form of subjection a source of euphoria to the disenfranchised cadets? Because, at the same time as it points performatively to some other danger external to itself, it is—necessarily—an act in itself: the performance of putatively exogenous violence is by the same token the actual practice and execution of violence by the palace itself; it therefore reveals to its victims the spectacle of the naked coercion at the heart of palatine hegemony, even as it masks it. No matter how often the masquerade recurs, it is never entirely a memory, a folkloric commemoration of something past, but each time, again, an embodied experience of contemporary violence that resurrects the ineffable but unforgotten violence of the past, bringing the struggles of contemporary youth into a dialectical relation with the unfinished struggles of their forebears. In the following chapter I examine how cadets, in addition to their agonistic engagement with the masks of the palace, contest the elite discourse of masking by producing their own masks and performing their own masquerades in the outlying villages of the chiefdom.

CHAPTER SEVEN

The Death of Tears: Mortuary Rites and the Indeterminacy of Dance

Does not the fantasy of an alternative society and its exteriorisation "nowhere" work as one of the most formidable contestations of what is? — Paul Ricoeur (1986, 16)

It would be difficult to exaggerate the popularity of masking in the Grassfields as a whole, and in Oku in particular. In every village in the chiefdom, each established lineage is likely to have at least one mask group housed in its main compound (*kɔbɛy kərarene*), and participation in mask societies is practiced universally by men from early childhood through old age. Nor does village masking exclude women. When three- to nine-year-old boys start to mask, their sisters will be watching and dancing on the periphery of the group, learning appropriate forms of participation at this early stage (Argenti 2001). Later in life, adult women become central to masked performances, despite the rhetoric of female exclusion: not only do they prepare the food for the dancers, musicians, and other participants, which is an essential part of the celebration, but they also dance and sing in their own right. At a more fundamental level, moreover, lineage-group masks are performed *for* women and are in many ways *about* women.[1] Finally, as women age, they are welcomed into the women's *fəmbiɛn* society—a society renowned in the Grassfields not only for its political activism at both the local and national levels but also for its ritual potency and its own "mask" (*kəkum fəmbiɛn*).[2] So central is masking to the social life of Oku that it occupies a small army of acolytes, who produce the necessary paraphernalia, run the secret societies, and organize the many rites of passage for new members and the performances in honor of deceased ones.[3]

So far, this book has concentrated on the palace masks and the palatine discourse of power. These masks, however, represent only a small minority of the plethora of masks and masking groups in the chiefdom. This chapter turns to the much more numerous masks of the peripheral lineages of the outlying villages of the chiefdom, which perform in groups (known as *kəkum kənɔn, əmkum əmnɔn*), and to the counterdiscourse that they may engender among those excluded from the palatine hierarchy.

All grown men are likely to be members of at least one masking group or society, if not several, in their village, and many men found new masking societies in their youth. Although nominally placed under the control and patronage of a compound elder, the majority of these mask societies are established by bachelors returning to their compounds after a long sojourn abroad. These young "children of the compound" have typically been living outside the kingdom for an extended period, occasionally as civil servants or entrepreneurs, more often as traditional healers, wage laborers, or petty traders. When speaking about masks, Grassfields people are careful not to contradict a general myth that masks originate in the liminal spaces (the forests, gorges, or watery areas) of the kingdom or outside the kingdom altogether. Thus, myths about the origins of mask groups in the forest surrounding the kingdom often tell of a hunter who suddenly surprises a mask in the forest and coaxes it to return to his compound in the village. These myths of the liminal, wild, or foreign origins of masks now equate forest and town, however, and young men returning from waged labor in the plantations on the coast or the towns outside the polity are said to "bring the masks back" with them from the new urban hunting grounds of the nation-state.

Joining the secret societies that possess the mask groups is a costly endeavor, while officiating in such a society is very time-consuming, as is dancing. During the dry season men may be asked to perform as often as once a week or more, with each performance involving at least a whole day of preparation and festivities, and journey time often adding another two days to the event. Given the violence inherent in the dominant model of masked dance performed by the palace societies, as discussed in previous chapters, and the fact that it is precisely the young men of the outlying villages of Oku who are called on to be the victims of the masks' stampedes at the palace, the villagers' passion for masking may seem paradoxical. Particularly when one considers that the lineage-group masks are clearly modeled on the palace Fuləŋgaŋ performance, why, one might well ask, do the young seem to re-create in their villages the forms of domination to which they have been subjected by the palace masquerades? The structure of the village-based secret societies is in many ways a microcosm of the hierarchy of the palace elite, complete with titles, offices, regalia, costly rites of passage, fines for transgressions, traditional medicines, and so on. And many of the frightening elements of the palace masks are also taken up by the village masks, as if the cadets excluded from influence at the center of the chiefdom intended perversely to re-create their domination by the palace all over again in their own compounds, embodying their subjection to palatine authority over and over again. As I argue later in the chapter, it would clearly not suffice to conclude that the cadets of the villages of Oku are laboring under some sort of false consciousness that forces them to reproduce the means of their own subjection. There are subtle but important differences between the masquerades of the palace and the village lineages, differences that make of village masking not simply a wholesale reproduction or an imitation of palace masking but rather a transformation of it.

Just as the motivation and the allegiance of the young spectators at the palace masking ceremonies were ambiguous, so too the allegiance to the palace by the young cadets who founded their own mask societies and by the dancers who join them in performing the masks cannot be taken for granted. This chapter and the next chart the subtle transformations that the dominant palace model of group masking, as evinced by the *kwifon* Fuləŋgaŋ group discussed in chapter 5, undergoes as it is devolved to the village. Ultimately, the chapter explores whether the discourse of masking disseminated by the palace—according to which all masking groups are local replications of its central, authoritative canon as exemplified by the Fuləŋgaŋ masquerade and the royal *kəkumndjaŋ* procession—is not countered by a model in which cadets look not only inward but also outside the kingdom and the capital for their inspiration and seek to engage directly with an experiential reality that is not mediated by the palace nor territorially bounded.

One of the prime methods the palace uses to exert control over village masking societies is its insistence that new ones present themselves at the palace to obtain official approval from the fon before they may perform publicly.[4] Partly for this reason, the young cadets who found new groups hand them over to the patronage of their elders, who in turn curry favor at the palace in hopes of having the groups accepted as legitimate. In addition to mere approval, the fon, if he is so inclined, may award special privileges and marks of honor (*bur'maa*) to those masks (or patrons) he particularly admires, further stamping the mark of the palace on new mask societies. It thus seems at first glance as if village masking is simply an extension outward, toward the periphery of the chiefdom of the palatine discourse—a means by which the palace elite maintain their hegemony performatively at the heart of every village. Certainly, there is an irradiation of influence from the palace to the periphery of the chiefdom by means of certain conservative masking institutions at the village level, and I chart these later in the chapter. Nevertheless, these exist in a state of constant tension with dissonant processes at the local level that perpetually undermine elite, conservative traditions by the introduction of new practices and the alternative interpretation of old practices. The process whereby the fon grants acceptance to new masks is a case in point. Intended as a demonstration of centralized control over the performative practices of the periphery, it is often fraught with tension, in practice, as the following case suggests.

How to Catch a Mask: Myths of Origin and Stories of Acquisition

Kɛŋkɔs is the feather-headed group mask (known as a "feather mask," *kəkum evəl*) of Ba Keming's compound in the village of Mbock-Jikijem in which I lived from 1992 to 1994. The present head of the compound, Fay Keming, is the first one in his lineage to have been installed as a titled lineage elder (known as a *fay* or *ŋkfum*). His father, Wantɔk Keming, was a son of the fon born of a royal wife during his rule.[5] Unlike many other mask groups in Oku, Kɛŋkɔs is the only one of its name in the kingdom. Fay Keming and others will tell the casual observer that it came from the neighboring chiefdom of Kom at the time when Nianggo was head of the compound. The idea that the mask group "came" as if of its own volition is common in Oku. In practice, compound heads or their male dependants negotiate with the owners of a mask that they wish to acquire for the rights to reproduce it in their own compound.

Most of the mask groups in the kingdom are nevertheless associated with an origin myth that recounts the arrival of the masks from the forest—much like the myths about fons. These are elaborated to different degrees for different groups, with separate areas of the forest in Oku cited as the point of origin of different groups, and other details and peculiarities cited to differentiate one myth from another. In addition to these myths, initiates recount stories about the acquisition of a mask group from another compound in the relatively recent past—usually in living memory. The two types of narrative are not seen as contradictory, self-negating, or problematic; rather, they are context dependent, with each type appropriate for different people in different situations. Just as the stories of acquisition are not discussable by noninitiates, so too origin myths, related mainly by women and children, are wholly inappropriate for use by adult initiates. One aged informant, Fay Keming of Eghok Ntul (a close adviser to the fon), once refused to discuss origin myths with me, apparently because of my gender. "Are you a woman?" he asked indignantly; "those stories are only for fooling women!" (*sə bɛl əbkui*). The following story, as it was told to me by Nobfon, the mask group's caretaker, and Fay Keming, the present head of the compound, is not an origin myth (for "fooling women") but a narrative of acquisition; it is the type of story told by adult males, especially married men and initiates, to one another regarding the acquisition of a mask.

At the time when the palace wanted to hold a new fon in 1956, Ngum Ngek of Ba Keming's compound was sought for the office, and [as other prospective titleholders are reputed to have done before him] he ran away to [the neighboring chiefdom of] Kom. Nobfon [then a young man] went into exile with Ngum Ngek, and lived with him in Kom for many years, but when Nianggo [the successor to Ba Keming's compound] died, Nobfon returned to Oku, leaving Ngum Ngek in Kom, where he later died. When Nobfon returned to his compound in Oku, he brought with him the xylophone that he and Ngum Ngek had been playing in Kom for the past six years. It was only when they had been playing this xylophone in Ba Keming's compound for some time that the mask [*kəkum*] came to the compound. [This is often the case with the "arrival" of new masks. The xylophone will be made (or brought from elsewhere) and played in the compound courtyard for some time, the music being perfected all the while, until a driver mask (*kəshiɛŋɛnɛ*) bursts forth into the courtyard one day, sending the women and children running for cover. It is thus a single mask rather than the whole group that first makes a dramatic appearance in the compound. The first one to arrive, presaging the arrival of the others, is always the driver mask. In the case of Kɛŋkɔs, Fay Keming related with great mirth]. The driver went running straight past the small crowd that had gathered in the compound to witness its arrival from Kom, and continued at high speed down the road to the Catholic church. Che Keming—he was not yet a titled *fay* in those days— chased it down to the church followed by some of the enthusiastic crowd, then on through bush paths to the village quarter of Ketel [a few kilometers down the mountain]. Keming finally caught up with the mask there, gave it two live fowls to assuage it, and convinced it to follow him back to the compound.

Nobfon and his brother Fay Keming then went on to tell me the story of the mask group's (mandatory) appearance at the palace to present itself to the fon for approval.

The group danced, then the fon praised the masks' "father" for having acquired them, telling him that a xylophone was a thing for women to behold, but a mask group was a thing for men: he had made a man of himself. [As is the tradition in Oku], the fon then gave a name of his own choosing to the new group, calling it *ntshar' laasə*—red bangles [after one of the masks that was wearing a pair of them]. [As usual] he then offered gifts to one of the masks: a cutlass, a ŋkɛŋ plant, and a club. But the mask threw all three gifts onto the ground right under the eyes of the fon, who in turn declared in a fit of anger that the mask would never dance with anything in its hands from that day on. That was how this mask came to be called dry/empty hands [*əbyɔ əbyumə*]. Undeterred by this first refusal, the fon then gave a spear to *kemeŋse*, one of the other masks in the group, which still dances with it today. On the same day, Fay Keming's son's wife bore a son, and to commemorate the event he was named Befntok —"spoils the palace." [Nobfon and Fay Keming burst into laughter at this point in their story.][6]

Nobfon referred to *əbyɔ əbyumə* that day as "the mother of the masks" (*nɔ əmkum*), because it was the first one to appear in their compound.[7] According to the origin myth, which posits the arrival of the masks of their own volition, all the other masks in the group came "behind it" (later in time), "like her brood behind the mother hen." In spite of this, it has a distinctly male persona. Nobfon, Fay Keming, and other initiates of the group refer affectionately to it and its antics at the palace, and it has a personality that distinguishes it from any other mask in the group or, for that matter, from any other driver mask in Oku. When it goes out to perform the solo display (*shiɛŋgə*) to announce the imminent arrival of the rest of the group, it moves in an extraordinarily slow and mournful manner—highly uncharacteristic of the typical *shiɛŋə* performance, which is full of bravado and suppressed violence. At this stage, says Nobfon, "you cannot guess to look at it that it will dance at all, but when it dances, it dances with power and energy!"[8] "It smashes stones!" Fay Keming added, in praise of its dancing.[9] The preliminary, slothful appearance of the mask is in stark contrast not only to the dance of the group as a whole but also to its original arrival at the compound as recounted by Fay Keming. For the mask to dance as if it had no power when it first appears is perceived by those of the mask's compound and others in the village as a rhetori-

FIGURE 29. Ɔbyɔ ɔbyumɔ (empty hands) of the mask group
Kɔŋkɔs performing its idiosyncratic, listless shiɛŋgɔ.

cal device protesting the fact that the fon effectively disarmed the driver
mask when it appeared at the palace: what good is an unarmed driver?
Indeed, during the performance of the mask group as a whole, another
mask plays the role of the driver.

The headdress of the driver in a feather-headed mask group is often
a small hard skullcap or helmet known as a ŋkaa, which the driver wears
with dreadlocks and two small teeth or claws at the back, tipped with a
red substance generally presumed to be medicinal. An outsider, on first
seeing a feather-headed mask group, might think that members do not
have individuated masks because they do not wear carved masks portraying different faces. They do, however, have all the identities of "wooden-
headed" groups: the two "captains" (kam), one at the front and one the

back; two or three women (ŋgɔn—the word means "marriageable young woman/virgin" but also applies to this particular mask); the driver; and kənfiibin, "he who takes the dance." These identities are distinguished in various ways. The ŋgɔnsə and kənfiibin, like the kəshiɛŋɛnɛ just mentioned, have helmet-type headdresses rather than feather ones. The two kam have feather headdresses but wear gowns woven with human hair (kəbam nɔ ŋgsə, literally "bag of hair").[10]

Although according to origin myths a kəkum is a forest creature that is acquired by a compound by being lured into the courtyard by the regular and skillful playing of a xylophone, narratives of acquisition belie these myths, revealing the man-made reality of masks and including details of how they were commissioned and produced. The origin myths constitute a genre or canon that upholds the palace discourse of masking, excluding women, children, and the noninitiated from the secret of their production and making of the masks something terrible and fearsome. In contradistinction to this, narratives of acquisition could be seen as an opposing genre that constitutes a counterdiscourse and subverts the hegemony of the palace. Within the canon of these narratives, the seriousness, conservatism, and secrecy of the elite discourse are confronted with a ribald, humorous, and revelatory oral tradition that is much less homogeneous, is willfully nonmystical and realist, and introduces laughter and farce to the realm of masking.

From a Bakhtinian perspective, it is possible to see the political relevance of the playful, the comic, and the grotesque in popular or folk culture—the culture of those excluded from elite forms of culture. In his work on Rabelais, Bakhtin ([1957] 1968) examines the historic role of carnival in medieval Europe and delineates his theory of the grotesque: a world of inversion, reversal, and degradation that confronted the inequality, the mysticism, the seriousness, and the asceticism of official power structures with an anarchic double of corporeal profanity, joy, irreverence, and radical egalitarianism. As the ever-present flip side of official political power and class distinction, Bakhtin's analysis of carnival presents it not as a momentary rite of rebellion in Gluckman's functionalist (1963) sense but as an ever-present dimension of the lived world. As such, the carnivalesque was not a mere performance for passive spectators that was restricted to certain exceptional feast days and ultimately intended to return the world to its precarnival normality, but rather an inherent aspect of the agonistic relations between the classes that constituted nothing less than a "second world" or "second life" that was a permanent aspect of the struggles and tensions of the political world (Bakhtin [1957] 1968, 5–6, 11, 33). The key to this second dimension of the lived world was laughter, understood as a ritual, communal form of ecstasy in which all the people united and participated.

In the story of the arrival of the first mask of Kɛŋkɔs, we also find the element of laughter as a central feature. When the mask first arrives, it breaks normal rules of behavior and protocol by running straight past the compound, causing confusion, chaos, and hilarity. Later, it behaves in an irreverent and outrageous manner at the palace blessing ceremony by insulting the fon. Finally, this lese-majesté is considered so comical by one of the mask's owners that he enshrines the event by naming one of his children after it: Spoils the Palace (Befntok). On the face of it, the masks of the village simply reproduce those of the palace and must seek the blessing of the fon in order to be legitimized. However, the grotesque Rabelaisian aspect of village masking inverts the seriousness of the palace masks, ultimately opening the door to the second world for those normally excluded from power while simultaneously effectuating a "comic uncrowning" of the king (Bakhtin [1957] 1968, 11).

Death and the Indeterminacy of Dance

Dancing on the Grave: Youth, Elites, and the Will to Life in the Grassfields

The mortuary rites occasioned by a death—a series of ceremonies known as the "death of tears" (*ɛykwo əmshie*) to distinguish it from the memorial celebration that comes years later and is known as the "death of dancing" (*ɛykwo ebinenene*)—are complex and protracted in Oku, lasting at least four days. I describe them below only insofar as they involve the participation of masking and other related performances.[11] The news of a death spreads quickly in a village, and its communication is from the very first a form of song: the women closest to the deceased immediately move from the deathbed through the village, calling out in loud modulated wails that are recognized as the announcement of a death as well as an expression of personal grief. Older women will not only wail but also sing eloquent laments about the life of the deceased, of their relationship to him or her, and, in the case of the newly widowed, of their anxieties in the face of a future of isolation, poverty, and loneliness. The burial, which usually happens the next day, is again punctuated by singing—this time by the young men, who stamp the grave down as the earth is poured back in over the cadaver. Prefiguring the choreography of the masked dance that will happen a year or more later on the occasion of the memorial celebration, the men climb into the burial pit and dance on the coffin, packing the earth rhythmically over it with their feet as the earth is shoveled in. As they do so, they punctuate their rhythmic stamping with ribald songs about death known as "grave-stamping" songs (*tshin isɛy*).

Some of these songs are political in nature, referring to recent historical events and to rumors about local and state-sponsored violence against Oku people. Nevertheless, the spirit of such occasions, especially during "good dies" (marking the death of someone who had led a full life and had had children), is irreverent and joking. As they stamp, the young men tease in particular the women closest to the grave, calling out to them,

FIGURE 30. Young men stamp the grave of Pa Tombuh in Ediom, Jikijem (October 17, 1992), as they sing.

"you, get crying!" (*ɛyə dii*!), and making them laugh in spite of themselves, or they poke fun at an elder firing his Dane gun in an ungainly fashion: "who's he trying to kill?" Some of the favorite refrains during my research went as follows:

CALL: You call!
RESPONSE: Your call kills us!
CALL ONLY: Harvest the corn!
CALL ONLY: A ho! Get stamping![12]

One of the longer songs is wryly called "The Good House Is in the Ground":

CALL: O house!
CHORUS (repeated after each call): The good house is in the ground!
CALL: You will die!
CALL: You will go!
CALL: Fons [must also die]!
CALL: Even *nkfəmse* [titled lineage elders]!
CALL: O house!
CALL: My brother [exclamation of alarm]!
CALL: Will die!
CALL: My stepbrother!
CALL: My/your friend![13]

Another of the longer songs is known as "Jelly Coil," named for a fashionable hairstyle among young women:

CALL: A child bears a child and throws it into a pit latrine.
RESPONSE: Oh wu o wu oo! [The response is the same for every call and has no meaning.]
CALL: A child throws her child away because of jelly coil!
CALL: The child cries here and is heard in Buunjin [name of a quarter in the village of Ngham]!
CALL: When they step on the infant and it bites them, they think of their mother! [Young, inexperienced mothers return to their parents' compound when in difficulties.]
CALL: *Dung, dung, dung*, chasing a husband [lit., "behind" a husband]! [*Dung, dung* relates to the young woman's buttocks swinging suggestively as she seeks to seduce a man.]

CALL: A child throws away a child just because of jelly coil!

CALL: The prostitute throws away her child because of jelly coil!

CALL: Leaves a corn beer house to enter a beer house!

CALL: The child cries here and they hear it in the husband's house![14]

The singing in all of these songs is high-spirited but the humor black. In the song "You Call!" the one who sings the first line, or call, of the song addresses god (Feyin Mbom), the spirits (*mjin*), or alternatively death itself in an apparently serious and respectful manner, but in the response line of the song—"Your call kills us!"—the respondents unveil the full meaning of the couplet, which is satirical, taunting an anthropomorphic death for its malign interventions in the world of the living. The call "Harvest the corn!" similarly taunts death, entreating it to do its best in the well-known Grassfields metaphor for death of reaping the harvest (a metaphor also common in the West, in the tradition of the grim reaper and his scythe). Part of the ambivalent humor and tension of this simple call arises from the fact that the singers do not take up a clear position in relation to the authorial voice of the call: as in the last song, they may be the living who are subject to the unpredictable caprices of death, but because of the lack of a personal pronoun in the call, they may also be understood to be intoning the voice of death itself calling for his harvest of human beings. That no moral position is taken in relation to the "harvest" in the call also heightens its tension and ambivalence. Without any evident moral position, the call can be seen as either a dark celebration of death or as a protest against its injustice.

The call "A ho! Get stamping!" is a call of encouragement by the lead singer to the other young men stamping the earth over the deceased. As they stamp, they shake their right fists in the air in front of themselves, a gesture often performed in other dances with Dane guns and based on the way spears were used in battle. The bodily memory of the use of the spear in battle in the distant past is thus transposed to the ceremonial use of the Dane gun in the present, and then to the burial of one's covillager. The martial gate of the dance suggests that the deceased had died on the battlefield, or that this confrontation with death was itself the battle, with death being taunted by the young men's ludic agonism and their professed impatience to reach their true home underground. At the same time, the organization of the work gang as a line of men being marched onward by an imperious, domineering master who shouts out orders recalls the role of the kashieŋenɛ or driver mask in relation to the line of masks discussed in the next chapter.

While the song "You Call" is metaphorical in its reference to death, the longer song "The Good House Is in the Ground" is explicit, referring to the inevitability of returning to one's "home" in the land of the dead, which, like the resting place of corpses, is often depicted as subterranean. As in the case of the next song, it is also explicitly insubordinate, satirically pointing out that elites such as fons and lineage elders die too. Although it is unacceptable in normal circumstances to mention the death of a fon (which is euphemized as his temporarily being "lost"), the ribald antics of the burial ceremony provide the young men the license to critique their elders by evoking, to the ominous rhythm of their stamping, the leveling effects of the human condition.

The final song, "Jelly Coil," refers to a hairstyle popular among young women in which hair is straightened and made glossy by the application of a manufactured gel sold in local markets. The song suggests disapproval and is apparently a conservative remonstration or protest against young women's supposed narcissism—a tendency also parodied in the masks representing young women and discussed in the next chapter. One may wonder why young men seem to be taking up the position of conservative elders in warning women of the dangers of seduction and the lure of modern cosmetics and fashions. Their concern with women's supposed narcissism and failure to nurture a child may, however, also be read as a veiled critique of those young women who would seek to seduce elders and become child brides of elite polygamists, thus denying impoverished young bachelors the chance to marry. The accusation of women throwing unwanted babies into the latrine—what might approvingly be interpreted by elites as a conservative form of misogyny—may connote young men's anxiety that their lovers will destroy their relationships, and even abort or kill their children, in order to remain eligible brides for elderly elite suitors.

Whatever the possible second meanings of the songs as a discourse about elites and social polarization in the chiefdom, the very juxtaposition of death with ribald songs about devious sexualities, and illicit relationships, and the grotesque representation of death as darkly comical all serve to render the burial an opportunity for carnivalesque deportment among the young men who stamp the grave down. Just as the stories about village masks, mentioned earlier, relive the seriousness of palace masking as a grotesque joke, so too the death of commoners in the village repeats the death of kings as farce.

At the same time as the songs reiterate the uncrowning inscribed in the narrative about Kɛŋkɔs, however, they also introduce the theme of birth and regeneration. The ground in Oku is sacred not only as the place of death but also as the realm of the ancestors from which all new life emerges (Argenti 2001). In this way, the ribald lines in the songs associating death with the ground and with agricultural labor are not simply a form of black humor but rather a celebration of the regenerative capacities of the earth. In this light, the grotesque elements of the songs referring to women's sexuality emerge as the very opposite of conservative censure or mere vulgarity and reveal the corporeal celebration of fertility as represented by a womblike earth.[15] The insults and abuse that the Kɛŋkɔs mask levels against the fon and the lurid suggestions the song makes about women are thus part and parcel of the same genre or discourse—the will to life that unites the marginalized against the stultifying permanence of autocratic power and the finality of social existence in biological death for those without children.[16] The ritual insults and the sexual innuendo of the young men's songs seek to subvert the twin obliteration of gerontocratic power and childless death by celebrating change, regeneration, fertility, and renewal.

Although in the previous song the call and response are identical to each other, each line repeated by the group after being sung by the caller, some more complex songs are sung with the call differing with every response, as in one much-loved song referring to Mbeze, a chiefdom on the northwest border of Oku, as well as to Nso', a large chiefdom on Oku's eastern border with which Oku has also periodically had fraught relations. Mbeze, still called by many Oku people by its old name Mbezenaku,[17] is said to have seceded from Oku to become an independent chiefdom at some point in the past, and wars have periodically been fought between the two chiefdoms along their disputed boundary ever since. This call-and-response song refers to the late fon of Mbeze, who is reputed to have died in a car crash in Nigeria when on an expedition to buy weapons with which to fight the Oku people:

> Oh! Ground of Oku!
> Fon of Mbeze!
> He got lost!
> Fon of Mbeze!
> He die-died!
> Fon of Nso'!
> He's a traitor!
> The fon came up here!
> He divided the land!

Ate! Ate!
Went back down!
Fon of Mbeze
He wanted death!
Eh! wuluwulu! It's a Mbeze man!
Gendarmes! Oh! Are in Ibalitchim [a village in the north of Oku near to
   Mbeze]![18]

In this song, the presence of death again provides an opportunity for
ribald excess and innuendo at the expense of the elite—in this case the
fons of neighboring chiefdoms. Where the verses of the last song made
veiled references to local elders' exploitation of young women (and thus
of the young men they doom to bachelorhood), these implicate neighboring rulers in memories of political insecurity and the deaths associated with the armed disputes that have often flared up on the periphery
of Grassfields chiefdoms. The initial reference to the fon of Mbeze leads
to another to the fon of Nso', a chiefdom that once claimed Oku as a
tributary state. The lyrics recall that Oku once occupied the same position
of dependency in relation to Nso' as Mbeze did to Oku. In both cases,
the foreign fons are castigated as blood-thirsty criminals. The late fon of
Mbeze meets his death while trying to smuggle weapons in from Nigeria,
while the fon of Nso' is depicted as a corrupt leader "eating" the land, a
metaphor that also implies he was a cannibal witch and highlights his role
as a slave dealer abducting Oku people for sale into slavery in the period
when Oku was said by the Nso' to be a subject principality that owed fe-
alty to them. In insulting the fons of neighboring chiefdoms, however, the
young grave stampers indirectly traduce fonship itself, ultimately including their own fon in their calumny in the guise of nationalist fervor.

Finally, in the last line of the song, a new theme is suddenly introduced:
the appearance of the paramilitary police in the village of Ibalitchim.
This line is not entirely disconnected from the content of the preceding
lines of the song. It evokes memories of a specific event in the course of
the dispute with Mbeze when gendarmes arrived to mediate the quarrel
but ended up badly mishandling the situation, panicking, and retreating
through Ibalitchim in their open-topped vehicle, indiscriminately spraying
the villagers with gunfire as they went. Many Oku people died that day,
killed by the state security forces they had hoped would protect them from
an aggressive neighbor. Local political struggles thus inevitably implicate
state intervention in the Grassfields, connecting the references to corrupt
and cannibal fons with the further references to a predatory and quasi-

anarchic state. However, the gnomic indeterminacy of the line—"Gendarmes, Oh! Ibalitchim!"—also enables people to interpret it in light of another event.

In a separate incident, a gendarme once murdered a young woman during a dispute in the village of Jikijem (Argenti 1998). The incident happened in public, at the crossroads, and the assembled crowd, consisting mainly of women, reacted with such fury that the gendarmes again, in fright, retreated through the village of Itchim and on down the mountain to the border village of Ibalitchim. The cry "Oh! Ibalitchim!" is thus polyphonic, referring at once to the tragedy of the boundary debacle but also to the second killing and the flight of the murderous gendarmes. In its aporia, the song thus juxtaposes separate historical events: the spears and Dane guns embodied in the dance recall the abductions of the era of the slave trade, while the songs recall the wars with Mbeze and the deadly incursions of the postcolonial state (as does the martial, marching step of the dance). The song forges these into an overdetermined corpus of memory that defies discrete chronological emplacement (and the closure and forgetting to which it inevitably leads), retrieving the losses of the past on the occasion of contemporary deaths. Moreover, the song recalls violent death in the form of farce and play, introducing to the monolithic seriousness of the official burial ceremony a festal atmosphere that celebrates transformation and rebirth. Subtly subversive of the rule of elders though the songs of the bachelors are, they are nevertheless essential to the ceremony, to which they contribute the seminal and regenerative element of life and fertility in its bacchanalian aspect, making of the sepulcher a womb in the very act of making a fool of the king.

When the deceased had been a member of a military society (*manjɔŋ* or *mfu'*), the idiom of the battle is taken up by the warlike stance of the military societies, whose members come to sing and clash their cutlasses rhythmically in the courtyard as the younger men stamp down the grave. The sudden appearance of their sonic mask in the courtyard—which noninitiates are prohibited from seeing—adds to the atmosphere of chaos as it sends women and children running for cover. In the case of the burial of a woman, the military societies do not attend. Instead the only female secret society in the kingdom, *fəmbiɛn*, gathers and sings during the burial.

Crying Death: Masks of the Night

The drivers of the mask groups to which a man belonged during his lifetime appear by the graveside at his burial, but the groups as a whole do not. When the driver masks appear alone for the newly dead, they are said to be mourning their lost member. On these occasions, the driver masks do not reveal their usual fierce demeanor or carry the cudgel they normally dance with; instead they walk about empty-handed and with dust on their feet in a sign of mourning, the dry feet connoting death. A mourning driver mask walks slowly, taking small steps, and it keeps its arms crossed over its chest, with its hands grasping each opposing shoulder—a sign of sorrow or mourning often adopted by people as well. The mask appears silently, with no musical accompaniment and no followers from its mask society.[19] It does not dance but meanders slowly among the crowd, making its way to the graveside, where it peers in and sometimes throws a handful of earth over the coffin. It then goes off to the mask house of the compound hosting the ceremony to rest and be fed in seclusion before leaving for its own compound.

During the first night after a burial, the men and women hardly sleep but instead sing and perform the *tshin εykwo,* an extremely energetic dance that involves leaping into the air and slamming one's feet into the ground in a manner reminiscent of the stamping on the grave earlier in the day.[20] During this night, if the deceased was a man, the mask societies of which he was a member—and which, during the day of burial, had been announced by the respective driver masks—come to "cry" his death (*dii εykwo*) at the compound under cover of darkness. This event is concentrated in the compound where the deceased has been buried during the day, but it covers the whole village and often neighboring villages as well. A mask in its night state is to be avoided at all costs by nonmembers, and people fall silent when one goes by on the road, doing everything to avoid attracting its attention. At times, the night mask nevertheless enters the compound, especially when the compound is the locus of the burial or the death celebration, and begins to sing in the courtyard. The women are especially wary of them at such times, sometimes turning their faces to the wall inside a locked house to avoid the slightest possibility of seeing one and becoming barren, going mad, or contracting epilepsy. Thus the whole surrounding area of the burial place (*beni kwo,* the "place of death") becomes the locus for a soundscape of mourning as the invisible night masks make their way along the roads in the dark, sending people running into nearby compounds with their disembodied and macabre mourning songs. The masks emerge from the secret society houses after complete darkness has fallen, followed by a few members singing songs of mourning (*eyɔf*) interspersed with sounds of alarm and of warning to others (*ezəmə*),[21] and they travel to the "place of death" (*beni kwo*), the burial site. People occasionally say of the masks at this stage that they are "angry" at the loss of a member and that they are "crying as if they had gone mad."[22]

In spite of the night masks' inapproachability, each mask society has its distinctive style of crying, and not only men but also women know how to recognize most of them by their sound at night. In fact, a woman's fear and revulsion of the night masks must be balanced against her fascination and repressed attraction for them. The night masks often sing in tongues, using foreign languages (most often Itang Ikom, the language of the neighboring chiefdom of Kom) and their voice modulators to make their phrases unclear, but this does not put women off. One of the women in my compound once expressed her disappointment that she would not be able to get to a compound holding a new death celebration one night because the sun had set and she would be in danger of seeing a night mask. She told me how she enjoyed hearing them sing of the past of the deceased, of the compound, and of the secret society, and how she stifled laughter at the insults they hurled at each other in their competitive displays when several were present in a compound at once. In telling me this, she revealed that she understood their veiled calls despite their being in a foreign language and spoken through distorting reed instruments. At such times, when up to five or six masks were "crying" in the courtyard with their attendant drums and whistles, she could distinguish each one by name. Sometimes, one of them would come and taunt an individual woman at the door of her house with a simulacrum of the rejected lover, calling her name repeatedly through its reed mouthpiece in an unearthly voice: "How can you sit by the fire in there when I'm out here in the cold? Find food! Find food, and feed me!"

At such times, she would not of course expose herself to the night mask but would open the door just enough to hand a cake of cooked maize to one of the mask's attendants. This woman's pleasure and fascination with the night masks were intensified rather than dampened by the dangers they posed to her. Despite the repulsion and horror that the night masks inspire in women, then, and the normative rules of avoidance proscribing any contact between women and the masks, the women at a death celebration engage in a flirtatious, illicit relationship of seduction with the masks, which call to them in hushed tones across the door lintel like clandestine lovers. This relationship recalls the illicit relationships that did in fact take place in the Grassfields in the past between cadets (who dance in the night masks) and young women who had been married to elders, often against their will. Warnier (2007, chap. 7) records that in Mankon such illicit affairs were euphemized in terms of sharing food, with the lover being said to "follow the sound of the pestle" made by the woman's pounding in preparation for the meal. In such illicit relations, the commensality of eating fades ambiguously into the antisocial behavior of witches, who are also said to "eat" their victims. In particular, those who commit incest, which is defined to include affines as well as kin in the Grassfields, are known as "witches of the day" and are said to "eat" their lovers in a manner analogous to that in which "witches of the night" eat their victims (Kaberry 1969, 179). Just as with the night masks, the trope of eating in these cases alludes to relationships that threatened to traduce or subvert the oligarchy of the elders.[23] The night mask therefore seems to address several contradictory levels at once regarding relations between cadets and married women: the visceral horror inspired by incest, and which included relations with women the cadet was only distantly related to though affines, seems to be transposed onto or embodied in the horror inspired by the menacing night mask. At the same time, however, the masks, despite their sinister traits, are attractive and charming to married women, recalling that illicit affairs were commonplace and pleasurable despite the horror they might normatively inspire.[24]

The deployment of the symbolic violence and the threat of pollution of the night masks may initially seem paradoxical: although the palace masks, as we have seen, aim their violence at the cadets in the palace courtyard, these cadets mobilize the violence of their village masks against their own kin and affines in their villages during the course of the nocturnal "crying" of the masks, seemingly reproducing the violence of the palace against themselves. Are the villagers, in appropriating the violence of the palace masks at the village level in this manner, complicit in extending the hegemony of the palace and the elders into their villages? On one level, they certainly are. Masking is of necessity a Faustian bargain for cadets in the Grassfields. Although an opportunity to prove one's manhood and economic independence, founding a mask group also entails negotiating with the palace authorities for its acceptance and reproducing the hierarchy of the palace in a microcosm within the secret society of the mask. Undoubtedly, mask groups give the young men who perform wearing the night masks the opportunity to invert their subjection to the violence of the *kwifon* masks at the palace, transforming themselves from pedestrian victims of the masks' onslaught into prowling beasts themselves. But they achieve this inversion at the cost of extending the violence of the palace masks out from the center to the periphery of the chiefdom.

Yet it is clear that the performance of the night masks by village lineage mask societies is not mere replication or mimicry of the palace masks and of the political violence of the palace. Rather, it is a mimesis of the palace masks that introduces a Derridean play of difference (*différance*) to its exemplar. In becoming masks, the cadets of the villages of Oku do not become palace masks or the palace elites who possess and perform them. Nor do they reproduce the violence of the palace masks wholesale in the village but rather introduce subtle differences to it as they reenact it. In the first place, while they threaten violence, they never deploy it— in contrast to the rampaging palace masks. Second, although the *kwifon* masks exclude cadets and women from participation in their "displays" at the palace—except as passive spectators on the periphery of the performance—the crying of the night masks is covertly transgressive, seducing the women into a vicarious relationship with the cadets, who cannot normally approach them publicly. The crying of the night masks is thus at once a eulogy for the deceased, a mimetic transformation of the violence of the palace, and a covert source of illicit pleasure and seduction for the young bachelors and women, many of whom have already been taken as wives by elders and elites but may still pine for their ineligible young lovers. At the same time that the youth confront the inequities of the elite, they transform death into a rite of fertility and regeneration. The night masks do not ultimately dwell on the loss perpetrated by death, nor on the hegemony of the palatine masks, but open out onto another world of possibility that is unformed, yet to come, and undetermined.

The Mother of Fɔmbiɛn, the Women's Mask

During the mortuary rites for elderly women who had been members of the *fɔmbiɛn* society, in the morning or early afternoon, the *fɔmbiɛn* society members present go out from the women's death house to "uproot the cocoyams" (*tshɔk əblɔm*): to harvest some of the crops that the deceased woman had been farming. While they are returning to the compound, one hears the music they play before seeing them. Paramount among the instruments played during this procession is the "mother" of *fɔmbiɛn* (*nɔ fɔmbiɛn*), a flat stone that resonates when struck. It is hidden from view when played, and although most people know what it is, they are not allowed to refer to it as a stone but must simply call it by its given name.[25] Similarly, a bamboo blowpipe they play is referred to as the "drum" of *fɔmbiɛn* (*ntshum fɔmbiɛn*). Although this instrument is not hidden from view the way the "mother" is, referring to it as a blowpipe can bring a heavy fine. The other instruments they play in this procession are the loud *kəmbak* (a calabash surrounded by a beaded net bag, which rattles against it when shaken) and the *kəŋkwas* (a raffia stem carved with a washboard surface, one side of which is rubbed with a brass bracelet).[26]

When the *fəmbiɛn* society members return, they not only have the fresh green cocoyam leaves protruding from the baskets on their backs but are literally covered in green branches they have cut in the bush. Most of them hold five- or six-foot-long branches with which they hide the "mask" in their midst. As they approach the compound, the *kwifon* members present go out to meet them with more branches that they have cut and help to hide the women's "mask" with them. This is the only "mask" that women lay claim to in the kingdom. Not only is it devoid of any actual mask, however, but it has no costume other than the greenery that shimmers around it as it enters the courtyard: the swaying curtain of branches does not hide the mask but constitutes it; it *is* the mask. Indeed the mask could be said to be invisible, for as the group enters the compound, it crosses the courtyard and makes its way to the women's death house, where all the greenery is held against the door as the mask passes inside. Suddenly, as if the mask had volatilized, the branches are all dropped to the ground at once, amid the triumphant laughter of the *fəmbiɛn* society women, to reveal the emptiness they had concealed. The branches, however, had concealed something—but if not a mask, then a sound, for it is from within the space concealed by the branches that the music of the "mother" of *fəmbiɛn* (*nɔ fəmbiɛn*) emerges. In this sense, the musical instrument is the mask of *fəmbiɛn*. Impossible to locate in a single place, entity, or sensory experience, the mask is indeterminate and ineffable.[27]

Once they have returned to the compound and their mask has entered the women's death house, the *fəmbiɛn* members start to dance in the courtyard. As they dance, the mother of *fəmbiɛn* is played by a society member crouching in the midst of the group, and the instrument is hidden by a male umbrella while it is played.[28] At this stage, they can be joined by other women and by *kwifon* members, who will dance on the periphery of the group, but male non-*kwifon* members cannot join in. As they dance they are brought gifts of wine, food, and salt tied in banana leaves by the other guests. When they have finished performing, one of the women distributes these gifts to the other members present, who are to redistribute them to the *fəmbiɛn* members of their own villages when they return home.

The "mask" of the village women raises many of the same questions as those raised by the night mask of the young men. Its ownership by the autocratic and hierarchical *fəmbiɛn* society, to which only elderly women belong and which is closely associated with the palace *kwifon* society, would appear to colonize the periphery of the chiefdom and the position of women with the dominant discourse of the palatine elite, reinforcing gerontocratic hierarchies in the borderlands of the chiefdom as the price for allowing women a mask of their own (albeit an invisible one). Nor can it be said that this mask is a mere parody of the masks of *kwifon;* it is taken seriously by the *fəmbiɛn* members, who behave in a welcoming and familiar manner toward the *kwifon* members present and severely reprimand any male or female nonmembers who happen to get too close to them and their "mother." Yet who can put into words the turmoil into which every man is placed by seeing the branches that hide the "mask" of *fəmbiɛn* come falling to the ground to reveal the unspeakable emptiness in their midst? The indeterminacy of a mask that it not visible but rather is a disembodied and often hardly audible sound seems to fill the *kwifon* members who help the women to hide it with their branches with glee, as if they took pride in the occult powers of their sibling secret society.

At the same time, the revelation of a mask as a hollow space or an absence seems to have critical implications for what in essence is the conundrum of men's masks: that what they represent does not exist. The periodic uprisings by women's *fəmbiɛn* and associated societies in the Grassfields since the1950s (Ritzenthaler 1960), and their resurgence as a pro-SDF opposition party force in the prodemocracy movement of the 1990s, pitted elderly women against the state and against those local elites seen to be in league with the CPDM ruling party. In such instances, the women's societies can suddenly turn against the palace authorities that so depend on them, organizing mass sit-ins in palace courtyards and government buildings alike to bring about political change (cf. Takougang and Krieger 1998, 232–33).

The Slave Auction

Women's use of indeterminate and ambiguous rites is nowhere more in evidence than in their ritual scapegoating of other women. On the fourth and final day of the mortuary ceremonies, allegedly barren women are occasionally singled out and ritually cleansed in order to restore their fertility. The barren women sometimes come forth of their own accord, but most often they are singled out and overpowered by some of the other women present. Their clothes are stripped off them in public by the other women, who then wash them from head to foot in the courtyard using the medicated water intended to wash the faces of the other mourners.[29] Once the washing is over, some of the women present beat the barren women with whips made from *Dracaena deisteliana* (*ŋkɛŋ*) plants drenched in the medicated ablution.[30] They beat them hard with a plant that is otherwise a symbol of peace and fecundity but now also a whip. As the barren women are being beaten, they run from their tormentors but not in a haphazard fashion: they run once around the women's death house. They then rush inside the house, where they are fed a luxurious meal of meat and corn meal and then rubbed from head to foot with camwood (recalling the treatment given to the *nokan* slave twins at the palace and, before that, to actual slaves by their "fathers" at the time of their sale). All this time, the barren women cry. Informants emphasized that they cry not because of the beating but because they have no children. Once they have eaten their meal, they are taken back out to the courtyard with a rope of banana bark tied to their wrists, where—again recalling the display of the slave twins at the palace and in a reenactment of the secret slave markets of the past—they are "sold at auction" to the highest bidder. Those doing the bidding, although married women, pose as prospective "husbands" for the barren women. Not only do they play at being husbands but, at the same time, their role is overdetermined by memories of the slave buyer:

"Who'll top that bid?" "I'll top it!" the women shout with great hilarity.[31] When a woman is finally "sold" to the highest bidder (who may pay with anything, a handful of grass, kola nuts, or the like), the new husband/slave owner runs home with her to "his" compound, dragging her by the lead tied to her wrist (again echoing the leads tied to the wrists of the twin figures at the palace). In spite of the rough treatment that the women receive, and the mockery they undergo, this event is not thought of solely as punishment for being barren (although some women are believed to be barren out of their own bad faith or involvement in witchcraft) but considered first and foremost a powerful cure. The hilarity of the occasion for the "slave traders" does not detract from their belief that the "slaves" will bear a child as a result. For the "slaves" themselves, however, the emotions they experience must be much more ambivalent. What is certain is that they do not laugh but cry during their ordeal. The sinister overdetermination of the slave buyer with an affinal relation—the "husband" of the bought woman—evokes at once the role of the Judas in the family who facilitated the abduction of a close relative, and the thinly veiled euphemism of the slave owners who habitually presented themselves as "fathers" to their newfound "children" but often took their girl slaves as wives. At the same time, it recalls the practice of selling women accused of witchcraft into slavery—including barren women, who were said to eat the children inside their wombs.

Slaves and Scapegoats: The *Pharmakos* of the Grassfields

The origin myths relate masks to the forest, where they are said to dwell like restless ghosts in the land of the ancestors, periodically emerging back into the world of the living like intrusive memories of the violence of the past. As if to demonstrate the acuity of the myths, the driver masks of the masking groups to which men belonged during their lives return to their gravesides on the day of burial. Shuffling mutely by the graveside and crying in the night, they are the dead of the past returned to the present. Like death itself, the masks conjoin and confuse one world with the other and collapse the past into the present. But lineage elders reject these myths, representing them as mere ruses with which to mislead women and children. In conversation with each other, men prefer to recount the stories of acquisition that relate the "true," "factual" events to do with the inception of a mask. As we have seen, these contrast the space of the forest with that of postcolonial modernity, replacing the call of the wild with the "call of the city" (Devisch 1995a, 602), but do they thereby set up an opposition between the forest and the city? Do they repudiate the sylvan cosmology of ghostliness and recurrence, and reject atavistic references to the past in favor of the modernist ideal of the economic promise of the urban center? The close relationship between the stories of acquisition and the origin myths suggests that they do not.

The city does not stand in diametrical opposition to the forest in the cosmology of the Grassfields. It does not engender forgetting and the abandonment of the past in favor of the all-too-often-unfulfilled promises of the modern nation-state. Rather, as Devisch (1995a) has shown for youths in Kinshasa and the film *Clando* reveals beautifully for Cameroon, the city is subsumed within the imaginary space of the forest and the night, playing the roll of a surrogate hunting ground for those who venture into its chaotic and undomesticated spaces. The stories that recount the "trapping" of a mask in the hunting grounds of the city thus reinscribe the space of the forest onto the modern wilderness of the postcolonial state, representing the cadets returning home successfully with their booty in the guise of latter-day hunters home from their nocturnal foray into the forest. The overt divisions that the elders would seem to erect between women and children on the one hand and male elders on the other by means of their alternative discourse of masking (opposing their stories of acquisition to the origin myths that are mere ruses "to fool women") thus turn out, upon closer consideration, to represent cognate models. By reinscribing the origin myths onto the space of the nation-state, elders effectively reproduce the myths in a modern form rather than rejecting them, and the role of women and children—far from being superannuated—is shown to be intrinsic to masking.

Likewise, the grave-stamping songs that seem to criticize women and their illegitimate and disastrous attraction to the space of modernity also turn out, at the same time, to eulogize them as martyrs and heroes who saved the chiefdom from the ravages of the predatory nation-state. This juxtaposition of apparently incommensurable and opposing discourses is further underlined in the crying of the night masks; although they are one of the gravest dangers that women confront, these masks are also attractive—their dances evoking not only the specter of death and madness but also of pleasure, love, and seduction. They seem on the face of it to terrorize women, but they simultaneously offer women and their lovers a source of illicit pleasure in a society that would monopolize it as the prerogative of elite men. And although the overt discourse of masking associates men with the space of the forest from which masks are said to originate, the *fɔmbiɛn* ceremony inscribes the close connection of women to the land, sending a delegation into the bush to dig up the crops of the deceased and bring them triumphantly back into the compound's courtyard covered in the green branches of the undomesticated land beyond the village boundary—the land from which women, midwives of the earth, produce virtually all the food that men eat.[32] Women also have a mask because they too venture into the space of the wild—the space of death, of ghosts and ancestors, and, not long ago, of the manhunt—and corral its forces to nurture the living.

The washing of the women—on the face of it also a denigration of women, a denial of their fertility, and a form of violence that replicates the violence of the past—brings to mind the scapegoat rituals of ancient Greece.[33] Symbols of barrenness, the scapegoats by the same token represented a means of achieving fecundity and rejuvenation for the city.

Derrida ([1972] 1997, 130–33) points out that they were known as *pharma-koi;* a cognate term of *pharmakon,* which referred to an illness and a drug at once. The term *pharmakos* likewise referred primarily to witches, magicians, and poisoners but also to scapegoats, at once powerless wretches and slaves but also sources of untold power and danger: "Beneficial insofar as he cures—and for that, venerated and cared for—harmful insofar as he incarnates the powers of evil—and for that, feared and treated with caution. Alarming and calming, sacred and accursed" (133).

Like the *pharmakos,* the barren women flogged with the rejuvenating dracaena plant (a plant that grows again from a cutting) are symbolic slaves and witches, but they also provide the means of chasing out the infertility caused by witchcraft and the debilitating effects of the slave trade to which witchcraft referred. Their beating with the wet dracaena plants makes of these barren women embodiments of fertility, and rather than being banished from the community as suspected witches still are today, these young brides are taken home by their "husbands" to perform their role as wives at the heart of the polity. Once again, the political role of the palace in banishing witches is inverted by this ultimately benign and subversive intervention, which transforms the banishment of witches and the sacrifice of slaves as performed by the palace *kwifon* society into its inverse: the restitution of the childless woman, marginalized by the elite discourse, to the heart of her village, with the beatings of the women ironically acting as a defense against those (elite men) who might truly have killed or banished the women into slavery in the past.

The poetics of death as invested in the mortuary rites of the Grassfields described here address experiences of loss and of disappearance in terms of bodily practices that evoke the untold losses of the dark past of the region. One death throws countless mourners back into the world of ghosts and ancestors that forever threatens to break in upon the world of the living, exposing them to a living death: the recurring presence of a latent past. At the same time, however, the past does not return simply as death or as annihilating violence but also as *difference.* The space of death is mediated in the mortuary rites in such a way that it is always presented anew: first experienced as tragedy, the cadets reproduce death as carnival. The means by which the cadets transform the subjective experience of death parallels the way in which they also mediate experiences of subjection at the palace mask performances, on the one hand, and evoke memories of past tragedies on the other, ultimately embodying the annihilating history of slavery as an alteric social vision that is stripped of its totalizing horror.

Whereas the dominant discourses alienate and marginalize women and cadets, the performances that work through the experience of bereavement and death, and the memories of a history of living death to which they give rise, effectively reinscribe women and cadets into the fabric of the village, prying life from the very jaws of death, remembering from oblivion, and creating subjectivities with which to confront the objectification inherent in political domination.

Dancing Death: Memorial Celebrations, the Politics of Ritual Laughter, and the Embodied Memories of Youth

Carnival laughter ... is not an individual reaction to some isolated "comic" event. Carnival laughter is the laughter of all the people ... it is universal in scope; it is directed at all and everyone, including the carnival's participants ... this laughter is ambivalent: it is gay, triumphant, and at the same time mocking, deriding. It asserts and denies, it buries and revives. Such is the laughter of carnival. — Mikhail Bakhtin ([1957] 1968,11–12)

Unlike the "death of tears," which despite its ritual humor is predominantly an occasion for mourning, memorial celebrations are unambiguously happy events, and although people in Oku say they are "crying" a death (*dii εykwo*), memorial celebrations generally are referred to as "dancing" a death (*bin εykwo*). A memorial celebration is always held in the compound of the lineage head of the deceased and can be held any time after the burial has occurred but usually takes place approximately one to three years afterward. Memorial celebrations are also timed to occur just after the corn harvest, to ensure that there will be plenty of food with which to "entertain" (*ntal*) the guests and masks and not too much work to be done on the farms. Sometimes, several ancestors will be commemorated in one celebration. The decision to hold a "dancing death" and the date chosen are usually determined through consultations with a diviner, who might blame a spate of misfortunes in a compound or lineage upon the jealousy of ancestors who have yet to be commemorated. There is no public crying at these events, and their mood is altogether much more lighthearted. Although at "new deaths" mask groups are only represented by their driver mask or by their invisible night masks, the entire masking group performs at the "dancing death," thus giving the celebration its name.

As with mortuary rites, the feasting and dance of memorial celebrations are spread over four days.[1]

Day 1: "Opening the Death" (Tshɔk Ɛykwo)

Unlike the commemoration of new dies, the memorial celebration for old dies is performed on particular days of the week. The celebration always begins on *ŋgɔkse,* a day of rest and the market day in Elak, the capital. This opening day of the celebration is known as the *tshɔk ɛykwo,* literally the "unstopping" or "pulling out" of the death celebration (as with a cork from a bottle). In an echo of the burial ceremony, the first day of the celebration is marked by the firing of Dane guns at daybreak. As the morning progresses, family members and mask associations from other villages and chiefdoms begin to arrive. When on their way to the celebration from a mask house situated in a different village, the members of a group travel along the paths in everyday dress with one of their masks in full costume (usually the *kam yɛ ebam,* the last one in the line of masks, known in pidgin as the second captain, which either wears an elephant or buffalo headdress). The members all follow behind it, head-loading the rest of the costumes and headdresses (which must not be seen when not being worn) and their xylophone in large bags and singing mournful songs particular to their mask group (*eyɔf*) as they go. They travel with their headloads in single file along the narrow paths, in the same manner as the caravans of porters did in the past.

Before the dancing starts but once quite a few guests have arrived with gifts of food and wine, the "opening of the house of death" (*dise nda ɛykwo*) occurs. For this ritual event, which also takes place at a burial ceremony, a large clay pot (these days an aluminum one is often used) is brought out to the courtyard and filled with the palm wine that the guests have been bringing until it flows over the brim. If the deceased was a royal eligible (*wantɔk*), the wine with which to "open the house of death" will be sent from the palace. In this case the wine (referred to as *m ɔmə ntɔk,* "water of the palace"), once poured, must be drunk by a young virgin girl before being served to the waiting crowd. The serving of wine is followed by the serving of food, sometimes is corn and beans (lit. "the meal of breath/spirit," *esaŋ keyus*), as on the day of burial. More usually, chicken is served: five roasted chickens are brought into the courtyard, cut into pieces on a board with a cutlass, turned in palm oil and salt in a large wooden dish decorated with a carved animal head, and then served to those standing by. A self-appointed group of younger participants then collect food and wine from the various families' cooking houses (*etshia*), which they carry up to the roadside to serve to those not directly involved with the death celebration. This practice is known as the *ntal ntɛk,* the "entertainment" of the village. The masquerade dances then go on to celebrate the male ancestors of the compound from midafternoon until sunset.

As the mask groups arrive at their destination, they move into the designated mask house in the compound to prepare for their first performance. Although they are readying themselves, the groups sometimes send out their driver masks to perform the solo dance known as the *shiɛŋə,* which gives the *kəshiɛŋɛnɛ* its name. Because *ŋgɔksen* is a day set aside for the palace *kwifon* society to hold court and try cases (cf. Chilver and Kaberry 1967), however, it is forbidden to beat a drum until late afternoon (*kəmbɔl əbɛy*), and the masks therefore do not come out until evening. The first mask to dance is always the one from the main or "big" compound (*kəbɛy kərarene*) where the celebration is being held. Each mask group first sends out its *kəshiɛŋɛnɛ* to perform the *shiɛŋə* on its own. Soon after a *kəshiɛŋɛnɛ* retreats to the mask house after its performance, it comes out again herding the whole group into the compound courtyard. The mask groups then go on to dance in memory of the male ancestors of the compound until sunset. They never dance in the night, and there is no crying (*edii*) of masks in the night of an old die. It is said that the masks are no longer angry or grieving at a dancing death the way they had been during the interment of their society member. The sensation of dread and danger that typifies the death of tears is thus replaced in the dancing death with a mood of joy and celebration, in an atmosphere of peace and safety.

Day 2: The Day of the Death of Men (Kətshi Ɛykwo nə Lumene)

When several ancestors are being celebrated at once, day 2 of the ceremony (on the day of the week known as *əbkwɛy*) is dedicated to the memory of the male ancestors of the compound. This day, much like the previous one, is spent in dance. The only difference is that none of the opening ceremonies is performed, and the masks from villages farther afield take precedence over those of the host village, because the latter had priority in dancing the day before.

Day 3: The Day of the Death of Women (Kɔtshi Ɛykwo nɔ Ɔbkui)

Day 3, held on the day of the week known as ɔbkwotui, is dedicated to the memory of the female ancestors of the compound and again involves masquerading, except that certain rules must be regarded with respect to the mask groups. Some of the groups do not perform for women's death celebrations because their medicine is considered too dangerous. Others perform, but the lead mask of the group (the captain or *kam*) does not wear the medicated necklace of twisted dried creepers it wears when dancing for the memorials of male ancestors. Not only do the masks with members from the host compound participate on this day, but masks from the birth compounds of those female ancestors who married into the host compound also come and dance. In other words, the "father" (*bamkum*) of a mask group may send his group to dance at a compound on this day if one of the deceased women there was related to him not only consanguineously but also affinally.

Day 4: Singing the Death (Eyɔf Ɛykwo)

On day 4, *kɔmɛywi*, the final day of the celebration before the ritual washing that marks the formal end of the celebrations (on the day of the week called *edintui*) the military societies *manjɔŋ* and *mfu'* attend and chant to the rhythm of a drum and their clashing cutlasses. At one point during this public display the "beast" (*nyam*) of *manjɔŋ*—its secret weapon that *manjɔŋ* warriors used to take into battle—makes a sudden appearance, and the women and children run and hide indoors as they hear the warning cries of the approaching men. Generally, this is a day of winding down, when people begin to depart, and the masks do not perform. The celebration as a whole is timed to go on until the next day known as *nsãmnen*, on which day the spirits (*ŋkvosay*) who had been in attendance go away, leaving the worlds of the living and the dead separate once again.

The Dance

Although each group has its own, distinctive way of dancing, the masked dances of Oku and of many other Grassfields chiefdoms can be sketched out in general terms. First, as mentioned earlier, the driver mask (*kəshiɛŋɛnɛ*) comes out of the mask house to announce the imminent arrival of the group as it is preparing to emerge into the courtyard. This performance is inevitably a wild show of force by the mask known as the disciplinarian of the group. On the occasion of a memorial celebration, the driver mask, in stark contrast to its pitiful appearance at the graveside of a deceased member, comes storming out of the mask house armed with its ponderous clubs, spears, or both and often runs amok through the compound. Its acolytes follow, jostling about the mask in their efforts to establish some control over it. The mask inevitably turns to vent its fury on them too, often threatening them with its club as they cower at its feet. To entice it forward again, they call to it with urgent phrases of encouragement, proudly displaying their fearful mask to the assembled guests and paradoxically enjoying its threats of violence, even when these are directed against them. The violence of this initial performance is ambiguous but ultimately celebratory rather than sinister. In fact, the performance of the driver at the two separate death rites can be seen as a reversal of the general tenor of the mask group as a whole. On the first occasion, just after the death, while the driver is listless and grieving, the rest of the masks appearing in the night are angry and violent. On the second occasion, during the "dancing death," the driver is uncharacteristically angry and violent on a day otherwise typified by peaceful, celebratory, and beautiful performances by the rest of the masks. Ultimately it is the pleasure and joy of the mask group as a whole that win out over the sinister violence of the driver.

Shortly after the driver mask's escapade, the group's xylophone players set up the separate keys of the instrument on the freshly cut trunks of two banana trees in the center of the compound courtyard. It is considered important that the instrument be played on these fresh tree trunks, which give the music a cool/wet (*sanə*) sound. Coolness or wetness is also a highly desired quality of masks: these dances are, first and foremost, pleasurable events for all to behold and partake in. To this end, the father of the masquerade often sprinkles the feet of the masquerades with cooling, medicated wine just before a dance, and the headdresses of each *kəkum* have water (or wine, in the case of the Samba masquerade) spat upon them in a fine mist by their attendants. This spitting of wine onto a masquerade is always done within the secrecy of the enclosure before the dance, as is the rubbing of the headdresses with oil. The beading of the wine on the oily surface of the mask is referred to as the "sweat" that keeps it cool/wet during its exertions. As if to emphasize the value placed

on coolness and self-possession, masks and people alike are always careful to keep their heads from shaking during a performance. To shake one's
head in dance is a sign of madness and lack of control. The only exception
to this rule is the performance by Samba, a secret society with a single
eponymous mask that represents a horse.

After the excursion of the driver mask into the courtyard, the musicians start to play the xylophone and drums, and the masks are enticed
out of their hiding place and into the courtyard—just as they were first
lured out of the forest by the xylophone players when the group was first
founded.[2] The dancers always form a single-file queue on the edge of the
dance space and enter it at a signal from their captain, or *kam,* who takes
the lead. They dance in a circle around the xylophone in a counterclockwise direction, stamping their feet energetically on the ground and elicit-
ing a loud percussive effect from the ankle rattles they wear.

Although the palace *kwifon* society's Fuləŋgaŋ mask group predominantly fills onlookers with a sense of dread as it performs its comparatively
lackluster, joyless shuffle, village lineage masquerades are electrifying performances whose excessive ecstatic energy seduces everyone present to
join in. And although the danger of contact with the palace Fuləŋgaŋ masks
precludes any sincere participation by nonelite onlookers, anyone witnessing the performance of a lineage mask inevitably becomes a participant in
the action: as the masks dance around the xylophone, the women of the
compound to which it belongs join in gleefully, making their own parallel
circuit around the musicians, or they dance in a line just outside the trajectory of the masks, ululating with pleasure as the masks pass (see fig. 31). The
men from the masks' compound, for their part, or friends of the performers,
join in by taking the spears and whisks out of the masks' hands and dancing
around the ring with them for a few turns. When they return the spear or
whisk to the mask, they include a coin along with it as a gift (*faalə*).

The basic set of wooden headdresses worn by the masks is generally
uniform across groups. These known types of masks represent categories
of people or animals, and each one is named and has its allotted place in
the line of masks (see fig. 31).[3] First comes the *kam* or captain, its headdress representing the head of an elder. Next comes the *ŋgɔn,* representing a young virgin or marriageable woman. Those belonging to lineages
with ties to the royal family (Mbele) have cowry shells encrusted around
their heads, in likeness of the headband of cowries worn by the wives of
the fon. There are two or three *ŋgɔn* in a line of masks; they are known
for their whimsical style of dance and often have to be shepherded back

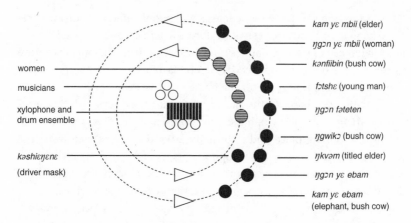

FIGURE 31. The organization of a typical lineage group masquerade (kɛkum kɛnɔn).

into line by the driver mask. The third mask is known as *kənfiibin,* and its headdress represents a bush cow—one of the large mammals that used to roam the montane forests of Oku. It dances with a spear in hand. Next comes *fɔtshɛ,* who represents a young man, then comes another virgin, followed by *ŋgwikɔ,* also a bush cow. The seventh in line is again a person, this time a titled elder (*ŋkvəm*), with a headdress depicting the elaborate lobed cap that goes with the title. Then comes the third virgin, followed by the "leader of the back" (*kam yɛ ebam*) or second captain, this one with a headdress depicting not an elder, as with the lead *kam,* but an elephant, or sometimes a bush cow. This one also carries a spear.[4] Many mask groups possess fifteen masks or more and add several other types of mask to this basic set.

Ŋkɛŋ and Mbɛlɛy at the Palace of Edin

Edin or Din, a small chiefdom on the northern border of Oku, is unusual for a Grassfields chiefdom because it has not one but two palaces, one for each branch of the royal family. This situation is said to have resulted from a dispute, which led to a schism within the original ruling family. The mother of the newly appointed Fay Mbu of Jikijem comes from the Əbdzəə branch of this divided royal family, and, one day in early January 1994, Fay Mbu's compound accordingly sent a delegation to commemorate a "son of the palace" or royal eligible at the Əbdzəə palace. The compound into which a woman marries has an obligation to go to celebrate her family's death rites. In this case, the deceased prince was a member of Fay Mbu's mother's matriline, or kənyi.[5] The deceased (who had died about five months earlier) had not yet had a memorial celebration performed for him, and Fay Mbu's compound was therefore the first to come to celebrate. The women of the compound set off in the morning, carrying food with them, and the men went along separately with Ŋkɛŋ, the compound's mask group, in the early afternoon.

In their capacity as followers of the mask group (ŋgaŋsə kəkum), the men of the compound accompanied the mask to the chiefdom of Edin. They were led along the way by the last mask of the group in the dancing line (the second captain or kam yɛ ebam), in full dress. In the case of Ŋkɛŋ, this costume is composed of a bush cow mask (nial) with a dark blue gown and a whisk in its right hand. Behind it came a group of perhaps nine men and young boys, carrying the "things" of Ŋkɛŋ inside old jute coffee bags. Ngum Valentine, one of the men of Fay Mbu's compound, was at the head of this group with the elaborately decorated spear (kədiɔŋ) of the lead mask (kam yɛ mbii). The men sang eyɔf as they walked, a skill the younger boys in the group had not yet acquired. This type of singing, as opposed to the eyɔf sometimes sung by elders during a masked dance, has a style and intonation characteristic of the mask group, which makes it recognizable to most who come from its village even before they have seen it. Certain phrases are also called out as part of the eyɔf of Ŋkɛŋ, most of them in the languages of various neighboring kingdoms, but one is in Eblam Ebkwo: "Burn the incense!" Niɔk kəlɛy!—a reference to the incense made of tree sap that is burnt on the bedposts of corpses before burial. Women got off the road and out of sight as they heard us approaching, and as we passed men walking on the paths, they did not greet us as usual but passed by wordlessly, just as they would if we had been wearing our full masking attire.

The group arrived at the palace in Edin as the sun was setting, the women of Jikijem having already found themselves places to settle and prepare food in the houses of the fon's wives. The women did not greet us on arrival, and an attendant at the palace immediately led us into the palace mfu' military society house. The building would serve as our mask house during our stay. Once inside, the lead mask disrobed, and the "things" of the mask were put down by the followers, who then went out to greet the women, set up the xylophone, and play some of the mask's melodies. Soon afterward, the mask group known as Mbɛlɛy—belonging to Tatangkum, the village head of Jikijem's compound—arrived in the same fashion as Ŋkɛŋ just had. Although Ŋkɛŋ had come to honor the commitment of the people of Fay Mbu's compound to its affinal relatives, Mbɛlɛy had come because the woman in question had not only married into Mbu's compound but she had been born in Tatangkum. One mask group (Ŋkɛŋ) thus came to honor the wife of the (preceding) head of Mbu's compound, the other (Mbɛlɛy) to honor the head of Tatangkum's daughter. That evening, after the sun had gone down but darkness had not yet fallen, the driver masks of Ŋkɛŋ and Mbɛlɛy came out to perform their solo displays in the palace courtyard, one after the other. The driver of Ŋkɛŋ emerged from the mask house crouching low, with its two clubs held over one shoulder with its right hand, its strange, zoomorphic face angled upward, looking for all the world like a prowling beast. All its followers came close on its heals, egging it on by singing fast and loud *eyɔf.* As was its style, the driver moved slowly, stooped over, but with its "neck" (the masker's head) angled backward, periodically and suddenly turning around and stretching up onto the tips of its toes, slamming a wide hand violently down onto the backs of its crouching followers, who responded with esoteric phrases with which to assuage it before it turned around, crouching to inch forward once again. Eventually, the driver and its tightly packed group of followers made their way to the palace door, upon which the driver, using its stout cudgels, set up a cannonade of ominous blows to demand its customary gift of food (*ntal*) from the fon, who, as head of the compound, was playing the role of the "father of the death" (*ba ɛykwo*).[6]

Early the next morning, having spent the night in the *mfu'* house, the members of Ŋkɛŋ prepared to dance. The younger children in the entourage that had come from Jikijem rubbed the masks with oil to make them shine.[7] Oku dancers provide their own ankle rattles and face nets, and are allocated the gown and headdress of a particular mask for each dance. The lead mask (*kam* or captain) of Ŋkɛŋ is always dressed with two gowns, one thrown over top of the other to give it an impression of solidity, bulk, and volume. One, known as a "shimmering bag" (*kəbam kəliarene*), is made of shiny black rayon pelt, and—being more highly valued—it is worn outside the older, traditional but less reflective "bag of hair" (*kəbam nɔŋse kətu*) made of human hair woven onto a jute cloth.[8] At about ten in the morning the masks filed out in a line to the edge of the dancing space in the palace courtyard and stood waiting for the xylophone to play the short, fast prelude that announces the imminent entrance of the masks.[9] The drum and xylophone soon changed from their previous tune to the expected prelude, then switched again to the entrance tune, and the line of masks started to dance in place, sounding their foot rattles in unison.

FIGURES 32 and 33. Irene Mbo coaxing the lead mask of Ɔkɛŋ into the dance space at the palace of Edin.

They did not enter the dance space, however, but stood stamping in place a few meters away from the xylophone while the women of Jikijem danced on the other side. After a few moments, Irene Mbo (Noh Ndise), one of the women with ties to Mbu's compound, broke from the group of women and came dancing gently forth, hardly lifting her feet from the ground as she oriented her hunched body toward the first in line of the masks, the *kam*. She approached it, then backed away again, always with her face turned bashfully away and her body submissively doubled over in the tantalizing dance known as the *liete*,[10] a dance that is often essential to entice the lead mask into the dance space. Although this dance can be performed by men or women, it is most often performed by women, either for the lead captain or the "leader of the back" (*kam yɛ ebam*). The dance appropriates the fearful figure of the colonial officer and the captain of the slave ship—at once evoking these unspeakable memories and domesticating them as the women seduce the captain, drawing him out of the space of death in the forest into the space of the courtyard, the safe heart of the compound.

Soon after this disarming prelude, the masks all entered the dance space and started to dance in a counterclockwise direction around the xylophone. As they came around the instrument, they passed close to the group of women dancing demurely on the spot. Despite their relative immobility in relation to the masks, these women radiated an intense joy as they danced, and some of them came forth to offer gifts of coins to some of the masks, which they threw down at the masks' feet so as not to touch their hands. The wife of Fay Mbu (actually his predecessor's wife) who had been instrumental in organizing the celebration then came forth from the group of women bearing a live fowl, which she handed to the lead mask. This gift is normally offered by the head of the compound, in his position

FIGURE 34. A woman leads the last mask of Ŋkɛŋ (with buffalo headdress) around the dance space by the tip of its spear.

as "father of the death" (*ba ɛykwo*), where the celebration is being held. In this case, however, it was appropriate that this woman, who had married into Mbu's compound, should thank her compound mask for recognizing her and her matrilineage by dancing for the death of her brother. Furthermore, although the fon of Edin was nominally the host of the death celebration in progress, he could not join in this celebration until the period of mourning for the deceased was officially terminated with the announcement of a death celebration by his closest relatives in Edin.

While all this was happening, another woman was dancing the *liete* with the suddenly tame "captain of the back" (*kam yɛ ebam*) by holding the tip of its spear in the palm of her hand and leading it gently around the dance space (see fig. 34). Also, in the same moment, the men of Fay Mbu's matriline were firing guns and making gifts of palm wine to the mask group by depositing calabashes of it around the xylophone.[11] As the dance went on, some of the women expressed their pleasure and participation with the high-pitched ululation interspersed with phrases of praise known as *elər'*. After Ŋkɛŋ had gone through its different dance steps and retired back to the mask house, Mbɛlɛy prepared to dance.[12] When Mbɛlɛy had danced and returned to the mask house, the wine that had been accumulating by the xylophone was brought in, augmented by a gift of wine from the fon. All the men inside the house then sat down, and the eldest among them poured the wine into their cups. After drinking, they shared cakes of corn meal prepared by the women of Jikijem along with the fowl that had earlier been presented to the *kam* of Mbɛlɛy and roasted by some of the young boys in our entourage.

This event belies the notion that masquerades are a strictly male preserve. Grassfields men often emphasize that they join mask groups so that their masks will come to dance at their death celebrations, but women just as often instigate the appearance of a mask group at a memorial celebration, although this fact is only alluded to indirectly, with the respectful reference to women in certain situations as *ŋgɔn djuo*. This title is actually movable or deictic, and conditional upon the relationship of the woman to the compound from which the mask comes.[13] Although the *ŋgɔnsə djuo* in the line of masks are defined simply as beautiful virgins or marriageable young women, these meanings of the term are not the ones used in relation to actual women. Instead, with reference to women rather than masks, the *ngɔnsə djuo* are the women attending the memorial celebration who were born in the compound from which a mask attending the celebration comes but who have since married out of it. In contrast to

FIGURE 35. The two female masks (*ngɔn*) of Ɗkɛŋ dance out of the line at the palace of Edin. (Cf. the description in this chapter of the same event performed by the female masks of Mbɛlɛy in the village of Nganggang.)

FIGURE 36. The driver (*kɔshiɛŋɛnɛ*) of Mbɛlɛy threatens one of its masks back into line.

the masks, they are by definition married women. Their affection for their compound of birth is thus expressed in the special relationship that they keep with the mask groups of their natal compound, and which represent them as forever-youthful virgins, as they were in their compound of birth. In this case, the woman from Tatangkum who married into Mbu's compound was a *ŋgɔn djuo* to the mask group of Tatangkum.

When a compound from which a woman comes, or into which she has married, has a mask group, it must be sent along to support her when she attends a death celebration, and any compound that fails to do so will be said to be uncaring about the women married into it. Thus to a certain degree masquerades are appropriated by women to punctuate their presence at a death celebration, in the framework of a public performance that the *ŋgɔn djuo* then reward with gifts and food. It is these women, the *ŋgɔn djuo,* and not the female mourners in general (*ɔbkui ŋkfɔ*), who dance so enthusiastically alongside the masks. In their public involvement with the mask during its performance, the women married or born into a compound display the support they enjoy there through the masks that appear in their name. Affinal as well as matrilineal ties are thus expressed in this situation, since a woman's father's compound sends its mask group as does her husband's compound. Even in indirect cases, when a mask group has come to dance for a deceased member of the mask society, women from its compound still take advantage of their relation of *ŋgɔn djuo* to it during their joint performance.[14] Bakhtin (1968, 7) makes the point that carnival is not a spectacle seen by the people but rather that it embraces all the people. During carnival, all the people join together and live in it as one. Likewise in the village death celebration—and in contrast to the violent and alienating masks of the palace—there is no audience for a lineage masquerade; there are only participants.

Kɛŋkɔs and Mbɛlɛy in Nganggang

It was only the day after we had returned from Edin that another memorial celebration was opened in Nganggang, a village on the low-lying northern border of Oku with Edin. The masks from Jikijem went down the day after our return from the palace of Edin, but I stayed behind in Jikijem with some of the other men who had participated in the first celebration to rest from the long walk, the dancing, and the sleepless night in the mask house. After a day's rest I set off down the mountain from Jikijem with some members of the mask group Ŋkɛŋ. After a few hours, we reached the compound holding the celebration and made our way directly to the compound's mask house. There we met the dancers of Kɛŋkɔs, the feather-headed mask group (*kəkum evəl*) of Ba Keming's compound in Mbock-Jikijem mentioned in chapter 7. They had preceded us and were preparing to perform. The mask known as *əbyɔ əbyumə* (the mask that came to be known as "dry/empty hands" after it threw down the presents of the fon in a fit of peek) was readied to go out first. True to its name, the mask emerged from the mask house without clubs in its hands, or followers behind it, walking silently about the compound with its arms crossed rather than performing the formidable *shiɛŋə* of proper driver masks. It meandered silently for thirty minutes or so before going back inside the mask house and reemerging with the group as a whole.[15]

After the appearance of its self-effacing outrider, the whole Kɛŋkɔs group then went out to dance, with an amazing twenty-one masks in the line. The masks began by stamping the ground rhythmically on the edge of the dancing space. As soon as the xylophone players started playing, though, some women came into the space before the masks had had the chance to move in and danced around the xylophone in the counterclockwise direction that the masks would also follow. Their encouragement failed to entice the masks of Kɛŋkɔs, which are famed for the indecision they display on the edge of the dance space, to follow them in. Rather than coming in with the start of the music or soon after, as most mask groups do, the leader of Kɛŋkɔs began dancing gingerly in, with the other masks following it. But each time the masks had completed barely a quarter turn around the ring, they danced out again, retracing their steps backward several times in a row.

While this ambivalent entry was under way, some of the women took turns trying to entice the *kam* into the ring with the seductive *liete* dance, but each time they seemed to have succeeded in luring it in, the *kam* scuttled nervously back out again. Finally, having overcome its uncertainty, the lead mask led the rest of the masks into the ring at terrific speed. Unencumbered by the heavy wooden headdresses worn by other groups, the feather-headed masks danced for a very long time, charging through the three traditional dance steps and adding an extra one at the end, which astonished those not familiar with the group, who had thought from the first mournful appearance of the listless outrider and the subsequent uncertain entrance of the lead mask that the group would not be up to much. The members of Kɛŋkɔs are proud to relate how this dramatic technique never fails to dumbfound the audience. During the performance, the women stopped dancing around the xylophone and moved to one side of the dance space to dance in place.

Unusually, the mask known as "empty hands" that comes out to announce the imminent arrival of the Kɛŋkɔs group is not the driver of the group. Once the group as a whole comes out, another mask takes over the role of the driver (*kəshiɛŋɛnɛ*) during the dance, clearing bystanders out of the way and leading the masks that fall out of step peremptorily back into the line. This driver dances with two spears and a "horse whip." Although many Grassfields masks dance with horsetail whisks, the use of a whip is unusual. As with the whisks, the horse whip recalls the mounted Fulani raiders who once terrorized the peoples of the Grassfields on horseback.

FIGURES 37 and 38. The driver (*kəshiɛŋɛnɛ*) of the mask group Mbɛlɛy performing the solo *shiɛŋə* before the group dance in the village of Nganggang on the Oku–Din border.

In addition, it provides this surrogate driver mask with a weapon with which to drive the other masks onward—one that was once also used by slave drivers. This driver mask is further distinguished from the other masks by its helmet-shaped headdress with dreadlocks hanging from it, like that of əbyɔ əbyumə rather than the feather headdress of the other masks. While the group danced, it was given a fowl by one of the ŋgɔnsə djuo and a calabash of wine by the head of the compound and "father of the death."

After this performance, back inside the mask house, some of the dancers changed into the "things" of the mask group Mbɛlɛy, which had also come. First its driver went out to perform its solo display, fast and aggressively, with its followers close behind it singing eyɔf. No oil was available that day to rub on the masks, so instead the dancers rubbed the masks they were given with green leaves to impart a momentary shine. As the kəshiɛŋɛnɛ of Mbɛlɛy was performing, another mask group was dancing, and once we heard from the mask house that this group had finished, Mbɛlɛy went out to dance. Once again, the ŋgɔnsə djuo women danced around the xylophone once it had started to play. When they had completed a couple of turns around the musicians, they moved to dance in a fixed place outside the circular trajectory of the masks. For a little time, however, the group of women and the masks danced next to each other in their parallel orbits around the musicians, the women dancing inside, and the masks encompassing them in a larger circle. As the women collected in their fixed position, some of the men of Tatangkum, to which Mbɛlɛy belongs, entered the dance space to dance, where they were given the sticks of the two captains and the driver and danced proudly around the space with them before returning the sticks to the masks with a small gift of coins.[16]

Both during the preparations inside the secret society house and in the dancing ring during the performance, two elders—Mbey and Sam Nchamcham of Edin—intoned the plaintive song known as eyɔf, a lament whose lyrics are improvised to the music played for a masquerade. First Mbey sang:

Oh! When one begets a child, the child is already his voice/mouthpiece.
Oh! Ndiketshui [man's name] is walking/being thus, what is the matter?
Oh! A man is the fon of his compound but soon leaves [dies] and another takes his place.
I'm worrying/tormented about the world, what could people be thinking?

Oh! What are the children of Mkong Mote [a past fon] getting up to in the
land of the fon of Oku?
Go and divide it up, go and come back, and see dry mouth [see wondrous
things].
Oh! I'm remembering this father today [the deceased for whom the
celebration is being held[17], the fon of Bah's compound.
Is the fon of Bah's compound [the deceased] gone to return again?
Oh, Ma! Oh, Ma! [Exclamation of sorrow]
Tell it from house to house that the book of the land of the red people is being
written [a reference to me taking notes].[18]

Sam Nchamcham then came in:

Oh! See the meat/wealth of Oku disappearing.
Oh! Call it out loud!
Oh! See how one must prepare for a child to eat his house [succeed him as
compound head]!
See the successor of Laate—Oh! Already on the stool[19]—Oh!
When you [Laate's father] had chosen him [Laate] you went to the Land of
Ngum [a past king of Oku, i.e., the Land of the Dead].
See that a man must choose his successor [lit. the "devourer of his house"]!
Laate, you ate the stool—Oh! [i.e., inherited the compound].[20]

As the dance continued, Japhet Chiente, an elderly bachelor (and therefore a cadet) from Jikijem, began to sing:

Oh! How I am suffering in Njinikijem [a village outside Oku] with no one to
hear!
Oh! I'm worrying/tormented about my skin/self, with no one to sympathize
[with me].
I'm feeling sorry for myself for having entered a land where there is no house
[i.e., a foreign land devoid of kin].
Struggle—struggle, a man's friend suffers a great deal in his place.
I have died today like this—Aaah!
Oh! A person struggles, but there is no one to hear/sympathize.
The mother entered with her child of Njinikijem but there was no one to buy
[marry?] it.
The father and the mother left without the child.
I fear for myself, Fokom [man's name—a dead friend?],

I fear for my world/life.

You struggle, struggle, but the river floods and washes away the seeds that you
planted [line from a *ndjaŋ isɛy* burial song].

I fear for myself in Njinikijem.

The river flooded in Njinikijem and washed away the seeds of my people [i.e.,
drowned my children].

I fear for myself.[21]

In the midst of the dancing and the laments, the "father of the death"
entered the dance space with a live cock and pulled feathers from it, which
he stuck on to the "sweat" of the headdress of the lead mask before giving the bird to the group. Before being given to the group as a whole, a
fowl is always shown to its leader, and some of its feathers are often offered in this highly noticeable way so that, even in the fog of dance, people
have the opportunity to notice the flapping wings, the raised hand, and the
white feathers fluttering on the shimmering, oily face of the *kam,* and to
know that the compound head has properly thanked the mask for coming.
Afterward, some of the men of the compound of Tatangkum standing in
the center of the dance space next to the xylophone took the bird from
the mask. Meanwhile both the lead mask and the driver danced inside
the ring formed by the other dancers. As they passed the other masks,
they steered them along the circular trajectory around the xylophone en-
semble and signaled each successive step to them. Despite their best efforts, one or two of the *ŋgɔnsɔ* masks would swoop in toward the center
of the space from time to time: "just to show off, beautiful women always
show off," I was told by one of the participants. Caricaturing the idealized
deportment of young women, the female masks broke loose from the controlled choreography of the group to swirl and stoop gracefully together,
arms spread out straight to display their beautiful gowns of resist-dyed indigo cloth (nominally restricted to the royal family) to their fullest advantage. Each time, however, the *kɔshiɛŋɛnɛ* would soon catch up to them and
chase them back into the line. After this performance, Kɛŋkɔs came out
and danced a second time, after which the celebration came to an end.

The head of the compound holding the death celebration, the "father
of the death," must offer gifts (*efaalɔ*) to the mask groups that attend. Depending on his wealth, generosity, and ties to the compounds from which
the masks come, he can give many different things to them. On that day,
apart from the cock already mentioned, the "father of the death" gave
palm wine, a bag of salt (symbolically counted as a goat), and a real goat

to the various mask groups. The men married to women from the compound holding the celebration (the compound's əbtshii) also are expected
to come with gifts with which to support the father of their wives during
the celebration. During the course of the day, he redistributes these gifts
to the masks that have come to dance. As mentioned earlier concerning
the old die in the palace of Edin, the masks thus confirm women's ties to
their compounds of origin. Because these men came with gifts, they gave
on behalf of their wives, who were the ŋgɔnsə djuo to the compound.[22]

Time and Social Memory

What is one to make of the lineage masquerades of the Grassfields? The
sheer richness and complexity of the lineage-group masking genre and
the memorial ceremonies with which it is associated threaten to make any
attempt at a concluding analysis a gross oversimplification. For one thing,
many of the elements described in this chapter seem to be at odds with
each other, if not contradictory:

· the pleasure that masks seem to elicit in dance versus the horror that they
  clearly inspire at night;
· the violence of the policing driver masks versus the beauty of the masks that
  they guard and discipline; and
· the joy of the ululating women and of the dancing men versus the sorrow and
  pain of the lamenting elders.

Most paradoxical of all, of course, is the stark contrast between the pleasure taken in masking and the cataclysmic violence of the historical phenomena that the dances appear to reenact. The appearance of these masks
calls forth strong and understandably ambivalent emotions from those
involved with them: the terror tinged with suppressed sexual attraction
of the women listening to the night masks; the ludic, pent-up violence and
the elation of the young acolytes egging on their drivers in the moments
before a group dance; or the pain, melancholy, and catharsis of the elders'
songs of loss and suffering. What is clear is that it is of no use to describe
the tensions evident in the masking complex in terms of dualistic oppositions. To do so would wrench asunder the constitutive elements that make
of masking a coherent phenomenon, albeit one fraught with tension.

Rather than decorticating the very tension that gives village masking
its transcendent depth and human richness, it would be more fruitful to

begin by contrasting it with the masking tradition of the palace, to which it is closely related but from which it clearly differs in significant respects. As with the palace mask group Fuləŋgaŋ, the dancers of lineage mask groups are organized like a line of porters or of slaves in a caravan, driven on by the pitiless "captains." Indeed, not only do the village masks hold their ungainly headdresses during the dance with exactly the same bodily postures as slaves and porters once carried their headloads, but one of the headdresses regularly found in village mask groups actually depicts the head of a young man topped with the type of basket still used for head-loading to this day. Known as a *ŋkɛm,* the basket lends its name to the eponymous mask.

The relationship between the masked dance and the bodily memories of the past is most clearly revealed, however, by the threatening driver masks armed with their weapons that march alongside the line of village lineage masks.[23] Indeed, far from being pale imitations of the palace masks, the village masks seem to piece together and to reveal what the palace dance obscures and dissimulates: at the palace, the fearsome Mabu mask emerges to threaten the crowd with its solo display of might (*shiɛŋə*), but it does not police the Fuləŋgaŋ group of which it is a member, joining instead in the line like the other masks during the dance. For audience members to be able to make the connection between the violence of the mask and the erstwhile role of the slave driver and the labor recruiters, they must piece together the palatine and the village performances that are presented distinctly from one another. The village masks, however, provide the Rosetta stone to the sublimations or fracturing to which the palace masks submit the past. In placing the driver mask alongside the line of dancers and making it vent its fury on the other masks in the line, the village masks return the driver to its proper place alongside its "slaves" and reveal the connection between the line of masks and the slave cara-van that is obfuscated in the separate palace performances.

Yet, while the masks of the palace fracture and dissimulate the full significance of the memories they allude to, they remain ineffably fear-some (*bɛmə*), whereas the masks that reveal the full violence of the past most plainly in their performance are paradoxically objects of affection, pleasure, and delight. While the palace's Fuləŋgaŋ group and its individual masks could be said to embody the violence of slavery and forced labor in all of its horror, the past is remembered in a crucially different manner by the village masks. While they reenact the slave marches more clearly than do the veiled performances of the palace, they simultaneously trans-form the desperate terror of that era into a festive dance that is lived by its participants above all as an intensely pleasurable event. While the sorties of the palace masks subject their audience to a humiliating form of unmediated violence that seems to reinstate the political relations of slavery in the palace courtyard intact, village masks—at the same time that they reconstitute the fractured past of the palace performances in its full horror—enjoin all to participate and to take pleasure in the beauty of the performance on an equal footing, excluding no one and creating of a community fractured by political polarization a new whole in which the cadets and scapegoats are suddenly heroes and heroines, the "slaves" of the masking line an image of beauty and pleasure, and the women of the compound symbols of desire, nurture, fertility, and regeneration for all to behold and to celebrate.[24] Where the palace perpetuates by concealing the terror of the past, the village masks dispel it by revealing it.[25]

Finally, the laments sung by the male elders present give verbal expression to these nondiscursive references to the violence of the past, albeit in an aoristic, aporetic manner that transcribes the political violence of the distant past onto the recent past of personal memory: the reincarnation of time noted by J.D.Y. Peel (1984) for the Ijesha. The song of Chiente, for example, opens with a lament on the tragic brevity of life—a child is no sooner born than he becomes a mouthpiece, replacing his father as compound head—and then it goes on to refer to the practice of selling or pawning children and of offering them for fosterage: "The mother entered with her child of Njinikijem but there was no one to buy it./The father and the mother left without the child." Once a way out of economic hardship for desperate parents, pawning and fosterage could also turn out to be a child's first steps toward enslavement in the Grassfields. Parents knew this and resisted pawning their children but sometimes had to in times of famine. Chiente is well placed to sing of these practices. Unable to marry, he spent the majority of his life in exile and returned to Oku a childless and destitute old man—a classificatory child despite his age. When he sang this song, he was living in a one-room hovel in Jikijem. In the line just quoted, Chiente is therefore alluding, however elliptically, to his own poverty, exile, and resulting classificatory childhood, but the phrase is not coined on the spur of the moment. The lament is improvised, but on the basis of a set of known phrases that are perpetually reused and modified through the generations to fit the singer's personal circumstances and intention.

This line of the lament could be said to "remember" more than Chiente does himself at the moment of his singing, having originally been coined to refer to the ravages of the slave trade and the tragedy of famine and fosterage. In this way, the past perdures, but not as an involuntary repetition or an intrusive memory. Rather, requiems first coined for generations of the dead of the precolonial and colonial pasts now return to add depth and background to the suffering of the recently deceased, whose lives are still vivid memories for contemporary generations. Furthermore, not only do the laments remember the dead but they highlight the personal indignities and frustrations of contemporary singers, indignities and frustrations with which all the celebrants can identify. This form of memory work also has a reflexive aspect, for just as the past adds background to the present, so too contemporary experiences of loss and humiliation provoke evocations of the historical past that keep it alive as a form of embodied memory of suffering, which constitutes a living memory.[26] The memorial celebration crystallizes these living memories of a past-present, placing them in counterpoint to the heroic discourse of the palace masks and providing a paean to the people's own subjective experience of centuries of violence.

The memorial celebration also prompted Mbey to reflect on the tragedies of his own life. Although he is one of the most respected master carvers in Oku and a member of *kwifon,* Mbey was also living in exile when he sang that day, having moved from the compound near the palace of which he was the head to the border village of Febwo, near Nganggang, to escape the witchcraft attacks to which he was subject in his home compound. By fleeing the compound he had just inherited, he lost everything he had.[27] Like Chiente who comes in after him, Mbey sings of the tragic brevity of life in the first five lines of his lament. The fourth line, "I'm worrying/ tormented about the world, what could people be thinking?" is a standard expression of anxiety. When people are "thinking about the world," they are acknowledged to be in an isolated depressive state. This lament then gives way to an ambiguous phrase that recalls the grave-stamping song in chapter 7. Mbey sings:

Went and divided it up, went and came back
and saw their mouths dry.[28]

The grave-stamping song had similarly referred to the fon of Nso' as "coming up" and "dividing the land":

The fon came up here
He divided the land!
Ate! Ate![29]

The term *gia-gia* in the grave-stamping song is a continuous form of the verb *giate*, "to divide," used by Mbey.[30] Mbey's song of an unnamed person going, dividing, and returning thus clearly echoes the well-known grave-stamping song and shifts the celebratory mood of the memorial feast back to the original event of his friend's death, dragging the time of death back into the present celebration and effectively collapsing the chronology that would provide the distance from the past, the forgetting, and the closure of an official memorial. However, it also reverses its elegiac effect by inscribing the ribald humor of the grave-stamping song onto the memorial celebration. The ritual laughter that was misplaced at the time of the burial is thus mirrored by Mbey's inappropriate mourning during the festivity of the "dancing die." This ambiguity is echoed in the indeterminacy of Mbey's referent. Because the referent is left unnamed, it could be the fon of Nso' of the grave-stamping song (and by extension the fon of Oku, to whom it subversively points), but it could also be Mbey's friend, whom he likens to the fon in that he was head, or "fon," of his compound: "Oh! A man is the fon of his compound."

Finally, the line of the lament clearly also refers to Mbey's life experience: in the following line of his lament, Mbey, like Chiente, is referring to his own life, turning the meaning of line 2 away from the deceased by singing ambiguously, in line 3, of his exclusion from his own compound: "Oh! A man is the fon of his compound [but soon] leaves and another takes his place." Although "leaving" would normally be understood as a euphemism for death in such songs, and especially in relation to succession, in this case it can also be understood literally in relation to Mbey's own life history. It was not death but disputes and suspected witchcraft that drove Mbey to leave his compound prematurely. When Mbey asks rhetorically in line 8 whether the deceased compound head for whom the celebration is taking place has gone to return again, his elegy provides its own answer, returning the memory of the deceased to his compound and to the celebrants some years after his death. Moreover, as it returns his memory to the present, so to the requiem fuses it with the memories of Mbey's own suffering as a result of political intrigue, returning him too to his compound, if only fleetingly.

The death of close kin and friends thus elicits a host of references irradiating outward from the anguish caused by the loss of the individual being commemorated in the memorial rites, and including the suffering that the bereaved have experienced throughout their lives. This is true for the women who go through the village wailing immediately after a death as much as for men singing at a memorial celebration. In addition, because the songs make use of a limited number of tropes, allusions, and metaphors, the men's laments take on wider referential qualities for their listeners, juxtaposing personal experiences of contemporary suffering with the history of political violence to which the members of the floating population have for centuries been subject in the Grassfields. By means of the laments, the memory of a single death or the loss of one family member or friend is made to bear a metonymic relationship to deeper, more inchoate memories and serves as a point from which a fathomless well of timeless suffering is plumbed. The pathos of the laments and the depth of feeling they evoke emerge from the connections they draw between the single death and the unplumbed reservoir of suffering sedimented into the language of the songs. In its latency, the violence of the past bridges the centuries to haunt future generations, who give it new life in their explorations of their personal experiences of private grief and contemporary political domination alike.[31]

The laments put into words what the masks embody, evoking the otherwise unvoiced violence of the past to address the pain of personal grief, the suffering of exile, and the uncertainty and inequity of contemporary life.[32] Conversely, memorial celebrations are understood and experienced in terms of a history of violent affliction that was never fully experienced as it happened. One of the implications of this lacuna is that history happens in a perpetually delayed present in the Grassfields: the political past of the Grassfields—the violence of state formation and imbrication into the global economy—is what *will have been* experienced in the recurring personal losses of daily life and death. And if the past comes to be experienced through present tragedies and struggles, contemporary political relations are informed by latent bodily memory and aporetic, overdetermined requiems. The dances of the Grassfields thus make the unremembered past and the tragedies and struggles of the present knowable by collapsing them one into the other, making everything happen *at once.* The laments sung at memorial celebrations are quite literally elegiac: not only are they elegies to the dead, but by means of their aoristic relationship to time, they take on a transcendent, revelatory quality. The memorial celebration is referred to as the "dance of death," or the "dancing death" (*bin εykwo*), emphasizing that it is not only a celebration but also, again, a death. The memory of a death strikes not once but over and over again, but—even in its recurrences—always *for the first time,* collapsing and fracturing chronological time as it does so. Although the dance of death presences the death again, however, performing it as a perpetual recurrence of past deaths, it returns death in its festal form, as dance, seduction, laughter, and triumphal celebration.

"Dancing death" is by definition a pleasurable if emotionally complex and melancholic activity in the Grassfields, and the masks are an unending source of pride and of aesthetic pleasure to all those involved with them, including the members of the floating population of marginalized cadets and young women who are scapegoated by the palace masks and excluded from the palace hierarchy. Where the palace masks are sinister and often characterized by an aesthetic of ugliness, the village lineage masks are beautiful, and whereas the palace masks evoke the past in order to justify and thereby to dissimulate the domination and the violence of the palace, the lineage masks are inclusive and under the control of the cadets who found and dance them.

So central is this contrast that mask performances often make their agonistic relation to the palace clear for all to see—hence the snub given to the fon by the driver of Kɛŋkɔs when it was made to appear at the palace, and the grotesque commemoration of the event by naming a newborn child of the mask's compound "Spoils the Palace." In other words, although the political violence of the past permeates village masquerades as much as it does those of the palace, it permeates them in a new context, denuded of the hegemonic scaffolding erected around it in the dominant discourse of palatine hegemony. No longer justified as a necessary evil, village masking looses its sinister aura. The communal euphoria that is so characteristic of village masking and that so differentiates it from the palace performances thus marks the appropriation that the genre undergoes as cadets and women take control of it.[33] In their hands, for the first time, the true depth of the political polarization of the Grassfields is unveiled. Again, the dances of the peripheral lineages are elegiac: they are tragic and heartbreaking, but they are beautiful and cathartic because they provide a lens through which silent centuries of violence are embodied and brought to bear on the experience of the present.

In masked dance, the most marginal members of the floating population appropriate the violence of which they have always been the victims and redeem it in new representations that expose and transform their suffering and the fallacies of the palatine discourse. In positivistic terms, it may seem illogical for women (some of whom in the past were in the structural position of potential slaves) to use memories of slavery to perform fertility rites for the barren, for cadets in the same condition of subservience and insecurity to appear to ape the masquerades of the palace, and for elderly bachelors to celebrate the masks of the lineage hierarchies that have alienated and excluded them. But the dances of the village lineages are not those of the palace. The masks are beautiful and virile; they are the young cadets themselves who secretly don their disguises to dance in their compound courtyards and even at the palace itself. The women's seductive *liete* dance reveals the full extent of the transformation to palace masking that the village lineage performances achieve. In the course of the *liete* dance, the women of the compound perform in public the seductions that they were prohibited in private, dancing the amorous conquests of the young lovers they are denied by their early marriages to polygamous elderly elites.

While the palatine discourse of masking emphasizes the dangers of masks to women, the village masks inevitably hesitate on the edge of the dancing ground, waiting for the women to lure them in and revealing, like the night masks, a secret collusion between the maskers and the *ngɔn djuo*—the women who married out of the compound and who remain forever "eligible virgins" to their compound's masks. Likewise the men known throughout Oku as the best singers are inevitably elders who have lived tragic rather than exemplary lives; these are not the titled elders of the palace hierarchy but the black sheep who have often been excluded from it on account of witchcraft accusations and exile. Their elegies again reveal the hollowness of the palace discourse of masking, counterposing the experiences of subjection at the palace with the cathartic revelation of the true measure of their lives and the real cost of state formation in the Grassfields.

CHAPTER NINE

Histories of the Present, Histories of the Future

Everything is near and unforgotten. — Paul Celan, from a letter to Erich Einhorn (1944)

All of it is now it is always now. — The slave girl Beloved, remembering the Middle Passage from Africa to the United States, in Tony Morrison (1987, 210)

We believe in the fiction of past, present, and future, but it may also be true that everything happens simultaneously. — Isabelle Allende (1985, 490)

Nothing conclusive has yet taken place in the world, the ultimate word of the world and about the world has not yet been spoken, the world is open and free, everything is still in the future and will always be in the future. — Mikhail Bakhtin ([1963] 1984, 165–66)

Remembering in the Time of the Postcolony

In the Grassfields, as we have seen, forms of violence and mass destabilization that were originally of exogenous origin were gradually appropriated by a minority of elites within the region. The result was that
by the late precolonial period, the terror that was the slave trade was no
longer a large-scale campaign waged by foreign invaders but an insidious small-scale process of cannibalism perpetrated by the Judases in the
community. The same historical cycle could be said to have recurred in
the twentieth century: the colonial period reintroduced large-scale forms
of coercive displacement, forced labor, and high death rates controlled by
a foreign power. By midcentury, however, this process had been largely
taken over by the elites of the strongest states in the Grassfields, who had
established themselves as middlemen for the colonial authorities, wield-

ing power locally on their behalf while perpetuating the hegemony of the palaces. Finally, with the emergence of the postcolonial state, the violence of a modern, centralized autocratic regime was once again internalized as a few entrepreneurs—often of commoner origins—obtained access to the single party, effectively becoming the gatekeepers not only of industry but also of political representation. Again, they were rapidly inculcated as neo-notables into the palaces of the Grassfields, which were thereby called into service on behalf of the state (Argenti 2005a). As in the late precolonial period, the great majority of the young, the poor, and women were once again marginalized and exploited by their own elites and a new predatory state.

Like the historical cycles of the Grassfields in which large-scale exogenous incursions have three times been appropriated and framed in terms of a local idiom by the palatine elite, the performances of palace masks and elites effectuate a process of sedimentation that interleaves experiences of exogenous and local violence within a Grassfields performative genre. The result is a recapitulation of the history of the Grassfields in which unforgotten centuries of tension between violent insertion into the Atlantic and later global trade and mass emigration, on the one hand, and palatine discourses of locality and cultural authenticity on the other are brought to bear on the contemporary experience of ordinary people. If history is about a fixed, determined past from which one can clearly delimit oneself, the memories embodied in the dances of the Grassfields burst the dam of the past, allowing its murky waters to come flooding forth in the guise of the menacing masks of the palace. Although the audience at the palace may be swept away on the terror of the past, however, these spectacles of power also presence the contemporary relations of violence, suffering, and inequity that still characterize Grassfields political reality and give their immediate salience to the performative remembering of slavery, forced labor, witchcraft, cannibalism, and human sacrifice.

Not only are cadets victims of the recurrence of the past in the form of embodied practices but also in the form of the literal return of the past, as the Grassfields continues to be plunged into insecurity and violence by unaccountable exogenous forces personified most clearly in the massacres perpetrated by the paramilitary forces. It is therefore not only due to cognitive or psychological factors that the past recurs in the present, then, but also because of political failures that make of the African postcolony today as much a space of death as it was in previous eras. In the living death of the postcolony, in which the past perdures not only as remembering but, all too often, in the ongoing repetitive experience of political violence and social polarization, the poetic indeterminacy of masking represents not an affliction but a response. It may seem that I have stretched credibility by suggesting that nondiscursive practices can embody memories of events that happened centuries ago. Like the violence they represent, the dances shape perceptions of time in line with the belatedness of their original exemplars. As unclaimed experience and encrypted memories come to be remembered as dance, they lose their determinacy and are thus opened up to overdetermination. In a political context that has remained insecure and has retained its fundamental hierarchical inequities over centuries, future instances of violence in turn will also come to be indexed by bodily practices that evoke the violence of the past and of a past-present that still recurs in the Grassfields today. Dance thus forges connections between present and past suffering, and forever bears witness to the futurity of suffering in a space of terror—a space in which what happened yesterday is (always) happening now. In the Grassfields, the past is commemorated not only through memorial practices but also by contemporary forms of violence. The reason the past is evoked so vividly in the dances of the Grassfields is because its structures of inequity perdure atavistically in current social relations.

Because masking is an embodied practice, it represents a nondiscursive, and therefore gnomic, form of remembering. Its very ambiguity can become a tool with which to pry open the Pandora's box of histories that have been silenced by extreme violence. This is not to say that masking is merely a performance, with a set script and choreography and a neat distinction between "performers" and "audience." Nor is it the return of the violence itself in all its meaningless immediacy. Rather, masking treads the line between art and life, retracing the steps that the fractured timescape of violence would elide, while pulling life toward myth in order to remember it in the image of a new world. Because masks remember the violence not as such but as an image of what the world might be, they engender memories of what has yet to be—memories of the future.

Masking Violence/Revealing Violence

Those who make use of indeterminate genres to express themselves despite the strictures of authoritarian social systems and autocratic regimes are making a Faustian bargain. The indeterminacy of nondiscursive representations of the past is advantageous not only to the oppressed but also to those who have something to hide. The memory of hundreds of thousands of slaves transshipped in the transatlantic slave trade and of the countless others absorbed into the local and regional trades of which the Grassfields formed a part is kept hidden by elite discourses of power that represent fons and their retinues as benign, paternalistic figures and even as heroes who saved their people from oppression and protected them from enslavement. The mythical representation of the past, offering only gnomic pronouncements in the place of clarity, makes it possible for the palace elite to elide the violence that their ascendancy necessitated, representing the sylvan, feral origins of fons as proof of their access to sources of unfathomable wealth and sacred power. In the elite discourse, the hidden forest-palace and the chthonian watery haunts of the fon stand at once for access to sources of global wealth and for contact with the ever-legitimating realm of the ancestors. Moreover, the unashamed emphasis in the myths on the genocide of local populations as the basis for the genesis of new chiefdoms offers fons the opportunity to communicate the coercive violence of their rule in a heroic genre: the permissible, limited violence against dehumanized strangers that begets the chiefdom denotes, at the same time that it dissimulates, the illegitimate coercive violence that the palaces deployed against their own people in subsequent historical eras.

Likewise in the performance of state embodied by the palace masks, the fundamental dependence of emerging hierarchies on the labor and sale of cadets—often from their own chiefdoms—is elided by means of the indeterminacy of speechless performance, which displays the terrifying power of the palace while simultaneously, and quite literally, masking it. The masking of palatine power thus facilitates a displacement: the conceit that the performances are not representations of the power of the palace but rather demonstrations of the exogenous dangers posed by foreign raiders and witches. The masks of the palace at once "display" (*shiɛŋə*), and even at times deploy, the violence at the heart—indeed in the intestines—of state formation in the Grassfields, while simultaneously projecting that violence outward in order to preserve the legitimating effect of the discourse of paternalism. The palace discourse would have it that the masks are at once what the palace protects the cadets *from* and what it protects them *with*.

As we have seen, however, the poetics of masking that make the discursive conceits of the palatine elite possible also allow for counterdiscursive readings. With respect to the myths of origin, for example, the cadets who help to promulgate the myths do not do so as passive recipients of the palatine discourse but rather because the indeterminacy of the myths allows for alternative readings. Just as indeterminacy is a boon to the palace elite, so too the marginalized make use of the multiple levels of interpretation possible in the myths to emphasize different aspects altogether of the histories they evoke. What makes the early fons folk heroes to them is not the fact that they are fons or elites, but precisely that they were not fons but cadets and members of the floating population when they were banished from their places of origin. And when they gleefully point to the bloody massacres of defenseless autochthonous peoples committed by these fons, are the cadets applauding the sacrificial violence that founded the state, or rather are they bearing witness to the point at which refugees turned into raiders and began to loose their legitimacy and the devotion that they enjoyed as marginalized outcasts?

The ambiguity of the violence of the palace masks can likewise be turned on its head by the cadets who go to the palace intent on provoking the wrath of the masks. Although the palatine discourse makes use of the undomesticated appearance and the foreign associations of its masks to project its violence outward, the cadets force the palace masks to chase them and to beat them, thus revealing in its starkest terms the violence of the palace against its people. Seen from this point of view, the uncontained violence of the palace masks is nothing less than a reenactment of the violence engendered by state formation against countless generations of cadets. The chase that the cadets initiate by their mere presence in the palace courtyard surreptitiously becomes the means to bear witness to centuries of youth, suddenly brought back to life to unmask what masking masks: the unspeakable anthropophagy of state formation.

Nor do the cadets restrict themselves to revelation by means of passive victimization. At the hands of the village lineages that populate the borderlands of the chiefdom on the periphery of palatine influence and control, experiences of violence and humiliation at the hands of the palace masks are transformed in mimetic representations that reinscribe masking not as a form of subjection to authority but as an elegiac, transcendent, and simultaneously ludic and festal practice that pulls the audience members in and unites them in the dance. Occasioned by death, the village dances are nonetheless about laughter, love, and seduction. The eloquent laments that the marginalized elders sing to their accompaniment are likewise based in the pain of loneliness, alienation, bachelorhood, and childlessness, but they tell of friendships and small victories and reclaim lives and experiences that would be forgotten by the official histories of the palace discourse. To the official memories of terror promulgated in the palatine myths and masks, the cadets reply with the countermemories of renewal and revitalization embodied in their own distinct celebratory masking tradition.

History and Utopia

This work has focused on remembering and the weight of the past in the present, but it has also questioned unreconstructed approaches to historical time as a unilineal and unidirectional chronological progression. With respect to the Grassfields, the masks of the village lineages in particular could be seen to look forward as much as they do backward in the remembering they embody. Not only do they emphasize rebirth and renewal rather than death and domination, but—taken as a whole composed of the initial burial ceremony followed by the commemorative celebration—they actually transform burial into rebirth and death into life. In this manner, the carnivalesque, grotesque aspects of village masks confront the memorial practices of the austere and fearsome palace masks with practices of remembering that orient themselves to a future that is open and heterogeneous rather than to a past that is monolithic and monstrous. In that they forever seek to overcome and to destabilize the official palatine memories that haunt the present and introduce complex temporal structures that revisit the past in order to revise the present, the practices of remembering of the village masks could be said to be utopian, and therefore to be politically radical.[1]

At the same time, however, the utopianism of dance is not born of Panglossian naïveté but of the experience of deep suffering inflicted during centuries of inequity. It seeks not a cloistered removal or retrenchment from the world but rather represents a radical intervention in the world. If the utopianism of dance evokes the past, it is not because the past is dead and gone but because the past returns in the social inequities and political polarizations of the present. The imitation of the past reveals not what has disappeared, then, but what doggedly perdures: it reveals the atavism of social formations that continue to marginalize and to exploit youth in Cameroon, despite the advent of decolonization, the birth of the nation-state, and the recent introduction of multiparty democracy. Likewise, in its suggestion of possible future worlds, the dance is not merely a form of temporary escapism but—as the recurring youth uprisings in Cameroon suggest—a vision of the political horizon toward which all eyes are turned.

The utopianism of cadets' countermemories is therefore no less "real" than the memories of the palatine discourse. The reversals and inversions of critical utopianism may be situated "nowhere" (Ricoeur 1986, 15ff.), but in a nowhere that serves as a position outside the dominant discourse from which to attack it. Critical utopias are therefore as real as the dominant discourse that they continuously confront. Like the hierarchical relations promulgated by the palace, cadets' alternative practices are lived as part of social reality, and they inform the tenor of social and political relations outside the dance, just as the embodied discourses of palace masking also do. Their ecstatic existence doubles and at the same time transforms the somber hierarchies of the palace with momentarily lived alternatives that envision other possible worlds. Embodied remembering replaces the elite, officially sanctioned, and menacingly oppressive Time of the King with the opposing experience of a fractured timescape that appropriates and re-presents past horror and catastrophe with bodily practices of bacchanalian hilarity and pleasure. These practices may be said to be as ideological as the palatine discourse, but because they are not only cogitated but also incorporated and lived as a present, they have real implications in the present in which they recur and for the future in which they are still to come. The utopianism of the marginalized cadets is therefore not adequately conceived of simply as a form of false consciousness or an escapist fantasy but rather must be acknowledged as an alternative, critical interpretation of the past through which to live in the present and to envision possible futures.

In other words, the mimetic transformations of the village lineage dances introduce a supplement that comes between the event and its re-enactment, and it is this supplementarity that constitutes remembering, thereby transforming the nature of the experience itself. Nor is it just the exemplar of the palace masks that is transformed by the village masks. More fundamentally, village masking practices transform the memories of the past—of slavery and colonial violence—that the palace masks embody. Where the palace masks repeat history as tragedy, the village youth could be said to do so as farce. In the village, the horrific memory of the slave driver and the line of slaves, or of the colonial labor recruiter and the line of porters, recurs as it does in the palace group masquerade, but this time with a transcendent quality, stripped of its horror as it is reclaimed and opened up to new forms of contemplation. The monstrousness of the past is not monolithic, however.[2] It is lived as terror and subjection but also relived in its grotesque, ironizing form as celebration.

In standard psychiatric and psychoanalytic thinking, chronological conflations are thought of as resulting from intrusive, involuntary memories arising from traumatic precursors, and consequently they are seen purely negatively as symptoms or as an affliction. The use to which the afflicted in Africa put such experiences of time, however, reveals that suffering itself can provide a form of knowledge and of insight, if not of empowerment.[3] The memories that appear to intrude into the monstrous, achronological present of regimes of terror are not only symptoms; they are not pathological, nor are they inaccurate or false. On the contrary, such memories highlight the historical and political continuities that both pathologizing medical discourses and positivistic historical discourses equally elide. In this sense, regimes of therapy could be said inadvertently to have similar effects on experiences of time and structures of memory as the regimes of terror whose victims they purport to care for.

Where standard psychological approaches would view the conflation of past events into a single realm of experience as symptoms of traumatic stress, and where historical approaches would describe the equation of the precolonial with the colonial and the postcolonial eras as a failure to record or to understand one's history, the indeterminacy of the performances of Grassfields masks reveals the essential continuities denied by positivistic approaches to knowledge and experience. Reading between the lines of the available historical material, we have seen that the distinctions that are upheld among the era of the slave trade, the colonial era, and the postcolonial era are all largely indefensible. As we know, the era of slavery bled over into the colonial period and was in effect indissociable from the experience of forced labor—distinguished from it only rhetorically. Likewise, the introduction of the postcolonial era has not marked a change in the economic or political condition of exploitation and oppression for ordinary people on the ground in Cameroon but only a perpetuation of the same socioeconomic conditions under a new group of elites. The falsehood then is not the "subjective" experience of the cadets of the Grassfields but the doxic reproduction of an empiricist chronological model that would place substantive distinctions between periods of time that were not in reality distinguishable.

Such an unreconstructed historical model is false for two reasons. First, it introduces a modernist teleological paradigm according to which social formations in the Grassfields over the centuries have been characterized by change and transformations—even by progress and evolution—where in fact consecutive phases of insertion into global modernity have visited more repetition than they have change on the political relations of the Grassfields. The second falsehood is that under such violent conditions, it remains possible any longer for the people of the Grassfields to place events in time, and thus to "put them behind" themselves. As we have seen, the past of the Grassfields cannot be forgotten because it cannot be chronologized: its unclaimed experience forms the basis for the recurring present of contemporary generations of cadets.[4] And here the between-character of masking is revealed: between life and art, violence and performance, terror and celebration, past, present, and future. Because the dance is incorporated, it is indeterminate and aporetic, and this ultimately guarantees its perpetual return, its futurity. This futurity in turn makes of its incorporations of past terror and violence forms of ecstatic, liberatory revelation that transform the claustrophobic oppression of the past into recurring experiences of possible futures.

Shibboleth: Belatedness and Encryption in the Grassfields

Borrowing from the tenets of the trauma paradigm the notion that extreme violence is not open to experience by its victims at the time of its occurrence, but only later in its reenactments, Cathy Caruth (1991c) and others have argued that such extreme experiences fracture time and introduce what she terms belatedness: the return in the form of reenactments of memories that were effectively repressed at the time of their occurrence. Without taking on board the elements of the trauma paradigm that we have already critiqued, it is still nonetheless possible to see the value of a notion of belatedness for understanding embodied memories of political violence in the Grassfields. None of the data discussed in this monograph suggests that the experience or the meaning of the extreme violence of the slave trade and forced labor was hidden from individuals by the psychological effects of posttraumatic stress, nor do the data suggest that reenactments of that seminal violence by later generations represent pathological, involuntary, or intrusive forms of memory. The dances of the Grassfields cannot usefully be represented as symptoms.

Nevertheless, it may still be the case that the full significance of individual incidents—each Chamba slave raid, each abduction by a Judas, each colonial labor recruitment drive—is not given in the singular moment of their occurrence and experience. Rather, it is only the *longue durée* that places each incident, each experience, within the wider context of the struggle that gives it its meaning—a meaning that is open to perpetual reinterpretation as time passes. In Homi Bhabha's words (1990, 308), the past can become "an anteriority that continually introduces an otherness or alterity within the present," and the challenge is then to "narrate the present as a form of contemporaneity that is always belated." The history of the Grassfields is belated by the indeterminacy of the unresolved atrocities of the past, which have yet in their reenactments fully to be disclosed, to be determined. What the past will have been is not yet known. It is still the site of a struggle between youth and elites in the Grassfields today. The past of the Grassfields is belated not by the despair of trauma, then, but by the hope and anticipation of ongoing political struggle. Nor is it situated in individual psyches but rather in the body of the people. The belated past marks the transition from the individualized and fragmentary experiences of the atomizing effects of violence to communal, enculturated forms of experience that bridge between individuals, creating and re-creating the social formations that will elaborate it and carry it forward into the future. Despite their predicament, the youth of the Grassfields would be the first to agree with Bakhtin that "nothing conclusive has yet taken place in the world," that the world is "open and free," and that "everything is still in the future and will always be in the future" ([1963] 1984, 165–66).

Just as we can make the case for the heuristic benefits of the concept of belatedness once it is divested of its individualizing implications, so too our understanding of the effects of political violence and the reasons for its recurrence and reenactment through time may be enhanced by reference to the notion of encryption. In a preface written for Nicolas Abraham and Maria Torok's work on Freud's Wolf Man case, *Cryptonymie: Le verbier de l'homme aux loups,* Derrida (1976) refers to the realm of "deep memory" by analogy as a "crypt" or a "forum"—a place hidden within or beneath another place, closed off from that outside itself of which it is nevertheless an inherent part. Derrida thus emphasizes the simultaneous inclusion and exclusion of experiences of extreme violence. The crypt is formed in violence, by violence, and yet also in silence. For this act of violence to remain silent and unheard, one places it as far as one can apart from oneself, but this place is in fact deep within the self. The cryptic enclave thus becomes a space of incorporation rather than of introjection, as is the case with "normal" experience and narrative memory. This failure of introjection, in other words, is at the root of a somatic embodiment of memory.[5] In the case of the death of close family members, the memory of the loved one may take up residence inside the crypt, *forum,* or *for,* where he or she will remain "safe": "dead, safe (save) in me" (Derrida 1976, 17).[6] By means of incorporation, the dead thus become the living dead inside us.

Once again, an argument based on a Western, Judeo-Christian, psychoanalytic model of the person is not applicable outside the cultural sphere of its elaboration, but the concept of the crypt might still be uncoupled from the individualized model of the person and applied to the comparatively dividual self of the Grassfields as well as to the social body of the cadets or the chiefdom as a whole. This is not to suggest a return to the mystical notion of a Jungian collective unconscious or to Levy-Bruhl's collective representations. A group consciousness need not be reified in order to envisage that experiences of extreme political violence are constituted not in the atomistic moment of the individual perpetration itself, but over time and intersubjectively between the members of social bodies of victims and social bodies of perpetrators, in their interactions with each other both within and between their groups. As we have seen, the violence of the past is not generally open to discursive contemplation in the Grassfields but embodied in bodily practices that bring people together for joint performances. In dance, individuals join together to re-present as a group what first happened to individuals. Because the dance actively disindividuates the experience of violence at the same time as it embodies it, the violence becomes encrypted in the social body of the people. The disappeared of the slave trade and the colonial period are not entombed deep within individual psyches but rather immanent in the embodied relations between the individual masks in the dance, and between the masks and audience members that the dance brings together. In this manner, the dead are encrypted not in individuals but in the relations between individuals that the dance brings to life.

In his 1986 work *Schibboleth,* Derrida turns his attention to the poetry of Paul Celan, focusing on one key word in Celan's oeuvre that encapsulates the indeterminacy of representation. This work of Derrida's reveals more than any other the crucial role that indeterminacy plays in mimetic representation, and he applies this idea to the question of the traumatic history of the Second World War, the central subject of Celan's work. In the world of the Old Testament, the word *shibboleth* was found in a whole family of languages and had a multiplicity of senses: river, stream, sheaf of wheat, olive branch. But it is remembered above all for having become a password: after a battle in which the army of Jephtah defeated the Ephraimites, the retreating Ephraimites were forced to pronounce the word as a test of their identity. They could not pronounce the *shi* of *shibboleth* and so were instantly killed. Derrida sees in this catastrophe the source of an indetermination: the unpronounceability of the word led to the massacre, but the massacre made the word inenunciable from then on.

Referring to a massacre it dare not name, the word becomes overdetermined and begins to appear again and again to refer to further catastrophic events throughout Western history, and each one of these events is consequently referred back to the first seminal massacre. Paul Celan makes use of the word *shibboleth* regularly in his poetry, using the word's lack of determination—and its resulting overdetermination—to evoke the catastrophe of the death camps, which he had himself survived. Derrida highlights the aporetic uses to which Celan puts fragmentary dates in his poems—with the year or the day elided—to make them refer to several historical events, several wars, several massacres, at once. Indeed, "In Eins" ("in one," "at once") is the title of one of his most renowned poems. Celan's dates are thus themselves shibboleths, and likewise the originary massacre to which the word *shibboleth* refers is overlaid in Celan's poetry with references to other massacres: the Shoah, the Spanish civil war, the October Revolution, the fall of Vienna. Furthermore, Derrida (1986, 49) notes that the deliberate indeterminacy of the poems, their aporetic nature, allows for the inclusion of future events, and future readings of past events that have not yet come to be known. Aware of the silencing effects of extreme violence, Celan wrote his poems in an anterior future: for what will have been known, *what will have been.*

In their mimetic relation of re-presentation and re-inscription in relation to the untold events of the past, the dances of the Grassfields can usefully be thought of as shibboleths. Their references to horrific ordeals are replayed in a way that makes events that were never fully subject to experience when they first took place visible as if for the first time; their performance makes them *happen* for the first time. Simultaneously, the dances introduce elements of beauty and of hilarity to the original horror—but without, for all that, eliding the horror. This is the secret of the uncanny tension that these performances are able to foment: at once horrific and beautiful, frightening and attractive, the dances introduce the play of difference that makes the ultimate meaning of what is represented irreducible. Dance in general is resistant to reductions of any kind—whether verbal or textual. Because the dances, sharing in this respect one of the qualities of poetry, are aporetic, they put gestures, movements, and forms into play that may be interpreted in many different ways.[7] By means of aporia, one performance is overdetermined with references to many different times and events, underscoring the subjective reality of the haunting of the present by the ghosts of the past. In their resistance to totalizing interpretations, these dances are thus opposed to monumental forms of remembering that would fix in the past what refuses to remain in place and can be known only in its reenactments—that is to say, only in its appearance in a present and a future that are always already doubled and split in their indissoluble relation to the past. The unspeakable past of the Grassfields is what *will have been* known only in the performative incorporation of its remembering. While this implies that the past will never and can never be known in a totalizing, monolithic way, it also suggests that it will always inform the present—that it will never be subject to the ultimate forgetting that Derrida has called "incineration" (1986, 83 [trans. mine]) and Dori Laub (1991) "the annihilation."

The indeterminacy of the dance also marks a fundamental ambivalence, however. Its role as a shibboleth retrieves from oblivion the unutterable recurring past that can and must never be forgotten: "the hell of our memory" (Derrida 1986, 83 [trans. mine]). But this indeterminacy can invert its effect. The password, mispronounced, becomes one's last word. The means of safe passage is also an ordeal. The poetic indeterminacy of coded references and secret words may provide the oppressed a manner of resisting by knowing-without-saying, of encrypting, and of remembering, but the shibboleth, in the wrong hands, can also suddenly reverse its effect, becoming an impassable frontier, a means of discrimination for the oppressors.[8] So it is that the palatine elites of the Grassfields make use of masked dance for radically different ends than do the cadets who are excluded from access to the palace, traducing the references of the dances and inverting the experience of their remembering. The mimetic aspects of dance that make it a means to bear testimony to political violence and to presence silenced histories are thus at once (*in eins*) the means by which the discourse of the elite can be elaborated to become hegemonic and the divisions of history reinstated. Thus is dance the site of a fierce struggle in the Grassfields: a struggle for remembering, for meaning, for representation, for commemoration, for knowing, and for forgetting.

Because the past was never fully known as a present, it returns as silent, embodied remembering, but because it has been encrypted within the dance it will always be present. The past that could not be known as it happened is doomed to happen again in sempiternity. Are the dances merely denotative of what happened then, or is the truth what is happening here, now, in the performative poetics of the dance? Is the dance a present that refers to the past, or rather an anterior future through which contemporary events will come to be known? This is the shibboleth—the return of the unpronounceable date, the unspoken catastrophe, destined to silence, remembered in dance, and forever projected back into the present. The masks of the Grassfields are here now; they are the faces of the unburied dead and the disappeared. Unrestful and unforgotten, they are doomed to be known only in their returns. See them shuffling by the graveside; hear them crying in the night. They will always have been ghosts.

As you go forth, you know [what lies] behind.[9]
           — Oku proverb

Notes

Preface

1. The language density of the Cameroon Grassfields is the highest in Africa. The region has been divided into four subsections: Momo, Ring, Metchum, and Mbam-Nkam. Although the languages of the Grassfields have been said to share 55 percent of their basic vocabulary with each other, they have distinct noun-class and tonal systems and are not on the whole mutually intelligible. Barriers to communication are overcome by widespread multilingualism and the use of West African pidgin as a vehicular language. For studies and classifications of the languages of the Grassfields, see Guthrie (1948, 1953), Hyman (1972, 1979, 1980), Hyman, Voeltz, and Tchokokamet (1970), Hyman and Voorhoeve (1981), Johnston (1919), Schaub (1985), Voorhoeve (1971), Warnier (1985, 3–5), and Williamson (1971).

Chapter One

1. As Rosalind Shaw (2002, 1–2) points out, it has often been noted by those setting out to study slavery in West Africa that informants are seldom forthcoming, and often irritated and evasive on the subject, giving the false impression that the slave trade has been forgotten altogether. It would be more accurate to say that such memories constitute "open secrets" "known by all, but knowingly not known" (Cohen 2001, 138, as quoted in Buckley-Zistel 2006, 132). However, while Cohen is concerned with the history of Western massacres and genocides of the twentieth century and Buckley-Zistel with the recent Rwandan genocide, African memories of slavery, an institution that is comparatively distant in time, are not best conceived of as a reserve of cognitive knowledge but rather as embodied practices

2. Here I use "social memory" in the sense developed by Paul Connerton ([1989] 1998).

3. In Eblam Ebkwo, the language of Oku, children are called *yon* or *yon ɔbtɛlɛ* (small children). The latter phrase differentiates between biological children and

youths, who are known specifically as *yondε war'*. The term *war'* literally refers to stirring, rustling, or rattling. Youths are thus known as "noisy children," or "agitated children." The term *war'* also alludes to grumbling or murmuring, and at meetings elders admonish youths not to "murmur" (*ya sə war*). Bachelors are known merely by the word for arm or hand, *əbkoy*, which specifically identifies their incompleteness, inferiority, and subjugation to classificatory adults, who are known as "people" (*wel, yel*). The term "arm" may also connote the use of bachelors for labor, as in the English expression "farmhands" for farm laborers. It may also have alluded to the role of bachelors as warriors: the right hand is referred to as the "spear hand" or "hand of war" *(əbkoy eyoŋ)* and identified as specifically male, in contradistinction to the left hand, the "woman's hand" *(əbkoy əbki)*.

4. *Cadets sociaux*, the same term as used by Meillasoux (1981), is rendered as "juniors" in the English translation of his work *Maidens, Meal and Money*.

5. In his analysis of Cameroon, Bayart ([1979] 1985, 233–81; 1992, 29–64) therefore refers to *cadets sociaux* rather than to *cadets*. *Cadets sociaux* are not always young, but they are by definition subject to elders. Furthermore, although the English term "youth," like the French *cadet*, tends to connote young men, Bayart's *cadets sociaux* refers to women as well as men, since both are subject to elders. Deborah Durham (2004) takes Bayart's insights a step further in her work on Botswana, revealing the ways in which "youths" are not only victims of this category but can also appropriate it in their political struggles against elders and the state.

6. Meillasoux (1981, 78ff.) goes so far as to suggest that cadets are only temporarily disfavored because they will one day become elders. Age, he claims, even understood in its social sense, is only a "transitional moment in the life of an individual" (80). By taking the terms of hierarchical distinction literally in this manner as if they really did refer to biological age, Meillasoux falls into the semiotic trap set by the elders: eldership is not a question of age but of power. As he acknowledges himself, referring to Rey (1971, 1975), in those societies that were subjected to the European slave trade for which they were the suppliers, juniors did not become elders but commodities to be sold. In such cases, as in the region that would come to be known as the Cameroon Grassfields, age was no more automatically transitional than was social rank.

7. Concerned as it is with the task of establishing a strong state in the midst of linguistic and cultural diversity, the Cameroonian government now looks to Grassfields rulers as an extension of its influence at the local level, using them as administrators and party supporters whenever possible (Argenti 1998; Goheen 1996; Geschiere 1993). The *fon*ship is thus gradually made to resemble an anodyne subcategory of the nation, with *fons* now officially ranked by the government into first class and second class, with first-class *fons* earning state salaries. Clearly illustrating the government's hegemonic project to extend its "tentacular grip over civil society" (Mbembe 1990, 60), Grassfields polities are incorporated into normalized national territories (the kingdom of Oku was thus "granted" subdivisional status

in 1992), and new elites increasingly replace "illiterate" elders, thus threatening the legitimacy of the chieftaincy in local people's opinion.

8. One of the main objects of the so-called authenticity campaigns—e.g., in Gabon under Bongo, Ghana under Nkrumah, Togo under Eyadéma, the CAR under Bokassa, or Zaire under Mobutu—was to facilitate a slippage that enabled the new elites to equate themselves with traditional elders and to treat their people—of whatever age or status—as children, defined for the most part as recalcitrant ingrates in need of stern leadership (cf. Bayart 1992, 59; Geschiere 1997, 37; Mbembe 1985, 16–18; and Toulabor 1992, 134ff.). Nevertheless, it must be said that the process of infantilization in African societies was never unilineal, unambiguous, or monolithic in its effects: in the Cameroon Grassfields, the "children" use their status regularly to make demands of the "fathers," and ungenerous kings have been shunned and alienated by their subjects. At the national level, activists demanding an enquiry into the case of the Bepanda 9, a group of men arrested in the city of Douala in 2001 on suspicion of having stolen a gas canister and summarily executed by the security forces holding them, voiced their protest on the basis that the victims were *jeunes* (youths), and thus by implication powerless, innocent, and consequently deserving of the protection of the state. This type of patron–client relationship recalls the implicit agreements between youth and elders in the precolonial Grassfields, in which youths in danger of enslavement would willingly relinquish any claim to freedom or independence in favor of submission to an elder or "father" who could grant them protection from capture by slave traders.

9. Today, 70 percent of Africa's population is under thirty years of age, and the majority of the total population is under the age of eighteen.

10. Bayart, Ellis, and Hibou sum up the situation regarding multiparty politics in Cameroon among other African countries in the following words (1999, 4–5):

> The process of democratisation has been captured, under the guise of competitive elections, by the authoritarian groups already in control of state power.... Efforts to combine the requirements of a market economy with the demands of popular sovereignty have ended in failure. There can be no doubt that most of the hopes raised by the promise of democratisation have now been dashed.... After the tide of reform movements had ebbed, the element of continuity between old and new regimes in both their social and political complexions became generally plain.... Hence what we are actually witnessing is the reproduction of the authoritarian condition which was widespread in the postcolonial period

11. See, e.g., Arnoldi (1995), Nunley (1987), Drewal and Drewal ([1983] 1990), Daniel (2005), Reed (2003), Strother (1998), Thomas (1993), and Thompson (1974).

12. Those sociologists and political scientists include, e.g., Bayart ([1979] 1985, 1989, 2000), Bazenguissa-Ganga (1999), Biyaya (2000), Kgobe (1997), MacGaffey

and Bazenguissa-Ganga (2000), Mbembe (1985), and Seekings (1993). For anthropologists, see, e.g., De Boeck and Honwana (2005), Durham (2000), Christiansen, Utas, and Vigh (2006), Cruise O'Brien (1996), Devisch (1995a), and Rasmussen (2000). For an anthropological study of youth from a global perspective, see Amit-Talai and Wulff (1995). For an early exception to this belated interest, see Gandoulou (1989a, 1989b).

13. Following Foucault (1974, [1975] 1977), Said (1995), and Mudimbe (1988), we can say that the framing or scaffolding to which African cultural production has been subjected in academia and the media constitutes a discourse rather than a simple, transparent representation. In this sense, to speak of "African art" or "African dance" is to speak first and foremost of the European cultural project according to which the West has constituted *itself* in relation to exotic, nonmodern, and remote others.

14. In keeping with the interests of the culture and personality school, Mead focused on what she saw as the psychological value of the dance in lifting children out of their shyness. In a society that discouraged individuality, the dance represented "a genuine orgy of aggressive individualistic exhibitionism" that served to compensate for the repression evident in other spheres of a young girl's life (1928, 98). Following Radcliffe-Brown's integrationist argument, John Blacking (1973, 51–52, 107–8) argued for an interpretation of Venda music and dance as a transcendental experience leading participants to experience a world outside time and beyond the frailty of individual human being: "Old age, death, grief, thirst, hunger, and other afflictions of this world are seen as transitory events. There is freedom from the restrictions of actual time and complete absorption in the 'Timeless Now of the Divine Spirit,' the loss of self in being" (1973, 52).

15. For a more extensive discussion of this subject, see Paul Spencer's (1985) thorough review of early anthropological theories of performance. For further reviews of the literature on dance and masking, see Argenti (1997), Drewal (1991), Kasfir (1988b), Royce ([1977] 2002), and Wieschiolek (2003).

16. Paul Spencer's ([1988] 2004) work on the Maasai of Matapato also falls into this school.

17. For another critique of Gluckman on the same basis, see Stallybrass and White (1986, 13).

18. Cf. Simon Ottenberg (1975, 131) on the masks of the Afikpo of eastern Nigeria: "The play asserts traditional norms and beliefs thereby supporting traditional leadership and its values. The players are not asking for a social revolution, but rather the proper execution of traditional leadership patterns."

19. See also Turner's (1968) study of *nkang'a,* the Ndembu female initiation rite, which he analyses in a similar manner, and Argenti (forthcoming) for a critical discussion. In focusing on the rites associated with circumcision and coming of age, Turner in effect delimited his study of youth to a conservative and highly controlled sphere of ritual performance that was bound to confirm his views regarding the cyclical nature of rites of passage and the reproduction of society. Although

he based his analysis on the model of *rites de passage* developed by Van Gennep (1909), he may ironically have done more justice to his data by focusing on Van Gennep's later work on French carnival and charivaris (1943–58, 1:196–212). As with most African masking, French and other European carnival activities of the late Middle Ages were organized under the auspices of the bachelors' associations and youth groups (which were known as Abbeys of Misrule) and were not strictly restricted to certain calendrical dates or predictably choreographed ceremonies. Rather, the inversions to which they gave rise were always overtly antiestablishmentarian, often anarchically unpredictable, and periodically violent—even potentially revolutionary (Bakhtin [1957] 1968; Davies 1971; Le Roy Ladurie 1979; Van Gennep 1943–58). What Le Roy Ladurie (1979, 349–50) says of carnival (and which also goes for the carnivalesque in general, which can erupt in society at any moment in opposition to the censure and domination of oligarchic authority) equally applies to the social relevance of youth performative practices in the Grassfields, which this book goes on to examine: "Carnival is not only a dualistic, prankish, and *purely momentary* inversion of society, destined in the last analysis to justify in an 'objectively' conservative fashion the world as it is [*comme il va*]. It is rather more an instrument of satiric, lyric, epic knowledge for groups in their complexity; therefore, an instrument of action, with eventual modifying force, in the direction of social change and possible *progress,* with respect to society as a whole" (as translated in LaCapra 2003, 55n10 [original emphasis]).

20. Although Jean-Pierre Olivier de Sardan (1993, 185ff.) has criticized Paul Stoller (1984) for interpreting this movement in terms of an intentional mockery or parody of the colonial administration, one should not deduce that the movement has no political significance. One of the points often overlooked by those who deplore the lack of politicization of African peoples is the degree to which overtly political activity is simply not practicable in authoritarian regimes. Within a context in which young people's organizations and meetings are prohibited unless they explicitly represent the youth wing of the party in power (often the single party), and in which imprisonment without charge, torture, and extrajudicial execution are routine, young people and the disenfranchised in general seek expression in mundane practices that can pass for religious, theatrical, or folkloric when the need arises, thus avoiding state censure. Bruce Kapferer's ([1983] 1991) study of the *tovil* healing performances of southern Sri Lanka provides one of the clearest arguments for the political relevance of possession. In his monograph, Kapferer reveals that demonic affliction is a class-specific illness, affecting only the poor, and that the healing rites for demonic affliction open the way to the transformation of the social sphere of the patient. In Kapferer's analysis as in Nunley's (1987), the world of demons is not a vestigial "folk" throwback to a bygone era but a contemporary commentary by the disenfranchised peasantry upon a violent political reality of oppression and exploitation. Demons are thus thoroughly modern entities—the contradiction of a bourgeois political order represented by the quasi-fascist tendencies of orthodox Buddhism—and they are always waiting to break

free in the war-ravaged slums of Sri Lanka. Possession by demons is metaphorical of subjugation to a monstrous "demon state" that is seen to be feeding on its people. For an African example of this phenomenon, see Nadia Lovell's study of possession in Togo as "muted defiance" (2006, 241ff.).

21. This recalls the nickname of Wan Mabu (Child of Mabu), an exuberant, acrobatic, and unpredictable mask belonging to the royal Ngele society in Oku, which is sometimes playfully referred to by its young acolytes and admirers as Minister of Youth and Sports. In this case as with the Ode Lay, young maskers and mask followers make use of local masking practices to address their marginalization by contemporary postcolonial, globalized systems of power. The satirical appropriation of such lofty bureaucratic accolades recalls the irreverent inversions of medieval European youth associations, with their Abbots of Misrule, Princes of Pleasure, and Grand Patriarchs of Syphilitics, to name but a few (Davies 1971, 43–44). As I discuss with respect to contemporary African cases, however, such appropriations are not straightforwardly satirical but ambiguously mimetic, creating a second reality with which the marginalized unemployed youths can parallel and infiltrate the hegemony of the postcolonial state.

22. For a further highly insightful analysis of this phenomenon, see Adelheid Pichler (forthcoming), who describes the Cuban Palero Mayombe ceremonies in which embodied memories of the punishment of slaves are reenacted. In the contemporary reenactments, however, the ordeals are stripped of their original horror and experienced as pleasurable events.

23. The famous pop musician Papa Wemba has sung about the dream of reaching Paris and seeking the coveted articles of clothing known to initiates as *griffes:*

> At Roissy-Charles-de-Gaulle
> My Love, chérie
> Know that I am waiting for you
> That day, chérie
> This griffe, it's Torrente
> This griffe, it's Mezo-Mezo
> This griffe, it's Valentino-Uomo.
> Papa Wemba, *Matebu* (trans. mine)

24. Although this may amount to nothing less than "a subversion of the cultural classification of a political order" (Friedman 1990, 318), it must also be kept in mind that its critical element only consists in the fact that the *sapeurs* are excluded from the wealth they so desperately desire. In other words, such movements are not to be read in simplistic Marxist terms as the rejection of the capitalist system from which their adherents are excluded, but as a plea for social inclusion and participation by a section of the population that has been marginalized by poverty, unemployment, rapid urbanization and social change, and state paternalism and authoritarianism.

25. See Palmié (2006), Röschenthaler (2006), and Warnier (2006).

26. Bakhtin ([1957] 1968) delineates three distinct stages of carnival. The first stage was a prehistoric, "primitive" period in which "ritual laughter" was inseparable from religious devotion, and insulting deities and laughing at them was seen as a positive ritual element with generative ritual force. The second was the Roman period, which he saw as an intermediary stage in which the state began to dissociate laughter from the serious business of worship and political display. In this period political leaders were still humiliated, mocked, and derided, especially during their coronations, but the serious and the comic began to be separated from one another, the former made official, the latter demoted as ineffectual, frivolous, and base. Finally, in the medieval world, the separation was completed in the third stage, with the state surrounding itself in the pomp and circumstance of the monolithically serious and allocating specified ritual festive times of year for the display of carnivalesque behavior.

27. As Bakhtin put it ([1957] 1968, 21): "To degrade is to bury, to sow, and to kill simultaneously, in order to bring forth something more and better. To degrade also means to concern oneself with the lower stratum of the body, the life of the belly and the reproductive organs; it therefore relates to acts of defecation and copulation, conception, pregnancy, and birth. Degradation digs a bodily grave for a new birth; it has not only a destructive, negative aspect, but also a regenerating one.... Grotesque realism knows no other lower level; it is the fruitful earth and the womb. It is always conceiving."

28. Homi Bhabha (1990, 293) identifies a similar alienation in the transnational experience of metropolitan modernity, which, he argues, also requires "a kind of 'doubleness' in writing; a temporality of representation that moves between cultural formations and social processes without a 'centred' causal logic." He refers to Derrida's ([1972] 1997, 210) proposition that in such circumstances, "the present is no longer a mother-form around which are gathered and differentiated the future (present) and the past (present) ... [as] a present of which the past and the future would be but modifications."

29. Throughout this work I use the term "remembering" rather than "memory" for two reasons: on the one hand, to emphasize the embodied nature of the social memories I describe, in which I do not refer to a body of cognitive data stored in individual minds, and on the other to emphasize that the memories I refer to do not represent petrified records of an unchanging, empirical past but rather intersubjectively constructed, open, pluralistic, and contested fields of action that are open to revision and transformations over time. Frederick Bartlett ([1932] 1995) makes the same semantic distinction to emphasize the role of memory as an ongoing social process, and Jennifer Cole (2001, 21–24) follows his usage to emphasize not only the way in which the past is recalled but, further, the literal re-membering of the social fabric that the Betsimisaraka of Madagascar perform to overcome the debilitating effects of colonial violence.

30. Achille Mbembe (1992; 2001, 103) shows how binary models of resistance

versus passivity, autonomy versus subjection, state versus civil society, hegemony versus counterhegemony, and totalization versus detotalization have clouded our understanding of postcolonial relations in Africa.

31. Clare Ignatowski (2006, 18) makes this point for the Tupuri of northern Cameroon in her recent study of their *gurna* performance, in which she refers to Labov's (1972) and Piersen's (1999) suggestion that the performance arts provide a sphere of indirect speech and communication in which conflicts can be aired without face-to-face confrontations.

32. Thus Dori Laub (1991, 81–82), writing on the Holocaust, reveals that the system of the Nazi death camps was foolproof in that it excluded the possibility of witnessing. To bear witness to a crime—and thus to inscribe its presence in history—one has to be able to stand outside of it and to look on, to bear witness. But the nature of the Holocaust was such that no one was able to stand outside or beside its events. Most crucially, even the victims of the Shoah were not able to bear witness to their own demise, and Dori Laub calls this aspect of the Shoah "the annihilation": not only did the event erase six million lives, even as it erased all record of its having done so, but it erased the possibility of effectively bearing witness. Countless victims of the Shoah have recounted that its most pernicious effect was that for decades afterward they internalized what had been affirmed about their otherness and their inhumanity, and came to believe that it was correct and even to admire their persecutors (Bettelheim 1943, 448–51). Thus the Shoah produced among its surviving victims first and foremost a prolonged silence (Caroll 1990; Langer 1991, 61; Laub and Podell 1995; Levi 1989, 83–84). In a context in which events are not communicable even to oneself as a victim, there is always the danger that one will come to doubt one's own experiences (cf. also Caruth 1991a, 1991b; Langer 1991, 88, 98–99).

33. As Rosalind Shaw (2002, 4) has argued with respect to memories of slavery among the Temne-speaking people of Sierra Leone, "the past is remembered not only in words but also in images and non-discursive practical forms that go beyond words." Shaw's model of memory has been critiqued (e.g., by Stewart 2004) on the basis that where memories are not made explicit, or where there is no verbal exegesis to prove that nondiscursive practices are overtly recognized to embody the traces of past events, they cannot be said to exist as memories. Such critiques are based on a cognitivist definition of memory as the conscious recollection of concrete forms of knowledge, and as such they are largely self-fulfilling prophesies. They first define memory narrowly according to one particular paradigm and then say that "phenomena falling outside our definition of memory cannot be considered memories." Rather than starting off from within the ramparts of an a priori definition, this work approaches social phenomena with memorylike attributes (including repetition, transmission between generations, emotive salience, and social and political significance) and considers whether extending the memory paradigm to include them might enrich our understanding both of memory and of the phe-

nomena considered in this light. It is already widely accepted that memory need not be individual but can be a social phenomenon existing in the relations between people (Connerton [1989] 1998, Halbwachs 1992). Moreover, Bourdieu's work clearly shows that memory need not be verbalized or explicit but can be practical or embodied, and that it can be handed down from generation to generation non-verbally (1972; 1980). This study examines dance as a site of such embodied, collective memory. Although choreography is famously difficult to describe adequately in language or by any sort of explicit notation (whether Labanotation, Benesh, or Eskhol-Wachmann), it is remembered by the dancing body, which "knows"/feels what is right and what is not (cf. Wieschiolek 2003). The practical memory of the dance is thus inseparable from its performance: although it remains largely in-effable, it undeniably constitutes a body of practical memory. Moreover, it often cannot be remembered by an individual but must be reproduced by a group, in which case the memory of the dance resides in the group as a social memory in Connerton's sense ([1989] 1998). It cannot be reified as something existing outside the time and place of its performance. But this study goes further than looking at dance as a practical memory of itself, as it were, suggesting that dance and other embodied practices might also constitute the locus of social memories of the past which—like the dance but for very different reasons—are also ineffable, such as memories of political violence.

Aside from practical memory, memories of past events can also be elusive and evanescent, evading discursive exegesis. These are what Walter Benjamin has re-ferred to as "flashbulb memories." Benjamin's autobiography, *Berliner Kindheit,* makes it clear that childhood memories, among others, tend to manifest themselves only briefly and disappear again in a flash (Benjamin [1950] 2006). The events of childhood surface for a moment, then sink back into forgetfulness. In this moment of appearance, they can achieve a shocking intensity, but they are fleeting traces, difficult to retrieve from forgetting (cf. Gebauer and Wulf [1992] 1995, 276–77). And how likely would an anthropologist be to elicit verbal testimony regarding episodic memories of the sort that flash up for an instant in association with certain movements, places, smells, or experiences? If one adds to the embodied nature of certain fields of remembering the vagaries introduced by the effects of violence, the question regarding not only remembering but even the experience of chrono-logical time becomes far more complicated. As the epigraphs at the head of this chapter suggest despite the disparate disciplinary backgrounds of their authors, memories prompted by violent events involve the embodiment of precisely that which is *not* available to discursive consciousness: these are "buried memories" that "fester in the present," perpetually reminding people that they have been pre-vented from remembering (Werbner 1998, 8–9).

34. Phantoms or ghosts not only appear as visions of the dead but can also take the form of bodily practices handed down as transgenerational memories. Nicolas Abraham has called these "the tombs of others" ([1975] 1994, 76).

35. In his brilliant article on Yoruba conceptions of time and history, J.D.Y. Peel (1984), although he focuses on oral history (*itan*) rather than performance, cuts through the clouded debate on time in anthropology and shows that the Yoruba of Ilesha in southwestern Nigeria experience time as both linear and cyclical. Moreover, they are quite explicit, and indeed eloquent, about their understanding of the recurrent aspects of history, seeing the other world of the spirits and the dead as somehow "out of time," and its interventions in the world of the living as therefore recurring or eternal. Hence the Yoruba term *lailai* is used in place of both the English expressions "once upon a time" and "for ever and ever, Amen" (1984, 118). Key political events in Ijesha history are thus experienced and remembered not as singular events but a recurrences of past events akin to reincarnations that periodically "enter the world" again (*nwaye*) and that are regularly commemorated in contemporary ritual (1984, 127–28).

36. As Niel Whitehead (2004, 1) has put it with respect to state violence engaged in by liberal democracies, "anthropology has proved resistant to coming to terms with violence . . . Indeed, . . . we have yet to understand and incorporate into anthropological theory serious studies of violence." He goes on to argue for an anthropology of experience that would prioritize individual meanings, emotive forces, and bodily practices to replace the now dominant anthropology of identity (2).

37. In his landmark work on oral tradition, Jan Vansina (1985, 54) laments that "weakness in chronology is one of the greatest limitations of all oral traditions," but such "weakness" seen from the point of view of the time of the people may in fact provide an accurate model of the subjective experience of the resurgence or "pulsation" (Bhabha 1990, 299) of the past in the performative present.

38. In Isabelle Allende's words, "I thought that if I would put into writing what I wanted to rescue from forgetting, I could reconstruct the lost world, resuscitate the dead, reunite the dispersed, detain the memories for ever and make them mine. Then nobody could take them away from me" (as quoted in Unnold 2002, 162). On the role of literature in addressing the trauma of political repression, see also Felman and Laub (1992), LaCapra (2001), Laub and Poddell (1995), Vickroy (2002), and Ramadanovic (2001).

39. In his critical analysis of *Beloved*, Peter Nicholls (1996, 60) notes that the ghost represents the upsetting and uncontrollable intrusion of the violent past of slavery in America upon the present of each subsequent generation. In her ability to possess people in the house, Beloved reifies the embodied character of the past as it intrudes uninvited into the lives of the ex-slaves—to whom "freedom," like "liberation" for the surviving victims of the Holocaust, will always be a pyrrhic victory and a hollow word. As Nicholls explains, "Morrison evokes the texture of a temporality which makes anachronism the condition of the psychic life" (59).

40. In this respect as in many others, however, the Grassfields chiefdoms cannot all be described as a unitary social system: Jean-Pierre Warnier (pers. com.) has emphasized that he was able in the 1970s to find several informants who would

freely speak of their knowledge of slavery in the chiefdoms of Mankon and Bafut (see also Warnier 1975, 1985). As he points out, one of the reasons for this difference in an otherwise culturally interrelated region probably stems from the power relations obtaining at the time of the slave trade: while Oku was a small, relatively dependent kingdom that survived by making alliances of clientship with more powerful neighbors, Mankon and Bafut were strong, expansionist polities. What this meant in broad terms was that Oku was primarily a source of slaves and that its people experienced the slave trade as a catastrophic and often violent disappearance of loved ones, children, kin, and affines, while Mankon and Bafut were slave-trading kingdoms that more often than not experienced the institution of slavery as a form of wealth accumulation. Moreover, the Chamba and the Fulani raids of the eighteenth and nineteenth centuries penetrated from the north into Oku, exposing its people to the violence and terror of full-scale *razzias,* but stopped short of the heavily fortified kingdoms of Mankon and Bafut to the south, which were never invaded until the colonial era, and even then they successfully routed the German military expeditions and kept them at bay for over ten years, from 1891 to 1901. Another point to consider is that those who were elderly in the 1970s were the last living members of the community to have had direct experience of the slave trade in the Grassfields. Until this period, it was still possible to speak to ex-slaves and to slave traders. Field research carried out from then on, such as mine in the 1990s, has been conducted exclusively with informants who have not had personal experience of slavery. Those alive today, therefore, represent the first generation for whom slavery is entirely a matter of transgenerational rather than personal remembering.

41. According to Derrida,

> Differance, the disappearance of any originary presence, is *at once* the condition of possibility *and* the condition of impossibility of truth. At once. "At once" means that the being-present (*on*) is its truth, in the presence of its identity and in the identity of its presence, is *doubled* as soon as it appears, as soon as it presents itself. *It appears, in its essence, as* the possibility of its own most proper non-truth, of its pseudo-truth reflected in the icon, the phantasm, or the simulacrum. What is is not what it is, identical and identical to itself, unique, unless it *adds to itself* the possibility of being *repeated* as such. And its identity is hollowed out by that addition, withdraws itself in the supplement that presents it. ([1972] 1997, 168 [original emphasis])

42. Bayart describes a criminal gang operating at the heart of Cameroon's political system: "The 'Beti lobby,' which is occupied in plundering the state in the shadow of president Biya, operates at the interface where the lineage societies of the Centre-South and the South meet the country's formal political institutions" (1999, 41). In Bayart's analysis, the ruling party in Cameroon is doubled by a "shadow state" that uses the visible government institutions as a front under

whose aegis members of the Beti lobby wield power clandestinely for their own, criminal ends (22). The Beti lobby has also been referred to as a "national board of directors," whose members wield power invisibly without holding public office. The recent murder of a dozen clerics in Cameroon is attributable to the need of the national board of directors to eliminate witnesses in possession of compromising information. Former colleagues and potential rivals of group members are also regularly murdered for these reasons.

43. The Southern Cameroons National Council is an Anglophone opposition movement that seeks the devolution of power from the center and the federation of the state to allow for more autonomy in the Anglophone region of Cameroon. It has been illegalized by the government on the basis that it seeks to instigate secession from the state by violent means.

44. In rural areas of the Grassfields, I have collected information regarding nocturnal raids on the homes or shops of suspected SDF opposition party members, many of whom were forced into hiding during the army deployments of 1992 and 1997. In the village of Jikijem where I lived, one of the local representatives of the SDF and a titled lineage elder (*fay*) was forced into hiding in 1997. In his absence, his compound was burnt to the ground and his family members beaten.

Chapter Two

1. For a critique of Grassfields claims to Tikar origin, see David Price (1979, 1987).

2. This project, although it focuses on oral testimonies relating to the past, is distinct in its aims from Jan Vansina's (1985) use of oral accounts as a quasi-textual body of evidence from which to reconstruct the historical past. In my interest in the origin myths of Oku, I am not primarily concerned with the empirical historical information about the past that they contain, although this information is instrumentally important to my enquiry. Rather, in this chapter I focus on what oral traditions tell us, on the one hand, about the way in which the palace elite have sought—both now and in the past—to validate their position through a political charter of past greatness and legitimacy, and on the other hand, about the way in which those marginalized by the elite try to reinterpret the myths to encapsulate memories of past oppression and atrocity. Although Vansina fully realizes that accounts of the past may in fact relate to the contemporary interests of the tellers and those who employ them, his focus is firmly on what these accounts reveal about the past once they are divested of the noise of contemporary political agendas (1985, 92). My interest, however, is in this noise itself: rather than trying to determine "what happened," this chapter highlights the ways in which the remembered past has become the object of a struggle in the Grassfields. Vansina assumes that there is one authentic or correct version of the past to be unearthed. He seeks to interpret

the statements in origin myths quite literally for the evidence of people, places, and specific events to which they might provide clues and gives advice on how to determine which accounts are "correct" or "false," "authentic" or "inauthentic" (48–54). Apart from the specific events to which they purport to relate, however, myths carry complex morals or precepts that are often highly complex, ambiguous, and indeterminate. The focus of this exegesis of the Oku origin myth is not on the clues it might provide to the historical past then, but on its moral complexity and the competing interpretations to which it gives rise, interpretations that coexist and struggle for dominance without any one of them necessarily being more "correct" or "legitimate" than any other.

3. Jeffreys (1946) points out that the very names of many Grassfields groups mean "the wanderers." Cf. Fardon (1990, 149) for a Chamba origin myth, and Brain and Pollock (1971, 8) and Pradelles de Latour (1985, 31, 46) for the Bangwa myth. For sources highlighting similar phenomena beyond the Grassfields region in West and central Africa, see De Boeck (1994), Feierman (1974), Herbert (1993, 165), de Heusch (1982), Drucker-Brown (1992), Last (1991), Turner (1967, 93–111), and Vansina (1985, 72–73; 1990, 56–57, 156).

4. See Argenti (1996, 15–19) for a full version of the myth, and Koloss (2000, 34–35) for a version collected from a 1977 school textbook in which the contending fon is not from Kom but Kijem. Koloss (2000) also offers a translation of a version gathered by Fr. Emonts (see Emonts 1927) in which the contender is the fon of Babungo. Cf. also Mbunwe-Samba (1993) for a similar myth among the Wimbum, and Nkwi and Warnier (1982, 14) for Meta and Babungo variations. Throughout the Grassfields, bodies of water are seen to be passages to the world of the deities and the ancestors, as many children's tales attest. In fact, many elements of the charter myth of Mawes reappear in a children's folktale in neighboring Nso' (see Asheri 1969, 17–20).

5. Devisch (1995b, 103) has analyzed the similar role of the otter in Yaka cosmology.

6. The compound houses the *kwifon* society—the regulatory body that provides the palace guard and the fon's body guard, and serves judicial functions.

7. Or in lakes: in the kingdom of Bafut, the Achum shrine within the palace is referred to as a lake in which only the fon and a few adepts can swim (Chilver and Kaberry 1963, 28).

8. Chilver (1961, 252) records that elephants were never hunted in the Grassfields proper, where they were rare even before colonial contact in the late nineteenth century, but in the more sparsely populated forests and on the plateaus at the periphery of the central highlands.

9. This division between an autochthonous population with ambiguously valued religious power, on the one hand, and a foreign invader with secular, military power on the other is universal in the Grassfields. See Argenti (1996, 15–19), Bah (1996), Brain and Pollock (1971, 8), Chilver and Kaberry (1960), Davis (1991), Emonts

(1927, 154–55), Jeffreys (1961b, 139–40), Kaberry (1959a, 1959b), Mbunwe-Samba (1996, 33–36), and Pradelles de Latour (1985, 33). A comparable political division is to be found among the coastal Duala (Austen and Derrick 1999, 21–22) and indeed throughout much of the African continent. See Needham (1980, 66–73) for a discussion of the analyses of divine kingship in Evans-Pritchard (1948) and Wilson (1959); and Vansina (1990).

10. The term *Tikar* is translated by the Bamum as "those who wander" (Njoya 1952, 260; Kaberry 1962, 283; Jeffreys 1946). Interestingly, an explicit claim to Tikari origin, commonly made by the ruling lineages of the northwestern Grassfields, was not made by any of my informants, who did not mention the Tikar by name, despite the close links of Oku with Nso'. I did not use the elders of the palace hierarchy as my main informants, who would no doubt claim Tikari links in line with their "brother" polity Nso'. Like Nso' and all the other polities claiming Tikari origins, Oku possesses a Ngiri (Ngele) princely society, and one of its masks, Morifum, has as the root of its name Rifum, one of the Tikari dynasties (Chilver and Kaberry 1968, 23; Kaberry 1962; Tardits 1980, 117). While origin myths, including claims to Tikari origin, have commonly been gathered from the palace elites of the polities of this region, further research among commoners and those less closely associated with the palace elite may elicit more origin myths that make no mention of the legitimizing myth of Tikari origin. For a deconstruction of the Tikari origin myth, cf. Nkwi and Warnier (1982, 26–28), Price (1979), and Warnier (1985, 264–66).

11. The chiefdom of Bafut is a perfect example: at the time that the Germans first encountered them in 1889, the Bafut consisted of a heterogeneous conglomerate of disparate groups depicting themselves as conquered peoples, refugees, or captives. Yet no matter how heterogeneous and self-consciously victimized the group was, it was considered militarily formidable by its frequently raided neighbors (Chilver and Kaberry 1963, 8).

12. On the Kidjem diaspora, cf. Chilver and Kaberry (1967, 131–32; 1968, 20, 26–27) and Shanklin (1985, 115n7).

13. This myth clearly borrows from a widespread tale about a king who entraps an individual in this manner rather than a whole people. In this version, which is told in Oku as a children's tale, a cruel fon tries to dispatch a clever trickster-hero in this fashion but fails. Vansina (1985, 90) has recorded versions of this myth hundreds of miles to the south in the Congo and Zambia, where it is related as an origin myth by many different peoples.

14. Although in the myths the founding fons are presented as hunters or forest people, they are nonetheless inevitably seen to have come originally from somewhere not within but beyond the forest, and therefore to be more sophisticated and cosmopolitan than the "people of the earth" whom they subjugate.

15. As Warnier points out, in the hierarchical chiefdoms of the Grassfields it is

predominantly the poor and the marginal who are accused of practicing witchcraft, in contrast to the peoples of the forest zone to the south of the Grassfields, who aim witchcraft accusations at the rich and where, it is argued, such charges represent a leveling mechanism (Malart-Guimera 1981; Geschiere 1982, 1995; Laburthe-Tolra 1981, 1988). This is true not only in Mankon but also in Oku, where those accused of practicing witchcraft (*evuŋ*) tend to be cadets and even children.

16. The focus in this body of myths and practices on violence as the basis for state formation, on ritual scapegoating (a feature of Grassfields performance and politics I return to later), and on the ambiguous identification of rulers with foreigners and outcasts recalls the work of René Girard so strikingly that it would be odd not to mention it here. His notion of a "sacrificial crisis"—first presented in *Violence and the Sacred* ([1972] 1977) and further elaborated in *Things Hidden since the Foundation of the World* ([1978] 1987)—in which mimetic acts of social violence are repeated across time with each new generation, bears a strong resonance in the Grassfields, where as I argue later, history is more marked by repetition than it is by change. His further insight in *The Scapegoat* ([1982] 1986) that scapegoating can serve as a means to interrupt a sacrificial crisis by projecting the source of internecine conflict outside the community, or seeming to do so by the expedient of focusing collective acts of violence on one outcast or a group of outcasts within the community—such as slaves—also clearly applies to the situation in the Grassfields. Girard has, however, been criticized for the Christian teleology and for the functionalism inherent in his model, which clearly seeks first of all to reduce all ethnographic examples of violence to his theory, and second to show that ritual scapegoating ultimately has a salutary effect on social and political relations in a community, serving to restore order and ultimately to shore up the power of the state. As Kapferer (1997, 210–19) makes clear in his critique of Girard, this form of universalism precludes complexity and hides the tensions, opposing interests, and multiple perspectives that may exist in society. Thus, while Girard's work is clearly useful in highlighting the pattern inherent in the politics of scapegoating in the Grassfields, this work goes on to note not only that this pattern exists, but also that it is a discourse promulgated by the elites that is opposed by the cadets in these divided communities, who have not historically been interested in promoting social harmony.

17. Just how desperate these exiles were is illustrated by the dangers they faced once they left the relative protection of their own settlements. Warnier (1975, 38off.) gives examples of losers in succession disputes leaving Mankon with their supporters and being massacred or sold into slavery by the neighboring chiefdoms of Bafut and Bali-Kumbat where they had sought refuge.

18. Eugenia Shanklin has additionally confirmed that Kom people also admit to having sold their children into slavery in times of hunger (pers. com. to Jean-Pierre Warnier; Warnier 2007, chap. 8).

19. When a rite of propitiation for one's ancestors known as a *ntaŋlɛ* needs to be performed for these descendants of slaves, it is performed outdoors, on the road leading to the person's chiefdom of origin rather than in a compound, as it would be for a person who could trace his or her ancestry to a specific lineage, be it in Oku or another chiefdom. In these cases, the rite is known as "*ntaŋlɛ* on the road home" or "on the road to the country of origin" (*ntaŋlɛ dji kɔtum*). The slave origins of individuals are thus remembered today in Oku in the denial of a place in a local lineage.

20. "At any one time during the pre-colonial period, there was a certain fraction of the Bamenda Plateau population which shifted residence or affiliation from one chiefdom to the next. That fraction of the population will be called the 'floating population'" (Warnier 1975, 385). Janet Roitman (pers. com., Feb. 3, 2004) notes that this term has a colonial etymology, having first been used in Cameroon by French colonial officers. As she points out, the fact that this group was first objectified (in pejorative terms) by the state according to dominant notions of what constituted the settled norm limits the extent to which we can apply the category without reference to its colonial implications. Certainly, elders and elites had no category exactly matching that of the floating population, but they were aware of disaffected, roaming groups and categorized them at times as witches, slaves, criminals, and enemies to be captured and sold, or alternatively as siblings or children to be taken in.

21. In Eblam Ebkwo, the language of Oku, the term "children" (*wan, yon*) is set in categorical opposition to the term for adult (*wel, yel*), but this latter term also means "person." By means of this slippage, children are excluded from the category of the person. Bachelors are likewise explicitly excluded from the status of a full person in that they are referred to as "arms" or "hands" (*ɔbkoy*—the term refers to both).

22. Life expectancy would have been around forty at the time.

23. The polities of Oku, Nso', and Mbiame thus grounded their close alliance in terms of descent from one ruler, Wu Chichi, who is credited with having had three children: Chie, an unnamed second son, and a daughter named Yeaney. According to the Oku version of the myth, Chie, the eldest, founded Oku; the second son, Nso'; and the son of Yeaney, Mbiame.

24. This conceptualization of Europeans as metamorphous beings associated with the underworld of the sea was of course—and still is—widespread along the coast of West and central Africa in the form of the Mammi Wata cult. Cf. studies by Bastian (1997), Drewal (1988), Frank (1995), Gore and Nevadomsky (1997), Jewsiewicki (2003, 110–34), Ogrizek (1981–82), Salmons (1983), and Wendl (2001). The likely historical origins of this cult in the transatlantic slave trade remain to date underexplored. For instance, despite Drewal's (1988) evidence of the relatively recent Indian iconographic influence for the figure of the siren, the image of the treacherous piscine seductress with white skin and "slippery" hair (as straight hair

is often known in the Grassfields) seems likely to have been prompted, in the first instance, by the figureheads—often depicted as sirens—on the prows of European slave ships.

25. Elites accumulated, stored, and traded the surplus crops grown by their wives and daughters (including domestic slaves in the role of classificatory wives and daughters) and the kola nuts, palm oil, and palm wine produced by their sons (and classificatory sons) in local and regional markets, storing their profits in cowry, bead, iron, and later brass currencies that they could invest in the rotating credit associations (known as *njangi* throughout the region) to which they belonged (Chilver 1961; Rowlands 1979; Warnier 1985, 1995b). By the time it was their turn to reap the dividends of their weekly or monthly deposits into one of these associations, they had accumulated enough for trade in the prestige sphere.

26. Brain (1972, 53) says of slaves in Bangwa, in the Bamileke area of the Grassfields, that they "are automatically involved in witchcraft accusations and dangers."

27. Thus was the recaptured slave Josia Yamsey first captured in the Grassfields. According to his account, recorded by the missionary Rev. W. Johnson in Sierra Leone in 1820,

> I went . . . to [a] Place call[ed] Banjum [Banjun?] because one of my Brothers lived there & I went to stay with him. But soon after the King of that country sent some people to catch me and he sold me to a man who kept me in his farm to drive the Elephants out of the farms which came every night and troubled me very much. I was so much troubled that I at last tried to run to my Brother again who was King in Bambah, but when I got about half way I was caught again by another headman who send me back again to my old master. They then try one woman with read [*sic*] water ["red water," the sasswood ordeal?], another headman made my master Palaver for that; then he took me and paid me for that palaver to that headman.
>
> I stayed there a little, then that Headman sold me for a Hoe to a country which is called Bamum, that man which buy me for a Hoe was a trader he go all about to Buy & sell slaves. He took me to another Place which is called Lo and there sold me in the market for salt. I saw plenty people there in the market they were all tied together like beasts and I was put amongst them. (Yamsey, as quoted in Johnson 1820)

28. Nkwi and Warnier (1982) make the point that although the Yoruba and Hausa language areas cover millions of people settled over thousands of kilometers, it is possible in the Grassfields to cross a language area in a morning's walk and to step between two mutually unintelligible languages by crossing from one village to another. Elderly Nso' informants interviewed by Chilver and Kaberry in 1960 confirmed that Nso' slaves were sold as far as possible from the polity (Chilver 1961, 245). Warnier (1995b) provides further detail on the different types

of slave trade and confirms that even with respect to the regional trade, fraudulent traders avoided detection when selling members of their own polity by handing them over to middlemen who sold them as far away as possible from their place of origin.

29. To this day, the initial greeting that friends and kin call out to one another in Oku is the question "Where are you going?" (*Wɛ ndu way?*), recalling a time when no one would leave home without letting someone know where they were going. Still now, in fact, it is considered highly undesirable to set out on any journey—no matter how short—without a companion, and those who are forced to build their houses in isolated spots far away from their compound or village are likewise considered exposed and vulnerable. Similarly, hunters never wander at will in the forest in search of game but only in certain delimited sectors so that they can be sought if they fail to return, making their abduction easier to detect.

30. Tardits (1980, 165–67, 363–64, 806–16) and Warnier (1985, 127–29) also allege that the larger, more centralized polities such as Bafut, Kom, and Bamum took to raiding their smaller neighbors on their own during the course of the nineteenth century, although they seem to have used the resulting captives predominantly to satisfy their need for domestic labor rather than for slaves for the long-distance trade. Warnier (1995b, 257–58) adds that Nso' also engaged in "wars of capture" during this period. Nor were the smaller polities, such as Oku, which did not engage in warfare, immune from trading in slaves (Chilver 1961, 242; Nkwi and Warnier 1982, 146).

31. The shadow-play of the forest would gain even more salience during the colonial period as a result of attempts to suppress the open dealing in slaves, which led to the establishment of secret forest markets and even of large slave settlements in the depths of the forest (Chem-Langhëë 1995, 184, 186; Chem-Langhëë and Fomin 1995, 197).

32. The great majority of the forests of the Grassfields region had given way to the farmers' hoes by the nineteenth century, but to this day fons still emphasize their close connection to this precious hegemonic resource. Many of the palaces of the Grassfields still sedulously tend a small symbolic copse of forest trees within their confines, most often in the *kwifon* regulatory society's compound (Argenti 2002a).

33. Dike and Ekejiuba (1990), as quoted in Röschenthaler (2004, n. 6), mention an oracle used by the Aro of southeastern Nigeria (on the Cameroon border) that was said to "devour" its supplicants if it found them guilty. In reality, they were not killed but secretly sold into slavery.

34. The representation of fons as wild predators and slaves as potential prey finds its parallel in the coastal epic of *Jeki la Njambe,* in the course of which the hero captures and kills various wild animals by trickery, pretending to be their sister's son—a favored Duala expression of hegemony over their hinterland trading partners (Austen 1996a, 35; Austen and Derrick 1999, 78). The epic places the

trickster hero in the position of the fon and the foreign traders dehumanized by the Duala in place of the slave.

Chapter Three

1. In addition to these masks, two other bodies in the palace possess masks in Oku: the fon himself and the society of royal eligibles, or princes (*ngiri* or *ngele*). For more on these masks, see Argenti (1996), Gufler and Bah (2006), and Koloss (2000). For descriptions of the masks of other Grassfields chiefdoms, see Brain and Pollock (1972), Dillon (1990), Engard (1989), Fowler (1990), and Warnier (1985).

2. Cf. Engard (1989, 147) on the several personas and different names of Mabu in the Grassfields polity of Bafut.

3. In the neighboring polity of Nso', where the *kwifon* society used to force those it had condemned to death to hang themselves (Goheen 1996, 56), Mabu belongs not to *kwifon* but to Ngiri, the Royal Society. In Nso' as in Bafut, where it is known as Mugbu (Chilver and Kaberry 1963), and in Meta, where it is referred to as Tekene (Dillon 1990), the executioner wore a simple woven hood. Warnier (1979, 27) describes the Mabu of the Grassfields polity of Mankon, and the palace Takoengoe subsection of the Kwi'fo (*kwifon*) society to which it belongs, as polluted by the power to pass judgment and met out punishments (including the death penalty). As a result of the pollution incurred by the violence of its mask, Takoengoe is also known as the Bad Kwi'fo, and Warnier adds that "Takoengo transcends nature and culture... [and] consumes everything" (27 [trans. mine]). Cf. Geary (1979, 65), who agrees that the embodiment of evil, destructive forces constitutes a basic feature of the Kweifo' (*kwifon*) society in the Grassfields polity of We and that these forces associate the society with the bush. Kaberry (1962, 289) describes the *ngwerong* regulatory society of Nso' in similar terms, noting that its judgments were all carried out in the king's name, "although he escaped the odium."

4. Labɛ, another palace mask, is similarly ambiguous. Belonging to the fon himself rather than to the *kwifon* society, it used to have a military function, appearing in battle. Like Mabu, it is robed in a gown of human hair. Its large helmet mask is made of long thick dreadlocks of human hair tipped with cowry shells. It carries spears and a cudgel. Although its dreadlocks associate it with the realm of the undomesticated forest and the wild, its weapons nonetheless identify it as a human being. Whether it is to be seen as a faithful warrior protecting the people from outside invaders or as an exogenous raider itself is not clear. When it appears today, military society (*manjɔŋ*) members run ahead of it, firing their Dane guns and shouting "shoot the stranger!" (*tem wel balak*). Notwithstanding the mask's putative role in protecting the community from external raiding, it was used in the past to administer beatings to *local* people and is infamous for once having attacked Oku people indiscriminately in the local marketplace. To make matters worse, the

fon of Oku at the time admitted that he had been masking Labɛ when the incident took place (Gufler and Bah 2006). Accordingly, when it performs today, it is against local people that it metes out its violence, slamming its hand down on their backs as they crouch before it. Despite the chants of the military society members, then, it would seem that the violence of Labɛ, the mask of the fon, is most often aimed not at strangers but at the people of Oku themselves.

5. Ian Fowler (1990, 287) describes how two Nko masks coexist in the *kwifon* compound in the palace of the neighboring polity of Babungo, and he shows that they are closely associated with the lineages of ironsmiths and smelters there. Fowler exposes the tensions between the palace *kwifon* society and the ironsmiths' and smelters' lineages in Babungo, and points out how these are embodied in the Nko performance, which culminates in the arrival of the smiths with their hammers, intent on "killing their child"—in this case not an otter but the *kwifon* society itself, whose sacred bells they produce. The connection of Nkɔk to iron smithing also seems to be alluded to in a photograph Koloss (2000, 119) has taken of the Nkɔk of Oku, in which the mask is holding a lump of iron slag in each hand. Elements of the antipathy between smiths and the palace are also evident in the polities of Big Babanki (Diduk 1987) and Bafut (Engard 1986, 470), where Engard saw the mask forced into a posture of submission before the fon after one of its rampages. In Bamessing, Nkoh also consists of two masks, a male and a female. In this case, it is not the female but the male that carries a "child" on its back (Silvia Forni, pers. com., Aug. 14, 2003).

6. Not only does the choice of an otter and its mummified state connote access to the realm of the dead, but the image of the child is evoked in the way the otter is tied to the mask's back and in its explicit naming as the "child" (*wan*) of Nkɔk. As I have argued elsewhere (Argenti 2001), children, like otters, are thought to be liminal creatures who straddle the realms of the living and the dead, having just recently arrived from the world of the ancestors, where they lived before birth.

7. The cap is woven from white and blue cotton yarn and is flat on top, bearing an interwoven pattern of crosshatched lines in indigo-dyed yarn and dividing the whole into a multitude of small white hexagons. From the points of each of these hexagons emerges a one-centimeter-long stud. The caps are said to "shimmer" (*ngwarle*) on account of their complex geometric and studded surface, and consequently are fearsome or "bad" (*bɛmə*). The walking stick is made from a shoulder-high branch of hardwood with a joint at the top, like a thumbstick. Its base is reinforced with a conical iron ferrule, which enables its owner to plant it outside the doorway of a house before entering. The fork at the top of the stick then serves as a place to hang the bag, a practice necessitated by the interdiction on entering a house with an Aga bag. It is for hanging them in this way outside a house that the bags have small loops rather than a shoulder strap, as do ordinary bags.

8. On such occasions, in addition to their caps and bags, Aga members carry a unique spear, known as *ngo,* with an oversized, ceremonial blade smithed in the

neighboring polity of Babungo. They wear loincloths of indigo tie-dyed cotton and smear camwood on their foreheads.

9. Jackson (1982, 64) argues for the interpretation of silence in ritual contexts as a palpable presence rather than an absence. Peek (1994, 477–78) points to the use of such silence in many African societies as a reference to the world of the dead, who no longer speak, and by the same token to the world of the ancestors and deities.

10. It is noteworthy that the word *agah* means "war" among the Igbo, just across the border in Nigeria (McCall 2000, 55). As McCall describes in great detail, the term gives its name to the Igbo war dance, the *iri agah,* which commemorates the killing and beheading of enemy soldiers.

11. Silvia Forni (pers. com., Aug. 14, 2003) reports that *nɛkiɛ* jesters have a policing function in Nsei (Bamessing): controlling the crowds at the palace during major ceremonies.

12. As has been said of court jesters before, however, to be a licensed fool means just that—to behave with the license afforded by the king; within its boundaries and never truly at his expense (Eagelton 1981, 148). The humor of the jesters is accordingly always at the expense of the audience members at the palace and never aimed at undermining the fon or the *kwifon* society.

13. At the other end of the continent, Yoshida (1991, 216) notes the falsetto voice in which otherworldly speech is conveyed among the Chewa of Zambia (cf. also Peek 1994).

14. The proverb juxtaposes the forest's insatiable appetite for human life with that of the elites, elliptically referring to the elites' cannibal appetites for those identified as criminals in their communities—or at least for the wealth generated by selling them into slavery.

15. It is perhaps for this reason that Koloss (2000, 163), attempting to reconstruct the enthronement ceremony (which he never witnessed), on the basis of informants' reports, alleges that the "sheep" was beaten until it was "nearly dead." Kaberry (1969, 184) describes a rite of expiation for incest in the neighboring chiefdom of Nso' in which the guilty parties are also made to strike a goat. As Kaberry points out, the animal is literally a scapegoat, absorbing as it does the sins of the culprits.

16. So too when the *kwifon* society finds a defendant guilty, a member of *kwifon* taps him or her with his hand. This tap signals that the plaintiffs are now within their rights to administer a punishment, and they beat the defendant in earnest.

17. Simon Tame (pers. com., 1993), the erstwhile director of the World Wildlife Fund–financed Kilum Mountain Forest Project based in Elak Oku, has been told simply that it was "a large monkey that lives in the forest and looks like a man." The species is uncertain. Baboons currently live around the summit of Mount Kilum, and chimpanzees did too as late as the 1980s. Some gorillas currently live in the Takamanga forest to the west of Wum in the western Grassfields and may in the past have been more widespread (Tame, pers. com.).

18. The name of the palace mask Mabu in Bambui is *məbu'u*—with the same root as that for slave, *abu'u,* but with a different noun-class prefix. The name of the palace mask Nkɔk is *nko'o,* possibly related to the term *nkɔ,* meaning "ape."

19. In Ghaŋ vəŋóo, the language of Babungo, *bú* means "dog." Cf. Schaub (1985, 395). Additionally, there is a second Babungo term for "slave": *vŋóo* (Ian Fowler, pers. com.).

20. To make a conscious connection between the two words, speakers of Eblam Ebkwo, Itang Ikom, and Lam Nso' would have to know the other Ring languages in which slaves are explicitly referred to with terms sharing the root *-buk* or *-bu'.* This detail, however, should not be taken as a sign that the possible interpretations of Mabu would be lost on most people. Grassfielders are noted for their multilingualism, often speaking three languages and understanding several more. In other words, the references of *-buk* and *-kɔs* to slaves and the connections between apes and slaves in the perspective of a pan-regional linguistic system function in the manner described by Lévi-Strauss (1979) for a South American masking complex, in which each one of several different language groups possesses part of what constitutes one single tradition. Within such a complex, the conundrums of one language group serve to elucidate those of another. Within the pan-regional linguistic system of the Grassfields, the meanings of word roots from one chiefdom influenced the connotations of the same root in other chiefdoms, even though the term's primary meaning differed from place to place. By means of this system of translingual associations, the term referring to apes in Oku and neighboring polities was colored with allusions to slaves and slavery.

21. It is perhaps for this reason that Koloss (1992, 3) identifies Mabu as a representation of a human being.

22. Lewis ([1971] 1989, 92) mentions a strikingly similar appropriation of the slave whip in the *numbi* cult dances of ex-slaves in southern Somalia. For Lewis, the dance represents a "role reversal," with the slaves effectively becoming slave drivers for the duration of the performance. In the Grassfields, where the offspring of slave dealers might well themselves be enslaved, such a clear-cut distinction is hard to make. Comaroff (1985, 226) describes the use of brass staffs in the rites of South African Tshidi Zionists. Known as "cudgels" and alluding to the weapons used in precolonial male initiation, these also recall colonial military dress swords and swagger sticks or batons.

23. In both cases, these royal gifts were known as *bur'ma* (or *mbu'me* in Nso').

24. The strong prohibition against fons entering a market may have to do with the association of markets with the slave trade and the need for the fon to distance himself from this trade.

25. For further details, see Tamwa Hamkong (1983), Nkwi and Warnier (1982, 88, 96), and Warnier (1985, 138; 1995b, 262–63).

26. I am indebted to J.D.Y. Peel, who recently discovered this document in the Church Missionary Society archives, for making it available to me.

27. Because the floating population was a result, or a symptom, of slavery, this analysis could be said to beg the question, amounting as it does to the statement that slavery existed to contain the demographic and political effects of slavery. Yet the discourse of slavery operated on just such an oxymoron, producing the spectacle of slavery as exogenous supernatural aggression as a form of justification for centralized rule—for which slavery in its various forms was an economic necessity. Vaughan (1977) similarly reveals that the essence of slavery to the Margi lay in the representation of slaves as outsiders to the rest of society, and rather than emphasize the benign means by which slaves were absorbed into kinship systems and their children born "free," he emphasizes that slavery involved the institutionalization of this marginality such that slavery can be characterized as a self-perpetuating "limbic institution" that prevented rather than facilitated the incorporation of outsiders.

28. This tactic is of course similar to contemporary nationalist techniques (Bhabha 1990). In the case of the Grassfields one can detect a continuum from precolonial slavery through to the later relationship of palace elites to colonial and postcolonial regimes (Argenti 2002a, 2005a).

29. The watery origins of certain fons and associated deities may similarly be associated with the widespread belief that the European slave traders who provided the exotic trade goods were themselves aquatic spirits whose home lay beneath the sea. Clarke (1848, 4) makes it clear that this belief was widespread in the nineteenth century:

The poor slave on the coast of Africa has too long been taught, that if sold to the white man, it is to be eaten by him upon the sea! His fear . . . on this point [has] grown with him from infancy. When this is kept in mind, the missionaries cease to wonder that children fly before them . . . and that slaves from the interior shrink behind free men, or steal away into the woods, and suppose the time has come when they are to be sold to the white monsters from the salt water, who have no land to supply them with yams and rice, and who buy to devour the unfortunate black man

Cf. Knut Knutson (1882–96, in Ardener 2002, 130): "the evil report that had been whispered in [the slaves'] ears, that the white men would eat them when they arrived abroad." Also see Esser (1898, as translated in Chilver and Röschenthaler 2001, 74), describing his journey from Mundame to Bali in the Kamerun hinterland with his carriers:

I was sometimes shocked by the sight of our own bodies, because, among all these deep black, strong and beautiful shapes, we appeared almost abnormally white. The Blacks were at first most amazed that the water gave us White folk the same trouble as it gave them. In their view, the water was the element, the home country, of the White men, believing, as they did, that they came up from the depths of the sea, via the shore, to encounter them. They claimed that the White man was a fish being, because he had white flesh like that of a fish

When Zintgraff had first arrived in Bali, the fon Galega had made a point of taking him by the wrist—a breach of royal etiquette—and holding up his hand for all to see, proclaiming that Zintgraff's skin did not burn and that he could not have emerged from the water (Chilver [1966] 1996, 3).

30. Hence fons' foreign wives produce "children of the palace," and gifts of palm wine from visiting dignitaries or wine tappers from peripheral villages are transformed into "water of the palace" for redistribution to the fons' subjects. Just as the gifts of exogenous origin that end up in the palace treasuries are referred to in the many languages of the Grassfields as the "things of the palace" (cf. Argenti 1996; Geary 1983), so too foreign slaves—often known (like fons) euphemistically as "strangers" in African languages—were gradually domesticated by being absorbed into the palace hierarchies of the Grassfields as retainers, or by being married to local women (cf. Kopytoff and Miers 1977, 14–20). Nevertheless, even the "free" descendants of slaves remained marginal to the rest of society for generations—in some cases, to the present day.

31. People in the outlying villages of Oku speak of "returning" to Elak when they are setting off from home for the palace, referred to simply by the name of the capital, Elak. This honorific form of speech equates the palace with the polity, representing it as one's true "home" no matter how peripheral one's compound may be to it.

Chapter Four

1. On the colonial argument that slavery was "benign," see also Kopytoff and Miers (1977). Recent analysts have likewise emphasized the movement of slaves into the kinship system and their supposed social mobility as evidence that Grassfields modes of slavery were essentially benign (e.g., Chem-Langhëë 1995; Njiasse-Njoya 1995; Nkwi 1995). As Kopytoff and Miers (1977, 20) have pointed out, however, while the mobility of some slaves from the status of strangers without rights to that of kin with the right to a wife, to land, and even to titles is often pointed to as evidence of the benign nature of the institution, this mobility was only intergenerational: slaves' children were the ones who might enjoy the rights and privileges of relative inclusion into the society, whereas the slaves themselves would remain marginal and "foreign" for the duration of their lives. Furthermore, slaves who were sold out of the Grassfields into Banyang country were settled in dedicated slave settlements, where they remained a despised category intergenerationally. The fact that Njiasse-Njoya (1995) stresses that it was only "criminals" and "recalcitrant wives" whom the Bamoum enslaved among their own people only begs

the question of how such categories became salient in the first place: clearly the young men and women who were most marginalized by the elite palace hierarchy and the most likely to voice their dissent were by the same token stigmatized as insubordinate and subversive "strong-heads," thereby justifying their enslavement. Although represented as a threat to the polity, such cadets were in truth the victims of its hypertrophy.

2. Eckert (1999, 140) notes that the Duala kings were still making provisions for their slaves in their wills in the 1930s, and that his Douala informants told him of neighbors snatched as children in the Grassfields in the 1920s—one hundred years after the effective end of the transatlantic slave trade from Cameroon in the 1820s (Chilver 1961, 237). This testimony accords with Chem-Langhëë's evidence that slave markets existed in the Grassfields kingdom of Nso' until the early 1920s (Chem-Langhëë 1995, 184). Eckert also notes the practice reported by Buell ([1928] 1965, 2:314): "Of many old men to buy girl babies from native parents at a low price, and sell them when they come to maturity at a large profit. While technically, the native law as to dowry has been followed, the system is really a kind of slave traffic."

3. The children of the slaves kept in dedicated slave settlements by the Banyang still retained the social status of their parents in the 1950s, and in 1953 Ruel observed a court case among the Banyang concerning a dispute between the members of a freeborn village and its neighboring slave settlement (Ruel 1969, 13, 166–68). In 1995, Chem-Langhëë and Fomin (1995, 196) wrote that the Banyang still used euphemisms such as "strangers" and "our other brothers" to refer to those descended of slaves—the same terms they had used to highlight the marginal position of their slaves in the past. In the same year, Chem-Langhëë (1995, 187) was able to write of the Grassfields chiefdom of Nso' that "some of the slave sections of lineages and slave sublineages have been carefully preserved to this day." Chem-Langhëë and Fomin (1995, 198–99) relate the court case brought by a man of slave descent against the chief of Fotabe village for preventing him from buying all the stages of the Ekpe society (to which slave traders notably used to belong). The claimant interpreted the chief's denial of his right to enter the society as a deprivation of the right to citizenship—a right traditionally denied to slaves. In 1981, the judge dismissed the claim as "premature and frivolous." The case was appealed and was still pending as late as 1995.

4. Jean-Pierre Warnier (pers. com., Nov. 1, 2003) met a woman in Mankon in the 1970s who recalled, when she was a girl, her father bringing a young female slave that he had just bought back to the compound. The day after her arrival, the slave was sent to work on the farm with Warnier's informant and her mother. When the slave arrived at the farm, however, she simply burst into tears, and the informant's mother could not convince her to work. When they returned home that evening, the compound head was informed, and he sold her again soon afterward.

5. Paralleling the increase in internal slavery that accompanied the end of trans-

atlantic slavery and the establishment of the "legitimate trade" in palm oil in Sierra Leone (Shaw 2002), the German presence on the coast of Cameroon actually
stimulated an increased demand for slaves by the Duala (Austen [1977] 1995, 142,
143). From 1900 onward, the value of a slave rose at all the sale sites along the supply line from the interior to the coast. This inflation coincided with the establishment of large-scale cocoa plantations by the Duala aimed at satisfying the demand
for cocoa by German traders (143). Austen and Derrick (1999, 218n114) argues,
contra Clarence-Smith (1989), that the German colonial administrators were not
ignorant of the Duala's use of slave labor but that they tried to hide it from their
superiors and the missionaries. The administrative court set up by the Germans in
Duala in 1892 heard twenty-one cases regarding the restoration of slaves to their
owners during its first four years, including one in which the defendant was forced
to sell a slave. Despite the fact that the Germans passed a decree illegalizing the
internal slave trade in 1895, it was still possible in 1901 for Manga Bell, the leading
Duala chief, to persuade the government to pardon two slave traders "because no
natives really understood that such transactions were illegal" (Austen [1977] 1995,
143 and nn. 19, 21). As noted earlier, it was not until 1902 that the decree was applied in practice, and even then the administration did not apply it to those who
were already enslaved but only to new instances of kidnap and trafficking. Such
cases could only realistically be brought in Duala, where the Germans had a strong
presence. In the newly discovered Grassfields area, the sparse and much harassed
administration could not have stopped the trade even if it had been an objective
of theirs, and cases of internal slavery such as that described in note 4 would have
been common.

6. The German administration in Togo adopted the same policy, considering the
populations of the interior a labor reserve for the plantations they set up along the
coast (Piot 1999, 40–41).

7. The fon's interpretation of Zintgraff's status was prescient. From 1891, in addition to the Vai or "Kruboys," the German troops would be made up of Dahomean
soldiers who were bought at Behanzin by the German officer Gravenreuth from a
Dahomean king who, according to Rudin, had captured them with the intention of
using them for human sacrifice. Gravenreuth, en route to Cameroon, bought the
three hundred male and female slaves but guaranteed them their freedom only on
condition that they sign a contract obliging them to serve for five years without
pay. They were transshipped to Duala in 1891, where they were treated so badly by
their German officers that a mutiny broke out in 1893. The main cause had been
the malnourishment of the Dahomeans and the public floggings to which the Germans subjected the women among them (Austen 1996b, 67; Austen and Derrick
1999, 104; Geschiere n.d.; Rudin 1938, 193–94; Van Slageren 1972, 59; Steer 1939,
161; Rüger 1960; 1968, 91–147; Vieter 1989). As Peter Geschiere (n.d.) points out,
however, "the deeper cause was that the 'Dahomeans' felt they were still treated
like slaves." To justify the fact that they were not paid, Leist, the acting governor of

Kamerun, stated that the men among them had been provided with wives by the German government and that "a Dahomean could [therefore] earn extra income by offering his wife to soldiers without a woman."

8. Chilver (1967), Jeffreys (1962), O'Neil (1996), Ruppel (1912, 846), Skolaster (1924, 303–4), and Wirz (1973b, 193ff.) have all recorded instances of Bali kidnapping and enslavement of men, women, and children from enemy and allied chiefdoms alike in the 1920s.

9. As Rudin (1938, 396) admits despite his pro-German imperialist stance, "the antislavery movement was one of the many strange animals that the traders mounted on their way to market."

10. For more on Hutter's descriptions of the battles he witnessed and took part in, see O'Neil (1996, 87) and Hutter (1902).

11. After the death in 1908 of the German captain Glauning, who had been leading many of the punitive expeditions, his successors undertook an investigation and concluded that the punished villages had been exhausted of their human resources and should be allowed to "rest" (Chilver 1967, 502; O'Neil 1996, 98).

12. In 1931 Chief Nono of Bangwa wrote a letter to the fon of Bali complaining of Bali abuses in the German era:

> My dear Chief of Bali,
>
> I am writing to you about the deception that you visited upon me some decades ago. When the German white men came to Bali, you deceived me, telling me that there were some red-skinned beasts in Bali. They were eating people everywhere they went. You told me that I had to give you 230 girls, 84 ivories, and 1,600 charges of gunpowder, or the beasts would come and eat all the people in my country. . . . You had deceived me, telling me that the whites were beasts that ate people. Since the whites have come here, they have yet to eat anybody. (As quoted in Debarge 1934, 20; and Van Slageren 1972, 83 [trans. mine])

Dongmo (1981, 122–24 [trans. mine]) quotes a 1942 document written by a Mme Dugast and held in the national archives in Yaoundé (also quoted in Bayart 1989, 99–101; and Mamdani 1996, 150–51). It relates to labor recruitment in the Francophone southern Grassfields, or Bamileke region, which was ruled by the Germans until 1915, and again clearly illustrates the ways in which the power to recruit was still seen by all involved as an economic opportunity in the interwar years:

> The *Office du Travail* said to the head chief: "You must give me forty men." His eyes shining, he calls to the village chiefs and passes on the message: "They want sixty men from me. Give them to me quick." The village chiefs decide among themselves how many each should give to supply the sixty men. "I can give ten." He calls his messengers and tells them in secret "Give me fifteen men." Then the messengers,

armed with their trusty whips, set upon the villages and seize anybody they meet by day or night.... In huts and fields, they hunt men. Showing no pity, they hit and wound, but so much the better. "You want to be freed? Give me a chicken. Give me five francs. You haven't got any? Too bad for you." They take as many as they can in order to free as many as possible in exchange for remunerative presents. How they enjoy the recruiting season! ...The village chief has received the 20 men demanded of him, but then it's his turn to intervene: "Let those who want to be freed make me a present; who would like to buy himself back? ...In a few days, the 60 men are found and assembled in front of the head chief. Now the buying out comedy starts again: "Who wants to give me a present? Anybody who gives me a goat will be free to return home." Even if the sacrifice is enormous, people prefer it to the certain ruin of going to work in a plantation. "Me, I'll give the goat," says one. "I don't want your goat," replies the chief, who for a long time has had his eye on the wife of the wretched man.

On similar abuses in other parts of French Africa, see Cooper (1996, 82ff., 160, 191–92) and Olivier de Sardan (1984, 167–72), and for British Africa see Killingray (1986).

13. Chem-Langhëë and Fomin (1995) state that the construction of military stations in the hinterland by the Germans made slave raiding impossible and encouraged the adoption of small-scale approaches by slave traders, such as kidnap or abduction for prearranged orders from clients. Warnier (1995b) likewise argues that the slave trade existed largely without slave raiding in the Grassfields, even before German control.

14. Bali trading parties armed with German guns brought slaves taken from their neighbors down to Douala for sale to traders. German breechloaders and the *basoge*, the irregulars of the *Balitruppe* trained by Hutter (*basoge* is probably a neologism, adding the plural prefix *ba* to the German *soldat*), provided the means by which the Bali were able to bypass the middlemen of the slave trade, a trade that they and others in the Grassfields continued into the late 1920s (Chem-Langhëë and Fomin 1995). Many of the laborers sent by the Bali to the German plantations, although supposedly Bali, were in fact domestic slaves working in Bali households or simply freemen taken from vassal chiefdoms; many Bali who had entered government service used their savings and their status to become slave traders (Chilver 1967, 497, 508).

See Cooper (1996, 29ff.; 2000) for an analysis of the "conditions analogous to slavery" generated by forced labor in colonial Africa. Like the Germans in Cameroon, the French administration organized *razzias* or "virtual slave raids" for the recruitment of forced labor in the Kong district of the Ivory Coast between 1928 and 1931 (Cooper 2000, 35–37). The independent inspector Maret's contemporary description of the practice was unequivocal: the administration was involved in forcibly rounding up workers on behalf of public and private employers, "just as the traders had delivered, before our arrival, their sinister human merchandise to the slave traders who carried them toward the islands of America.... The only difference is that today they are delivered for six months ... only" (Maret, 1931, as quoted in Cooper 1996, 34). Coercive recruitment was still a problem in 1939, ninety years after France had officially abolished slavery (Cooper 1996, 85). Meanwhile in the British territories, success in obtaining young laborers for white settlers from an African chief was similarly observed to depend "on how far he could be induced to exceed his instructions" (Assistant District Commissioner Kilifi, 1918, as quoted in Cooper 1996, 43; 2000, 131), and in Rhodesia, the official term "recruitment" was simply a euphemism for abduction, where those kidnapped to work in the mines were referred to in local languages as *chibaro,* "slaves" (Cooper 1996, 44; 2000, 131; Van Onselen 1976).

15. There is even evidence that Flegel, one of the German military officers traveling with Zintgraff, actually engaged in a slave raid with a Fulani raiding party in the northern Grassfields (Chilver 1967, 484), while Brauchitsch, a German officer and the *Bezirksamtmann* in charge of Douala, bought a young Duala woman for sexual purposes (Austen and Derrick 1999, 107)—a practice that was apparently "general among whites" and defended by the cynical Governor Puttkamer on the basis that "it kept a girl out of a cruel harem" (Rudin 1938, 304–5). There is no shortage of reports regarding atrocities committed by Germans in Kamerun (e.g., Ardener 2002; Chilver [1966] 1996; Fanso and Chilver 1996; Fanso and Chem-Langhëë 1996; Van Slageren 1972, 57), but to pretend that these are the only historically relevant aspects of German colonial rule would be to miss equally prescient aspects of their legacy. As Austen and Derrick (1999, 93) point out, the "myth" of extreme colonial oppression is only one among three for which the Duala remember the Germans. Although they are based on facts, such myths obscure the ambiguities of colonial history. Many in the upper echelons of the German administration sincerely believed that developing the territory would go hand in hand with an amelioration of the plight of its slaves and subjugated peoples. Esser's 1898 memoir, for instance, makes frequent reference to his abhorrence of slavery and his respect and admiration for the Bali people (e.g., Chilver and Röschenthaler 2001, 65, 74ff.). It is clear that he viewed salaried labor in the plantations as much in Christian missionary terms, as a form of salvation, as in socioeconomic terms. Likewise it is evident that Zintgraff was deeply attached to the Bali people, once telling Kemner, a German plantation manager, that his return to Bali in 1896 had been the happiest moment of his life (Kemner 1937, 148; Chilver 1967, 493). Moreover, the affection and respect he had for the Bali was reciprocated. He was still remembered in the 1960s as a *Bali nda'ni*—a true Bali—and his erstwhile mistress, the princess Fé Ditamina, aged over ninety in 1963, spoke to Chilver affectionately of his devotion to her (Chilver 1967, 493). As Chilver points out, however, these aspects of Esser's and Zintgraff's personalities have to be balanced against the "chicanery and terror" (493) that they must have suspected their recruitment agreement with Fon Galega would have engendered.

16. Governor Puttkamer even allowed his troops to keep any women they cap-

tured in the course of punitive raids, reasoning that reversing this precolonial practice would reduce their incentive (Rudin 1938, 304).

17. In a May 13, 1913, communiqué, Lieutenant von Adametz—the new station
commander for the Grassfields who was keenly aware of the contradictions in the
imperial government's policies of pacification, centralization, and labor recruitment—wrote:

> If Herr van der Loo [manager of the West Afrikanische Pflanz ungs-Gesellschaft
> Victoria] could realize the evil results this recruiting in large numbers has had for
> the Bali people he would abstain from estimates of what the Bamenda district can
> supply.... It was in the interest of chiefs to catch as many laborers as possible. The
> Bali population [i.e., Bali and all the surrounding states of the Western Grassfields
> so far discovered by the Germans], as a result of this "mass-recruiting," is being
> reduced. The flower of the Bali population lies on the Cameroon Mountain [site of
> the German-run WAPV plantation]. In a gang of three hundred Balis, according to
> my records, there were ninety-four deaths in one year [1912]. (As quoted in Chilver
> 1967, 510)

Cf. the French local administrator Aubin's leaked complaint to the French government of 1943 that was intercepted by the colonial authorities in Ivory Coast and
which evokes the same frustrations with respect to forced labor recruitment: "I am
disgusted to fill ... the role of slave trader. We recruit labourers to a terrible extent
in this god forsaken place and we have come to exceed the maximum possible.
Headquarters remains obstinately deaf to our cries of alarm and ... kills ... all possibility of a future in this country" (as quoted in Cooper 1996, 151).

18. These figures are for the Gestapo-run labor camps and not for the extermi-
nation camps set up toward the end of the war to implement the "final solution."

19. For the period1926–35, women outnumbered men by 18–24 percent in all
of the provinces of the fledgling British Cameroons except for the province of Victoria, where the plantations were (Kuczynski 1939, 257–59). In Victoria, there were
twice as many men as women. In 1937, the population of the province of Bamenda
was 226,630. In that year, there were 19,590 laborers on plantations in the British Cameroons. Of these, 9,693 were classed as coming from the "rest of British
Cameroon," that is, not from Victoria or Kumba where the plantations were (Kuczynski 1939, 252–78). The great majority of these would have been from Bamenda
province. This seems in keeping with René's estimate that by 1905 the *Balitruppe*
was sending over 1,000 men a year from the Grassfields to the plantations, that
the area was swarming with recruiting agents from the plantations, and that they
had already recruited 10,000 laborers from the Grassfields (René 1905, 103). If the
total Bamenda population was 226,630, and we assume (generously) that half of
these (113,315) were men, and of these half again (56,657) were young and able-
bodied, then we reach a proportion of 1 in 5 or 1 in 6 Bamenda youths working

on plantations in 1937 (56,657/9,693 = 5.84). By comparison, Clarence-Smith estimates that in the year 1913, during the German colonial period, 40,000 plantation contracts were officially registered. The majority of these were migrants from the Grassfields, and approximately one-fifth of them were not forced but "voluntary" laborers escaping "the despotic regimes of their chiefs" (1989, 500).

20. This figure indicates a slight drop from the 16,000–18,000 I estimated for the eighteenth century in chapter 2. Warnier (1995b) revises his previous, much lower estimate: he originally put the number of slaves annually sold into the external trade at 200–260, or 1.66 to 2.16 per 1,000 (1985, 194–95). In discussing this earlier estimate, he already admits that the true number may be anywhere "up to five times higher" than the figures he proposes (1985, 195). After further research Warnier (1995b, 255) considers his original calculation "a considerable underestimate," revising it upward to 15,000 per annum. See Austen (1998) for a discussion of Warnier's (1985) estimate of the proportion of slaves traded to Douala and Old Calabar, and Nwokeji and Eltis (2002), who provide a lower annual estimate for the years 1822–37 of 500 per year (2002, 205).

21. See Franz Thorbecke's four-volume *Im Hochland von Mittel-Kamerun* (1914–16).

22. The weight limit was originally set by the government at 25 kg but was increased in 1908 to 30 kg, with the addition of a further 5 kg "for the personal needs of the carriers" (Rudin 1938, 331).

23. André Gide, who traveled to Cameroon in 1926–27, a decade after the French had taken control of the territory from the Germans, shows in his memoir that little had changed on the ground for the porters. Paid FF 1.75 per day of carriage (one way only), they were expected to pay for their own food out of their salary. Gide notes that they were refused food or only sold it at extortionate prices in many villages where they were strangers (1927–28, 367–68). He also reports that a good proportion of his carriers were ill at any one time and that he was advised by a French labor clerk not to give them extra pay to cover their food: he would be spoiling them (123, 316–20).

24. In principle, beatings were supposed to be meted out only under the supervision of a government representative—if possible, in a colonial irony worthy of Conrad's *Heart of Darkness*, by a medical doctor. Apart from the grotesquery of this proposition, the tiny number of government labor inspectors, let alone doctors (even by 1912 there were only twenty-nine in the entire country), made it impossible to carry out, and traders ignored the ruling as a gross interference in their right to ensure the discipline of their carriers (Rudin 1938, 336–37, 350–51).

25. The government once justified its actions by pleading that only a small rope was used and that it was untied whenever any Europeans showed up (Rudin 1938, 326).

26. In Oku, caravan portage for the British was known as "plucked work" (*tshɔk efɛl*) or alternatively as *ngundu,* a term of obscure etymology. It was the fon who

personally chose porters. Middle-aged informants of mine remember their fathers having been chosen—"plucked"—by the fon as caravan porters. Silvia Forni (pers. com., Aug. 14, 2003) was told by one of her Bamessing informants that one of his grandfathers had been "carried away" by "white-men," who came to the palace and ordered that the fon provide them with porters: "When my grandfather was called to assist these white people, he went and went with them forever. And that was all about him. . . . So we don't know whether our family is existing in the white-men country or not." The same informant, when asked the term for "slaves," replied: "*Bɔ;* these were the men that were taken and sent away." Colonial portage has evidently been conflated here with memories of the transatlantic slave trade, and is presumed also to have ended in transportation to the Americas. The idea that the grandfather or his "family" may be living in the country of the whites recalls the equation of the United States with the realm of death by Congo peoples (MacGaffey 2000) and Angolans alike (Miller 1988, 4–5). According to them, transportation to the New World resulted not only from literal transshipment in the era of the slave trade but also in the present by way of death: having been the place to which people disappeared forever, the United States then became the otherworldly abode of ancestors.

27. Ardener ([1970] 1996, 250) notes that the Bakweri term for pledging or pawning one's children was *sómbî*, from which he suggests that the Haitian term *zombie* originates. The near identity of many other Haitian words with Bakweri vocabulary suggests that this population supplied a significant proportion of the country's slaves. The resurgence of the belief in pawning one's kin in the colonial era suggests that, like the peoples of the Grassfields, the Bakweri assimilated their experience of plantation labor to their previous experience of transatlantic slavery.

28. His inquiries into *ekong* quickly revealed more details about what buying people entailed: "They take your shape," an informant told him about the *éconeur.* "They make a sort of big doll. It's there on the bed, and everyone cries. But you, you are standing next to it and you see everything. They've put something in your mouth and you can't speak. You are like a dog, obedient to a master that has killed it" (de Rosny 1981, 98–99 [trans. mine]).

29. So too, as Achille Mbembe notes, the violence of the European colonial presence would later penetrate even the sleep of Cameroonians (1996, 388).

30. On this point, see Austen (1993), and for strikingly consistent beliefs by peoples on other parts of the Slave Coast, see MacGaffey (1986, 2000) and Shaw (2002).

31. A cargo cult of sorts seems to have emerged briefly among children in the period leading up to and just after independence. Chilver (pers. com., Sept. 21, 2003) states that "in the 1960s it was a commonplace among schoolboys that [the rows of houses] would follow independence." Chilver interpreted such statements as a reification of the notion that many Cameroonian politicians were regularly

traveling to the world of the European in search of "independence" and that this was the palpable form it might take once they had returned with it.

32. A similar account is supplied by the Rev. Enow in Buea (1994, 39). An old woman from his congregation came to see him early in the morning and complained of being very tired; then she went on to relate the following story: "I have been driving all night. I drive a plane. We use the plane to transport food, rain etc. from places of plenty to the Buea area. Very recently, White people have been attempting to seize the plane from us. If I hadn't been skillful, having piloted the plane for over thirty years, they would have long gone with it."

33. Pool was soon able to confirm this information with his own acquaintances. Tangwa, a neighbor of Pool's, dropped by one day when Francis, a sociology student from Yaoundé University, happened to be staying with him. The student started to ask Tangwa about *tvu'*, and in particular whether a member of such a *njangi* might be able to get out of his debt by offering a replacement for a human being:

"Okay, so if you want to go and pay for the [human] meat you've eaten what do you do? Do you take money to the witch market?"

"You've eaten a man," Tangwa said, his voice becoming louder, "so you can only pay with another man. They will say: *you have eaten my brother,* now you have to pay with a man."...

"Can you give a fowl instead?" Francis interrupted, looking slyly at me.

"A fowl," Tangwa shouted indignantly as he leaned forward.

"Is a fowl a man? If I give you a man are you going to give me a fowl in return?" (Pool 1994, 151 [emphasis added])

Once again, the ethos of the trade in human beings clearly perdures in the tenor of such comments.

34. In a lesser form of cannibalistic consumption, *əbvuŋ* are also said to have the power to disturb people in their sleep through an activity known as "to *sam*" a person (*sam wel*) and conceived of as pressing down (*jiikə*) on them, making it difficult for them to breathe. A *kəvuŋ* can press down on any person who has offended him, not only on members of his family.

35. Children seem to be suspected of witchcraft at least as often as adults in the Grassfields, and certainly more often than elders. A similar case involving schoolchildren from the neighboring chiefdom of Noni is said to have occurred in the mid-1970s (see Geschiere 1997, 160–62). Filip De Boeck (2005) provides a detailed case study of the prevalence of witchcraft accusations against children in the Democratic Republic of Congo, again highlighting that children—like others accused of witchcraft in Africa—routinely confess to their alleged crimes (albeit often under duress), often with detailed and gruesome stories.

36. In a clear illustration of this phenomenon, Ferme (2001) notes that everyone

among the Mende is said to be "for" someone else—an ambiguous relationship that also included slavery as one of its outcomes.

37. Niehaus (2005), critiquing Geschiere's (1997) contention that zombie discourses accuse elites, argues that this is only the case in normative terms, whereas in practice accusations are leveled against impoverished, marginal, or young people. This argument cannot justifiably be applied to the Bakwery and other coastal Cameroonian cases that Geschiere discusses, however, where it is clearly documented by the likes of Ardener ([1970] 1996), de Rosny (1981), and others that the accused *are* elites. Yet as Geschiere again points out (1997, 159), Niehaus's point seems to apply to the Grassfields, where the political polarization and the strong vertical hierarchies make elites largely immune to witchcraft accusations. As Niehaus (2005) argues of the South African lowveld and in contradistinction to the coast of Cameroon, despite the normative view that it is the elites who are the Judases in the Grassfields, it is cadets who are actually accused of witchcraft.

38. As Mbembe seminally put the point in his work on youth, "Africans have never eaten so badly as they have since the independences" (1985, 122 [trans. mine]).

39. Moving from the hunger of the people to the obesity of the elite, Achille Mbembe (1992) again traces the uses of the imagery of eating in relation to the prebendalization of Cameroon in the 1980s and notes that the body is the principle locale for popular idioms depicting power and its abuses.

40. This notion closely resembles the pre-*ekong* witchcraft beliefs of the Duala (which still persist alongside *ekong*): "[The witches] eat you in their mouths like meat: one meat eats another meat. It's the strongest witchcraft of all, the sorcery of the water, the one of the caiman. It's the first witchcraft of Cameroon. You are not sold. You continue to live, to walk. But you feel a little pain, you begin to sing gently, and when they bring you to the hospital, you can't understand. You don't know that it's a supernatural [*ndimsi*] matter" (Loe, as quoted in de Rosny 1981, 99–100 [trans. mine]).

41. Somewhat complicating matters, the data that Pool presents (1994, 153) make it clear that his informants are also conversant with forms of witchcraft that they refer to with the terms *kupey* and *munyongo*—which they also refer to as "national witchcraft." This form of witchcraft also posits the existence of invisible plantations and is identified with those who have been working on the plantations in the south. Francis Nyamnjoh (1985, 15) further states that his informants in the Grassfields chiefdom of Bum called Msa witchcraft *kubeh* (i.e., *kupe*) or *munyongo* (i.e., *nyongo*). The point, however, was explicitly emphasized to me by Oku informants, as it was to Pool by his informants, that *kupe* and *nyongo* are recent imports brought back from the coast by plantation laborers and are not of Grassfields origin (hence their identification as "national" as opposed to "local" witchcraft). This aspect suggests that Bakweri-type *nyongo* beliefs have been brought to the Grassfields as a result of labor migration to the plantations, and specifically

that they are hybridizing original *msa* and *kəvung* beliefs with the elements of *nyongo* relating to zombies and witch plantations. The data that Geschiere cites (1997, 155–57; referring to Alobwede d'Epie 1982; Balz 1984; and Ejedepang-Koge 1971) on the witchcraft beliefs of the Bakossi who inhabit Mount Kupe further highlight the degree of borrowing, replication, and integration of witchcraft beliefs throughout the region from the coast to the Grassfields. Like the Wimbum, the Bakossi believe that the initiated are able to go to secret locations on this forested mountain, where they gather "mysterious closed bundles" that may contain either riches or misfortunes.

42. See also Piot (1999, 68), who extends this model to the Kabre of Togo, among whom, he argues, witchcraft beliefs are essentially a modern phenomenon, emerging in the 1920s as a result of their experiences of forced labor on the German coastal plantations. It seems, as Piot suggests, that the cultural elements the Germans identified as quintessentially "African" were in fact a reaction to the Germans' own forcibly imposed capitalist modes of production and their inversion of the logic of gift exchange. In German Kamerun as in Togo, from an emic perspective, forced labor extended the capitalist logic of slavery, replacing the Judas figure with the officially appointed chief-cum-labor recruiter and marking a further traducement of ideal social and economic relations.

43. Illnesses, and in particular protracted wasting illnesses, were often attributed to witches (*kəvuŋ, əbvuŋ*) or angry ancestors (*nkvosay, ŋkvosaysə*), who were said to be consuming the ill person in some intangible way, while the person apparently remained in the world of the living. Similarly, people often interpreted dreams of goats as signs that they had been bewitched. In particular, they identified difficulty in breathing as evidence that witches were "pressing" (*jikə*) upon them, and the common dream that a goat was standing on one's chest was interpreted as a sure sign that one was being consumed by witches, who were pressing the life breath (*kəyui*) out their victim. The notion that one's inner strength is being surreptitiously consumed by others again vividly taps the cannibal discourse, and it simultaneously recalls the use of the slave rope by slave traders to sap the strength of the slaves they acquired.

44. The percentage of labor recruits who returned to their villages was often shockingly small. Rudin (1938, 328) quotes reports from German officials that show that the norm, during the last decade of the nineteenth century, was as few as 30–50 percent returned.

45. The limit to the work week, as imposed by the government in 1902, was ten hours a day, six days a week. Before the government's mandate, plantation managers had presumably been forcing their employees to work longer hours (Rudin 1938, 329). On conditions in the plantations, cf. Knutson, as quoted in Ardener (2002, 135ff.); Kuczynski (1939, 50–58); Rudin (1938, 250–51, 304, 325–29, 335–37); and Steer (1939, 80).

46. We know, for instance, that by 1892, "numerous Grassfielders had been to

the coast and seen the [German] Governor and the factories" (Chilver [1966] 1996, 32). We also know that many of the survivors of plantation labor returned home; complaints were even made by colonial officers about the plantation managers' practice of sending sick personnel home at the first sign of illness—a cheaper alternative to treating them on site. Most certainly these returnees recounted their experiences, much as returning emigrants are still required to spend many days after their return from the cities and towns of Cameroon or abroad recounting the latest news, political developments, and the particularities of their personal experiences.

47. It is noteworthy that the social structure of the Duala, in contrast to the hierarchies of the Grassfields, was markedly acephalous and egalitarian, with the terminology of titles and ranking being borrowed from European terms once the need arose, but the actual differences in status these implied were largely ignored. To this end, Austen (1998, 5) notes that "the Duala political system seems to have few attributes of a state" and that one of the few titles, *kine*, has been borrowed from the English "king."

48. On this point Ferme (2001, 6–7) notes the Mende of Sierra Leone's "hermeneutic of concealment" and makes the point that "ambiguous practices and discourses are common in situations of political danger." Argenti-Pillen (2003, 102ff.) cautions, however, that ambiguous forms of reference may predate the contemporary political violence that the ethnographer witnesses. Ambiguous forms of reference to violence, pain, and illness have been a part of South Asian cultures for millennia and have, at their core, the concern of an orator not to reproduce suffering in an interlocutor by referring to it explicitly (Chilton 1987). This concern is then redeployed in situations of conflict, shifting from the sphere of illness or domestic violence to that of state-sponsored violence. Nonetheless, as Scheper-Hughes (1992) has illustrated with respect to Brazil, centuries of violence can give rise not only to the adoption or redeployment of techniques of ambiguity and euphemism but also to the suppression of discursive strategies altogether—to submerged discourses. The absence of discursive strategies with which to address colonial intervention in the Grassfields evokes just such a submergence.

49. Rosalind Shaw (2002, 222–23) has described how elites among the Temne-speaking peoples of Sierra Leone used accusations of witchcraft against those with less power and wealth in their community as a means of selling them into the transatlantic slave trade. By a process that one could perhaps best describe as countertransference, the cannibalistic models upon which these accusations drew were based on the elites' own actions: "By authorising one of the principal ways in which persons were transformed into slaves, those who controlled witchfinding divinations accused those convicted of an invisible 'eating' of others analogous to that in which they were themselves engaged." This Freudian slip did not escape the young, the poor, and the marginalized most likely to become the next victims of a witchcraft accusation: "[The elites'] own participation in an 'eating' in which the . . . accumulation of new wealth was engendered by the disappearance of people into

oblivion was itself the object of ... stories and rumors that reversed the direction of formal divinatory accusation" (Shaw 2002, 223). As the testimony of Josia Yamsey quoted earlier underlines with respect to the Grassfields, slaves believed that their captors were cannibals and that they themselves were destined literally to be eaten. This belief was held by captives throughout the Slave Coast and even on the other side of the Atlantic (Clarke 1848; Palmié 1995; Shaw 2002, 230–31).

50. Or "la viande des autres," also the subtitle of Peter Geschiere's *Sorcellerie et politique en Afrique* (1995), the original French edition of *The Modernity of Witchcraft*. The aphorism was first coined by Mamadou Diouf in conversation with Peter Geschiere (Geschiere, pers. com., June 10, 2004). The Jesuit missionary Manuel Alvares, who worked in Sierra Leone in the early seventeenth century at the time of the transatlantic slave trade, noted the use of the idiom of cannibal witchcraft without realizing the political reality to which it referred: "[The Mane] entertain a malevolent and false belief about their illnesses and physical ailments, for they say, and they sincerely believe this, that God does not send death to them, rather it is their enemies and rivals who are eating them up" (Alvares, ca. 1615, as quoted in Shaw 2002, 213). In this period too, the predatory economy of the slave trade gave rise to a zero-sum view of the world in which one person's satiation could only be the result of another's wasting.

51. This practice brings us full circle to the phenomenon that Rosalind Shaw (2002, 223) has identified in seventeenth-century Sierra Leone, mentioned earlier in note 49, whereby slave-trading elites projected their own predation onto their victims by accusing them of witchcraft (thus providing themselves a motive for enslaving their victims).

Chapter Five

1. On masks and masking practices in the Grassfields, cf. Brain and Pollock (1971), Harter (1986), Northern (1973), Ruel (1969), Savary (1980), and Warnier (1985).

2. As Kasfir (1988b, 5) puts it: "The universe of forms which we call masks is simply part of a larger universe which might be called vehicles of transformation." Peek (1994, 484) similarly remarks that "the visual presentation of spiritual beings at festivals and other rituals is frequently secondary to their awesome acoustic dimensions," and he concludes that "because our experience of the world is multisensory, so must our study of that experience." In the Grassfields, as Geary (1979, 64) points out with reference to the *kweifo'* of the small chiefdom of We, to "see" a masquerade signifies having undergone a primary initiation that is largely acoustic.

3. The usual distance of the audience from the performer, artificial lighting effects, and music all serve to mask the violence of dance in classical Western staged

performance (although this aestheticization is now eschewed in some forms of modern dance), so that watching a dancer perform at close range, bereft of the proscenium arch of the stage and even at times of musical accompaniment, can be a shocking experience, revealing as it does the smell of perspiration and the sounds of halting breath and feet slamming painfully onto the ground.

4. In practice, the mask used for the Mabu in the Fuləŋgaŋ procession is not the same one as that used by the *kwifon* society's lictor mask when on its punitive expeditions or solo performances. This fact is not generally known outside the *kwifon* society, however, and the mask is considered to be essentially the same one whether it appears on its own or in the dancing line of Fuləŋgaŋ.

5. The death celebration of a *ntshii ndaa* belonging to the Mbele (royal) lineage is celebrated at the palace; for a *ntshii ndaa* of the Mbulum lineage it is celebrated at Fay Mentan's compound (close to the palace), and for a *ntshii ndaa* of the Əbjəŋ lineage the celebration takes place at Fay Ndifon Soom's compound just behind the *mfu'* house. The *kwifon* masquerades will go to these compounds and perform there. There is only one death celebration for a *ntshii ndaa,* which takes place the day after the burial. There is no commemorative celebration for a *ntshii ndaa.* In certain circumstances, for example during the interim period between the demise of the fon and his funeral celebration, all death celebrations of *nchiyse ndaa* are "locked." They are "reopened" after the funeral celebration for the late fon has passed and the new fon has been "moved out." Fuləŋgaŋ does not dance at death celebrations of princes (in the strict sense of the term, that is, sons of a fon) or princesses. If a "prince" (in the extended sense, that is, a male descendant of the fon of the third, fourth, etc., generation) is a *ntshii ndaa,* his death is celebrated at the palace by *kwifon.*

6. This is the case, provided that the man was married and had had children. Memorial celebrations are not held for women aside from exceptional cases, such as a queen mother.

7. For a full description of the enthronement ceremony, see Argenti (1996, 261ff.; 1999a). I was never a member of the palace *kwifon* society and provide as much as possible a commoner's perspective on these events and their significance, although I did have recourse to *kwifon* informants with respect to the exegesis of the Fuləŋgaŋ performance—a mask group that belongs to that society. For a description of these events from the perspective of the palace elite, see Koloss (2000, 105ff.), who did not witness any of the enthronement ceremonies but has attempted a reconstruction based on correspondence and interviews that he carried out a few years after the event.

8. For a full historical analysis of the "masks of the palace" belonging to the fon and those of Ngele, the princes' society, see Gufler and Bah (2006).

9. In fact, although Fuləŋgaŋ does possess medicines that are kept in the "house of Fuləŋgaŋ" inside the *kwifon* compound, its masks are not rubbed with medicines. The medicinal activity undertaken before a performance consists of the as-

perging of the feet of the dancers with medicine from a calabash bowl as they line up to move out of the *kwifon* compound. This custom, performed by one of the leaders of the "house of Fulǝŋgaŋ," is done, *kwifon* members say, to prevent the dancers from knocking their feet against a stone or sliding and falling in the rainy season (Gufler and Bah, pers. com.)—accidents understood to result from the curses of witches.

10. The common species of *Dracaena* known in pidgin as "peace plant" is used as a symbol of office for fons in the Grassfields. Often cultivated around people's houses, it is considered functional as well as decorative in that it is used in certain medicines and considered effective in warding off sickness. Because in its natural state it tends to grow in dark wet places, it is associated with coolness. The word *san* means both cool and wet and has positively valued connotations of fecundity, as opposed to heat and dryness, which refer to aging, death, bareness, and, by extension, unruliness and disorder, chaos, and insanity. See Argenti (2001) for details and Lan (1985, 93–94) for a homologous situation among the Shona of the Zambezi valley.

11. McCall (2000, 67, 69) notes that the leader of Ohafia war dancers from neighboring eastern Nigeria also holds a palm shoot in his mouth during the dance, in this case impersonating headhunters setting out on a raid. Here too the palm leaf is associated with war, and it was in fact used as a message to declare war between opposing factions. In the case of the Ohafia dance, the closed mouth that clasps the leaf recalls the danger of speaking out when conducting a raid.

12. See Argenti (2002a) for a description of my apprenticeship to him.

13. "Ka lu kǝkúm kǝtaa, lo kil ǝbfwa nǝ bɛmkǝ kɛn di."

14. "Kǝfaa-ki fɔ ŋgɛk sǝ mɛ!"

15. In contrast to the aesthetic principles of many West and central African mask traditions, the headdresses of the Grassfields are carved in a relatively naturalistic, representational style, making the bold and highly geometric features of a mask such as Mbi stand out all the more.

16. Although some Oku mask groups known as *ŋgaŋ* (which are not associated with the palace) also have feather gowns, they never wear wooden headdresses. They are said to be "headless," and the loosely woven mesh hoods that the dancers wear to conceal their features are interpreted, or read, as the headless "necks" of the figures. Masks that do make use of wooden headdresses are never adorned with feather gowns.

17. This right can be passed on by special dispensation (*bur'maa*) to the mask groups belonging to members of the royal (Mbele) lineage.

18. Banerman's Touraco is a rare forest-dwelling bird that survives uniquely in the montane forest of Oku; its red tail feather is used as the insignia of military society officers in the Grassfields.

19. According to Chilver (1961, 247), "Red cloth, to judge by Zintgraff's account of Fon Bo'mbi's dress, had reached [the chiefdom of] Bafut: local legend has it that

the uncertain attitude of Bafut towards his expedition was the result of coveting the red sailor-blouses of his carriers for dance outfits." At the same period in the chiefdom of Bali-Nyonga, red cloth was reserved for titled elders, who possessed the right to wear a small dorsal "moon" of it on their gowns (247).

20. The area involved included the chiefdoms of Bum in the north and Kom, Oku, Nso', Bamessing, Babessi, Babanki-Tungo, Fumban and Bambalang, Bangwa, and Bangangté in the south.

21. Cowry shells were so desirable to slave dealers along the west coast of Africa that European slave buyers had to supply up to one-half of the payment for a slave in cowry shells, despite the desirability of the other trade goods that they carried (Hogendorn and Johnson 1986, 110). The Royal African Company found the shells "almost a *sine qua non*" for trading at Whydah, Ardra, and the Bight of Benin (Davies 1957, as quoted in Hogendorn and Johnson 1986, 110).

22. A similar myth is presented by Verdier (1982).

23. This calculation is extrapolated from information provided by Jean-Pierre Warnier (1985, 90), who discloses that one brass rod was worth 250 cowries in the Grassfields in 1890 and that one slave was worth 150 brass rods (1985, 194). We can thus calculate that one slave was worth 37,500 cowries in 1890. Because the value of cowries had been depreciating in relation to brass rods, however, the value of a slave in cowries earlier in the century should be revised downward. Furthermore, before the eighteenth century, "heads" of cowries—then known by the Portuguese word for head, *cabess* or *cabeça*—referred to a value not of two thousand but of four thousand cowries. Because the price of slaves was subject to constant inflation along the entire Slave Coast throughout the centuries, it is likely that the four-thousand-cowry *cabess* of the sixteenth and seventeenth centuries referred to the value of one slave—thus one "head."

24. The sense of dread projected by this masking group is further marked by the fact that men cannot sing in its presence, as they often do when inspired by the beauty of lineage masking groups not associated with the palace. Nor are men allowed to cross the line of masks as they dance, or to hand coins to the maskers they appreciate, as they would with other groups. Rather, men and women who want to make such a gift are forced to throw their change on the ground for the masks' *kwifon* society acolytes to pick up.

25. Contemporary Fulani, though they are simply a peaceful transhumant pastoralist minority in the region, are still spoken of with barely concealed contempt by the sedentary peoples of the Grassfields as "people without a home," or "wanderers" who go "round and round" (*kaalɔ kaalɔ*). This stereotype recalls the terminology used with reference to prostitutes, who are called wanderers (*kɔdjɛl*, from *se djɛl,* "to walk"). Such resentment is no doubt related to the serious conflicts between Muslim pastoralists and Christian or animist farmers today in the region (Kaberry 1952; Pelican 2006), but it may also evince long-standing memories of the Fulani armed raiders of the nineteenth century.

26. Was it this Faustian bargain that the human sacrifices of the annual dances of the Grassfields palaces commemorated?

27. On such occasions the mask behaves in a solemn, reserved, and subdued manner. No other members of the society accompany it, and no musical instruments are played. The kəshiɛŋənə does not carry its customary weapons but only lingers in silence by the graveside for a short while, often keeping its arms crossed across its chest and clasped on both shoulders as a sign of grief. It sometimes throws a handful of earth over the coffin before slipping quietly away.

28. This mask has sometimes been referred to as a "runner mask" in the literature. This term is based on the role of messenger that the mask plays, that of being sent round the village to announce a forthcoming memorial celebration or to pass on other official messages. The term "runner," however, fails to account for the disciplinarian role that the mask plays in relation to the other masks in its group during a performance, which is its defining role. It is therefore more accurate to speak of a kəshiəŋənə as a "driver mask."

29. Here again, the manner in which forced laborers were recruited and delivered shows a continuity with the methods of the slave trade. After their capture, slaves were detained in stocks while awaiting the middleman trader and bound to one another by the neck, with wooden poles and collars, on their way from the Grassfields to the coast (Van Slageren 1972, 78).

30. Speaking not of masked dance but of mixed-gender group dances, Warnier (1995b, 261n8) has noted the "inexpressible boredom" of Grassfields dance, putting the lack of exuberance it betrays down to the tight control over sexual relations enjoyed by the elite of the Grassfields: "In almost 20 years of intermittent residence I have never observed the slightest touch of eroticism." As with mixed dancing, the severity of the bodily discipline of masked dances may relate to the control by elders, connoting in this instance their control not only over men's sexuality but over their commodification.

31. In English too, the etymology preserves memories of the continuity between colonial caravans and earlier slave marches: the "coffle," the line of slaves on a forced march, is derived from the Arab kafila, meaning "caravan."

32. The jesters' and other palace masks' association with the forest recalls the strong emphasis on "the bush" as a space of death inhabited by unrestful spirits in African folktales, suggesting that these too could be read in terms of an intrusive resurgence of collective memories breaking the containment of the past in standard or chronological histories. See, e.g., Amos Tutuola ([1982] 1989) and Ben Okri (1991, 1993), whose works are strongly influenced by the West African folktale tradition.

33. Jeffreys (1961a, 61) tells us that among the Bakweri to the south of the Grassfields, "any male who is found to have had sexual intercourse with [a widow] before she has been purified is said to have 'whitened her,' or has taken away the spirit of the deceased from her." Among the LoDagaa, white is associated with

death, and mourners are covered in whitewash (Goody 1962, 58). Gilbert (1987, 314) has noted that in Akuapem, Ghana, the king-elect's right arm is smeared with kaolin when he is brought to the palace for the first time. Gilbert reports that infants are similarly rubbed in kaolin when first brought out of doors. In this way, not only is the king-elect likened to the neonate, but both king and neonate are considered to be joining the living from the realm of the ancestors. Theeuws (1954, 18–19) notes that kaolin is also used in Luba kings' funerals; here he mentions a figurine called *mboko,* "which represents a kneeling woman holding a bowl of white clay." See also Petit (1995) on kaolin use among the Luba.

34. Tardits has described an event, from accounts remembered by some of his older informants in the kingdom (now sultanate) of Fumban to the east of Oku, that may have furnished the template for the contemporary form of the rite. According to these informants, two twins used to be buried alive with the king: "The tradition relates that in the olden days two twins, one of whom was the chief of the twins of the palace, were buried at the same time as the king after having been emasculated: the practice can only be very ancient, associated with the death of the king Mbuambua" (1980, 707 [trans. mine]). The expanding conquest states such as Bamum, Bafut, and Bali and the Banyang chiefdoms that bought Grassfields slaves tended, however, to sacrifice slaves rather than twins. Njiasse-Njoya (1995, 232) mentions that the Bamum buried live slaves and royal wives with the deceased fon. In other chiefdoms, an elite palace servant took the place of twins. Price (1979, 94) notes the practice among the neighboring Tikar to the east of Fumban: "The role of the [custodian of the kings' skulls] has been to be buried alive with the king at his death, but it is said that the custom has lapsed." Price elaborates (1985, 102) that "he entered the grave and the body of the chief was placed on his lap in a sitting position.... At this point, *Tusa,* one of the king's councillors would swiftly kill him to spare him from being buried alive."

35. This effect, discussed in the trauma literature, has also been noted more widely. As George Orwell states in "Notes on Nationalism" ([1945] 1970) with respect to nationalist struggles, "Events which, it is felt, ought not to have happened are left unmentioned and ultimately denied.... Indifference to objective truth is encouraged by the sealing off of one part of the world from another, which makes it harder and harder to discover what is actually happening."

36. The Catholic Father Heinrich Vieter recounts (1989, 65–66) how one of five Dahomean boys he had bought from the German governor of Cameroon in 1892 was fond of making a case to him for a salary increase on this basis. Every few months, the boy (whom he had also baptized Heinrich) would come and ask him for more money. "I would reply to him: 'Heinrich, I had to spend a great deal of money to buy you, I can't afford to pay you more.'" But to this argument, the boy would reply that "After all, ... by the fact of having bought him, I had become his father" (66, my trans.).

37. Chem-Langhëë and Fomin (1995, 196–97) observe that the Banyang often settled their slaves at either end of a free village so that that their witchcraft pow-

ers would ward off malefactors and evil spirits. Brain (1972, 53) notes likewise that the Banyang of the southern Grassfields "automatically" accused their slaves when witchcraft was suspected.

38. Strictly speaking, these were the "wives of the palace" (əbkii ntɔk) rather than his personal wives; they were all inherited from his predecessor.

39. Kramer ([1987] 1993, 46–49, 73, 130) points out that palace collections dating from as early as the eleventh century have been found in Zimbabwe, including, from the thirteenth century onward, Persian *fayences* and Chinese plates traded across the Indian Ocean.

40. For further discussion of the nefarious associations of representing human beings in the Grassfields, see Argenti (1999b, 2002a) and Forni (2001, 164ff.).

41. Try as they might, neither the Germans nor their successors ever managed to quell the self-association of Grassfields rulers with Western military personnel and paraphernalia. In the kingdom of Nso', where the Germans committed some of their worst atrocities (Fanso and Chilver 1996), some of the palace roof supports still represented German soldiers in 1958 (Chilver, pers. com., 1996). Chilver noted these—which she says were carved after 1915—while carrying out research in Nso' in 1958. Asking about their "meaning," she was told they represented "power, like Jaman." Chilver ([1966] 1996, 125) further states that the frontage of the *mfu* military lodge in the kingdom of Nso' was decorated with German soldiers, and the fon's throne (destroyed by fire in 1959) was supported by caryatids in the form of German soldiers (Chilver, pers. com., 1996). In a clear persistence of this aesthetic principle, the Nso' palace guard in the mid-1990s wore locally produced uniforms of various colors replicating the khaki green uniforms of the national gendarmerie (Goheen, pers. com., 1996). Farther south, a photograph of the chief of Bahouan taken in 1955 (during the UPC insurgency) reveals, painted into the frescos on the palace wall behind him, French soldiers in fatigues who are stalking with guns pointed before them (Hurault 1962, pl. 15). Harter (1986, 94) has published a 1925 photo of doorposts in the southern Grassfields chiefdom of Fonjomekwet that are entirely decorated with German soldiers. A photo of a bed with German soldier caryatids (Harter 1986, 63), presumably taken by Harter himself, has its provenance given as "Pangui, Baloum," but it was evidently produced by the same carver who produced the Fonjomekwet door frame. See Lecoq (1953, pls. 16 and 44) for similar carvings in Bamendou and Bangam.

42. The closest pidgin expression referring to dry mouth is *wandas*—from the English "wonders"—a term used to describe the sort of phenomena likely to give rise to "dry mouth." To *see wandas* often refers to having witnessed witchcraft or its effects and is also used to refer to Europeans and the technology associated with them. The term also indexes the violence of witches and Europeans, however, and the warning "you go see wandas!" is used as a threat of bewitchment or, alternatively, of physical punishment. To have "seen wonders," for example, "Y don see wandas today-o!" thus refers to having been beaten.

43. Piot (1999, 37) similarly notes how the oral history of the Kabre peoples of

northern Togo in the village of Kudwe includes two exegeses regarding a corpse said to lie in the forest near the village: one version has it that this was a German soldier, another that it was a slave raider from northern Benin. Piot reflects that "it is not difficult to imagine why Kabre might conceptually equate the predations of the slave trade with colonization, and thus one predator with another" (38). Shaw (2002, 14–15) highlights this story as an example of how one historical event inevitably comes to be remembered "through the lens of another" and adds that we dichotomize between discursive and practical memories at our peril.

44. There is a precedent for this behavior in that the fon transcends gender and during his installation is represented by a statue of a woman who mysteriously appears in a wood near the palace (Argenti 1999a).

45. This reference would have been all the more clear to those who saw the women's procession in the colonial period, but it is still determined today by the same sense of dread it would have caused then. Rosalind Shaw (2002, 117–25) relates the life story of a female ritual specialist from Freetown who received visitations from spirits who informed her she had a "load on her head" and who compelled her to "take up the load." For this woman, becoming a diviner was thus equated in some way with being a carrier. Shaw goes on to stress that "carrying headloads is women's work" among the Temne. As in much of Africa, it is women who carry the agricultural and household produce on their heads, on their way to and from the fields, from the well or the spring to the house, and so on. The striking thing about the colonial period in Cameroon, however, was that the gendered tasks of carrying were thrown into disarray as men, women, and children were all indiscriminately recruited for portage by the thousands (see fig. 14, p. 103). To see the women of the palace carrying the exogenous "things of the palace" is to see the traduction of the normal order. Where women would have carried water and the produce of their fields with which to feed their children, they now headloaded the items of the prestige economy that linked the chiefdom to the wider political sphere and its economy of predation and social dislocation.

Chapter Six

1. They were especially discomfited on one notable occasion that year, when Sultan Njoya traveled to Buea, the German capital, with his newly trained *garde du corps*. A German officer inspected them, and on his command one of Njoya's soldiers presented arms so violently that he shattered his rifle. Later that day, the Bamum soldiers shamed the German officers by beating them in a tug-of-war (Tardits 1980, 227).

2. The invention of this script unsurprisingly gave rise to enormous interest among the German administration at the time, as it has ever since. For reports on it from the German period, see Gohring (1907a, 1907b) and Migeod (1909). Works from the French colonial period include Debarge (1928–29) and Delafosse (1922).

3. The cause of the Germans' anxiety may have been due to their memories of the uprising of their Dahomean troops in Douala in 1893. The group of men and women had been so badly maltreated by the Germans in Cameroon after being bought in Dahomey that they finally rose up against the Germans, sending them fleeing from their own capital to a ship in the harbor while the insurrectionists occupied the governor's house. From the ship, the acting governor Leist could see their leader wearing his own clothes, and even dressing his beard in the same manner as Leist's (Vieter 1989, 65). The French, who took over from the Germans, would later express a similar disquiet at Njoya's keen interest in Europeans, the administrator Ripert referring to him in 1923 as an unintelligent and arrogant "imitator" (Ripert 1923, as quoted in Tardits 1980, 997).

4. Thomas Abler (1999) has demonstrated the very widespread historical phenomenon of the appropriation of exotic military dress by imperial armies as a facet of their incorporation of local forces of irregular fighters in their colonized territories. This process of sartorial appropriation was not unidirectional, however, and the case of the entry of the Germans into the Cameroon hinterland demonstrates that for a protracted initial period it was not clear that either partner (the Germans and their local allies) in the Germans' colonial adventure in the Grassfields would be dominant.

5. The term *basoge* probably comes from the combination of the German for "soldier," *Soldat,* and the Bali prefix *ba-* meaning "people." The Nso' also attributed magical powers to the Germans and referred to them as spirit-beings when the Germans first came to the area. Because they were seen as warriors, the Germans were accommodated in the warriors' lodge during their stay (Fanso and Chilver 1996, 103).

6. Christraud Geary (1996b, 185) quotes Seitz (1908, 10) who makes it clear that the armed guard of Sultan Njoya of Bamum was also adept at performing military drills.

7. Njoya's bodyguards were trained by a Bamum soldier who had served on the coast in the regular German *Schutztruppe,* as were the Bali *basoge* (Tardits 1980, 227; Moisel 1908).

8. Ruel (1969, 305) notes that the German colonial officer Kommandant Von Besser was remembered by the Banyang simply as "Commander," which suggests that this military title passed from the German into pidgin with the arrival of the British in the First World War.

9. These bolt-action rifles, loaded with high-powered cartridges, represented an enormous tactical advantage over the locally produced Dane guns available until then in the Grassfields. Not only were they waterproof and much quicker to load, but they were much safer to fire than were the Dane guns (which regularly exploded in the user's face) and much more accurate (cf. Warnier 1980).

10. When I once paid him a visit at the palace in the early stages of my research, the fon of Oku jokingly referred to my research assistant as my *tapenta.*

11. Cf. Richards (1996, 30, 71) on the ways in which the forest became a source

of empowerment to those excluded from the state in Sierra Leone. Richards also emphasizes the importance of literacy to the RUF insurgents in Sierra Leone, many of whom saw themselves as "excluded intellectuals" (61–62). In Cameroon, similarly, the tract titled "Statutes with a Few Commentaries," reproduced in Mbembe (1996, 287, 407–18), includes an introduction by the UPC leader Um Niobè titled "Our Mission Is to Educate the People."

12. Warnier underlines the lack of any properly revolutionary motive among the Bamileke maquisards when he says that "the cadets, though they signalled their strength, failed to propose any alternative political order. In two words: the hierarchies are in agony while the hierarchical principle stays intact" (1993, 217). The phrase strikingly recalls Gibbon's judgment of the murders of the Caesars in Rome: "They attacked the person of the tyrant, without aiming their blow at the authority of the emperor" ([1776] 1993, 83). The fact that a small minority of the maquisards may have taken possession of the thrones left vacant by their rebellion, however, should not be seen as evidence of a premeditated attempt at a straight-forward coup d'état. Rather, the historical context suggests that the local youth were aroused by a much more broad-based, grassroots discontent with geronto-cratic authority itself in the region.

13. Hurault (1962, 127ff.) points out the extent to which the Bamileke chiefs were largely seen as puppets of the state with little real legitimacy, during his re-search in the midst of the UPC uprising in the 1950s. This ambiguous role is per-haps best encapsulated in a 1955 formal portrait photograph of the chief of Bah-ouan featured in the book. A blue-and-white royal cloth has been hung in front of the palace as a backdrop for the chief, who stands among the objects of the palace collection. It could be a royal portrait like any other from the region. A closer look at the palace wall partially hidden by the cloth and the eaves of the thatch roof, however, reveals murals of soldiers in contemporary colonial uniform, standing at attention in a line and presenting arms (1962, 126). The palace was burnt down two years after the photograph was taken, on the night of the October 18, 1957 (*Le Bamiléké*, December 1957, as quoted in Malaquais 2002, 316).

14. Other analysts, including Bayart ([1979] 1985), Gaillard (1989), and Le Vine (1964, 1971), have similarly concentrated their analyses on the political and his-torical dimensions of the movement, and in fact little is known of the member-ship, motivations, modus operandi, social configurations, performative aspects, and cosmological configurations of UPC and related activism in the Bamileke region. Achille Mbembe (1996) covers some of these aspects of the rebellion, but for the Bassa region to the south of the Grassfields rather than its distinct Bamileke in-carnation.

15. This assumption is all the more pernicious because it was used to justify the loss of life caused by the counterinsurgency measures instigated by the French colonial authorities and the Ahidjo regime they put in place at independence in 1960, in preference to the UPC.

16. As Le Vine (1964, 63) explains, the age-old problem of marginalized bach-

elors was at the center of the *problème Bamiléké:* "Under Bamiléké customary law, property passed from father to son is indivisible. Most often, land passed in this manner is too small to support several households. As only one son may inherit, the other must of necessity leave at the age of twelve or thirteen and seek employment elsewhere in manual labor, apprenticeship, commerce, or domestic service so as to be at most a minimal burden on the family. At sixteen or eighteen, many emigrate to other parts of the country."

17. Dominique Malaquais (2002, 326ff.) argues convincingly that the young marginalized cadets of the region were not strongly represented in the armed troops of the UPC guerrilla movement but that they were nonetheless fundamental to the uprising in their tacit support for the UPC, which took the form of passive resistance, nonviolent forms of protest and sabotage, strikes, and symbolic actions. These acts were all the more significant in that the cadets hugely outnumbered both the UPC fighters under whose aegis they had mobilized on this occasion and the chiefs and notables of the region.

18. For a contemporary assessment of the security services in Cameroon with special reference to the abuse of human rights, see the 1998 report of Sir Nigel Rodley, the Special Rapporteur on Cameroon to the UN, and the recent report on Cameroon by the Medical Foundation for the Care of Victims of Torture (Ball 2002).

19. The Brigade Mobile Mixte, made up of gendarmes and army troops together, and therefore a group with access to the army's fully automatic weapons as opposed to the semiautomatic rifles of the gendarmes, is particularly notorious, as are the antigang brigades that have been accused of summary executions in the lawless north of the country and in the port city of Douala.

20. The title of this chapter should therefore not be taken to mean that palatine or gerontocratic discourses of power are separate from colonial and postcolonial forms of hegemony. On the contrary, they are linked across time and space by overarching practices of violence and accumulation that belie the nominal distinctions between the local and the national, the traditional and the modern, or the colonial and the postcolonial. The types of power deployed across these eras and types of authority form a complex matrix of feedback loops and dialectical processes that cannot usefully be separated one from another or understood in isolation from each other. From a subjective point of view, the cadets of the Grassfields can "think" one system of authority in terms of the other without experiencing any cultural discontinuities between them.

21. It has been estimated that the *ville morte* operations brought about a 40 percent decrease in economic activity, resulting in an FCFA 4 billion daily loss for the state in tax revenue (Diallo 1991; Van de Walle 1993, 381, in Roitman 2006). It should be added that nonpayment of taxes and utility bills was one of the forms of civil disobedience practiced by the activists (Takougang and Krieger 1998, 129, 155n29).

22. At the same time, young men and women in Oku took to referring to the

princes' mask Wan Mabu—belonging to the royal Ngele society famous for its long-standing opposition to the palace—as the "minister of youth and sports." Antonio (1995), De Boeck (1998, 805), Nunley (1987, 64), and Smith (2004) report similar phenomena in other parts of Africa. And just as these young activists appropriated the titles of global discourses of modernity from the state, they sneeringly ascribed to it the traditional categories to which they are so often relegated themselves; thus they named the armored police vehicles that sprayed the crowds of young demonstrators with water canons Mammi Wata, after the water spirit.

23. One could see the corpses of these alleged thieves in and around the Bamenda markets on a regular basis in the early 1990s. Gathered around the body was always a small crowd of people engaging in discussion about the victim's alleged crime, his manner of dispatch, and so forth. I once saw a policeman idly looking on from the back of such a crowd and making no attempt to intervene. As Le Roy Ladurie (1979) illustrates with respect to the charivaris and carnivals of early modern France, and as has always been the case with the witchcraft accusations of the Grassfields, it was not the established order that these bacchanalian demonstrations threatened in practice but the weak and the poor, who could more easily be scapegoated.

24. As it turned out, most of the time was spent quarrelling over which villages had or had not contributed money to the palace for the fon's new car and some roof repairs for the palace building. The other topics on the agenda were only quickly covered by the fon himself and not discussed.

25. "We weh we di shidong fo hea we be stone, so make any man weh y be wata lokot!" The whole meeting was held in pidgin.

26. One can of course question the extent to which "voluntary labor" was ever really worth the name in colonial Africa. With colonial authorities colluding with chiefs over the restriction of access to wealth, land rights, and marriage, young men facing a life of indigence and perpetual "childhood" were often forced to seek wage labor as a least-bad option. Young men in a similar demographic situation during the precolonial era in the Grassfields had joined together into trading groups head-loading kola nuts on foot to the distant markets of Nigeria. Such journeys of course had their own dangers—the risks of illness, robbery, and enslavement—and one can only assume that the promise of earning a wife and becoming a full adult played a strong role in convincing these young men to risk their lives. Jean-Pierre Warnier (2006) has recently argued that young men from the Grassfields were better off as domestic slaves in Douala than they were in the position of "free" cadets in the Grassfields, and indeed many chose not to return home after they were freed in the colonial era.

27. The fon is therefore often referred to as a primus inter pares in the literature on the Grassfields. One could go further, however, and argue that the colonial and postcolonial relationships between fons and central government authorities both petrify and problematize the legitimacy of their positions (Argenti 2005a). Martin Chanock (1985, 169; 1991) similarly shows that elders in Malawi and Zambia col-

laborated with colonial authorities in the construction of a monolithic and time-less notion of "customary legal institutions" that was beneficial to both parties. Of course the invention of "customary legal institutions" was itself one battle in a long-term power struggle between youth and elders that had been anything but static. As Cooper puts it, the elders hijacked the colonial concept of "African tradition" to turn a "conflicted recent past into ancient custom" (2000, 128) and to enlist the help of the authorities in protecting their status as elders and slave owners.

28. "If the crowd gathered round the scaffold, it was not merely to witness the sufferings of the condemned man or to excite the anger of the executioner: it was also to hear an individual who had nothing more to loose curse the judges, the laws, the government and religion. The public execution allowed the luxury of these momentary saturnalia, when nothing remained to prohibit or to punish.... In these executions, which ought to show only the terrorising power of the prince, there was a whole aspect of the carnival, in which rules were inverted, authority mocked and criminals transformed into heroes. The shame was turned round . . . the cries of the condemned, caused offence only to the law" (Foucault [1975] 1977, 60–61).

The people were called on to witness the execution—in part to be terrorized but also in part to participate in the execution—much as they could be called on to protect the country in war. In practice, however, the crowd was just as likely to sympathize with the perpetrator who had now become a victim as with the executioner and the king. And the executioner and king were paradoxically tainted with the guilt of the criminal—to whose barbaric level they stooped in their very reenactment of his crime on his own body. In many dramatic cases, the crowd rushed in to save the dying man and to chase the executioners away, thus reversing the entire symbolic order of the rite. Even in those instances in which the crowd did not actively interrupt proceedings, their motivation to attend and their true sympathies could not be taken for granted. When they cheered, was it for king and country, or for the regicide about to become a martyr and a hero? When they witnessed the excess of violence meted out on the body of the condemned, did they see justice being done and the sovereignty of the king being restored, or was the king simply revealing his struggle for domination, his true barbarity, and his parity with the lowliest criminals in the land?

Chapter Seven

1. Women's central role in male masked performance has been observed in relation to Gelede masked dance by Drewal and Drewal ([1983] 1990) among others, while in the southern periphery of the Grassfields, women actually mask legitimately (Röschenthaler 1998). In addition to their role in the dance, women have their own esoteric societies in the Grassfields, which operate independent of male involvement (cf. Kaberry 1952, 97–101).

2. On the women's *anlu* uprising in the chiefdom of Kom in the 1950s, cf. Nkwi

(1985), Ritzenthaler (1960), and Shanklin (1990). On the *takumbeng* uprisings against the state in the Bamenda area in the 1990s, see Takougang and Krieger (1998, 232–33).

3. Among other artisans, dozens of carvers are employed in the villages of Oku in producing the necessary masks and drums, which are put to use not only in Oku but throughout the region (Argenti 2002a).

4. This practice takes the form of a ceremony in which the fon confers his blessing on a new mask group. This is done by "throwing water" (*mar'mɔɔ*)—palm wine from the royal reserves, known as "water of the palace" (*mɔɔmə ntɔk*)—onto the lead mask and the *kəshiɛŋɛnɛ* or driver.

5. A son born before the rule of the fon is not considered a *wantɔk* (*ghɔntɔk*), literally, "child (children) of the palace." Only those "conceived on the leopard bed"—that is, with a royal wife inside the palace—are legitimate *ghɔntɔk* with a claim to the throne one generation after their own father's rule. Any son of the fon has a *fay* appointed in his lineage, whether it be himself, his own son, or his son's son.

6. Befntok is now a middle-aged traditional healer, known as Dr. Sophia, living near his father's compound by the marketplace in Mbock-Jikijem.

7. Nobfon does not live in his main compound but in the neighboring village of Mbo. The mask group he has largely created himself, however, is kept in his classificatory father (actually his brother) Fay Keming's compound.

8. "Binə naasə ŋgaŋ, nə kədiar'!"

9. "Tshar' eti!" (i.e., under its stamping feet).

10. Engard (1989, 150) was told in Bafut that these gowns are designed to replicate the shimmering of the spots of the leopard.

11. For a fuller description, see Argenti (1996) and Jindra (2005).

12. CALL: Wɛ dzaŋə gə!

   RESPONSE: Dzaŋə yui γɛs!

   CALL ONLY: Dzən esaŋ!

   CALL ONLY: A ho! γɛn tshin!

13. CALL: Oo ndaa!

   CHORUS (repeated after each call): Ndaa ejuŋ lu ntie!

   CALL: We nɛy kwo!

   CALL: We ney nduu!

   CALL: Təfɔnə!

   CALL: Naa nə ŋkfəmsə!

   CALL: Oo ndaa!

   CALL: Ye bɛɛy wan nom!

   CALL: Nɛy kuo!

   CALL: Wan baam!

   CALL: Wel ejɛl!

14. CALL: Wan bii wan-a nduu maay ɛykfəl.

   CALL: Wan maay wan-a ge jɛli koil-a!

CALL: Wan tɔŋ fɛn ɛ yio Buunjin!

CALL: Ɛ jɘle kelum ɛ tam nyii!

CALL: Duŋ duŋ duŋ lum ɛybam!

CALL: Wan maay wan-a ge jɛli koil-a!

CALL: Kwale maay wan-a ge jɛli koil-a!

CALL: Fuy ndaa nkaŋ lii ndaa ɘmnduk-a!

CALL: Wan toŋ fɛn ɛ yio lum e ndaa!

15. To place a deceased person into the ground is not simply conceived of as burying a corpse in the Grassfields but rather as returning a person to the realm of the ancestors, where he or she will continue to live, eventually returning (Argenti 2001). For this reason, a communication channel is kept open, leading from the surface of the ground to the ear of the deceased, through which prayers can later be made (Bah 2000). As one sows, so too one reaps; just as one provides people to the earth, so too the earth provides people to the world. One cannot therefore properly speak of a realm of the dead in Oku but rather of a womblike second world in which the deceased are in a state of gestation. Bakhtin points out a similar ambiguity in the profane references to death in medieval European carnival, in which the earth "swallows up [death] and gives birth at the same time": "To degrade is to bury, to sow, and to kill simultaneously, in order to bring forth something more and better. To degrade also means to concern oneself with the lower stratum of the body, the life of the belly and the reproductive organs; it therefore relates to acts of defecation and copulation, conception, pregnancy, and birth. Degradation digs a bodily grave for a new birth; it has not only a destructive, negative aspect, but also a regenerating one.... Grotesque realism knows no other lower level; it is the fruitful earth and the womb. It is always conceiving" (Bakhtin [1957] 1968, 21).

16. I do not use the expression "will to life" (*Wille zum Leben*) with the biological determinism given to it by Arthur Schopenhauer but rather in the political context of the Grassfields, in which young bachelors are keenly and consciously aware that their chances of marrying and of having legitimate children are severely curtailed by the dominance of elders and elites.

17. *Mbezenaku,* a term rejected by the people of Mbeze, can be translated as "Mbeze of Oku," suggesting the chiefdom's subjection to Oku.

18. O! Ntie ɘbkwo!

   ɘbfɔn Mbezey!

   Ɛb nɘ lɔ lɛy!

   ɘbfɔn Mbezey!

   Ɛb nɘ kwo-kwon!

   ɘbfɔn Nsɔk!

   Ɛb lu wel ɘmnaɲ!

   ɘbfɔn kɔr' kɘ gwi-a

   Ɛb gia-gia ntie!

   Jie-jie-a!

   Kasɘ tshuo!

Əbfɔn Mbezey!

Ɛb nə kɛŋ ə ŋkfə!

Ȇ! wuluwulu, ē! lu wel Mbezey!

Jandarmɔsə! Ȏ! Ibal Etshem!

19. In this case, women do not flee from it. This is not because it is any less dangerous but because it is moving slowly. Women are thus less hurried in their efforts to keep their distance from it and make sure they do not face it.

20. In fact, *ntshin ɛykwo* literally means "stamp death," whereas the actual grave-stamping performances are referred to as *tshin isɛy* (stamp grave). The *ndjaŋ isɛy*, or *əbluŋ isɛy*, referring to "songs of the grave," are not grave-stamping songs per se but laments sung at burial ceremonies.

21. Kasfir (1988b) and Peek (1994) have noted the relative lack of attention in the literature paid to acoustic masquerades. Peek (1994) quotes Ritchie (1991, 194), who remarks that, for the Hausa, "to hear" (rather than the English "to see") is "to know." Similarly in Oku, one says "I hear" (*mə juo*) to mean that one understands, and "to hear" a language means that one not only understands it but is conversant in it. Unlike the visual, which is delimited spatially, the aural world is all encompassing, and thus all the more apt as a form of cross-world communication.

22. Angry at the loss of a member: "*kəkum yaps əblɛɛ*"; crying as if they had gone mad: "*kəkum dii ka kə djarə-djarə.*"

23. As Kaberry (1969, 185) points out, the most heinous form of incest a man could engage in in Nso', after that with his own mother or sister, was with a wife of his lineage head or a wife of the fon, with the latter punishable by death.

24. Illicit affairs did not necessarily entail incest, but because incest was (and is) defined very inclusively, the general tenor of the taboo was to prohibit relationships between bachelors and the wives of any of the elders in their patrilineage. Needless to say, even when an affair with an elder's wife did not entail incest, it still attracted opprobrium and social sanctions.

25. See Kasfir (1988b, 4–5) on the artificial restriction of the masquerade in Western literature. Masks are not simply three-dimensional objects but "vehicles for the process of transformation." Once the problem is reframed in this way, "we also encompass a number of events which until now have been treated only marginally as 'masks': acoustic masks, 'night' masks, and body painting" (4–5). Kasfir goes on to point out that the presence of the music as originating from a concrete instrument is often a closely guarded secret in West African societies and that they are made known publicly only through their sonorous presence. There is thus a relationship of secrecy whereby dancer : masquerade :: musical instrument : music. Conant (1960, 159) has recorded the use of "rock gongs" in northern Nigeria. As Peek (1994, 480) notes, this instrument, with its origin in the ground, makes it particularly apt as a vehicle for the "acoustic representation of the other world."

26. This instrument is also used by the male military societies.

27. Perhaps even more so than men's masks, the women's "mask" recalls the indeterminacy of spirits in other parts of Africa. Often these are defined only in the

vaguest terms. The *kubandwa* spirits of the interlacustrine area, for example, are said to be "like the wind" (Pennacini 2000; Crapanzano and Garrison 1977).

28. Men and women use umbrellas of different styles in Oku. The female one, built of banana leaves in a five-foot-long raffia stem frame, is designed to cover the woman's head and back as she is bent over for farming tasks. The male one is built of the same materials, but it is square, to be worn on the head while standing. It is this second umbrella—now seldom used by men, who prefer Chinese folding umbrellas—which the *fəmbiɛn* musicians use.

29. This washing replicates the full body washing, performed by a male healer in public in the stream nearest the compound, during the ceremony for a woman with a newborn child, know as *fœyse wan sə dji* (taking the child out to the road).

30. Found growing wild in the forest and also cultivated in the courtyard of established compounds, this plant has many ritual uses throughout the Grassfields. Known in pidgin as the "peace plant," it is associated with fons and often is used for asperging people with medications during rites. Because it grows in the wettest areas of the forest floor, it is seen to be "wet" and "cool," and therefore fertile.

31. "Tshia ndɛ wel? Tshia mɛ!"

32. Even in the case of the hunt, the large game chased by the hunters often ends up running out of the forest into the fields, where it is women who dispatch the disoriented animal with blows of their pointed hoe-handles.

33. Here too, as James Frazer recounts ([1922] 1995, 577–83), individuals were regularly singled out by the population and beaten or stoned on ritual occasions. It was primarily slaves who were chosen as scapegoats, sometimes on the occasion of a plague or other misfortune, but at other times in a yearly ceremony whose purpose was to guarantee the fertility of the harvest. The scapegoats were commonly beaten on the genitals with plants associated with fertility. The actual or symbolic killing of a slave and the violation of their regenerative powers thus paradoxically guaranteed the city health and fertility in the coming year. Representing the evil forces of death that infect the city from outside and must be expelled, scapegoats were nevertheless maintained by the city authorities at the heart of the city and treated like kings or gods before their death. On this subject, see also René Girard's theory of the scapegoat mechanism ([1972] 1977, [1982] 1986).

Chapter Eight

1. The news of a memorial celebration is first spread by word of mouth, sometimes with the help of the *keshiɛŋɛnɛ* of the compound mask group, which is sent around to its subcompounds to spread the word. The first guests then start to arrive in the evening of the appointed day, the men with fowls and palm wine and the women with their farming baskets full of corn flour and dried meat. As in the case of burial ceremonies, men and women are allocated separate "death houses" (*nda ɛykwo*) in the compound, and it is said that the ancestors are watching who

enters from their place at the fireside (ŋkui ŋkɔk) and noting what gifts the guests bring. Once the guests arrive, they eat, drink, and perform ndjaŋ dances on and off all night long. For the memorial celebration for heads of large compounds, an announcement is made to the palace that the celebration will be "opened." This procedure is known as efɛs ɛykwo.

2. The lineage-group masquerades of Oku share a few basic dance steps. These are known as eliine (also known as etəmene or esɔɔne), ebensene, and efəəne. Esɔɔ ne has the verb root sɔɔ, "to stab," and by extension "to stamp one's foot into the ground." Etəmene is derived from the verb tem, "to shoot."

3. The kam yɛ mbii, a mask with the "head" of an old man, comes first in line. It sometimes wears the red feather of a military society leader, and it sometimes has a long strand of hair emerging from the back of its head, on the extremity of which may be fastened a medicated object. The kam is usually dressed in a gown made of human hair that covers its whole body except for the hands and feet. It dances with an iron spear. It does not dance to the same rhythm as the rest of the masks in the lineup, but in counterpoint to them, and will often stop dancing except to send the signal for the next step during the moments between two dance steps. It does not do this simply by demonstrating the next step but rather dances briefly and often at higher speed than the group as a whole, in a fast prelude that the other masks respond to with a new step.

The ŋgɔn yɛ mbii, literally the "ŋgɔn of the front," is the first of the three ŋgɔnsə in the line of masks. Ŋgɔnse ("young women") depict formalized representations of beautiful virgins (they are never thought of as mothers) with rounded cheeks, beaming smiles, earrings, and, in the case of royal masks, a ring of cowry shells around the top of the "head." They wear gowns of the sought-after blue-and-white cloth known as fɛntshi that is otherwise reserved for the royal family and dance with decorative whisks in their right hands.

Kənfiibin is a name made of the words kənfii and ebin, "which takes on the dance," referring to the role this mask plays in acting as a secondary leader for the masks behind it that cannot see the kam. The kənfiibin is usually depicted as a bush cow, and it often carries a spear.

Ɖkie is the personal name given to the kəshiɛŋɛnɛ of each group. Kəshiɛŋɛnɛ is another composite, based on the root verb shiɛŋə, "that displays" or "that shows off." The verblike word shiɛŋə refers to the dance that masks perform when they dance singly. Single dance performances, such as that performed by Mabu, the kəshiɛŋɛnɛ of Fuləŋgaŋ of the kwifon society, are highly stylized performances that announce the imminent arrival of the whole group at the celebration of an old death. People scrutinize these performances to see if they are in keeping with the known style of the group and the mask in question. The pent-up violence of a shiɛŋə alludes to the disciplinarian role of the kəshiɛŋɛnɛ, which dances with two heavy sticks with which it threatens those who stray onto the dancing ground and brings wayward masks back into line (especially the female ŋgɔnsə, which have a reputation for wanting to dance out of line to attract the gaze of the men). The "head" of this mask usually bears a variation on a pattern that includes two abstract spiral shapes, not unlike rams' horns or the lobes on the caps of titled elders, along with the jaws and teeth of a carnivorous animal. It is thus one of the few zoomorphic masks in the kingdom.

Fɔtshɛ, which is not always included in a mask group, represents a younger man. Ŋgɔn fəteten, the "ŋgɔn of the middle," is the optional third young woman of the mask group. The mask ŋgwikɔ, literally "come catch me," like the kenfiibin, has the "head" of a bush cow (nial). Ŋkvəm is the title, otherwise known as fay, given to the lineage elders of large, established compounds by the palace. Its mask is carved with the two-lobed cap (kətandɔŋ) that these men characteristically wear. It sometimes dances with the elaborate, short ceremonial spear of fays (kədiɔŋ). Ŋgɔn yɛ ebam is the last ŋgɔn in the procession. Kam yɛ ebam, the "kam of behind," is depicted as an elephant (kətam) or a bush cow (nial) and is a mask for which Oku carvers are famous in the Grassfields. It dances with a long spear of the type made by ironsmiths from the chiefdom of Babungo.

All lineage masked dance groups include the masks just listed unless stated otherwise. They may also duplicate certain ones, or have unique ones that appear in no other group. One optional headdress regularly found in village mask groups is known as ŋkɛm, the term that refers to a type of basket used for head-loading. The mask actually depicts the head of a young man topped with such a basket. Mask groups normally have a minimum of seven masks (except for the mask groups known as "foreign" masks, kəkum məkalə, which usually dance with four or five) but have been known to appear with more than twenty. All masks have a face covering (which forms the "neck" of the mask) and ankle rattles. It is said that "they have not come from the road" (baa fəy djii), an expression used to describe something mysterious and potentially nefarious and which emphasizes the suspension of disbelief exercised in relation to the manmade nature of masks. They are summed up, in a few words, as unknown, wondrous things (kemanen kefaa). The construction of the mask is restricted to narrow stylistic parameters; skin exposure is kept to a minimum, and shoes, jewelry, or anything that might lead to the recognition of a dancer are never worn. Furthermore, masks are always matched with a particular gown, so as to give the impression of a unified, organic body rather than an ad-hoc composition of man-made parts. To this end, masks never speak audibly (except at night, when they are invisible, and with modulated voices), nor should they be addressed, especially by the name of the dancer, and especially not by women or children. Likewise, people do not speak of the rattles, gowns, masks, and so forth of masks, but identify them as body parts of the mask: its headdress is its "head," its gown is its "skin," and so on. Even when one needs to refer to these things separately from the rest of the mask, for example, inside the mask house, they have names taken from benign objects in Eblam Ebkwo such that a metavocabulary of euphemisms is used for all the paraphernalia. There is no word for "mask" in Eblam Ebkwo.

4. The wooden headdresses worn by these types of mask group (known as

kəkum kəkaŋ) make the different masks easy to differentiate one from another. However, there are two other main types of masking groups that wear no wooden masks but that in all other respects are just like those with headdresses: they also dance in groups to xylophone and drum ensembles, and they wear ankle rattles just like the masks with headdresses. The first of these is known as the *kəkum evəl,* whose headdress is made of feathers (*evəl*) rather than wood. The second is called *kəkum ŋgaŋ,* and it is said to be "headless." That is, although the dancer's own head is hidden by the cagoule of woven raffia fibers, as with all other masks, he does not wear a headdress of any sort. Because the disguised head of the dancer represents the neck of the mask that surmounts it, these masks are effectively acephalous. Although there are few differences that can be used to identify particular members of a single-feather or "headless" masking group, participants can still identify the individual masks by the names just listed according to position in the line, style of dance, and role vis-à-vis the other masks. Likewise, a *kəkum ŋgaŋ,* or "headless" mask, has recognizable positions within it according to the objects that each mask holds, the gown it wears, its position in the line, and the role it plays vis-à-vis the others. Some adepts prefer these two types of mask groups to the ones with headdresses because, unencumbered, they can dance faster and for longer periods.

5. Ties to the mother's side of the family are generally stronger (both emotionally and in terms of punishment for transgressions of obligations) than ties to the father's side.

6. This demonstration of appetite was deemed premature by Ngum Valentine, with whom I was standing watching the performance. He pointed out that the group as a whole should dance before its *kam yɛ mbii* or *kəshiɛŋɛnɛ* could legitimately go to the palace door or men's die house to demand the reward for the group. Rather than reprimand the dancer once he was back in the house, though, he only shrugged his shoulders. It is not in the nature of a mask, and certainly not of a driver mask, to behave itself.

7. Ideally, this is done with castor oil, *mdjaŋ*—pressed from the castor bean, *Ricinus communis* — but it is relatively expensive and hard to come by, so discarded engine oil is often used now. In this case, some were using *mdjaŋ,* others engine oil. One of the children then started to place *ŋkɛŋ* leaves inside the mouth of the bush cow mask used by the lead mask but was quickly rebuked by the elder men there. These leaves can only be used by the lead mask of groups that have received special dispensation (*bur'ma*) from the fon.

8. Karin Barber (1991, 202) has noted that cloth is a well-known image for people and wealth-in-people among the Yoruba. The epithet associated with one oba, or king, has him proclaim, "I could take off my clothes and wrap myself in people." The image of power radiating from the big man over his acolytes, subordinates, and slaves is associated with the sensuous qualities of the cloth he wears, and one *oriki* proverb actually refers to the doubling of robes: "one who wears one cloth on top of another, sweeping the ground with vigorous magnificence" (202).

9. The dancing space is always referred to as the *ewey*—literally, the "mar-

ket"—perhaps because it needs to be a flat, open area free of stones (to keep danc-ers' foot injuries to a minimum), or perhaps because markets were often held in or near palace courtyards in the Grassfields, where masks also dance. This name is in keeping with the elaboration of a para-nomenclature for everything associated with masquerades in Oku.

10. *Liete*, a diminutive of the verb *se lii*, "to take," is a term also used to refer to the pounding motion exerted with the cooking stick by women as they prepare maize pudding from corn flour in the evening. Once the water has been added and soaked up by the flour, the woman pulls small lumps of the dough toward herself with the stick as she sits by the large pot. With reference to the dance, *liete* has con-notations of this gradual, painstaking, delicate, and ultimately nurturing activity, which is essentially feminine.

11. Although women's gifts are known as *faalə*, men's gifts to masquerades are called *kɛŋ*, the term used to refer to the harvest of vegetables.

12. Because the two compounds of Mbu Bey and Tatangkum are both in Jiki-jem, and many young men are members of both these mask societies, and because enough men for two distinct groups of dancers could not come such a distance, sev-eral of those who had danced in Ŋkɛŋ simply changed costumes to dance again in the guise of Mbɛlɛy. Because the whole panoply of masks could not be brought due to their weight, even the two sets of masks for the masquerades were not wholly discreet: Mbɛlɛy borrowed some from the Ŋkɛŋ set to dance with.

13. Deborah Durham (2000, 2004) describes the ascription of the term "youth" in Botswana as deictic, that is, referring to a relationship *between* people rather than an inherent quality of any one person. For example, to be "young" is deictic in that it cannot apply to someone absolutely, but only in relation to other, "older" people.

14. This is especially evident in the performance of *ŋgwikɔ* from the village of Ichim, at whose appearance (even in the palace in Elak for the old die of the fon) the women from its compound—no matter where they married—immediately set up a shrill and striking ululation of delight and find great sticks to beat against the cudgels of the sprinting masquerades.

15. It is said that this mask once used to come out to perform in a spectacular fashion, atop a pair of perilously high stilts that were steadied by its numerous followers, and with which it would run across the rooftops of the compound. This practice was apparently stopped by the palace authorities, however, who confis-cated the stilts on the grounds that the palace masks had no such apparatus and therefore no village mask could have one.

16. It sometimes happens also that a masquerade, recognizing a man it likes (who may or may not recognize it), hands or throws him its whisk. In these cases, likewise, the recipient is free to dance around the ring with it before returning it with a few coins hidden in his hand.

17. This line of the song is partly in Itang-Ikom, the language of the chiefdom of Kom, and is consequently somewhat obscure.

18. Õ! Gə wel ne bii wan wen fenə shii giɛ wen-ã.

Õ! Ndikətshuii djɛl lɛ, gə ghɛ-ã?

Õ! wel nə sar' əbfɔn kəbɛy lɔle wel lii kəlik-ə-wen.

Mɛ kan mbi-a nə ghel kwa gə ghɛ-ã?

Õ! Gə ghonə Mkɔŋ Mɔte mɔm ghɛ ilar' nə əbfɔn əbkwo?

Ndu giate, ndu kasəgwi, mə yɛn əbtshuo əbyumene.

Õ! Kanə gə ndɔ ba-yin lan-vin ebfɔn-ə-bɛy nə Bah.

Gə əbfɔn-ə-bɛy nə Bah ndu kasə gwi-ã?

Õ! Ma! Õ! Ma!

Sui nda nə nda gə niar' ŋwale ilar' ne ebaŋ-ã.

19. The stool of the compound head, that is, see how soon Laate died.

20. Õ! ghɛy yɛn nə nyam əbkwo boy.

Õ! Gə ghɛy djaŋ-ndu!

Õ! yɛn wel sə lɔ əblɛm sə wan nda!

Jie-bɛy nə Lat—Õ! shil kətie—Õ!

Wɛ lɛmmen lɔ ndu djaŋ ilar' nə ŋgum.

Yɛn gə wel lɔ ɛb lɛm jie nda nə wen—Õ!

Late wɛ jie kətie—Õ!

21. Õ! mɛ luŋ-luŋ njin kədjɛm, wel bu sə juo-ã!

Õ! mɛ kan əbwun wɔm, wel bu sə tsham.

Mɛ kan əbwun wɔm-ɛ, lii kəlik nda bu-ɛɛ.

Luŋ-luŋ, bɛ wel bɔŋ dio e-wel ketu-ã.

Mɛ kwomen lan-vin liɛ-ã!

Õ! wel luŋ-luŋ, wel-ɛ-bu sə juo-ã.

Nɔ wan lii nə wan ndjin kədjɛm wel-e bu sə yun-ẽ.

Bay ghɛnə nyi lɔ lɛm wan.

Mɛ kan əbwun yɔm, Fɔkɔm,

Mɛ kan mbi yɔm.

We luŋ-luŋ jio lun lie ŋgɔsə.

Me kan wun wɔm Ndjin Kədjɛm.

Jio lun djin kədjɛm lii ŋgɔs-ə wel mə sɔŋ.

Mɛ kan əbwun wɔm.

22. In Eblam Ebkwo, the men married to the women of a compound are thereafter called "my child" (*wan wɔm*) by their wife's father or mother, and they are called "my husband" (*lum wɔm*) by the men of the compound, the brothers, and uterine (half) brothers of the woman they married.

23. In a recent development of the tradition of the *kəshiɛŋɛnɛ*, one of whose tasks is to keep the crowd from getting in the way of the dancing masks, certain participants now dress in contemporary paramilitary uniforms during masquerades and act as crowd control officers, threatening unruly children with their sticks (see fig. 20).

24. As Bakhtin ([1957] 1968, 7) says of carnival:

In reality, [carnival] is life itself, but shaped according to a certain pattern of play. In fact carnival does not ... acknowledge any distinction between actors and spectators. ... Carnival is not a spectacle seen by the people; they live in it, and everyone participates because its very idea embraces all the people. While carnival lasts, there is no other life outside it. During carnival time life is subject only to its laws, that is, the laws of its own freedom. It has a universal spirit; it is a special condition of the entire world, of the world's revival and renewal, in which all take part. Such is the essence of carnival, vividly felt by all its participants.

25. In a recent thought-provoking article, Michael Jindra (2005) argues that the proliferation of these commemorative celebrations may be relatively recent and linked to the democratization of ancestorship as introduced by missionary education from the turn of the twentieth century. If so, this development would fit in with the wider pattern of youth politics in the Grassfields, which saw cadets harness the opportunities offered by colonial occupation to contest their oppression.

26. Building on J.D.Y. Peel's (1984) analysis of Yoruba oral history (*itan*) as an immanence of "the past in the present," Karin Barber (1991,15) notes in her groundbreaking analysis of Yoruba *oriki* oral texts that

Oriki ... are not "history" in the sense of an overview or attempt to make sense of a sequence of events, but a way of experiencing the past by bringing it back to life. ... Through all the stages of their transmission they do not lose their relationship of contemporaneity to the events they refer to. ... They are not thought to be *about* the past: they *are* fragments of the past, living encapsulated in the present. In this way they do more than preserve a sense of continuity through the violent reversals of Okuku's history: they also keep "the past" close at hand, at the heart of present concerns

27. About a year after this death ceremony, he was involved in an armed conflict during a territorial dispute on the border between Oku and Edin. As a result, he had to go into hiding, leaving his family behind once again. This second tragedy can be seen as a result of his original exile, which had forced him into the disputed borderlands of Oku.

28. Ndu giate, ndu kasəgwi,
    mə yɛn əbtshuo əbyumene.

29. Əbfɔn kɔr' kə gwi-a
    ɛb gia-gia ntie!
    Jie-jie-a!

30. The present continuous in Western languages refers to a discrete and bounded period of time shortly before and after the action indicated. For example, the English expression "he *is dividing* the land" is conveyed in the present continuous, or "he *was dividing* the land" in the past continuous, and both can be assumed

to take only a short period of time. The Eblam Ebkwo doubling of a verb does not have the same meaning, however, because the past that it includes as part of the time duration of the action is not bounded in its staring point, nor is it bounded in the near future of the action taking place. In Eblam Ebkwo, the present or past continuous, therefore, marks indefinite durations of continuous time. Moreover, the songs, although I have translated them into the past tense in English for the sake of clarity, are sung in the present. Mbey literally sings of past events in the present tense, singing "*goes* and divides it up/*goes* and comes back." The same applies to the fon of Nso' in the grave-stamping song. These songs thus literally return the past to the present, depicting distant events in the present tense as if they were happening in the "now" of the singer. In this manner, the present continuous of Eblam Ebkwo suggests a different conception of time than the linear image of chronological time constructed in Western-language ideologies, and one in keeping with the belatedness of history and the recurring nature of embodied memory.

31. Karin Barber has noted the ways in which the "disjunctive, labile form" (1991, 35) of Yoruba *oriki* recitations is essentially composed of "an endlessly shifting tissue of quotations without any center or starting point upon which to anchor them" (37). The effect of speaking in borrowed fragments is to introduce a Bakhtinian polyvocality that brings the speaker and audience together into a dialogical and multiauthorial relationship. Furthermore, because the reported speech of *oriki* borrow from a distant past to address the present, this speech form collapses time, introducing an achronicity in which the past is experienced as an emanation recurring in the present (15–16, 63).

32. A friend from the chiefdom of Fumban, which has largely given up its masking traditions after the Islamic reforms first introduced by Sultan Njoya, has told me that old men have been known to cry when they see the masks of the Anglophone Grassfields perform there. The Grassfields have thus become emblematic of the resurgent past of Fumban to those who live there now.

33. Just as the violence of the palace mask is not an adequate explanation for the panic they strike in the hearts of the audience, so too the euphoria to which village masking gives rise cannot be explained by means of the aesthetic pleasure of their beauty, or even by the commemoration of the ancestor whom they mark. In the case of both the palace and the lineage masquerade, the performance gives rise to intense reactions not justified by the content of the event itself. Rather, the events are overdetermined with references to other, prior, far more momentous events, and the emotive responses to which they give rise can only be explained by taking these into consideration.

Chapter Nine

1. As Ricoeur (1986, 16–17) argues, utopianism can represent a plunge into unreality and delusion, but it can also engender a critical engagement with politi-

cal reality. Utopias can therefore have not only ideological but also liberatory or subversive effects (cf. Gardiner 1993, 26), and while revisionist utopias may serve the dominant discourse, critical utopian discourses may introduce social change, nurturing "a permanently open process of envisioning what is not yet" (Moylan 1986, 213).

2. As Stephan Palmié (2002) and Rosalind Shaw (2002, 263–64) have eloquently demonstrated, the history of Africa's insertion into global modernity in all its guises—the Atlantic slave trade, the corvée labor of the colonial era, and the mining of Africa's minerals for the profit of a tiny minority of elite politicians and entrepreneurs in the postcolonial era—exists now in the form not of a linear past constituted of discrete periods but of a monstrous present.

3. Rosalind Shaw expresses this quality of the timeless past when she says that "both past and present interfuse, shape, and mutually fashion each other, such that memories form a prism through which the present is configured even as present experience reconfigures those memories. Memory, then, works both forward and backward. . . . Modernities past . . . have formed a lens through which modernities present and modernities future are experienced" (2002, 265).

4. In the languages of the Grassfields, the exclamation "Jaman!" (German!) still refers to a moral quality and a discourse of power that transcend historical periodicity and gain their salience with reference to contemporary political events. Likewise, the fact that, well into the colonial era, slave traders disguised slave convoys as caravans of carriers by giving the slaves loads to carry on their way to the coast (Chem-Langhëë and Fomin 1995, 194) suggests how the embodiment of the caravan might by the same token serve to index bodily memories of slavery.

5. For more on the emergence of the crypt as a "secret vault" within the subject, see Abraham and Torok (1980), Torok (1987), and Abraham ([1975] 1994).

6. "Mort, sauf en moi" (Derrida 1976, 17), with *sauf,* meaning both "safe" and "save" in the sense of "except."

7. In this way, the dances of the Grassfields are akin to the *oriki* chants of the Yoruba described by Karen Barber (1991, 17): "[*Oriki*] are labile, elliptical, allusive, and often deliberately obscure or incomplete. An *oriki* chant is a form that aims at high impact, high intensity, which it achieves through juxtaposing apparent opposites. Although they are so highly valued and so tenaciously preserved, *oriki* are almost impossible to pin down."

8. As Derrida puts it, "the value of the shibboleth can always, and tragically, become inverted. Tragically because the inversion at times escapes the subjects' initiative, the good will of people, their mastery of language and politics. Call to arms or password in a fight against oppression, exclusion, fascism or racism, it can also corrode its differential value; the basis for alliance and of the poem, in its discriminatory guise it becomes a technique of policing, of normalization and of control [*quadrillage*]" (1986, 56 [trans. mine]).

9. "Wɛ lɔ ndu mbui, wɛ ke ebam." "Behind," *ebam,* here can be understood as referring to witchcraft and violence as well as to the past.

Reference List

Abler, Thomas. 1999. *Hinterland warriors and military dress: European empires and exotic uniforms.* Oxford: Berg.

Abraham, Nicolas. [1975] 1994. Notes on the phantom: A complement to Freud's metapsychology. In *The shell and the kernel,* by Nicolas Abraham and Maria Torok, trans. Nicholas T. Rand, 171–76. Chicago: University of Chicago Press.

Abraham, Nicolas, and Maria Torok. 1980. Introjection–incorporation: Mourning or melancholia. In *Psychoanalysis in France,* ed. S. Lebovici and D. Widlocher. New York: International University Press.

Adorno, Theodor. 1982. *Against epistemology: A metacritique. Studies in Husserl and the phenomenological antinomies.* Trans. Willis Domingo. Oxford: Basil Blackwell.

Africa Confidential. 1997. Biya election: The president's team arranged his assembly majority; next comes his own election. 38(13): 6–7.

Alobwede d'Epie, C. 1982. *The language of traditional medicine: A study in the power of language.* Thèse d'état, University of Yaoundé, Cameroon.

Amit-Talai, Vered, and Helena Wulff, eds. 1995. *Youth cultures: A cross-cultural perspective.* London: Routledge.

Amnesty International. 1992. Cameroon. AI Index: AFR 17/14/92 DITR: SC/CO/GR.

———. 1994. Cameroon. AI Index: AFR 17/2/94 DISTR: SC/CO/GR.

———. 1997a. April 16. Urgent action: Reports of torture amid large scale arrests. AI Index: AFR 17/05/97.

———. 1997a. May 12. Cameroon: Parliamentary elections must not lead to further human rights violations. AI Index: AFR 17/07/97.

———. 1997c. May 14. Urgent action: Reports of torture amid large scale arrests. AI Index: AFR 17/09/97.

Ankermann, Bernhard. 1959. *Völkerkundliche Aufzeichnungen im Grasland von Kamerun, 1907–1909.* Ed. H. Baumann and L. Vajda. Baessler Archiv, NF, vol. 7/2: 217–317.

Antonio, Africano. 1995. *L'UNITA et la deuxième guerre civile angolaise.* Paris: Harmattan.

Appadurai, Arjun. [1990] 1996. Disjuncture and difference in the global cultural economy. *Theory, Culture and Society* 7:295–310. Reprinted in *Modernity at large: Cultural dimensions of globalization,* ed. A. Appadurai, 27–47. Minneapolis: University of Minnesota Press.

Ardener, Edwin. [1970] 1996. Witchcraft, economics and the continuity of belief. In *Witchcraft confessions and accusations,* ed. Mary Douglas, 141–60. London: Tavistock. Reprinted in *Kingdom on Mount Cameroon: Studies in the history of the Cameroon coast, 1500–1970,* ed. Shirley Ardener, 243–60. Oxford: Berghahn Books.

Ardener, Shirley. 2002. *Swedish ventures in Cameroon, 1883–1923: Trade and travel, people and politics.* Oxford: Berghahn Books.

Argenti, Nicolas. 1992. African aesthetics: Moving to see the mask. *Journal of the Anthropological Society of Oxford* 23(3): 197–215.

———. 1996. The material culture of power in Oku, North West Province, Cameroon. Ph.D. dissertation, University College London (Senate House).

———. 1997. Masks and masquerades. *Journal of Material Culture* 2(3): 361–81.

———. 1998. Air youth: Performance, violence and the state in Cameroon. *Journal of the Royal Anthropological Institute* 4(4): 753–82.

———. 1999a. Ephemeral monuments, memory and royal sempiternity in a Grassfields kingdom. In *The art of forgetting,* ed. Adrian Forty and Susanne Küchler, 21–52. London: Berg.

———. 1999b. *Is this how I looked when I first got here? Pottery and practice in the Cameroon Grassfields.* British Museum Occasional Paper 132. London: Trustees of the British Museum.

———. 2001. *Kesum-body* and the places of the gods: The politics of children's masking and second-world realities in Oku (Cameroon). *Journal of the Royal Anthropological Institute* 7(1): 67–94.

———. 2002a. People of the chisel: Apprenticeship, youth and elites in Oku (Cameroon). *American Ethnologist* 29(3): 497–533.

———. 2002b. Youth in Africa: A major resource for change. In *Young Africa: Realising the Rights of Children and Youth,* ed. Alex de Waal and Nicolas Argenti, 123–53. Trenton, NJ, and Asmara: Africa World Press.

———. 2004. La danse aux frontières: Les mascarades interdites des femmes et des jeunes à Oku. In *Matière à politique: Le pouvoir, les corps et les chose,* ed. Jean-François Bayart and Jean-Pierre Warnier, 151–80. Paris: Karthala.

———. 2005a. Dancing in the borderlands: The forbidden masquerades of Oku youth and women (Cameroon). In *Makers and breakers: Children and youth in postcolonial Africa,* ed. F. De Boeck and A. Honwana, 121–49. Oxford: James Currey; Trenton, NJ: Africa World Press.

———. 2005b. Preface to *Some Oku rituals (Western Grassfields, Cameroon),* by Njakoi John Bah. *Archiv für Völkerkunde* 53:49–72.

————. Forthcoming. Youth: Rural. *New encyclopedia of Africa*. New York: Charles Scribner's.

Argenti-Pillen, Alexandra. 2003. *Masking terror: How women contain violence in southern Sri Lanka*. Philadelphia: University of Pennsylvania Press.

Arnoldi, May Jo. 1995. *Playing with time: Art and performance in central Mali*. Bloomington: Indiana University Press.

Asheri, Jedida. 1969. *Promise*. African Readers Library no. 16. Lagos: African Universities Press.

Austen, Ralph. [1977] 1995. Slavery and slave trade on the Atlantic Coast: The Duala littoral. *Paideuma* 41:127–52. Originally published as "Slavery among coastal middlemen: The Duala of Cameroon," in *Slavery in Africa: Historical and anthropological perspectives*, ed. Suzanne Miers and Igor Kopytoff, 305–33. Madison: University of Wisconsin Press.

————. 1983. The metamorphoses of middlemen: The Duala, Europeans, and the Cameroon hinterland, ca. 1800–ca. 1960. *International Journal of African Historical Studies* 16(1): 1–24.

————. 1993. The moral economy of witchcraft: An essay in comparative history. In *Modernity and its malcontents: Ritual and power in postcolonial Africa*, ed. Jean Comaroff and John Comaroff, 89–110. Chicago: University of Chicago Press.

————. 1996a. *The elusive epic: The narrative of Jeki la Njambe in the historical culture of the Cameroon coast*. Atlanta: African Studies Association.

————. 1996b. Mythic transformation and historical continuity: The Duala of Cameroon and German colonialism, 1884–1914. In *African crossroads: Intersections between history and anthropology in Cameroon*, ed. Ian Fowler and David Zeitlyn, 63–80. Oxford: Berghahn Books.

————. 1998. Douala: Slave trade on the periphery of the Nigerian hinterland. Paper presented at the symposium titled The Ports of the Slave Trade (Bights of Benin and Biafra), University of Stirling, UK, June 6–7, 1998.

————. 2001. The slave trade as history and memory: Confrontations of slaving voyage documents and communal traditions. *William and Mary Quarterly* 58: 229–44.

Austen, Ralph, and Jonathan Derrick. 1999. *Middlemen of the Cameroons' rivers: The Duala and their hinterland c. 1600–c.1960*. Cambridge: Cambridge University Press.

Awasom, N.F. 1984. The Hausa and Fulani in the Bamenda Grasslands (1903–1960). Thesis, doctoral de troisième cycle, University of Yaoundé, Cameroon.

Bah, Njakoi John. 1996. *Oku past and present: Three essays*. Private printing.

————. 1998. Marriage and divorce in Oku. *Baessler Archiv* 46:31–57.

————. 2000. Burial in Oku, Cameroon: An eyewitness account of the death celebration of Fai Ndongdei (Philip Njakoi). *Tribus* 49:49–64.

————. 2004. *Ntok ebkuo*: A Western Grassfields palace (Cameroon). *Anthropos* 99:435–50.

————. 2005. A royal ritual: The visit of the *ebfon ebkwo* to Lake Mawes. In *Some*

Oku rituals (Western Grassfields, Cameroon). With a preface by Nicolas Argenti. *Archiv für Völkerkunde* 53.

Bakhtin, Mikhail. [1957] 1968. *Rabelais and his world.* Cambridge, MA: MIT Press.

———. [1963] 1984. *Problems of Dostoyevsky's poetics.* Trans. Caryl Emerson. Manchester and Minneapolis: Manchester University Press and University of Minnesota Press.

Balandier, Georges. 1974. *Anthropo-logiques.* Paris: Presses Universitaires de France.

Ball, Olivia/Medical Foundation for the Care of Victims of Torture. 2002. *"Every morning, just like coffee": Torture in Cameroon.* London: Medical Foundation for the Care of Victims of Torture.

Balz, Heinrich. 1984. *Where the faith has to live: Studies in Bakossi society and religion.* Basel: Basler Mission.

Banya, K., and J. Elu. 1997. Implementing basic education: An African experience. *International Review of Education* 43:481–96.

Barber, Karin. 1991. *"I could speak until tomorrow": Oriki, women and the past in a Yoruba town.* Edinburgh: International African Institute.

Barley, Nigel. 1983. *Symbolic structures: An exploration of the culture of the Dowayos.* Cambridge: Cambridge University Press.

Bartlett, Sir Frederic Charles. [1932] 1995. *Remembering: A study in experimental and social psychology.* Cambridge: Cambridge University Press.

Bastian, M. 1997. Married in the water: Spirit kin and other afflictions of modernity in southeastern Nigeria. *Journal of Religion in Africa* 27(2): 116–34.

Baum, Robert M. 1999. *Shrines of the slave trade: Diola religion and society in precolonial Senegambia.* Oxford: Oxford University Press.

Bayart, Jean-François. [1979] 1985. *L'état au Cameroun.* Paris: Presses de la Fondation Nationale des Sciences Politiques.

———. 1989. *L'état en Afrique: La politique du ventre.* Paris: Fayard.

———. 1992. Le politique par le bas en Afrique noire: Questions de méthode. In *Le politique par le bas en Afrique noire: Contributions à une problématique de la démocratie,* 27–64. Paris: Karthala.

———. 1999. The social capital of the felonious state, or the ruses of political intelligence. In *The criminalization of the state in Africa,* ed. J.-F. Bayart, S. Ellis, and B. Hibou, 32–48. Oxford: James Currey.

———. 2000. Africa in the world, a history of extraversion. *African Affairs* 99: 217–67.

Bayart, Jean-François, Stephen Ellis, and Béatrice Hibou. 1999. From kleptocracy to the felonious state. In *The criminalization of the state in Africa,* ed. J.-F. Bayart, S. Ellis, and B. Hibou. Oxford: James Currey.

Bazenguissa Ganga, R. 1999. The spread of political violence in Congo-Brazzaville. *African Affairs* 98(390): 37–54.

Becker, Jean-Jacques. [1983] 1985. *The Great War and the French people.* Trans. Arnold Pomerans. Lemington Spa: Berg.

Bellman, B. 1984. *The language of secrecy: Symbols and metaphors in Poro ritual.* New Brunswick, NJ: Rutgers University Press.

Benjamin, Walter. 1968. The work of art in the age of mechanical reproduction. In *Illuminations,* ed. Hannah Arendt. New York: Harcourt, Brace and World.

———. 1978. On the mimetic faculty. In *Reflections: Essays, aphorisms, autobiographical writings,* ed. Peter Demetz. New York: Harcourt Brace Jovanovich.

———. 1979. Doctrine of the similar. Trans. K. Tarnowski. *New German Critique* 17: 65–69.

———. [1950] 2006. *Berlin childhood around 1900.* Trans. Howard Eiland. Cambridge, MA: Harvard University Press.

Bettelheim, Bruno. 1943. Individual and mass behavior in extreme situations. *Journal of Abnormal and Social Psychology* 38: 417–52.

Bhabha, Homi K. 1990. DissemiNation. In *Nation and narration,* ed. Homi K. Bhabha, 291–323. London: Routledge.

Biyaya, T.K. 2000. Jeunes et culture de la rue en Afrique urbaine (Addis-Abeba, Dakar et Kinshasa). *Politique Africaine* 80: 12–31.

Blacking, John. 1973. *How musical is man?* Seattle: University of Washington Press.

Blanchot, Maurice. 1995. *The writing of the disaster.* Trans. Anne Smock. Lincoln: University of Nebraska Press.

Bloch, Maurice. 1992. *Prey into hunter: The politics of religious experience.* Cambridge: Cambridge University Press.

Blood, Cynthia, and Leslie Davis. 1999. *Oku–English provisional lexicon.* Yaoundé, Cameroon: Summer Institute of Linguistics.

Boheemen-Saaf, Christine van. 1999. *Joyce, Derrida, Lacan, and the trauma of history: Reading, narrative and postcolonialism.* Cambridge: Cambridge University Press.

Bopda, Athanase. 2003. *Yaoundé et le défi camerounais de l'intégration: À quoi sert une capitale d'Afrique tropicale?* Paris: CNRS.

Bourdieu, Pierre. 1972. *Esquisse d'une théorie de la pratique.* Geneva: Droz.

———. 1979. *Distinction: Critique sociale du jugement.* Paris: Éditions de Minuit.

———. 1980. *Le sens pratique.* Paris: Éditions de Minuit.

Brady, Ivan. 1991. Harmony and argument: Bringing forth the artful science. In *Anthropological poetics,* ed. Ivan Brady. Savage, MD.: Rowman and Littlefield.

Brain, Robert. 1972. *Bangwa kinship and marriage.* Cambridge: Cambridge University Press.

Brain, Robert, and A. Pollock. 1971. *Bangwa funerary sculpture.* London: G. Duckworth.

Buchner, Max. 1914. *Aurora colonialis: Bruchstücke eines Tagebuchs aus dem ersten Beginn unserer Kolonialpolitik, 1884–1885.* Munich: Piloty und Loehle.

Buell, Raymond. [1928] 1965. *The native problem in Africa.* 2 vols. New York: Macmillan; reissued, London: Frank Cass.

Buckley-Zistel, Susanne. 2006. Remembering to forget: Chosen amnesia as a strategy for local coexistence in post-genocide Rwanda. *Africa* 76(2): 131–50.

Calame-Griaule, Genevieve. 1986. *Words and the Dogon world.* Philadelphia: ISHI.

Caroll, David. 1990. The memory of devastation and the responsibilities of thought:
"And let's not talk about that." Foreword to *Heidegger and "the Jews,"* by Jean-
François Lyotard, trans. Andreas Michel and Mark S. Roberts, vii–xxix. Min-
neapolis: University of Minnesota Press.

Caruth, Cathy. 1991a. Introduction: Psychoanalysis, culture and trauma. *American
Imago* 48(1): 1–12.

———. 1991b. Introduction: Psychoanalysis, culture and trauma II. *American
Imago* 48(4): 417–24.

———. 1991c. Unclaimed experience: Trauma and the possibility of history. *Yale
French Studies* 79(4): 181–92.

Celan, Paul. [1952] 2001. Todesfuge/Deathfugue. In *Selected poems and prose of
Paul Celan,* trans. John Felstiner, 30–33. New York and London: Norton.

Chanock, Martin. 1985. *Law, custom and social order: The colonial experience in
Malawi and Zambia.* Cambridge: Cambridge University Press.

———. 1991. A peculiar sharpness: An essay on property in the history of customary law in colonial Africa. *Journal of African History* 32(1): 65–88.

Chem-Langhëë, Bongfen. 1995. Slavery and slave marketing in Nso' in the nineteenth century. *Paideuma* 41:177–90.

Chem-Langhëë, Bongfen, Verkijika Fanso, and E. M. Chilver. 1985. Nto' Nso' and
its occupants: Privileged access and internal organization in the old and new
palaces. *Paideuma* 31: 151–82.

Chem-Langhëë, Bongfen, and E.S.D. Fomin. 1995. Slavery and slave trade among
the Banyang in the nineteenth and early twentieth centuries. *Paideuma* 41:191–
206.

Chilton, Paul A. 1987. Metaphor, euphemism, and the militarisation of language.
Current Research on Peace and Violence 10(1): 7–19.

Chilver, Elizabeth. 1961. Nineteenth century trade in the Bamenda Grassfields.
Afrika und Übersee 45(4): 233–58.

———. 1963. Native administration in the West Central Cameroons, 1902–1954.
In *Essays in imperial government presented to Margery Perham,* ed. Kenneth
Robinson and Frederick Madden. Oxford: Blackwell.

———. 1964. The Bali-Chamba of Bamenda: Settlement and composition." Report
No. 2 to the Bali History Committee. Manuscript.

———. [1966] 1996. *Zintgraff's explorations in Bamenda, Adamawa and the Benue
Lands, 1889–1892.* Oxford: Friends of the Buea Archives. Originally published
in Buea, Cameroon.

———. 1967. Paramountcy and protection in the Cameroons: The Bali and the
Germans, 1889–1913. In *Britain and Germany in Africa: Imperial rivalry and*

colonial rule, ed. Prosser Gifford and W. M. Roger Louis. New Haven, CT: Yale University Press.

———. 2002. Addendum to the Report to the Bali History Society: Slave trading in c. 1817. Manuscript.

Chilver, Elizabeth, and Phyllis Kaberry. 1960. From tribute to tax in a Tikar chiefdom. *Africa* 30(1): 1–19.

———. 1963. Traditional government in Bafut, West Cameroon. *Nigerian Field* 28(1): 4–30.

———. 1965. Sources of nineteenth-century slave trade. Two Comments: The Cameroons Highlands. *Journal of African History* 6(1): 117–19.

———. 1967. The kingdom of Kom in West Cameroon. In *West African kingdoms in the 19th century,* ed. Daryll Forde and Phyllis M. Kaberry, 123–51. London: Oxford University Press for the International African Institute.

———. 1968. *Traditional Bamenda: The precolonial history and ethnography of the Bamenda Grassfields.* Buea: Ministry of Primary Education and Social Welfare, West Cameroon Antiquities Commission.

Chilver, Elizabeth, and Ute Röschenthaler. 2001. *Cameroon's tycoon: Max Esser's expedition and its consequences.* Oxford: Berghahn Books.

Christiansen, Catrine, Mats Utas, and Henrik Vigh, eds. 2006. *Navigating youth, generating adulthood: Social becoming in an African context.* Uppsala: Nordic African Institute.

Christol, Frank. 1922. *Quatre ans au Cameroun.* Paris: Société des Missions Evangéliques de Paris.

Clarence-Smith, William Gervase. 1989. From plantation to peasant cultivation in German Cameroun. In *Proceedings/contributions: Conference on the political economy of Cameroon—Historical perspectives,* ed. Peter Geschiere and Piet Konings, 2:483–502. Leiden: African Studies Centre.

Clarke, John. 1848. *Specimens of dialects: Short vocabularies of languages and notes of countries and customs in Africa.* Berwick-upon-Tweed: Daniel Cameron.

Cohen, Stanley. 2001. *States of denial: Knowing about atrocities and suffering.* Cambridge, MA: Polity Press.

Cole, Herbert, ed. 1985. *I am not myself: The art of African masquerade.* Los Angeles: Museum of Cultural History, University of California.

Cole, Jennifer. *Forget colonialism? Sacrifice and the art of memory in Madagascar.* Berkeley: University of California Press.

Comaroff, Jean. 1985. *Body of power, spirit of resistance: The culture and history of a South African people.* Chicago: University of Chicago Press.

Comaroff, Jean, and John Comaroff. 1992. *Ethnography and the historical imagination.* Boulder, CO: Westview Press.

———. 2005. Reflections on youth from the past to the postcolony. In *Makers and breakers: Children and youth in postcolonial Africa,* ed. Filip De Boeck and Alcinda Honwana, 19–30. Oxford: James Currey; Trenton, NJ: Africa World Press.

Conant, Francis. 1960. Rocks that ring: Their ritual setting in northern Nigeria. *Transactions of the New York Academy of Sciences* 23:155–59.

Connerton, Paul. [1989] 1998. *How societies remember.* Cambridge: Cambridge University Press.

Cooper, Frederick. 1996. *Decolonization and African society: The labor question in French and British Africa.* Cambridge: Cambridge University Press.

———. 2000. Conditions analogous to slavery. In *Beyond slavery: Explorations of race, labor, and citizenship in postemancipation societies,* ed. Frederick Cooper, Thomas C. Holt, and Rebecca J. Scott, 107–49. Chapel Hill: University of North Carolina Press.

Crapanzano, V., and V. Garrison. 1977. Introduction to *Case studies in spirit possession,* ed. V. Crapanzano and V. Garrison. New York: John Wiley.

Cruise O'Brien, Donal. 1996. A lost generation? Youth identity and state decay in West Africa. In *Postcolonial identities in Africa,* ed. Richard Werbner and Terence Ranger, 55–74. London: Zed Books.

Daniel, Yvonne. 2005. *Dancing wisdom: Embodied knowledge in Haitian vodou, Cuban yoruba, and Bahian candomble.* Urbana: University of Illinois Press.

Davies, K.G. 1957. *The Royal African Company.* London.

Davies, Natalie Zemon. 1971. The reasons of misrule: Youth groups and *charivaris* in sixteenth-century France. *Past and Present* 50:41–75.

Davis, Leslie. 1991. The story of Lake Oku (Mawes), told by Zacharias Ndifon. Manuscript.

Debarge, Josette. 1928–29. Note sur l'écriture inventée par Njoye, Sultan du Bamum. *Archives Suisses d'Anthropologie Générale* 5:243–47.

———. 1934. *La mission médicale au Cameroun.* Paris.

De Boeck, Filip. 1994. Of trees and kings: Politics and metaphor among the Aluund of southwestern Zaire. *American Ethnologist* 21(3): 451–73.

———. 1998. Domesticating diamonds and dollars: Identity, expenditure and sharing in southwestern Zaire (1984–1997). *Development and Change* 29(4): 777–810.

———. 2005. The divine seed: Children, gift and witchcraft in the Democratic Republic of Congo. In *Makers and breakers: Children and youth in postcolonial Africa,* ed. Filip De Boeck and Alcinda Honwana, 188–214. Oxford: James Currey; Trenton, NJ: Africa World Press.

De Boeck, Filip, and Alcinda Honwana, eds. 2005. *Makers and breakers: Children and youth in postcolonial Africa.* Oxford: James Currey; Trenton, NJ: Africa World Press.

Delafosse, Maurice. 1922. Naissance et évolution d'un système d'écriture de création contemporaine. *Revue d'Ethnographie et des Traditions Populaires* 3(9): 11–36.

Deleuze, G., and F. Guattari. 1992. *A thousand plateaux: Capitalism and schizophrenia.* London: Athlone Press.

de Rosny, Eric. 1981. *Les yeux de ma chèvre: Sur les pas des maîtres de la nuit en pays douala (Cameroun)*. Paris: Plon.

Derrida, Jacques. 1976. Fors: Les mots anglés de Nicolas Abraham et Maria Torok. Preface to *Cryptonymie: Le verbier de l'homme aux loups*, by Nicolas Abraham and Maria Torok, 7–73. Paris: Aubier Flammarion.

———. 1986. *Schibboleth: Pour Paul Celan*. Paris: Galilée.

———. [1972] 1997. *Dissemination*. Trans. B. Johnson. Chicago: University of Chicago Press.

Devisch, René. 1995a. Frenzy, violence and ethical renewal in Kinshasa. *Public Culture* 7(3): 593–629.

———. 1995b. The slit drum and the birth of divinatory utterance in the Yaka milieu. In *Objects: Signs of Africa*, ed. Luc de Heusch, 97–110. Tervuren, Belgium: Snoeck-Ducaju.

de Waal, Alex, and Nicolas Argenti, eds. 2002. *Young Africa: Realising the rights of children and youth*. Trenton, NJ, and Asmara: Africa World Press.

Diallo, M. 1991. Qui gouverne le Cameroun? *Jeune Afrique* 1595 (July 24–30): 18.

Diduk, Susanne. 1987. The paradox of secrets: Power and ideology in Kedjom society. Ph.D. dissertation, Indiana University, Bloomington.

———. 1993. Twins, ancestors and socio-economic change in Kejom society. *Man*, n.s., 28:551–71.

Dike, K., and F. Ekejiuba. 1990. *The Aro of south-eastern Nigeria, 1650–1980: A study of socio-economic formation and transformation in Nigeria*. Ibadan: Ibadan University Press.

Dillon, Richard. 1990. *Ranking and resistance: A precolonial Cameroonian polity in regional perspective*. Stanford: Stanford University Press.

Dongmo, Jean-Louis. 1981. *Le dynamisme bamiléké (Cameroun)*. Yaoundé: Centre d'Édition et de Production pour l'Enseignement et la Recherche.

Drewal, Henry John. 1988. Performing the other: Mammi Wata worship in West Africa. *Drama Review* 32(2): 160–85.

Drewal, Henry John, and Margaret Thompson Drewal. [1983] 1990. *Gelede: Art and female power among the Yoruba*. Bloomington: Indiana University Press.

Drewal, Margaret. 1991. The state of research on performance in Africa. *African Studies Review* 34(3): 1–64.

Drucker-Brown, Susan. 1992. Horse, dog and donkey: The making of a Mamprusi king. *Man* 27(1): 71–90.

Durham, Deborah. 2000. Youth and the social imagination in Africa. *Anthropological Quarterly* 73(3): 113–20.

———. 2004. Disappearing youth: Youth as a social shifter in Botswana. *American Ethnologist* 31(4): 587–603.

Eagelton, Terry. 1981. *Walter Benjamin: Towards a revolutionary criticism*. London: Verso.

Échard, Nicole. 1991. The Hausa Bori possession cult in the Ader region of Niger: Its origins and present-day function. In *Women's medicine: The Zar-Bori cult in Africa and beyond,* ed. I.M. Lewis. Edinburgh: Edinburgh University Press for the International African Institute.

———. 1992. Culte de possession et changement social: L'exemple du bori hausa de l'Ader et du Kurfey (Niger). *Archives de Sciences Sociales des Religions* 79(2): 87–101.

Eckert, Andreas. 1999. Slavery in colonial Cameroon, 1880s to 1930s. In *Slavery and colonial rule in Africa,* ed. Suzanne Miers and Martin Klein, 133–48. London: Frank Cass.

Ejedepang-Koge, S.N. 1971. *The tradition of a people: Bakossi.* Yaoundé, Cameroon.

Emonts, Joh. 1927. *Ins Steppen- und Bergland Innerkameruns.* Aachen.

Engard, Ronald. 1986. Bringing the outsider in: Commensality and incorporation in Bafut myth, ritual, art, and social organization. Ph.D. dissertation, Indiana University.

———. 1989. Dance and power in Bafut. In *Creativity of power,* ed. W. Arens and Ivan Karp, 129–62. Washington, DC: Smithsonian Institution Press.

Enow, A.V. 1994. Appendix 1: African culture and Christianity. In *African traditional religion as anonymous Christianity,* ed. Tatah H. Mbuy. Bamenda. Mimeo.

Erikson, Kai. Notes on trauma and community. *American Imago* 48(4): 455–72.

Esser, Max. 1898. *An der Westküste Afrikas: Wirtschaftliche und Jagd-Streifzüge.* Cologne: Albert Ahn.

Evans-Pritchard, E. 1928. The dance. *Africa* 1:446–62.

Fanso, Verkijika G., and B. Chem-Langhëë. 1996. Nso' military organisation and warfare in the nineteenth and twentieth centuries. In *African crossroads: Intersections between history and anthropology in Cameroon,* ed. Ian Fowler and David Zeitlyn, 101–14. Oxford: Berghahn Books.

Fanso, V.G., and E.M. Chilver. 1996. Nso' and the Germans: The first encounters in contemporary documents and in oral tradition. In *Nso' and its neighbours: Readings in social history,* ed. B. Chem-Langhëë and V.G. Fanso, 102–31. Amherst: Amherst College.

Fardon, Richard. 1988. *Raiders and refugees: Trends in Chamba political development,* 1750–1950. Washington, DC: Smithsonian Institution Press.

———. 1990. *Between God, the dead and the wild: Chamba interpretations of ritual and religion.* London: Edinburgh University Press for the International African Institute.

Feierman, S. 1974. *The Shambaa kingdom: A history.* Madison: University of Wisconsin Press.

Felman, Shoshana, and Dori Laub. 1992. *Testimony: Crises of witnessing in literature, psychoanalysis, and history.* London: Routledge.

Ferme, Mariane. 2001. *The underneath of things: Violence, history and the everyday in Sierra Leone.* Berkeley: University of California Press.

Ferro, Marc. [1969] 1973. *The Great War: 1914–1918.* Trans. Nicole Stone. London: Routledge.

Fisiy, C.F. 1995. Chieftaincy in the modern state: An institution at the crossroads of democratic change. *Paideuma: Mitteilungen zur Kulturkunde* 41:49–62.

Fisiy, C.F., and P. Geschiere. 1993. Sorcellerie et accumulation, variations régionales. In *Itinéraires d'accumulation au Cameroun*, ed. P. Geschiere and P. Konings, 99–130. Paris: ASC-Karthala.

Fomin, E.S.D., and J. Ngoh. 1998. *Slave settlements in the Banyang country, 1800–1950.* Limbe.

Forni, Silvia. 2001. Molding culture: Pottery and traditions in the Ndop plain (North West Province, Cameroon). M.A. thesis, Department of Anthropology, Archaeology, and Territorial History, University of Turin.

Fowler, Ian. 1990. Babungo: A study of iron production, trade and power in a nineteenth-century Ndop plain chiefdom (Cameroons). Ph.D. dissertation, University College London (Senate House).

Foucault, Michel. 1970. *The order of things: An archaeology of the human sciences.* New York: Vintage.

———. 1974. *Archaeology of knowledge.* London: Tavistock.

———. [1975] 1977. *Discipline and punish: The birth of the prison.* London: Penguin.

Frank, Barbara. 1995. Permitted and prohibited wealth: Commodity-possessing spirits, economic morals, and the goddess Mami Wata in West Africa. *Ethnology* 34(4): 331–46.

Frazer, Sir James George. [1922] 1995. *The golden bough: A study in magic and religion.* Abridged ed. London: Macmillan.

Freud, Sigmund. 1926. *Inhibitions, symptoms, and anxiety.* SE 20.

———. 1939. *Moses and monotheism: Three essays.* SE 23.

Friedlander, Saul. 1992. Trauma, transference, and "working through" in writing the history of the *Shoah. History and Memory* 4(1): 39–59.

Friedman, J. 1990. Being in the world: Globalization and localization. *Theory, Culture and Society* 7: 311–28.

Fuglestad, Finn. 1975. Les Hauka: Une interprétation historique. *Cahiers d'études africaines* 58.

Gaillard, Philippe. 1989. Le Cameroun. 2 vols. Paris: Harmattan.

Gandoulou, Justin-Daniel. 1989a. *Au coeur de la sape: Moeurs et aventures de congolais à Paris.* Paris: Harmattan.

———. 1989b. *Dandies à Bacongo: Le culte de l'élégance dans la société congolaise contemporaine.* Paris: Harmattan.

Gardiner, Michael. 1993. Bakhtin's carnival: Utopia as critique. In *Bakhtin: Carnival and other subjects*, ed. David Shepherd, 20–47. *Critical Studies* 3(2)–4(1–2).

Geary, Christraud. 1979. Traditional societies and associations in We (North West Province, Cameroon). *Paideuma* 25:53–71.

————. 1983. *Things of the palace.* Trans. Kathleen Holan. Studien zur Kulturkunde 60. Wiesbaden: Franz Steiner Verlag.

————. [1988a] 1992. Art and political process in the kingdoms of Bali-Nyonga and Bamum (Cameroon Grassfields). *Canadian Journal of African Studies* 22(1): 11–41. Reprinted in *Art in small-scale societies: Contemporary readings,* ed. Richard L. Anderson and Karen L. Field, 84–102. Englewood Cliffs, NJ: Prentice Hall.

————. 1988b. *Images from Bamum: German colonial photography at the court of King Njoya.* Washington, DC: Smithsonian Institution Press.

————. 1994. *The voyage of King Njoya's gift: A beaded sculpture from the Bamum kingdom, Cameroon, in the National Museum of African Art.* Washington, DC: National Museum of African Art.

————. 1996a. Art, politics and the transformation of meaning: Bamum art in the 20th century. In *African material culture,* ed. Mary Jo Arnoldi, Christraud Geary, and Chris Hardin, 283–307. Bloomington: Indiana University Press.

————. 1996b. Political dress: German-style military attire and colonial politics in Bamum. In *African crossroads: Intersections between history and anthropology in Cameroon,* ed. Ian Fowler and David Zeitlyn, 165–92. Oxford: Berghahn Books.

Gebauer, Paul. 1979. *Art of Cameroon.* Portland, OR: Portland Art Museum.

Gebauer, Gunter, and Christoph Wulf. [1992] 1995. *Mimesis: Culture, art, society.* Berkeley: University of California Press.

Gell, Alfred. 1975. *Metamorphosis of the cassowaries.* London: Athlone Press.

Geschiere, Peter. 1982. *Village communities and the state: Changing relations among the Maka in south-eastern Cameroon since the colonial conquest.* London: Kegan Paul.

————. 1993. Chiefs and colonial rule in Cameroon: Inventing chieftaincy, British and French style. *Africa* 63(2): 151–75.

————. 1995. *Sorcellerie et politique en Afrique: La viande des autres.* Paris: Karthala.

————. 1997. *The modernity of witchcraft: Politics and the occult in postcolonial Africa.* Charlottesville: University Press of Virginia.

————. N.d. Violence and the production of history: Von Gravenreuth and the making of Buea (Cameroon) into a site of history. Manuscript.

Gibbon, Edward. [1776] 1993. *The decline and fall of the Roman empire.* Vol. 1. New York: Alfred Knopf.

Gide, André. 1927–28. *Voyage au Congo, le retour du Tchad: Carnets de route.* Paris: Gallimard.

Gilbert, Michelle. 1987. Ritual and power in a Ghanaian state. In *Rituals of royalty: Power and ceremonial in traditional societies,* ed. D. Canadine and S. Price, 298–330. Cambridge: Cambridge University Press.

Girard, René. [1972] 1977. *Violence and the sacred.* Trans. Patrick Gregory. Baltimore: Johns Hopkins University Press.

———. [1978] 1987. *Things hidden since the foundation of the world.* trans. Stephen Bann and Michael Mettect. Stanford: Stanford University Press.

———. [1982] 1986. *The scapegoat.* Trans. Yvonne Freccero. Baltimore: Johns Hopkins University Press.

Gluckman, Max. 1963. Rituals of rebellion in South-East Africa. In *Order and rebellion in tribal Africa,* ed. Max Gluckman, 110–36. London: Cohen and West.

———. 1965. *Custom and conflict in Africa.* Oxford: Blackwell.

Goheen, Miriam. 1996. *Men own the fields, women own the crops: Gender and power in the Cameroon Grassfields.* Madison: University of Wisconsin Press.

Gohring, M. 1907a. Die Bamum-schrift. *Der Evangelische Heidenbote* 80(6): 83–86.

———. 1907b. Der König von Bamum und seine Schrift. *Der Evangelische Heidenbote* 80(6): 41–42.

Goody, Jack. 1962. *Death, property and the ancestors: A study of the mortuary customs of the LoDagaa of West Africa.* London: Tavistock.

Gore, C., and J. Nevadomsky. 1997. Practice and agency in Mammy Wata worship in Southern Nigeria. *African Arts* 30(2): 60–69.

Griaule, Marcel. 1994. *Masques Dogon.* Paris: Institut d'Ethnologie.

Gufler, Hermann, and Njakoi John Bah. 2006. The establishment of the Princes' Society in Oku, Cameroon. *Anthropos* 101:55–80.

Guthrie, Malcom. 1948. *The classification of the Bantu languages.* London: Oxford University Press.

———. 1953. *The Bantu languages of western Equatorial Africa.* London: Oxford University Press.

Halbwachs, Maurice. 1992. *On Collective Memory.* Chicago: University of Chicago Press.

Harrison, Simon. 1993. *The mask of war: Violence, ritual and the self in Melanesia.* Manchester: Manchester University Press.

Harter, P. 1986. *Arts anciens du Cameroun.* Arnouville: Arts d'Afrique Noire.

Herbert, Eugenia. 1993. *Iron, gender, and power: Rituals of transformation in African societies.* Bloomington: Indiana University Press.

Herzfeld, Michael. 2003. *The body impolitic: Artisans and artifice in the global hierarchy of value.* Chicago: University of Chicago Press.

Heusch, Luc de. 1982. *The drunken king, or the origin of the state.* Bloomington: Indiana University Press.

Hirschman, A. 1970. *Exit, voice and loyalty: Responses to decline in firms, organizations and states.* Cambridge, MA: Harvard University Press.

Hobsbawm, Eric. [1969] 2000. *Bandits.* Rev. ed. New York: New Press.

Hogendorn, Jan, and Marion Johnson. 1986. *The shell money of the slave trade.* Cambridge: Cambridge University Press.

Holquist, Michael. 1990. *Dialogism: Bakhtin and his world.* New York: Routledge.

Hutchinson, T.J. [1861] 1967. *Ten years' wanderings amongst the Ethiopians.* London: Cass.

Hutter, Franz. 1902. *Wanderungen und Forschungen in Nord-Hinterland von Ka-merun*. Braunschweig: F. Vieweg.

Hurault, J. 1962. *La structure sociale des Bamiléké*. Paris: La Haye.

Hyman, Larry. 1972. A phonological study of Fe-Fe Bamileke. *Studies in African Linguistics* Suppl. no. 4.

———. 1979. *Aghem grammatical structure*. SCOPIL 7. Los Angeles: University of Southern California.

———. 1980. *Noun classes in the Grassfields Bantu borderland*. SCOPIL 8. Los Angeles: University of Southern California.

Hyman, Larry, E.F.K. Voeltz, and G. Tchokokam. 1970. Noun-class levelling in Bamileke. *Studies in African Linguistics* 1(2): 185–209.

Hyman, Larry, and J. Voorhoeve, eds. 1981. Les classes nominales dans le Bantou des Grassfields. Paris: SELAF.

Ignatowski, Clare. 2006. *Journey of song: Public life and morality in Cameroon*. Bloomington: Indiana University Press.

Jackson, Michael. 1982. *Allegories of the wilderness: Ethics and ambiguity in Kuranko narratives*. Bloomington: Indiana University Press.

Jeffreys, M. D. W. 1946. Wanderers. *African Affairs* 45(178): 37–40.

———. 1947. Notes on twins: Bamenda. *African Studies* 6(4): 189–95.

———. 1955. The cowry shell and the lozenge in African decorative art. *South African Museums Association Bulletin* 6(4): 83–94.

———. 1961a. Notes on Bakweri funeral customs. *African Studies* 20(1): 61–65.

———. 1961b. Oku blacksmiths. *Nigerian Field* 26(3): 137–44.

———. 1962. Traditional sources prior to 1890 for the Grassfields Bali of northwestern Cameroon. *Afrika und Übersee* 46(3): 168–99; 46(4): 296–313.

———. 1963. Some notes on the Rom people. *Nigerian Field* 28(2): 78–86.

Jewsiewicki, Bogumil. 2003. *Mami Wata: La peinture urbaine au Congo*. Paris: Gallimard.

Jindra, Michael. 2005. Christianity and the proliferation of ancestors: Changes in hierarchy and mortuary ritual in the Cameroon Grassfields. *Africa* 75(3): 356–77.

Johnson, W.A.B. 1820. Letter to the Church Missionary Society. March 24. CA1/O/126/121. CMS, Sierra Leone Mission.

Johnson, Willard. 1970. The Union des Populations du Cameroun in rebellion: The integrative backlash of insurgency. In *Protest and power in black Africa*, ed. Robert Rotberg and Ali Mazrui, 671–92. New York: Oxford University Press.

Johnston, Harry. 1919. *A comparative study of the Bantu and semi-Bantu languages*. Vol. 1. Oxford: Oxford University Press, Clarendon Press.

Joseph, Richard A. 1977. *Radical nationalism in Cameroun: Social origins of the UPC rebellion*. Oxford: Oxford University Press, Clarendon Press.

Joset, P.E. 1955. *Les sociétés secrètes des homes léopards en Afrique noire*. Paris: Payot.

Kaberry, Phyllis. 1952. *Women of the Grassfields: A study of the economic position of women in Bamenda, British Cameroons.* London: Her Majesty's Stationery Office.

———. 1959a. Nsaw' political conceptions. *Man* 59(206): 138–39.

———. 1959b. Traditional politics in Nsaw'. *Africa* 29(4): 366–83.

———. 1962. Retainers and royal households in the Cameroons Grassfields. *Cahiers d'Etudes Africaines* 3(10): 282–98.

———. 1969. Witchcraft of the sun: Incest in Nso. In *Man in Africa*, ed. Mary Douglas and Phyllis Kaberry, 175–95. London: Tavistock.

Kaberry, P.M., and E.M. Chilver. 1961. An outline of the traditional political system of Bali-Nyonga, Southern Cameroons. *Africa* 31(4): 355–71.

Kapferer, Bruce. [1983] 1991. *A celebration of demons: Exorcism and the aesthetics of healing in Sri Lanka.* London: Berg.

———. 1997. *The feast of the sorcerer: Practices of consciousness and power.* Chicago: University of Chicago Press.

Kasfir, Sydney. 1988a. Celebrating male aggression: The Idoma Oglinye masquerade. In *West African masks and cultural systems*, ed. S. Kasfir, 85–108. Sciences Humaines 126. Tervuren: Musée Royal de l'Afrique Centrale.

———. 1988b. Masquerading as a cultural system. In *West African masks and cultural systems*, ed. S. Kasfir, 1–16. Sciences Humaines 126. Tervuren: Musée Royal de l'Afrique Centrale.

Kemner, W. 1937. *Kamerun: Dargestellt in kolonialpolitischer, historischer, verkehrstechnischer, rassenkundlicher und rohstoffwirtschaftlicher Hinsicht.* Berlin: Freiheits-Verlag.

Kgobe, M. 1997. The national qualifications framework in South Africa and "out-of-school" youth: Problems and possibilities. *International Review of Education* 43:317–30.

Killingray, David. 1986. Labour mobilisation in British colonial Africa for the war effort, 1936–46. In *Africa and the Second World War*, ed. David Killingray and Richard Rathbone, 68–96. New York: St. Martin's Press.

Kilson, Martin. 1966. *Political change in a West African state: A study of the modernization process in Sierra Leone.* Cambridge, MA: Harvard University Press.

Klein, Herbert S. 1999. *The Atlantic slave trade.* Cambridge: Cambridge University Press.

Kleinman, Arthur, and Joan Kleinman. 1994. How bodies remember: Social memory and bodily experience of criticism, resistance, and delegitimation following China's cultural revolution. *New Literary History* 25:708–23.

Koelle, S. W. [1854] 1963. *Polyglotta Africana.* Ed. P.E.H. Hair and D. Dalby. Graz, Austria: Akademische Druck- und Verlagsanstalt.

Koloss, Hans-Joachim. 1992. Notes on kwifon and fon in Oku. Unpublished translation by E.M. Chilver.

———. 2000. *World-view and society in Oku (Cameroon).* Trans. Emily Schalk. Berlin: Dietrich Reimer.

Kopytoff, Igor, and Suzanne Miers. 1977. African "slavery" as an institution of marginality. In *Slavery in Africa: Historical and anthropological perspectives*, ed. Suzanne Miers and Igor Kopytoff, 3–81. Madison: University of Wisconsin Press.

Kramer, Fritz. [1987] 1993. *The red fez: Art and spirit possession in Africa*. Trans. Malcom R. Green. London and New York: Verso.

Kuczynski, Robert R. 1939. *The Cameroons and Togoland: A demographic study*. London: Oxford University Press.

Labov, William. 1972. Rules for ritual insults. In *Studies in social interaction*, ed. David Sudnow. New York: Free Press.

Laburthe-Tolra, Philippe. 1981. *Les seigneurs de la forêt*. Paris: Publications de la Sorbonne.

———. 1988. *Initiations et sociétés secrètes au Cameroun*. Paris: Karthala.

LaCapra, Dominick. 2001. *Writing history, writing trauma*. Baltimore: Johns Hopkins University Press.

———. 2003. Bakhtin, Marxism and the carnivalesque. In *Mikhail Bakhtin*, ed. Michael Gardiner, 2:35–59. Thousand Oaks, CA: Sage Publications.

Lambek, Michael. 2002. *The weight of the past: Living with history in Mahajanga, Madagascar*. New York: Palgrave Macmillan.

Lan, David. 1985. *Guns and rain: Guerrillas and spirit mediums in Zimbabwe*. London: James Currey.

Langer, Lawrence. 1991. *Holocaust testimonies: The ruins of memory*. New Haven, CT: Yale University Press.

Laplanche, Jean, and J.B. Pontalis. 1974. *The language of psychoanalysis*. New York: Norton.

Last, Murray. 1991. Adolescents in a Muslim city: The cultural context of danger and risk. Special issue on youth and health in Kano. Special issue, *Kano Studies*, 1–21.

———. 1992. The power of youth, youth of power: Notes on the religions of the young in northern Nigeria. In *Les jeunes en Afrique: La politique et la ville*, ed. Helene d'Almeida-Topor, Catherine Coquery-Vidrovitch, Odile Goer, and Francoise Guitart. Paris: Harmattan.

Laub, Dori. 1991. Truth and testimony: The process and the struggle. *American Imago* 48(1): 75–91.

———. 1992. No one bears witness to the witness. In *Testimony: Crises of witnessing in literature, psychoanalysis, and history*, ed. Shoshana Felman and Dori Laub. London: Routledge.

Laub, Dori, and Daniel Podell. 1995. Art and trauma. *International Journal of Psychoanalysis* 76:991–1005.

Lecoq, Raymond. 1953. *Les bamiléké*. With a preface by Robert Delavignette, governor general of the colonies. Paris: Présence Africaine.

Le Roy Ladurie, Emmanuel. 1979. *Le carnaval de Romans: De la chandeleur au mercredi des cendres (1579–1580)*. Paris: Gallimard.

Levi, Primo. 1989. *The drowned and the saved*. London: Abacus.

Le Vine, Victor T. 1964. *The Cameroons from mandate to independence.* Berkeley: University of California Press.

———. 1971. *The Cameroon Federal Republic.* Ithaca, NY: Cornell University Press.

Lévi-Strauss, Claude. 1979. *La voie des masques.* Paris: Plon.

Lewis, I.M. [1971] 1989. *Ecstatic religion: A study of shamanism and spirit possession.* London: Routledge.

Lovejoy, Paul, and Jan Hogendorn. 1993. *Slow death for slavery: The course of abolition in northern Nigeria, 1897–1936.* Cambridge: Cambridge University Press.

Lovell, Nadia. 2006. The serendipity of rebellious politics: Inclusion and exclusion in a Togolese town. In *Navigating youth, generating adulthood: Social becoming in an African context,* ed. Catrine Christiansen, Mats Utas, and Henrik Vigh, 228–52. Uppsala: Nordic African Institute.

Lyotard, Jean-François. 1988. *The differend: Phrases in dispute.* Trans. Georges Van Den Abeele. Minneapolis: University of Minnesota Press.

———. 1990. *Heidegger and "the Jews."* Trans. Andreas Michel and Mark S. Roberts. Minneapolis: University of Minnesota Press.

MacGaffey, Janet, and Rémy Bazenguissa-Ganga. 2000. *Congo–Paris: Transnational traders on the margins of the law.* Oxford: James Currey.

MacGaffey, Wyatt. 1986. *Religion and society in central Africa: The Bakongo of lower Zaire.* Chicago: University of Chicago Press.

———. 2000. The cultural tradition of the African forests. In *Insight and artistry in African divination,* ed. John Pemberton III, 13–24. Washington, DC: Smithsonian Institution Press.

Malaquais, Dominique. 2002. *Architecture, pouvoir et dissidence au Cameroun.* Paris: Karthala.

Malart-Guimera, Louis. 1981. *Ni dos ni ventre.* Paris: Société d'Ethnographie.

Malinowski, B. [1925] 1948. Magic, science and religion. In *Science, religion and reality,* ed. J. Needham. London: Sheldon Press.

Mamdani, Mahmood. 1996. *Citizen and subject: Contemporary Africa and the legacy of late colonialism.* London: James Currey.

Manganaro, Marc. 1990. *Modernist anthropology: From fieldwork to text.* Princeton, NJ: Princeton University Press.

Marie, A. 1976. Rapports de parenté et rapports de production dans les sociétés lignagères. In *L'anthropologie economique: Courants et problèmes,* ed. F. Pouillon. Paris: Maspéro.

Masquelier, Adeline. 1992. Encounter with a road siren: Machines bodies and commodities in the imagination of a Mawri healer. *Visual Anthropology Review* 8(1): 56–69.

Masquelier, B. M. 1978. Structure and process of political identity: Ide, a polity of the Mentshum Valley (Cameroon). Ph.D. dissertation, University of Pennsylvania.

Mbembe, Achille. 1985. *Les jeunes et l'ordre politique en Afrique noire.* Paris: Harmattan.

———. 1992. Provisional notes on the postcolony. *Africa* 62(1): 3–37.

———. 1996. *La naissance du maquis dans le Sud-Cameroun (1920–1960)*. Paris: Karthala.

———. 2001. *On the postcolony*. Berkeley: University of California Press.

Mbembe, Achille, and Janet Roitman. 1995. Figures of the subject in times of crisis. *Public Culture* 7:323–52.

Mbunwe-Samba, Patrick. 1993. *Wimbum ancestral voices: Cameroon folktale heritage*. Private printing.

———. 1996. *Witchcraft, magic and divination: A personal testimony*. Bamenda, Cameroon, and Leiden: African Studies Centre.

Mburu, J.M. 1979. Witchcraft among the Wimbum. B.A. thesis in philosophy, Regional Major Seminary, Bambui, Cameroon.

Mbuy, Tatah H. 1989. *Encountering witches and wizards in Africa*. Buea, Cameroon.

———. 1994. *African traditional religion as anonymous Christianity*. Bamenda, Cameroon: Unique Printers.

McCall, John C. 2000. *Dancing histories: Heuristic ethnography with the Ohafia Igbo*. Ann Arbor: University of Michigan Press.

Mead, Margaret. 1928. *Coming of age in Samoa*. New York: Morrow.

Meigs, A. 1990. Multiple gender ideologies and statuses. In *Beyond the second sex: New direction in the anthropology of gender*, ed. P.R. Sanday and R.G. Goodenough. Philadelphia: University of Pennsylvania Press.

Meillasoux, Claude. [1975] 1981. *Maidens, meal and money: Capitalism and the domestic community*. Cambridge: Cambridge University Press.

Meinert, Lotte. 2003. Sweet and bitter places: The politics of schoolchildren's orientation in rural Uganda. In *Children's places: Cross-cultural perspectives*, ed. Karen Fog Olwig and Eva Gulløv, 179–96. London: Routledge.

Mendoza, Zoila. 2000. *Shaping society through dance: Mestizo ritual performance in the Peruvian Andes*. Chicago: University of Chicago Press.

Migeod, F.W.H. 1909. The syllabic writing of the Vai people. *Journal of the African Society* 9(33): 46–58.

Miller, Joseph. 1988. *Way of death: Merchant capitalism and the Angolan slave trade, 1730–1830*. Madison: University of Wisconsin Press.

Mitchell, J.C. 1956. *The Kalela dance*. Rhodes-Livingston Papers no. 27. Manchester: Manchester University Press for the Rhodes-Livingston Institute.

Moisel. M. 1908. *Eine Expedition in die Grashochländer Mittel-Kameruns, II*. Special supplement. *Deutsche Kolonialzeitung* 15 (April 11).

Morrison, Toni. 1987. *Beloved*. London: Chatto and Windus.

Moylan, Tom. 1986. *Demand the impossible: Science fiction and the utopian imagination*. New York: Methuen.

Mudimbe, V.Y. 1988. *The invention of Africa: Gnosis, philosophy, and the order of knowledge*. Bloomington: Indiana University Press.

Needham, Rodney. 1980. *Reconnaisances*. Toronto: University of Toronto Press.

Nicholls, Peter. 1996. The belated postmodern: History, phantoms, and Toni Morrison. In *Psychoanalytic criticism*, ed. Sue Vice, 50–67. Cambridge, MA: Polity Press.

Niehaus, Isaak. 2005. Witches and zombies of the South African lowveld: Discourse, accusations and subjective reality. *Journal of the Royal Anthropological Institute* 11(2): 191–210.

Njiasse-Njoya, Aboubakar. 1981. Naissance et evolution de l'Islam en pays Bamum (Cameroun). Thesis (doctorat de troisième cycle), University of Paris I–Panthéon Sorbonne.

———. 1995. Slavery in the Bamum kingdom in the 19th and 20th centuries. *Paideuma* 41:227–37.

Njoya, Sultan. 1952. *Histoire et coutumes des Bamum*. Trans. H. Martin. Douala: Mémoires de l'Institut Français d'Afrique Noire (IFAN), Centre du Cameroun.

Nkwi, Paul Nchoji. 1985. Traditional female militancy in a modern context. In *Femmes du Cameroun,* ed. Jean-Claude Barbier, 181–91. Paris: Karthala.

———. 1995. Slavery and slave trade in the Kom kingdom of the 19th century. *Paideuma* 41:239–50.

Nkwi, Paul Nchoji, and Jean-Pierre Warnier. 1982. *Elements for a history of the western Grassfields.* Yaoundé: University of Yaoundé.

Northern, Tamara. 1973. *Royal Art of Cameroon.* Hanover, NH: Hopkins Center Art Galleries.

———. 1984. *The art of Cameroon.* Washington, DC: Smithsonian Institution Press.

Nunley, John. 1987. *Moving with the face of the devil: Art and politics in urban West Africa.* Urbana: University of Illinois Press.

Nwokeji, G. Ugo, and David Eltis. 2002. Characteristics of captives leaving the Cameroons for the Americas, 1822–1837. *Journal of African History* 43:191–210.

Nyamnjoh, Francis. 1985. Change in the concept of power amongst the Bum. M.A. thesis, Department of Sociology, University of Yaoundé, Cameroon.

Ogrizek, M. 1981–82. La Mammy Wata: Les envoûtées de la sirène. Psychothérapie collective de l'hystérie en pays Batsangui au Congo, suivie d'un voyage mythologique en Centrafrique. *Cahiers de l'O.R.S.T.O.M., Série Sciences Humaines, Médicines et Santé* 19(4): 433–43.

Okri, Ben. 1991. *The famished road.* London: Doubleday.

———. 1993. *Songs of enchantment.* London: Vintage.

Olivier de Sardan, Jean-Pierre. 1982. *Concepts et conceptions songhay-zarma: Histoire, culture, société.* Paris: Nubia.

———. 1984. *Les sociétés Songhay-Zarma (Niger–Mali): Chefs, guerriers, esclaves, paysans.* Paris: Karthala.

———. 1993. La surinterprétation politique: Les cultes de possession hawka du Niger. In *Religion et modernité en Afrique noire,* ed. J.-F. Bayart, 163–213. Paris: Karthala.

O'Neil, Robert. 1996. Imperialisms at the century's end: Moghamo relations with Bali-Nyonga and Germany, 1889–1908. In *African crossroads: Intersections be-*

tween history and anthropology in Cameroon, ed. Ian Fowler and David Zeitlyn, 81–100. Oxford: Berghahn Books.

Onwuejeogwu, Michael. 1969. The cult of the Bori spirits among the Hausa. In *Man in Africa,* ed. Mary Douglas and Phyllis Kaberry. London: Tavistock.

Orwell, George. [1945] 1970. Notes on nationalism. In *The collected essays, journalism and letters of George Orwell,* ed. Sonia Orwell and Ian Angus, 3:410–31. Harmondsworth: Penguin.

Ottenberg, Simon. 1975. *Masked rituals of the Afikpo: The context of an African art.* Seattle: University of Washington Press for the Henry Art Gallery.

Pain, Françoise. 1959. Evolution économique et sociale du Cameroun depuis 1947. Thesis, Faculté de Droit et des Sciences Economiques, University of Paris.

Palmié, Stephan. 1995. The taste of human commodities: Experiencing the Atlantic system. In *Slave cultures and cultures of slavery,* ed. Stephan Palmie, 40–54. Knoxville: University of Tennessee Press.

———. 2002. *Wizards and scientists: Explorations in modernity and Afro-Cuban tradition.* Durham, NC: Duke University Press.

———. 2006. A view from itia ororó kande. *Social Anthropology* 14(1): 99–118.

Peek, Phillip. 1994. The sounds of silence: Cross world communication and the auditory arts in African societies. *American Ethnologist* 21(3): 474–94.

Peel, J.D.Y. 1984. Making history: The past in the Ijesha present. *Man,* n.s., 19(1): 111–32.

Pelican, Michaela. 2006. Getting along in the Grassfields: Interethnic relations and identity politics in northwest Cameroon. Ph.D. thesis, Martin-Luther University of Halle-Wittenberg.

Pennacini, Cecilia. 2000. Religion and spirit possession in the Great Lakes, Africa: The *kubandwa* tradition in a regional perspective. In *Ambienti, lingue, culture: Contributi della missione etnologica italiana in Africa Equatoriale,* ed. Francesco Remotti, 119–50. Alessandria, Italy: Edizioni dell'Orso.

Petit, Pierre. 1995. The sacred kaolin and the bowl-bearers. In *Objects: Signs of Africa,* ed. Luc de Heusch, 111–32. Tervuren: Snoeck-Ducaju & Zoon.

———. 1996. Les charmes du roi sont les esprits des morts: Les fondements religieux de la royauté sacrée chez les Luba du Zaïre. *Africa* 66(3): 349–66.

Pichler, Adelheid. Forthcoming. Memories of slavery and ritual performance: Reflections on Palo Monte in contemporary Cuba. In *Remembering violence: Anthropological perspectives on intergenerational transmission,* ed. Nicolas Argenti and Katharina Schramm. Oxford: Berghahn.

Piersen, William. 1999. A resistance too civilized to notice. In *Signifying, sanctifying and slam dunking,* ed. Gena Dagel Caponi. Amherst: University of Massachusetts Press.

Piot, Charles. 1999. *Remotely global: Village modernity in West Africa.* Chicago: University of Chicago Press.

Pool, Robert. 1994. *Dialogue and the interpretation of illness: Conversations in a Cameroon village.* Oxford: Berg.

Pradelles de Latour, Charles-Henri. 1985. Le palais du chef dans une chefferie ba-miléké: Bangoua. *Paideuma* 31:31–47.

Price, David. 1979. Who are the Tikar now? *Paideuma* 25:89–98.

———. 1985. The palace and its institutions in the chiefdom of Ngambe. *Paideuma* 31:85–104.

———. 1987. Descent, clans and territorial organization in the Tikar chiefdom of Ngambe, Cameroon. *Zeitschrift fur Ethnologie* 112(1): 85–103.

Radcliffe-Brown, Alfred. 1922. *The Andaman islanders: A study in social anthropology.* Cambridge: Cambridge University Press.

Ramadanovic, Petar. 2001. *Forgetting futures: On memory, trauma, and identity.* Lanham, MD, and Oxford: Lexington Books.

Ranger, Terence. 1975. *Dance and society in eastern Africa, 1890–1970*: The Beni Ngoma. London: Heinemann.

Rasmussen, S.J. 2000. Between several worlds: Images of youth and age in Tuareg popular performances. *Anthropological Quarterly* 73(3): 133–44.

Reed, Daniel. 2003. *Dan Ge performance: Masks and music in contemporary Côte d'Ivoire.* Bloomington: Indiana University Press.

René, Carl. 1905. *Kamerun und die deutsche Tsâdsee-Eisenbahn.* Berlin: Mittler.

Reno, W. 1995. *Corruption and state politics in Sierra Leone.* Cambridge: Cambridge University Press.

———. 2000. Shadow states and the political economy of civil wars. In *Greed and grievance: Economic agendas in civil wars,* ed. M. Berdal and D. Malone. Boulder, CO, and London: Lynne Riehmer Publishers.

Rey, P.P. 1971. *Colonialisme, néo-colonialisme et transition au capitalisme.* Paris: Maspéro.

———. 1975. L'esclavage lignager chez les Tsangui, les Punu et les Kuni du Congo-Brazzaville. In *L'esclavage en Afrique précoloniale,* ed. Claude Meillasoux, 509–28. Paris: Maspéro.

Richards, P. 1996. *Fighting for the rain forest: War, youth and resources in Sierra Leone.* Oxford: International African Institute.

Ricoeur, Paul. 1986. *Lectures on ideology and utopia.* Ed. G. Taylor. New York: Columbia University Press.

Ripert. 1923. Une apprétiation sur le sultant Njoya. Administrative report. Yaoundé: Service des Archives Nationales; Fonds du Département Bamoun, Fumban.

Ritchie, Ian. 1991. Fusion of the faculties: A study of the language of the senses in Hausaland. In *The varieties of sensory experience,* ed. David Howes, 192–202. Toronto: University of Toronto Press.

Ritzenthaler, Pat. 1966. *The fon of Bafut.* New York: Thomas Crowell.

Ritzenthaler, Robert. 1960. Anlu: A women's uprising in the British Cameroons. *African Studies* 19(3): 151–56.

Rodley, Sir Nigel. 1998. Report of the special rapporteur, Sir Nigel Rodley, submitted pursuant to Commission on Human Rights resolution 1998/38; http://

www.unhchr.ch/Huridocda/Huridoca.nsf/TestFrame/3473ae924odf264b8025
688e0053378a?Opendocument.

Roitman, Janet. 1998. The *garrison-entrepôt*. *Cahiers d'Etudes Africaines* 150–52: 297–329.

———. 2005. *Fiscal disobedience: An anthropology of economic regulation in central Africa*. Princeton, NJ: Princeton University Press.

———. 2006. The ethics of illegality in the Chad basin. In *Law and disorder in the postcolony*, ed. Jean Comaroff and John Comaroff, 247–72. Chicago: University of Chicago Press.

Röschenthaler, Ute. 1998. Honouring Ejagham women. *African Arts* 31(2): 38–49.

———. 2004. Die Ambivalenz des Außerordentlichen: Talent und Macht als endliche Ressource im Cross River Gebiet. In *Africa screams*, ed. Peter Hammer, 126–41. Die Wiederkehr des Bsen in Kino, Kult und Kunst. Wuppertal: Peter Hammer.

———. 2006. Translocal cultures: The slave trade and cultural transfer in the Cross River region. *Social Anthropology* 14(1): 71–92.

Rothenberg, Jerome, ed. 1985. *Technicians of the sacred: A range of poetries from Africa, America, Asia, Europe, and Oceania*. Berkeley: University of California Press.

Rouch, Jean. 1955. *Les maîtres fous*. Film.

Rowlands, Michael. 1979. Local and long distance trade and incipient state formation on the Bamenda plateau in the late nineteenth century. *Paideuma* 25:1–19.

———. 1987. Power and moral order in precolonial west-central Africa. In *Specialization, exchange, and complex societies*, ed. Elizabeth Brumfield and Timothy Earle, 52–63. Cambridge; Cambridge University Press.

———. 1993. Accumulation and the cultural politics of identity in the Grassfields. In *Itinéraires d'accumulation au Cameroun*, ed. Peter Geschiere and Piet Konings, 71–98. Paris: Karthala.

———. 1995. Inconsistent temporalities in a nation-space. In *Worlds apart: Modernity through the prism of the local*, ed. Daniel Miller, 23–42. London: Routledge.

Rowlands, Michael, and Jean-Pierre Warnier. 1988. Sorcery, power and the modern state in Cameroon. *Man*, n.s., 23(1): 118–32.

Royce, Anya Petersen. [1977] 2002. *The anthropology of dance*. Alton, Hampshire: Dance Books.

Rudin, Harry. 1938. *Germans in the Cameroons, 1884–1914: A case study in modern imperialism*. London: Jonathan Cape.

Ruel, Malcolm, 1969. *Leopards and leaders: Constitutional politics among a cross-river people*. London: Tavistock.

Rüger, A. 1960. Der Aufstand der Polizeisoldaten (Dezember 1893). In *Kamerun unter deutscher Kolonialherrschaft*, ed. H. Stoecker, 1:97–149. Berlin: Deutscher Verlag der Wissenschaften.

————. 1968. Die Duala und der Kolonialmacht, 1884–1914. In *Kamerun unter deutscher Kolonialherrschaft,* ed. H. Stoecker, vol. 2. Berlin: Deutscher Verlag der Wissenschaften.

Ruppel, J. 1912. *Die Landesgesetzgebung, für das Schutzgebiet Kamerun.* Berlin: E.S. Miller.

Russell, S.W., Jr. 1980. Aspects of development in rural Cameroon: Political transition amongst the Bali of Bamenda. Ph.D. dissertation, University of Pennsylvania.

Sadembouo, Étienne, and Maurice Tadadjeu. 1984. *Alphabet général des langues camerounaises.* Yaoundé: University of Yaoundé.

Said, Edward. 1995. *Orientalism: Western conceptions of the Orient.* London: Penguin.

Sanders, Todd. 2001. Gender rituals of rebellion and patriarchy in Africa. *Gender Institute New Working Papers Series,* no. 3, March.

Sanduo, Lazare. 1955. *Mon Pays d'hier.* Dissertation for the seminary of Ndoungué, Cameroon.

Salmons, J. 1983. Mammy Wata. *African Arts* 10:8–15.

Savary, Claude. 1980. *Cameroun: Arts et cultures des peuples de l'Ouest.* Geneva: Musée d'Ethnographie de Genève.

Schaub, Willi. 1985. *Babungo.* London: Croom Helm.

Scheper-Hughes, Nancy. 1992. *Death without weeping: The violence of everyday life in Brazil.* Berkeley: University of California Press.

Schieffelin, Edward. [1976] 2005. *The sorrow of the lonely and the burning of the dancers.* New York: Palgrave Macmillan.

Scott, James. 1986. *The weapons of the weak: Everyday forms of peasant resistance.* New Haven, CT: Yale University Press.

Seekings, Jeremy. 1993. *Heroes or villains? Youth politics in the 1980's.* Johannesburg: Raven Press.

Seitz, T. 1908. Übergabe des Thronsessels des Häuptlings von Bamum als Geburtstagsgeschenk für den Kaiser anlässlich der Feierlichkeiten in Buea. 7 February. Fonds Allemands (1/38). Service des Archives Nationales, Yaoundé.

Shanklin, Eugenia. 1985. The path to Laikom: Kom royal court architecture. *Paideuma* 31:111–50.

————. 1990. Anlu remembered: The Kom women's rebellion of 1958–61. *Dialectical Anthropology* 15:159–81.

Sharwood-Smith, B. 1925. Assessment report on the Mogamaw and Ngemba speaking families of the Widekum tribe of Bamenda division. Manuscript. Buea Archives, Cameroon.

Shaw, Rosalind. 2002. *Memories of the slave trade: Ritual and the historical imagination in Sierra Leone.* Chicago: University of Chicago Press.

Simmel, G. [1923] 1950. The stranger. In *The sociology of Georg Simmel,* ed. K.H. Wolff. New York: Free Press.

Skolaster, H. 1924. *Die Pallotiner in Kamerun.* Limburg Lahn: V.K.P.

Smith, Daniel Jordan. 2004. The Bakassi boys: Vigilantism, violence, and political imagination in Nigeria. *Cultural Anthropology* 19(3): 429–53.

Smith, Mary. 1954. *Baba of Karo.* London: Faber and Faber.

Spellenberg, F. 1914. *Quartalbericht.* Banjoun 14-6-1914. Église Évangélique du Cameroun Archives, Douala.

Spencer, Paul. 1985. Introduction: Interpretations of the dance in anthropology. In *Society and the dance: The social anthropology of process and performance,* ed. Paul Spencer, 1–46. Cambridge: Cambridge University Press.

———. [1988] 2004. *The Maasai of Matapato: A study of rituals of rebellion.* London: Routledge.

Stallybrass, Peter, and Allon White. 1986. *The politics and poetics of transgression.* London: Methuen.

Steer, G.L. 1939. *Judgment on German Africa.* London: Hodder and Stoughton.

Steinberg, Michael. 1998. Cultural history and cultural studies. In *Disciplinarity and dissent in cultural studies,* ed. Cary Nelson and Dilip Paramashwar Gaonkar, 103–30. New York: Routledge.

Stewart, Michael. 2004. Remembering without commemoration: The mnemonics and politics of Holocaust memories among European Roma. *Journal of the Royal Anthropological Institute* 10(3): 561–82.

Stoller, Paul. 1984. Horrific comedy: Cultural resistance and Songhay possession dance. *Ethos* 11:165–87.

———. 1989. *Fusion of the worlds: An ethnography of possession among the Songhay of Niger.* Chicago: University of Chicago Press.

———. 1995. *Embodying colonial memories: spirit possession, power, and the Hauka in West Africa.* New York: Routledge.

Strother, Z.S. 1998. *Inventing masks: Agency and history in the art of the Central Pende.* Chicago: University of Chicago Press.

Sykes, Karen. 1999. After the *raskol* feast: Youths' alienation in New Ireland, Papua New Guinea. *Critique of Anthropology* 19(2): 157–74.

Takougang, Joseph, and Milton Krieger. 1998. *African state and society in the 1990's: Cameroon's political crossroads.* Boulder, CO: Westview Press.

Tamwa Hamkong, J. 1983. *Relations economiques traditionelles entre le Haut-Noun et Yabassi.* DIPLEG thesis, Department of History, University of Yaoundé.

Tardits, Claude. 1960. *Les bamiléké de l'ouest Cameroun.* Paris: Berger-Levrault.

———. 1980. *Le royaume bamoun.* Paris: A. Colin.

———. 1996. Pursue to attain: A royal religion. In *African crossroads: Intersections between history and anthropology in Cameroon,* ed. Ian Fowler and David Zeitlyn, 141–64. Oxford: Berghahn Books.

Taussig, Michael. 1993. *Mimesis and alterity: A particular history of the senses.* New York: Routledge.

Tedlock, Dennis. 1992. Ethnopoetics. In *Folklore, cultural performances, and popular entertainments,* ed. Richard Bauman. Oxford: Oxford University Press.

Theeuws, J.A. 1954. Textes Luba. *Bulletin du CEPSI* 27:1–153.

———. 1960. Naître et mourir dans le rituel Luba. *Zaïre* 14 (2–3): 115–73.

Thomas, Helen. 1993. *Dance, gender and culture*. London: Palgrave Macmillan.

Thompson, Robert Farris. 1974. *African art in motion: Icon and act*. Los Angeles: University of California Press.

Thorbecke, Franz. 1914–16. *Im Hochland von Mittel-Kamerun*. Hamburg: L. Friederichsen.

Thorbecke, Marie Pauline. 1914. *Auf der Savanne: Tagebuch einer Kamerunreise (1911–1913)*. Berlin: E.S. Mittler und Sohn.

Torok, Maria. [1975] 1994. Story of fear: The symptoms of phobia—the return of the repressed or the return of the phantom? In *The shell and the kernel*, by Nicolas Abraham and Maria Torok, trans. Nicholas T. Rand, 177–86. Chicago: University of Chicago Press.

———. 1987. Maladie du deuil et phatasme du cadavre exquis. In *L'ecorce et le noyau*, by Nicolas Abraham and Maria Torok, 229–51. Paris: Flammarion.

Toulabor, Comi. 1992. *L'énonciation du pouvoir et de la richesse chez les jeunes "conjuncturés" de Lomé (Togo)*. In *Le politique par le bas en Afrique noire*, ed. Jean-François Bayart, S. Ellis, and B. Hibou, 131–45. Paris: Karthala.

Turner, Victor. 1967. *The forest of symbols: Aspects of Ndembu ritual*. Ithaca, NY: Cornell University Press.

———. 1968. The drums of affliction: A study of religious processes among the Ndembu of Zambia. London: International African Institute in association with Hutchinson University Library for Africa.

Tutuola, Amos. [1982] 1989. *The wild hunter in the bush of the ghosts*. Ed. Bernth Lindfors. Washington, DC: Three Continents Press. First published in 1948.

United Kingdom Home Office. 2001. *Cameroon country assessment*. Country Information and Policy Unit.

Unnold, Yvonne S. 2002. *Representing the unrepresentable: Literature of trauma under Pinochet in Chile*. New York: Peter Lang.

U.S. Department of State. 2001. *Cameroon country report on human rights practices, 2000*. Washington, DC.

———. 2003. *Cameroon country report on human rights practices, 2002*. Washington, DC.

Van der Kolk, Bessel A., and Onno van der Hart. 1991. The intrusive past: The flexibility of memory and the engraving of trauma. *American Imago* 48(1): 425–54.

Van de Walle, N. 1993. The politics of non-reform in Cameroon. In *Hemmed In*, ed. T. Callaghy and J. Ravenhill, 357–97. New York: Columbia University Press.

Van Dijk, Rijk. 1998. Pentecostalism, cultural memory and the state: Contested representations of time in postcolonial Malawi. In *Memory and the postcolony: African anthropology and the critique of power*, ed. Richard Werbner, 155–81. London: Zed Books.

———. 1999. Pentecostalism, gerontocratic rule and democratization in Malawi: The changing position of the young in political culture. In *Religion, globalization and political culture in the third world*, ed. J. Haynes. London: Macmillan.

Van Gennep, Arnold. 1909. *Les rites de passage: Étude systématique des rites*. Paris.

———. 1943–58. *Manuel de folklore français contemporain*. Paris: Picard.

Van Onselen, Charles. 1976. *Chibaro: African mine labour in Southern Rhodesia*. London: Pluto Press.

Vansina, Jan. 1985. *Oral tradition as history*. Islington, UK: James Currey.

———. 1990. *Paths in the rainforest: Toward a history of political tradition in Equatorial Africa*. London: James Currey.

Van Slageren, Jaap. 1972. *Les origins de l'église évangélique du Cameroun: Missions européennes et christianisme autochtone*. Leiden: Brill.

Vaughan, James. 1977. Mafakur: A limbic institution of the Margi (Nigeria). In *Slavery in Africa: Historical and anthropological perspectives*, ed. Suzanne Miers and Igor Kopytoff, 85–102. Madison: University of Wisconsin Press.

Verdier, R. 1982. *Le pays Kabié*. Paris.

Vickroy, Laurie. 2002. *Trauma and survival in contemporary fiction*. Charlottesville: University of Virginia Press.

Vieter, Mgr Heinrich, 1989. *Les premiers pas de l'église au Cameroun: Chronique de la mission Catholique 1890–1912 récit de Mgr Heinrich Vieter*, trans. Jean Criaud. Yaoundé: Centenaire.

Vigh, Henrik. 2006. Social death and violent life chances. In *Navigating youth, generating adulthood: Social becoming in an African context*, ed. Catrine Christiansen, Mats Utas, and Henrik Vigh, 31–60. Uppsala: Nordic African Institute.

Voorhoeve, J. 1971. The linguistic unit Mbam-Nkam (Bamileke, Bamum and related languages). *Journal of African Linguistics* 10(2): 1–12.

Waage, Trond. 2006. Coping with unpredictability: Preparing for life in Ngaoundéré, Cameroon. In *Navigating youth, generating adulthood: Social becoming in an African context*, ed. Catrine Christiansen, Mats Utas, and Henrik Vigh, 61–87. Uppsala: Nordic African Institute.

Warnier, Jean-Pierre. 1975. Pre-colonial Mankon: The development of a Cameroon chiefdom in its regional setting. Ph.D. dissertation, University of Pennsylvania.

———. 1979. La polarité culture-nature entre le chef et *takoengoe* à Mankon. *Paideuma* 25:21–33.

———. 1980. Trade guns in the Grassfields of Cameroon. *Paideuma* 26:79–92.

———. 1985. *Echange, développements et hiérarchie dans le Bamenda pré-colonial (Cameroun)*. Studien zur Kulturkunde 76. Wiesbaden: Franz Steiner Verlag.

———. 1993. *L'esprit de l'entreprise au Cameroun*. Paris: Karthala.

———. 1995a. Around a plantation: The ethnography of business in Cameroon. In *Worlds apart: Modernity through the prism of the local*, ed. Daniel Miller, 91–109. London: Routledge.

———. 1995b. Slave-trading without slave-raiding in Cameroon. *Paideuma* 41: 251–72.

———. 1996. Rebellion, defection, and the position of male cadets: A neglected category. In *African crossroads: Intersections between history and anthropology in Cameroon,* ed. Ian Fowler and David Zeitlyn, 115–23. Oxford: Berghahn Books.

———. 2006. The transfer of young people's working ethos from the Grassfields to the Atlantic Coast. *Social Anthropology* 14(1): 93–98.

———. 2007. *The pot-king: Bodily conducts, material culture and the technologies of power (Le roi-pot).* Leiden: Brill; Paris: Karthala.

Wendl, Tobias. 2001. Visions of modernity in Ghana: Mami Wata shrines, photo studios and horror films. *Visual Anthropology* 14(3): 269–92.

Werbner, Richard. 1998. Beyond oblivion: Confronting memory crisis. In *Memory and the postcolony: African anthropology and the critique of power,* ed. Richard Werbner, 1–17. London: Zed Books.

Whitehead, Niel. 2004. Rethinking anthropology of violence. *Anthropology Today* 20(5): 1–2.

Wieschiolek, Heike. 2003. "Ladies, just follow his lead!": Salsa, gender and identity. In *Sport, dance and embodied identities,* ed. Noel Dyck and Eduardo Archetti, 115–38. Oxford: Berg.

Williamson, K. 1971. The Benue-Congo languages and Ijo. *Current Trends in Linguistics* 7:245–306.

Wirz, Albert. 1973a. La "Rivière de Cameroun": Commerce pré-colonial et contrôle du pouvoire en société lignagère. *Revue Française d'Histoire d'Outre-Mer* 60(219): 172–94.

———. 1973b. *Vom Sklavenhandel zum Kolonialhandel: Wirtschaftsräume und Wirtschaftsformen in Kamerun vor 1914.* Zurich: Atlantis.

Yoshida, Kenji. 1991. Masks and transformation among the Chewa of Eastern Zambia. *Senri Ethnological Studies* 31, Africa (4): 203–73.

Young, Allan. 1995. *The harmony of illusions: Inventing post-traumatic stress disorder.* Princeton, NJ: Princeton University Press.

Zeitlyn, David. 1990. *Sua in Somié:* Mambila traditional religion. Rev. ed. of a Ph.D. dissertation, Cambridge University.

Zintgraff, Eugene. 1895. *Nord-Kamerun.* Berlin: Gebrüder Paetel.

Index

Page numbers in italic refer to figures. For purposes of alphabetization in this index, ε = ə = e, ŋ = n, and ɔ = o.